"Two Strikes and the Bases Full," Drawing by Charles Dana Gibson *for* Collier's Weekly, *1904.*

THE ILLUSTRATOR IN AMERICA 1880·1980 A CENTURY OF ILLUSTRATION

Walt and Roger Reed

THE SOCIETY OF ILLUSTRATORS

"The Dover Coach," by Norman Rockwell. Collection of the Society of Illustrators Museum of American Illustration.

THE ILLUSTRATOR IN AMERICA 1880·1980

A CENTURY OF ILLUSTRATION

Walt and Roger Reed

design by Art Weithas

THE SOCIETY OF ILLUSTRATORS

PUBLISHED FOR THE SOCIETY OF ILLUSTRATORS BY MADISON SQUARE PRESS, INC., NEW YORK CITY 10010.
DISTRIBUTED BY ROBERT SILVER ASSOCIATES, NEW YORK 10016

Illustration by Norman Price from "The Rogue's Moon" by Robert W. Chambers

ACKNOWLEDGEMENTS

Much of the original research for the first edition of this book, published in 1966, is still valid and the help provided by the individuals then listed is gratefully acknowledged again.

For this expanded and updated new edition, many others have also been helpful. First, thanks go to my son, Roger, for suggesting the present format and for doing the extra work as co-author to make the project at all possible; secondly, to my wife, Mary, for her uncounted hours of research, letter writing and manuscript typing. Thanks also are extended to Bill Fletcher, Gerald McConnell and to the Board of the Society of Illustrators for making the project economically feasible, to Terry Brown of the Society for his contributions, to Art Weithas for the handsome design, to Janet Weithas and Arpi Ermoyan for the final editing, to Fred Goellner-Cortright for plentiful and valuable advice, to Bill Noyes for many of the color photographs, to all of the illustrators who provided photos, proofs and biographical information, to the cooperation of the publications holding copyrights and to institutions or individual owners of illustration originals for photos and permission to reproduce them. Special thanks go to Ben Eisenstat and Murray Tinkelman for their perceptive commentaries.

Walt Reed, Westport, Connecticut

Printed and bound in Tokyo, Japan by Dai Nippon Printing Co. Ltd.
through DNP (America), Inc.

Distributors to the trade in the United States:
Robert Silver Associates: 95 Madison Avenue, New York, N.Y. 10016

Distributors to the trade in Canada:
General Publishing Co. Ltd., 30 Lesmill Road, Don Mills, Ontario, Canada M3B2T6

Distributed in Contintental Europe by:
Feffer and Simons, B.V., 170 Rjinkade, Weesp, Netherlands

Distributed throughout the rest of the world by:
Fleetbooks, S.A., c/o Feffer and Simons, Inc.,
100 Park Avenue, New York, N.Y. 10017

Publisher: Madison Square Press Inc.
10 East 23rd Street, New York City, N.Y. 10010

Typography: PhotoGraphic Productions, Inc., Danbury, Ct.
Designer: Art Weithas

Dedication
To Roger Allen Reed
   (1920-1984)

CONTENTS

drawing by
Robert Fawcett

IS ILLUSTRATION ART?
by Albert Dorne
(1904-1965)

In recent years, it has been fashionable for art critics to couple the word "mere" with "illustration" in dismissing pictures that tell any kind of story. And, since illustration is usually commissioned, it has also been viewed as impure, commercial art when contrasted with the nobler motivation of the fine arts in which the artist is free to express his innermost feelings.

This distinction, if applied consistently, would reject a Fra Angelico, a Giotto or a Michelangelo, who made paintings of Biblical subjects on commission from wealthy patrons or the Church. To come closer to the present, many American painters such as Winslow Homer, William Glackens or Frederic Remington, whose works now command honored places in our museums, contributed much of their life's output to illustration. Certainly for them it was a valid form of art, and they gave their best to it.

More appropriate, to me, would be a distinction between good artists and bad artists. Throughout history there have been thousands of mediocre artists, many good ones, and a few who were great. In many cases we have no record of the original reasons the artists had for painting their pictures, and whether or not the pictures were painted to specification. This no longer seems very important. The real question is, what did the artist contribute of his own particular individuality to make his picture a masterpiece?

The form in which an artist chooses to create is secondary. He may work with stone, metal, canvas or watercolor paper; he may paint murals, portraits, illustrations or landscapes; his viewpoint may range from highly detailed academic realism to abstract expressionism. Each artist, however, works within the restrictions of his medium, his purpose, and his ability.

The illustrator, in his turn, is subject to the limitations of his assignments and a responsibility to his client. His success is measured by whether or not the function of the picture is realized — to tell a story or to present an idea effectively. He must, therefore, be able to communicate his intention clearly.

In translating the requirements of an advertising director or a magazine art editor into a picture, there is no reason why the same standards of art cannot as appropriately be applied here as for gallery walls. Many illustrators do, in fact, paint as many pictures for exhibition as they do for reproduction, without compromising their integrity in either area.

This is not to imply that *all* illustration is art. We have seen far too many pictures of stereotyped cliches or models with toothpaste grins promoting a product to be sold. In these instances, the vision of the advertiser or art editor, as well as the artist, is shallow and deserves but little respect.

Furthermore, some artists, and often the public, mistakenly confuse technique or facility with art. An artist must have much more than virtuosity. A painting may approach technical perfection and yet be completely vacuous. And even a crudely made drawing or painting can be important if the artist has a really worth-while statement to make.

This does not mean that the illustrator must always say something profound. He may use humor or exaggeration, present a glimpse of beauty, a fresh insight into a familiar scene, or even use a line in such a sensitive and expressive way as to stimulate the imagination. The artist may also be a reporter, adding his special dimension to that of the camera, the recording, or the printed word.

In other words, opportunities for the illustrator are limited only by the imagination of the individual. It is up to each one of us to realize his fullest potential both as individual and as artist.

This volume covers a period during which illustration became a vital art form in the United States. Since it is, perhaps, too early for a definitive judgment, each reader should draw his own conclusions from the varied contents of this book. He should do so because the final worth of the pictures will be based on these conclusions, plus the opinion that will ultimately be filed by posterity.

PREFACE

The first edition of THE ILLUSTRATOR IN AMERICA 1900-1960s was published in 1966 and has been out of print for almost 20 years. The decision to publish a new edition was based primarily on the fact that so many profound changes in the profession have occurred during that time. The addition of another two decades would record those changes and bring the history up to date.

However, the decision also presented an opportunity to revise the somewhat arbitrary chronology of the first book which began with the year 1900. By so doing, the book had placed some of the earlier artists into the later years of their careers. Also, some important illustrators who had died by 1900 were thus excluded. By moving back to the period beginning in the year 1880, these problems could be better resolved.

This edition, covering the one hundred years from 1880 to 1980, adds many new artists at the beginning and at the end of the book and many biographies of living artists have been brought up to date.

The color plates for the original edition have become lost in the interim and necessitated making new ones. While this has added to the expense of producing this edition, it has also provided the opportunity to use fresh material throughout the book and, in fact, to add much more color.

Some earlier artists whose work was done in an era when color printing was not yet invented spent their whole careers making black and white pictures. Even after color printing was available, publishers used it very sparingly because of the prohibitive cost. Many examples in the book will necessarily, therefore, remain in black and white. And, because of the impermanent nature of periodicals, the record of much of this art has vanished; the originals are scattered or lost. In such cases where the originals were not obtainable, it was necessary to reproduce from proofs in order to include particular pictures which best represent the artists.

Fortunately, there has been a resurgence of interest in illustration as art in the last twenty years, by critics and museums alike. Several major collections of American illustration are now in museums, such as the New Britain (Connecticut) Museum of American Art, The Society of Illustrators Museum of American Illustration in New York, the Brandywine River Museum in Chadds Ford, Pennsylvania, the Delaware Art Museum in Wilmington, and the Library of Congress in Washington, D.C. Also, many individual examples are included in museum collections across the country from the Los Angeles Museum in California to the Metropolitan Museum of Art in New York City. Such changes have been most gratifying to observe and several examples in this book have been drawn from these sources.

Even in its expanded form, too many competent and worthy illustrators have still had to be omitted from this volume and we regret that. Our purpose has been to honor as many of them as possible.

Walt and Roger Reed
Westport, Connecticut, 1984

1880
1890

drawing by Tom Lovell

THE DECADE: 1880-1890
Walt Reed

Any beginning date must necessarily be a confining limitation, cutting off what has gone before. Winslow Homer, for instance, was one of America's great illustrators, if for his Civil War coverage for *Harper's Weekly* alone. But his career as an illustrator covered only about fifteen years, from 1860 to 1875, even though his painting career continued until his death in 1910, so he is not included here. And, certainly Homer's career has been well documented in other publications. However, we have taken the opportunity to include a Homer subject to illustrate the problems involved in translating the artist's original work to print on the pages of a newspaper, magazine or book at the time when virtually all illustrations were reproduced by wood engravings.

Although the technical skill of the engravers was extraordinary, the method of reproduction had changed very little since the days of Albrecht Durer. The art work was drawn or traced directly on a block of wood (in reverse) as a guide for the engraver. It was then the job of the engraver to cut away the wood *between* the lines, thus creating the white areas in the final printed form. Oftentimes, as in the case of Homer, the original drawing was destroyed in the cutting process. Later, it became possible to transfer the artist's drawing photographically to the wood block, freeing the artist considerably, but the final printed result still tended to reflect the personality of the engraver as much as that of the artist. In fact, the artist and the engraver both signed the work and shared the credit.

However, it was the invention of photoengraving, as a mechanical process for reproducing drawings or paintings, that was responsible for the spectacular development and expansion of the whole field of illustration. The transition from the use of wood engravings to line or halftone photoengraving was a gradual one, dating from the early 1880s to as late as 1910. The early halftones (which also made full color printing practical) tended to be gray and muddy, requiring a great deal of additional handwork by the engraver. However, by 1900, leading monthly periodicals, such as *Harper's, Century,* and *McClure's,* were able to obtain halftone reproductions of good quality and hence began to make lavish use of illustrations. Many of the finest artists of the time were attracted to illustrating for the magazines and their names became widely known to the general public. The caste distinction between ''Fine'' and ''Commercial'' art as yet scarcely existed and many artists pursued simultaneous careers in painting for print and for the galleries.

This period thus marked the real beginning of illustration as a popular art and, as we now look back on it, the beginning of its Golden Age.

Walt Reed

ILLUSTRATORS 1880-1890

EDWIN AUSTIN ABBEY
DANIEL CARTER BEARD
REGINALD BATHURST BIRCH
ROBERT FREDERICK BLUM
BENJAMIN WEST CLINEDINST
FELIX OCTAVIUS CARR DARLEY
HENRY FARNEY
HARRY FENN
ARTHUR BURDETT FROST
WILLIAM GILBERT GAUL
EDWARD WINDSOR KEMBLE

MAX FRANCIS KLEPPER
LOUIS LOEB
FRANCIS DAVIS MILLET
THOMAS NAST
JOSEPH PENNELL
ALLEN CARTER REDWOOD
WILLIAM THOMAS SMEDLEY
WILLIAM LADD TAYLOR
THURE De THULSTRUP
ELIHU VEDDER
RUFUS FAIRCHILD ZOGBAUM

E. A. Abbey

EDWIN AUSTIN ABBEY, N.A., R.A. (1852-1911) was both illustrator and artist in the fullest sense. His work, beginning with small black-and-white illustrations for the old *Harper's* magazine, and culminating in the huge mural decorations for the Boston Public Library and the State Capitol in Harrisburg, Pennsylvania, was done with extraordinary artistic dedication.

Abbey's drive for authenticity was legendary among his fellow-illustrators and eventually led him to live in England where the original props and costuming required for his historical illustrations were still to be found.

Many of his later illustrations were rendered in water color or in oils for reproduction in full color, but he continued to use pen and ink as a serious art medium. The brilliant draughtsmanship of his pen-and-ink drawings for the plays of Shakespeare has never been surpassed.

A full record of his life and work is contained in the two-volume *Edwin Austin Abbey* by E. V. Lucas, published in 1921 by Charles Scribner's Sons in New York, and Methuen and Company Limited in London.

A permanent collection of his drawings, paintings, and pastels is retained in the Edwin Austin Abbey collection at Yale University in New Haven, Connecticut.

Illustration for Henry IV, *Part I, by William Shakespeare, published by* Harper's Monthly *magazine, 1906. Collection of Yale University Art Gallery.*

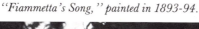

"Fiammetta's Song," painted in 1893-94.

"Richard, Duke of Gloucester, and the Lady Anne" from Shakespeare's Richard III, *Act I, Scene II, painted in 1905-06.*

"O My Fair Warrior," from Othello, *Act II, Scene I,* Harper's Monthly *magazine, October, 1904.*

REGINALD BATHURST BIRCH (1856-1943) was known as "the children's Gibson" because of the great number of pen-and-ink illustrations for children's stories and fairy tales he did for *St. Nicholas* magazine.

His drawings give the appearance of great spontaneity and directness resulting from his practice of using models only for his preliminary sketches and rendering the finished drawings freely from them.

Although Birch also illustrated for the *Century* magazine, *Harper's, McClure's, Scribner's, Collier's,* the old *Life, Youth's Companion,* and nearly 200 books, his best known illustrations were done for *Little Lord Fauntleroy,* by Frances Hodgson Burnett in 1886. These were responsible for a whole generation of Victorian boys' being forced to wear black velvet suits, lace collars and curls, patterned after Birch's prototype.

Birch was born in England, grew up in San Francisco, and studied at the Art Academy in Munich, Germany.

DANIEL CARTER BEARD (1850-1941) Today the artist is better remembered as the founder of the Boy Scouts of America, in 1910, with which he was completely involved for the latter part of his life. Mt. Beard, located near Mt. McKinley, was named in his honor.

Born in Cincinnati, Ohio, son of James Henry Beard, a National Academician, he studied at the Art Students League with John Sartain and J. C. Beckwith. His high sense of humor made him an ideal candidate to illustrate Mark Twain's *A Connecticut Yankee in King Arthur's Court,* and he was a regular contributor to *St. Nicholas Magazine.* He also wrote and illustrated books on animals and outdoor life as well as the *American Boy's Handy Book.* Active in the Society of Illustrators, he served as its president in 1914.

Reproduced from St. Nicholas *magazine, January, 1889.*

"I saw he meant business," frontispiece illustration for A Connecticut Yankee in King Arthur's Court, *1889.*

"*A Levee at the President's House in 1813,*" from The Century *magazine, 1901.*

B.WEST CLINEDINST.

BENJAMIN WEST CLINEDINST, N.A. (1859-1931) was one of the original ten founders of the Society of Illustrators in 1901. He was born in Woodstock, Virginia, and studied at the Ecole des Beaux Arts in Paris where he was a pupil of Cabanel and Bonnat. In addition to his illustrations for many magazines and books, he painted portraits of several national figures including President Theodore Roosevelt and Admiral Peary.

From 1903-'05 he was art editor of *Leslie's Weekly.* He exhibited widely and was elected to membership in the National Academy in 1898. The last years of his life were devoted to painting and teaching of illustration at Cooper Union in New York.

In this beautiful pen-and-ink rendering by ROBERT FREDERICK BLUM, N.A. (1857-1903) there is evidence of the influence of Fortuny, the Spanish master, but the soundness of draughtsmanship and form were his own.

Blum was born in Cincinnati, Ohio, and was apprenticed to a lithographer's shop in 1871. He studied nights at the McMicken Art School of Design in Cincinnati, later attended the Pennsylvania Academy of the Fine Arts in Philadelphia. Blum made many trips abroad, and the majority of his pictures are of foreign subjects. He lived for some time in Japan where he produced some of his finest drawings and paintings — one of which, "The Ameya, or Itinerant Candy Vendor," is owned by The Metropolitan Museum of Art.

"*Mr. Joseph Jefferson as Bob Acres,*" for Sheridan's comedy, The Rivals, Scribner's *magazine, 1880.*

"The Song of the Talking Wire," Collection of the Taft Museum, Cincinnati, Ohio.

FARNY
∅

HENRY F. FARNY (1847-1916) was the son of a promi-nent Republican refugee from France and his early years, 1853-1859, were spent in the wilderness of western Pennsylvania. There he made his first contact with the Seneca Indians, with whom he became friendly. The family eventually moved by raft downriver to the more civilized city of Cincinnati where Farny became apprenticed to a lithography firm. Needing further art training, he saved enough to go abroad to Rome, Vienna, Munich and Dusseldorf on two successive trips, sporadically working to support his classroom studies. On his return to the United States, he began to illustrate for Cincinnati publishers as well as for *Harper's.*

He also became interested and specialized in Indian sub-ject matter, and in 1881 made the first of many visits to the West, recording the contrasts of white and Indian interac-tion. Many of these drawings and paintings were published in *Harper's Weekly* and *Century* magazine which sent Farny and a reporter on the trips. There Farny met and drew Sitting Bull; later he introduced the famous warrior to General Grant. President Theodore Roosevelt was a per-sonal admirer of Farny's work.

After 1890 Farny concentrated on easel painting, relying on his large collection of Indian costumes, artifacts, photos and sketches for reference. The accuracy and artistry of his work combine to make him one of our major painters of the Old West.

Illustration for "Two Arrows," Harper's Young People, *1885.*

Darley

FELIX OCTAVIUS CARR DARLEY, N.A. (1822-1888) can well be considered America's first important illustrator. Self-taught, he created an immense volume of work over a long career. Beginning as a staff artist with a Philadelphia publisher, he learned to take on a wide variety of subjects. Later, in New York, his work was reproduced by many book publishers, *Harper's Weekly,* and other magazines. Among the important authors whose books he illustrated were Irving, Hawthorne, Longfellow, Poe and Cooper. He also wrote and illustrated his own book, *Sketches Abroad with Pen and Pencil,* published in 1869. An important project was the illustrating of *Our Country, A Household History,* containing over 500 illustrations in four volumes by Benson Lossing, printed in 1880.

Darley was the first of a new American school of illustrators which was to successfully challenge the dominance of English and Continental illustration during the mid-nineteenth century.

He also made designs for bank notes and exhibited at the National Academy, becoming a member in 1853.

Gilbert Gaul

WILLIAM GILBERT GAUL, N.A. (1855-1919) specialized in military subjects to which he gave a feeling of great authenticity. His characters were not paintings of polished, costumed models, but of real people revealed by carefully observed gestures. The uniforms looked lived-in, powder-stained, torn or patched. Like Matthew Brady's photos, the effect is one of raw honesty to which he added the drama of lifelike action.

Gaul was born in Jersey City, New Jersey, and was educated at the Claverack Military Academy. He studied art in New York City under the painter J. G. Brown. His illustrations appeared regularly in *Harper's Monthly* and other magazines.

He won a Gold Medal from the American Art Association in 1881 for his painting, "Hold the Line at All Hazards." "Charging the Battery" won a medal at the Paris Exposition in 1889.

"Taking a Break" Collection of Mr. and Mrs. Davies.

Frontispiece illustration for The Deerslayer *by James Fenimore Cooper.*

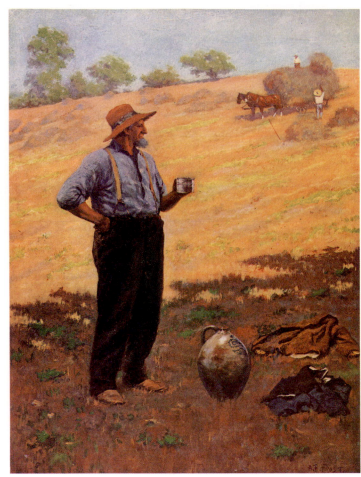

A. B. Frost.

ARTHUR BURDETT FROST (1851-1928) was our best illustrator of rural America. He usually treated his characters with humor, and in his drawings there was a directness and honesty which showed his sympathetic understanding of his subjects. His sound draughtsmanship was combined with an intimate knowledge of nature. The details in his picture are always very specific, as though drawn on the spot, and so artfully chosen and placed as to carry out the picture's idea in a natural and entirely convincing manner.

He may be best remembered now, however, for his charming illustrations for the *Uncle Remus* tales by Joel Chandler Harris. In the preface and dedication by Harris for the 1896 edition, he wrote of Frost "...you have conveyed into their quaint antics the illumination of your own inimitable humor, which is as true to our sun and soil as it is to the spirit and essence of the matter. . . . The book was mine, but now you have made it yours, both sap and pith . . ."

The Grasshopper and the Ant. Frontispiece for Scribner's *Magazine, December, 1894.*

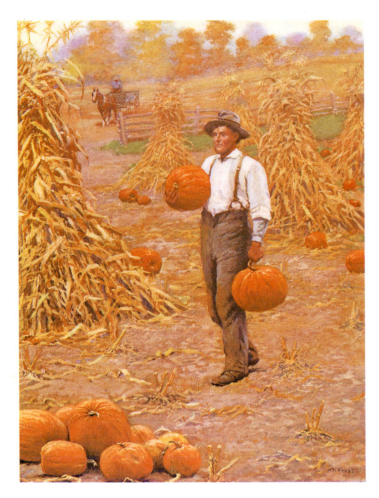

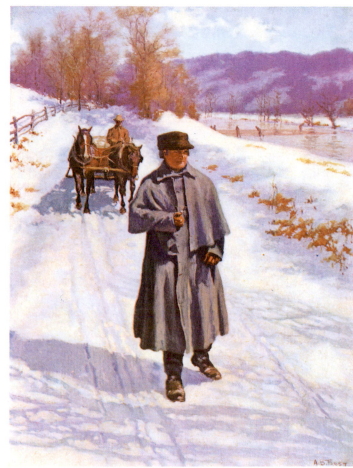

The Four Seasons, 1906. Although Frost was red-green color blind, that was not a great handicap since the majority of his work was reproduced in black-and-white. However, he managed to work successfully in color by reading the labels on the tubes and placing the colors in the proper order on his palette.

"Swinging on the Tee." Frost was an ardent sportsman and many of his favorite subjects were hunting, fishing and golfing. The golfing subjects, as here, tended toward humor.

"Br'er Fox and Br'er Rabbit," from The Tar Baby, *published by D. Appleton & Co., 1904.*

"Scollay Square — Boston," illustration for St. Nicholas Magazine, January, 1893.

HARRY FENN (1838-1911) was born in England and received his early art training as an apprentice under the Dalziel brothers who ran the famous wood engraving firm.

After completing his term, he took a vacation journey to Canada and, at nineteen, a side trip to America to see Niagara Falls. He stayed to work in the States for the rest of his career, interrupted only by a trip to study further in Italy. In 1870 he took on a major project for D. Appleton publishers to travel extensively throughout the country and illustrate *Picturesque America.* This was followed by several similar volumes and illustration work for *Harper's Monthly* and other magazines.

Fenn was the founder of the American Watercolor Society, a member of the New York Watercolor Club, the Society of Illustrators and the Salmagundi Club.

EDWARD WINDSOR KEMBLE (1861-1933) was a self-taught artist whose work reveals a strong sense of humor and an acute observation of character. His outlook was similar to that of A. B. Frost and, like Frost, he illustrated many of the *Uncle Remus* stories by Joel Chandler Harris.

Kemble illustrated several other famous books, including Mark Twain's *Huckleberry Finn,* and *Puddin' Head Wilson,* Harriet Beecher Stowe's *Uncle Tom's Cabin,* and Washington Irving's *Knickerbocker's History of New York.*

He had a special empathy for Black characters and drew them with an understanding and geniality uncommon in his day.

Huck Finn, as depicted in the 1884 edition of Huckleberry Finn by Mark Twain.

"McCulloch's men taking the first line of fortifications," from "The Storming of Fort Pillow," Harper's Monthly *magazine, September, 1899.*

Max F. Klepper

MAX FRANCIS KLEPPER (1861-1907) was brought to America from Germany by his parents in 1876. Later, he returned to study in Munich for four years. Back in New York, he began to illustrate for major magazines such as *Harper's, Scribner's* and *The Century.* He was expert in depicting animals of all kinds, particularly horses, which are featured in many of his illustrations.

— LOUIS · LOEB —

LOUIS LOEB, N.A. (1866-1909) Like the majority of the illustrators of his day, Loeb received his art training abroad. He studied under Gérome in Paris and exhibited in the Paris Salon in 1895 and 1897 before returning to the States. As an illustrator, his work appeared in *The Century, Harper's Monthly* and other publications. He was a Founding member of the Society of Illustrators.

Loeb was also an active etcher and painter for exhibition, winning a number of awards including the Hallgarten prize of the National Academy of Design in 1902 and the Carnegie prize in 1905. He was elected a full member of the National Academy in 1906.

"I want to find my Father's People," illustrated for *"Prisoners of Conscience,"* The Century Magazine.

Le Mans, August 1892, published by The Century *magazine*

JOSEPH PENNELL, N.A. (1860-1926) was a pictorial reporter interested chiefly in architectural subjects. He ranged the world on assignments for *Century, McClure's,* and *Harper's* magazines, sending back exquisite etchings, pen-and-ink drawings or lithographs of cathedrals, plazas, street scenes, and palaces. He also skillfully depicted the panoramic aspects of major construction or engineering projects — the Locks at Niagara Falls, the construction of the Panama Canal and the war production efforts in Britain, France and America during World War I.

He was a friend and great admirer of James McNeill Whistler, whose biography he wrote. He also wrote a number of books on various art and travel subjects, many in collaboration with his wife, Elizabeth Robins Pennell.

FRANCIS DAVIS MILLET, N.A. (1846-1912) went down with the S.S. Titanic, ending an illustrious career. Born in Mattapoisett, Massachusetts, he studied at the Royal Academy of Arts in Antwerp. During the Russo-Turkish War of 1877, he became a special correspondent for the London *Daily News* and was decorated by the Rumanian and Russian governments. He was also a correspondent for the London *Times* in Manila during the Spanish-American War.

In 1893, Millet was Director of Decorations at the Chicago Columbian Exposition. He also served as vice-chairman of the Federal Committee of Fine Arts, was executive officer of the American Academy in Rome and was a founder of the American Federation of Arts.

Millet, who was a National Academician, exhibited regularly there, painted a number of portraits, including one of Mark Twain, and several murals.

"Cossacks Raiding a Turkish Village," from "Campaigning with the Cossacks," Harper's Monthly, *January 1887.*

"The Tammany Tiger Loose — What are you going to do about it?"
Considered one of the most powerful political illustrations ever
published, it appeared as a double page spread in Harper's Weekly
on November 11, 1871 and helped to bring down the Tweed Ring.
This was the first appearance of the Tammany Tiger in a cartoon.
Nast is also credited with creating the images of the Republican
Elephant and the Democratic Donkey.

Th: Nast.

THOMAS NAST (1840-1902) whose work as a political
cartoonist and caricaturist had an immense influence on
American politics, was born in Bavaria and died in Guy-
aquil, Ecuador, while serving as the American consul-
general.

With a precocious art talent, he did his first professional
illustration for Frank Leslie's illustrated newspaper at the
age of fifteen. Later assignments included trips abroad to
England and Sicily and Calabria, following Garibaldi's
Army.

In 1861 he returned to America and soon became a staff
member of *Harper's,* producing many war related illustrations for *Harper's Weekly.* President Lincoln considered Nast
one of the most influential recruiters for the Northern
cause.

It was following the war, however, during the reign of the
Tammany political machine in New York, that Nast developed his most effective style in attacking the corruption of
Boss Tweed and his ring, eventually forcing them out of
office. Nast was also an accomplished painter and produced a number of oils relating to the Civil War and other
historical scenes.

"Money Bag" portrait of Tweed, Harper's Weekly, *1871.*

"Confederate Types," from Battles and Leaders of the Civil War
published by The Century *Magazine in four volumes in 1888.*

A.C.Redwood

ALLEN CARTER REDWOOD (1834-1922) Unlike
many of the artists who illustrated the action of the Civil
War from the sketches sent to the publishers, Redwood was
an active participant. He enlisted in 1861 and served in the
55th regiment of the Army of Northern Virginia. Captured
at the second battle of Bull Run, he was later exchanged
and advanced in rank to Major.

After the hostilities were over, many memoirs and histories of the war were published, and Redwood's artistic
services provided an authentic documentation from the
Southern side. Redwood also illustrated many other subjects in the postwar years for *Century, Harper's* and other
magazine and book publishers.

W.T.Smedley

WILLIAM THOMAS SMEDLEY, N.A. (1858-1920)
was born in West Chester, Pennsylvania, received his art
education at the Pennsylvania Academy of the Fine Arts in
Philadelphia and later studied with Jean Paul Laurens in
Paris.

He began his career in the early 1880's as pen-and-ink
artist for Harper and Brothers; later, as halftone engraving
was introduced, he changed to working in opaque water
color.

An active painter, Smedley was a member of the American Watercolor Society, National Association of Portrait
Painters, and National Institute of Arts and Letters. He
won many awards, including the Evans Prize, A.W.C.S.
1890; Proctor Prize, National Academy of Design, 1906;
and the Carnegie Prize, National Academy of Design,
1916. His work is also represented in the National Gallery
of Art, Washington, D.C.

"Alice Bruce and Randolph Marshall" from Life and Character
— Drawings by W. T. Smedley, *Harper and Brothers,' 1899.*

W. L. TAYLOR -

WILLIAM LADD TAYLOR (1854-1926) had a thorough art education in art schools in Boston, New York, and with Boulanger and Lefebvre in Paris.

Taylor returned to settle in Boston and to record a long series of subjects, usually of historical or regional nature. His interest in antiques and in recreating the era of their use was reflected in an excellent series of paintings of the nineteenth century in New England. Other series included "Old Southern Days," "Home Scenes," and "Frontier Scenes," the latter painted during the course of an illness and a year's stay in Colorado.

For many years these pictures were a regular feature as full-color, full-page reproductions in *The Ladies' Home Journal;* reprints of the pictures for framing were very popular. A large number of the pictures were also reproduced in a book, *Our Home and Country,* published by Moffat, Yard and Company in 1908.

"Evangeline," published by The Ladies' Home Journal *in 1899.*

THULSTRUP -

THURE DE THULSTRUP (1848-1930) was a Swedish subject born in Stockholm. He fought with the French Army during the Franco-Prussian War of 1870-71. Shortly after immigrating to the United States in 1873, he attended the newly organized Art Students League in New York. His first illustrations were made for the old *Daily Graphic* of New York; later he became a staff artist for Frank Leslie's periodicals. By 1881 he was a regular contributor to *Harper's* magazine, then to *Century, Scribner's, Cosmopolitan,* and other leading magazines.

His work is forthright and without frills, whether rendered in pen and ink, black-and-white wash, or in full color. His careful observance of fact and a strong compositional sense gave him the versatility to depict any subject convincingly, but he was especially competent with horses and military subjects.

Illustration for "Lieutenant-Colonel Forrest at Fort Donelson," Harper's Monthly, *February, 1899.*

Vedder

ELIHU VEDDER, N.A. (1836-1923) Of Dutch ancestry, Vedder was born in New York, and his artistic talents were precocious. At the age of twenty, he went to Europe to study, staying for four years. On his return to the United States, he quickly established himself as an illustrator and a painter. He became a full member of the National Academy by the age of twenty-seven, the youngest painter so elected. In 1867, he returned to Europe and settled permanently in Italy.

Among his murals are a mosaic in the Library of Congress and a commission for the Walker Art Gallery at Bowdoin College. His best known illustrations were done for the *Rubaiyat of Omar Khayyam* in 1884. He also wrote poetry, and his autobiography was published in 1910.

"The Questioner of the Sphinx," Scribner's Monthly, *November, 1880.*

R.F. Zogbaum

RUFUS FAIRCHILD ZOGBAUM (1849-1925) was a lifelong student of and expert in the depiction of battle scenes. (He wrote and illustrated a book titled *Horse, Foot and Dragoons,* published by Harper and Brothers as well as several scholarly articles for Scribner's, including "From Port to Port with the White Squadron" in the October, 1890 issue.) He specialized in American war illustrations: of the Civil War, the skirmishes with the Indians, and the Spanish-American War. In his pictures, there is an origi-

nality of approach and authenticity of detail that mark him as a master. Unfortunately, the great bulk of his work predated halftone engraving and was reproduced by the cruder method of wood engraving.

He painted the "First Minnesota Regiment at the Battle of Gettysburg," as a mural at the State Capitol in St. Paul, and the "Battle of Lake Erie" for the Federal Building in Cleveland.

"The Charge of the Dragoons" from "Mad Anthony Wayne's Victory" by Theodore Roosevelt, Harper's Monthly, *April, 1896.*

1890

1900

drawing by Charles Santore

THE DECADE: 1890-1900
Benjamin Eisenstat

The "Gay Nineties" was an appropriate description of this decade despite the depression of '93 and the hordes of newly-arrived immigrants. America slowly pulled itself out of that depression and those immigrants, though bewildered and poor, brought with them a tradition of self-reliance and a fervent belief in the future of their adopted country. It was a time of faith and optimism. Advances in industry, commerce, transportation and educaton went far beyond the wildest predictions. And heralding all this progress for a rapidly expanding readership was the glamorous business of publishing.

America's appetite for information and entertainment was served almost entirely by newspapers, magazines and books. Publishers, editors, writers and artists were the celebrities of the day. And since the most obvious and easily appreciated aspect of publishing were the pictures, the greatest heroes were the picture-makers, the illustrators.

With the introduction of photo-engraving, reproducing art work had become fast and inexpensive as compared to the old wood engraving process. This meant that the highly competitive publishing houses could use pictures as a means of increasing circulation. The most competent artists of the day were recruited by rival editors and their illustrations were eagerly awaited by the reading public.

Because there was no other mass access to visual communication, illustrators achieved public recognition comparable to the movie, television and rock stars of today. Charles Dana Gibson's career, for instance, was a matter of great public interest. When two magazines, *Life* and *Collier's* fought for his drawings, each raising the ante, it was front page news. Every aspect of his life was copy for journalists, photographers and cartoonists. His pen-and-inks of American manners and morals, of the matchmaking of opportunistic, down-at-the-heels European nobility with the daughters of the newly-rich American tycoons, and his documentary illustrations of England, France and Egypt were admired by everyone and copied by countless aspiring young artists. Now, almost a century later, many of these copies regularly turn up in galleries and auction houses, passing innocently or otherwise as original Gibsons.

Along with veneration at home, American illustrators were winning praise abroad. Gibson was lionized internationally and Howard Pyle, whose books were frequently published simultaneously in New York and London, received rave reviews on both sides of the Atlantic. Regrettably, American easel painters did not fare as well abroad. Nor were they held in great esteem in their own country. Our collectors and museums ignored artists like Thomas Eakins who painted in obscurity, while they spent huge sums in Paris, Munich, London and Rome for works long since forgotten.

Illustrators, of course, had higher visibility. The large circulation of sophisticated magazines, such as *Harper's, Scribner's, Century* and *McClure's,* insured their artists a large and intelligent audience compared to the limited patrons of galleries and museums. Then, too, there were no artificial divisions of "fine" and "commercial" art. The latter term was hardly used since major artists had not yet become involved in advertising, other than the prestigious posters of outstanding illustrator/designers, such as Edward Penfield and Will Bradley.

In those days there were few pronounced stylistic categories in art. Only a small minority of American artists were aware of European experimentation with impressionism, abstraction, etc. Practically all painting was based on variations of realism and many easel painters used genre themes that were consistently illustrative. Important annual exhibitions included works by men like Pyle, Guerin, McCarter, Church, DuMond, Granville-Smith, Wiles and others, which had been originally commissioned as illustrations. Their creators considered them art-with no apologies, a viewpoint held most convincingly by Howard Pyle.

When Pyle decided to act upon those convictions, he offered to teach illustration at the Pennsylvania Academy of the Fine Arts, the oldest art institution in America. Coldly rejected, he began his brilliant teaching career elsewhere. When his fame as a teacher spread, the Academy regretted its decision and invited him to join their faculty on his own terms. This time Pyle refused and the

Academy secured the services of Walter Appleton Clark. After Clark, Henry Bainbridge McCarter, whose romantic illustrations were widely admired, became the Academy's next choice and he was soon acknowledged as another outstanding teacher in the field of illustration. In fact, a number of Pyle's most noted pupils had also studied with Henry McCarter.

Much later, in the mid-thirties I was also a McCarter student at the Academy. By then he was respected as a painter, but few of us knew of his earlier fame as an illustrator. His emphasis was always on ART from the broad point of view and his students idolized him. Whatever was brought for criticism, be it a small black-and-white illustration or a large experimental canvas, he treated with equal respect and consideration. He was never caustic or cynical with any serious student, although he could be feisty with dilettantes. Most of all there was always encouragement. Perhaps it was this attitude that made the '90s "golden." It had been a time of high regard for the illustration profession. One aspired to be an artist first. Publication was a by-product. It must have been this dauntless striving for quality that lifted turn-of-the-century illustration to such heights.

Benjamin Eisenstat

ILLUSTRATORS 1890-1900

WILL H. BRADLEY
ALFRED LAURENS BRENNAN
CLIFFORD CARLETON
FREDERICK STUART CHURCH
WALTER APPLETON CLARK
WILL CRAWFORD
FRANK VINCENT DuMOND
MARY HALLOCK FOOTE
CHARLES DANA GIBSON
WALTER GRANVILLE-SMITH
JULES GUERIN
HENRY McCARTER

PETER SHEAF NEWELL
EDWARD PENFIELD
EDWARD HENRY POTTHAST
HOWARD PYLE
CHARLES STANLEY REINHART
FREDERIC SACKRIDER REMINGTON
WILLIAM ALLEN ROGERS
ALICE BARBER STEPHENS
THOMAS STARLING SULLIVANT
ALBERT BECK WENZELL
IRVING RAMSEY WILES

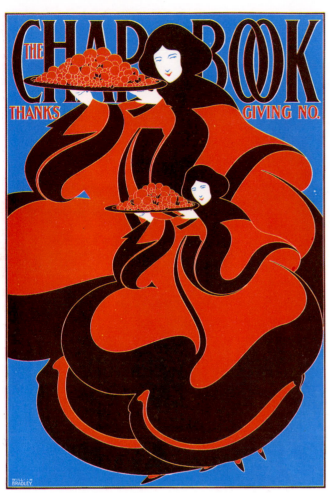

The Chap Book *cover, Thanksgiving number, November, 1895.*

WILL BRADLEY

WILL H. BRADLEY (1868-1962) began his career as a printer's devil on a local newspaper in Ishpeming, Michigan, initiating a life-long fascination with type and printing. He moved to Chicago in 1886 to launch his career as an illustrator, working in pen and ink for *The Inland Printer* and *Frank Leslie's Illustrated Newspaper.*

Greatly influenced by William Morris of the Arts and Crafts movement in England, Bradley incorporated Morris' theories in his work, along with the influences of Aubrey Beardsley and Art Nouveau. One of the first Americans to produce posters, he had a major influence on that art in the United States.

A multi-talented artist, Bradley organized his own publishing firm, the Wayside Press, designed type faces, wrote and illustrated stories in his magazine, *Bradley; His Book,* was a design consultant for several advertising agencies and corporations, ran an art service, served as art director for *Collier's Weekly, Good Housekeeping, Success,* and *Metropolitan* magazines. In 1915 he was employed by William Randolph Hearst as art supervisor for *Hearst's International* and other Hearst magazines, and also for several Hearst-produced motion pictures. He later wrote and directed his own film, "Mangold."

C. Carleton.

CLIFFORD CARLETON (1867-1946) was born in Brooklyn, New York, and studied at the Art Students League under H. Siddons Mowbray. Carleton was at his best with rural subjects, such as the watercolor painting reproduced here. He produced a great amount of work and illustrated for most of the leading magazines of his day, including the old *Life, Harper's Weekly, Harper's Bazaar,* and *Scribner's.* Books he illustrated include: *Pembroke,* by Mary Wilkins, *People We Pass,* by Julian Ralph, and *Their Wedding Journey,* by William Dean Howells.

"The Barn Dance," published by E. R. Herrick & Company, 1898.

"King Edward III and the Black Prince crossing Old London Bridge" from St. Nicholas Magazine, *February, 1888.*

Brennan

ALFRED LAURENS BRENNAN (1853-1921) was born in Louisville, Kentucky, and was one of the major talents in the use of pen and ink in his day. To the apparent influence of the Spanish master Fortuny, he added his own technical virtuosity and an unconventional point of view which makes his work always arresting and intriguing.

Like Fortuny, he made telling use of pure blacks and pure whites which effectively set off the intermediate values and fine detail. His elaborate compositions prevented his being as prolific as many of his contemporaries, but his work appeared regularly in publications such as *Harper's, Century,* and *St. Nicholas* magazines.

Walter Appleton Clark

The life of WALTER APPLETON CLARK (1876-1906) was cut tragically short by complications following a bout with typhoid fever, but even in that time he established himself as a mature and versatile artist.

While Clark was still a student at the Art Students League, one of his drawings on the classroom wall was seen by the art editor of *Scribner's* magazine. This led to his first commission as an illustrator. He thus fortunately began his career very early and worked industriously for the remaining ten years of his life.

He took on a wide variety of subjects and had a faculty for executing each assignment in an original and dramatic way. In addition to his illustrations for magazines and books, he also produced a series of large oils for a mural project based on the Canterbury Tales. These were published in book form in 1904 by Fox Duffield & Co. and one appeared as a cover for *Scribner's* magazine in 1905.

"The Knight," cover design for Collier's Weekly, *December 8, 1906. This was Clark's last cover. In the Sanford Low Collection of American Illustration, New Britain Museum of American Art.*

Illustration for "Sweet Bells out of Tune," published by Century magazine, March, 1893.

"Seeing the Art Editor," (a subject Gibson knew well from both sides of the door) from Our Neighbors, published by Charles Scribner's Sons, 1905.

"An Imitation of the Lady of the House," Life *Publishing Company, 1902.*

CHARLES DANA GIBSON, N.A. (1867-1944) could draw a pretty face. His drawings of women were so beautiful, so gracious, that it was the highest compliment to a young woman to say that she looked like a Gibson Girl. She was depicted on the stage; her likenesses were printed on pillow covers, painted on chinaware, molded on silver spoons. The Gibson Girl, although aloof and refined, was everyone's "ideal" sweetheart.

However, the popularity of Gibson's art was based on much more than a pretty girl. First, he was a master-draughtsman with pen and ink. He used a penpoint almost as a brush, "painting" in his values with sure capability.

Not that his sureness of technique was an overnight acquisition. Years later, John Ames Mitchell, art editor of the old *Life* magazine, who bought Gibson's first drawing, related that he "detected beneath the outer badness of these drawings peculiarities rarely discovered in the efforts of a beginner ... his faults were good, able-bodied faults that held their heads up and looked you in the eye. No dodging of the difficult points, no tricks, no uncertainty, no slurring of outlines ... there was always courage and honesty in whatever he undertook." Gibson's later virtuosity was

developed through many years of solid application and gradual refinement.

Most important, he was a commentator on the social life and mores of his day, with a satiric but gentle point of view. His people, like "Mr. Pipp," were those with whom everyone, rich or poor, could identify. This happy combination of abilities made Gibson the highest paid illustrator of his time. In 1904 Gibson accepted a contract from *Collier's Weekly* for $100,000 for one hundred illustrations over a period of four years, a contract, incidentally, that repaid *Collier's* many times over in increased circulation.

During World War I, Gibson, as President of the Society of Illustrators, formed and became the head of the Division of Pictorial Publicity under the Federal Committee of Public Information. The top illustrators of the day were recruited to design posters, billboards, and other publicity for the war effort.

After the war, Gibson became owner and editor of the old *Life,* a step which greatly curtailed his own drawing output. By the early 'thirties, he had retired to paint exclusively. In his long career, however, Gibson had compiled a warm and eloquent pictorial record of his era.

"Knowledge is Power," painted in 1889. Grand Rapids Public Library.

FREDERICK STUART CHURCH, N.A. (1842-1924) was born in Grand Rapids, Michigan, and studied art with Walter Shirlaw at the Chicago Academy. He went to New York for further study at the Art Students League and the National Academy of Design; several years later he was elected a full member of the Academy.

His forte was allegorical subject matter, and he found an enthusiastic public reception for his whimsical illustrations, etchings and paintings for exhibition. Along with A. B. Frost and E. W. Kemble, he was also an early illustrator for the "Uncle Remus" stories of Joel Chandler Harris.

WILL CRAWFORD (1869-1944), a staff artist for the *New York World,* had a special flair for humor. With thorough mastery of his pen, he loved to contrive very elaborate situations based on actual historical incidents, poking fun at or exposing what *really* happened. He did a number of these illustrations, called "Historic Bits," for the old *Life* magazine at the turn of the century. He was also a pungent political cartoonist and appeared regularly in *Puck* magazine, often with a full-color, double-page spread.

Crawford, who was born in Washington, D.C., began drawing for the old *Newark* (N.J.) *Call* while still in his teens and later also illustrated for *Collier's, Munsey's,* and *St. Nicholas.*

"The Branding" depicts the subjugation of a maverick Congressman. Published by *Puck* magazine, 1910.

F.V. DuMond

FRANK VINCENT DuMOND, N.A. (1865-1951) had a great influence on illustration through his classes at the Art Students League where, like the anatomy teacher, George Bridgman, he was a fixture for many years.

Probably not many of his students, particularly in his later years, quite realized how good he was as a practicing artist. His training was in the tradition of the French Academy where he studied with Benjamin Constant, Boulanger and Lefebvre in Paris. His early illustrations for *The Century, Scribner's* and *Harper's Monthly* were spectacularly beautiful. Among his outstanding works were the illustrations for Mark Twain's *Personal Recollections of Joan of Arc.*

MHF

MARY HALLOCK FOOTE (1847-1938) was from Quaker stock and raised in a liberal family, which fostered her artistic inclinations. Despite the prevailing attitudes against women in the profession, she was determined to be an artist and, after graduation from the Cooper Union Institute of Design for Women, began her career as a wood engraver. She soon was given book and magazine illustration assignments and was at the beginning of a successful career when she married a young mining engineer, Arthur De Went Foote, in 1876.

Her husband's career came first, and she lived for many years in various primitive mining towns in Colorado, Idaho and California. Despite the hardships of makeshift living and raising three children, she wrote sixteen novels and, when her husband was ruined in a business failure, resumed her illustrating career to support the family. Many of her pictures were published by *Scribner's* and *The Century* magazines. She also painted for exhibition, showing at the Columbian World's Fair in Chicago in 1893 and participated in the Armory Show in 1913; her painting, "The Old Lady," was purchased by the Art Institute of Chicago.

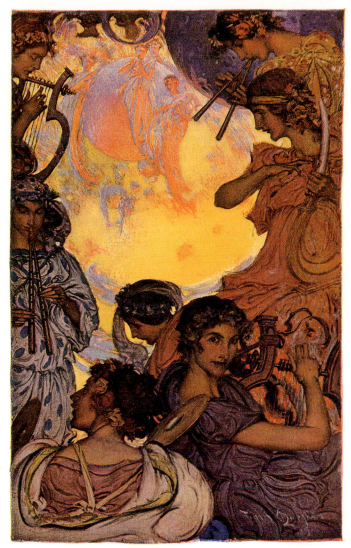

"The Hymn," Milton's Ode on the Nativity, The Century Magazine, *December, 1900.*

"Looking for Camp," published by Century *magazine, November, 1888.*

JULES GUERIN

JULES GUERIN (1866-1946) specialized in architectural illustrations in which the figures were subordinate to the setting. His larger view, usually featuring a man-made structure (ranging from the Pyramids to a colonial church) was presented in a very carefully designed and well-ordered composition. His use of color was particularly effective, usually a bold statement, yet with subtle modulations. His work was reproduced with many travel articles, often in collaboration with the author Robert Hitchens.

Guerin was born in St. Louis, Missouri, and received his art training in Paris where he studied under Benjamin Constant and Jean Paul Laurens. He exhibited at the Paris Exposition in 1900 and the Pan-American Exposition in Buffalo in 1901; received a silver medal at the St. Louis Exposition in 1904 and was elected a member of the National Academy in 1931.

Guerin was also a muralist; best known are his friezes in the Lincoln Memorial in Washington, D. C.

The Arch in Washington Square.

W. Granville-Smith

WALTER GRANVILLE-SMITH, N.A. (1870-1938) pursued dual careers as illustrator and painter; eventually, he devoted full time to painting for exhibition. Active in affairs of the Salmagundi Club and the National Academy, he was elected to full membership in the latter in 1915. Granville-Smith's paintings are represented in numerous museums and private collections.

He was born in Granville, New York, and studied at the Art Students League, as well as abroad. His illustrations were generally of a humorous or light-hearted turn, and he did many covers and illustrations for *Truth* magazine as well as for *The Ladies' Home Journal, The Century Magazine,* and others.

"The First Ball of the Season," typical of his subjects for Truth *magazine.*

Cover design for Outing Magazine, *May, 1903.*

HENRY McCARTER

HENRY McCARTER (1865-1943) occupied a special niche with his work — somewhere between the traditional approach to illustration and exhibition painting. His talents lent themselves best to the interpretation of poetry and although he did some fiction and travel subjects, verse was his specialty. Outstanding were his illustrations for "Claire de Lune" and "Le Piano" by Verlaine.

McCarter studied at the Pennsylvania Academy of the Fine Arts under Thomas Eakins and later in Paris with Puvis de Chavannes. His illustrations were published by *The Century, Scribner's, Harper's Monthly, Collier's* and other magazines. The artist was also an excellent teacher, lecturing at the Art Students League and for many years at the Pennsylvania Academy in Philadelphia.

Peter Newell

PETER SHEAF NEWELL (1862-1924) demonstrated a great sense of humor in his work, and the art editors of several magazines kept him busy exercising it. *Harper's Monthly* used his work regularly for their feature, "The Editor's Drawer." He also illustrated several books by John Kendricks Bangs, and other authors; particularly effective were his interpretations of Lewis Carroll's *Alice in Wonderland.* He wrote and illustrated a number of his own books as well; *The Hole Book, The Slant Book, The Rocket Book* and *Peter Newell's Pictures and Rhymes* all were popular successes.

Newell was largely self-taught with but three months' instruction at the Art Students League.

"The Faux-pas of the Misguided Ass," from "Fables for the Frivolous" by Guy Wetmore Carryl, Harper's Monthly, *1898.*

"The Battle of Bunker Hill" was thoroughly researched by Pyle and is the definitive painting of the subject. The scene represents the second attack and is taken from the right wing of the Fifty-second Regiment, with a company of grenadiers in the foreground. The left wing of the regiment, under command of the major, has halted, and is firing a volley; the right wing is just marching past to take its position for firing. The ship-of-war firing from the middle distance is the Lively; in the remoter distance is the smoke from the battery on Copp's Hill. The black smoke to the right is from the burning houses of Charlestown. From "The Story of the Revolution" by Henry Cabot Lodge; published by Scribner's magazine. February, 1898. Collection of the Delaware Art Museum, Wilmington.

Illustration for "The Story of King Arthur and his Knights," written by Pyle; published in St. Nicholas magazine, November, 1902, through October, 1903, prior to appearance in book form.

H. Pyle.

The illustrations of HOWARD PYLE, N.A. (1853-1911) are as exciting now as they were over 80 years ago, while pictures by many of his contemporaries today look dated and mannered.

Several special qualities combined to make Pyle America's foremost illustrator. Pyle was interested in pictures, first of all, as drama. As a young man his initial visit to a theatrical performance had made a great impression on him and influenced his point of view from then on. In his illustrations, Pyle sought to dramatize themes with universal appeal. The pictures portrayed basic human emotions: the ruthlessness of pirate greed, raw grief in the break-up of Lee's army after Appomattox, smug pride, humble petition.

Pyle's concept of a picture was never trite. He deliberately looked for new ways to tell a story and involved himself in his subject so thoroughly that his picture makes the reader an eye-witness to a vivid experience.

Having evolved his basic pictorial idea, Pyle developed his compositions; his pictures are fascinating to analyze. No area of a picture is wasted; each makes its contribution, through placement, line, tone, or color, to the whole story. Through the details, the viewer's eye is purposefully led toward the focal center.

Pyle wrote, as well as illustrated, many books himself. He did original research on the obscure subject of the buccaneers in the New World. It is from his famous *Book of Pirates* that our present-day concept of pirates has come. School children still read his *Men of Iron, The Story of King Arthur and his Knights, The Merry Adventures of Robin Hood,* and many other tales.

As a teacher, Pyle attracted a large number of students, inspiring them as much by his idealism as by the high standards he set for picture making. Over the years he taught at the Drexel Institute in Philadelphia, lectured at the Art Students League in New York, and eventually conducted special classes for gifted students both at Wilmington, Delaware and, during the summer, at Chadd's Ford, Pennsylvania. He made no charge for his teaching and, in fact, built a set of studios for the students to work in. N. C. Wyeth, Harvey Dunn, Stanley Arthurs, and Frank Schoonover were among the beneficiaries of this instruction, and passed along to others Pyle's unique approach as they, in turn, became illustrators and teachers.

At a time when it was customary and fashionable to study in Europe, Pyle had a strong conviction that students should seek their training and inspiration in America. Many of Pyle's greatest pictures came from his intense and loyal interest in Americana. His renditions of the Revolutionary War period and of Civil War subjects have since become standard pictures in our history books, among them Woodrow Wilson's *History of the American People,* and James Truslow Adams' *History of the United States.*

After Pyle's death, his students collected many of his original paintings as a nucleus for the present comprehensive collection of his work in the Delaware Art Museum. An excellent biography entitled *Howard Pyle,* was written by Henry C. Pitz and published in New York by Bramhall House in 1965.

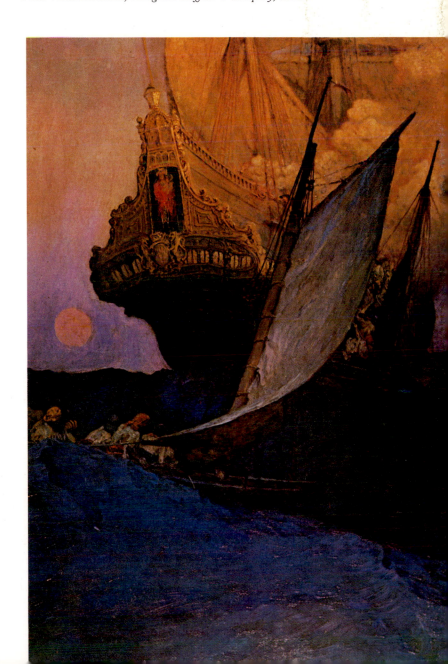

From Grandmother's Story of the Bunker Hill Battle *by Oliver Wendell Holmes, Houghton Mifflin & Company, 1892.*

"The Attack on the Galleon" from "The Tale of a Treasure Town," published in Harper's Monthly, *December, 1905. Collection of the Delaware Art Museum.*

The Old Post Road.

EDWARD PENFIELD (1866-1925) produced some of America's finest posters. His clean style and large silhouetted shapes resulted from much careful preliminary refinement and elimination of detail. Horses and coaches were a favorite subject with him, as typified by this Post Road illustration. A notable series of his illustrations were contained in his book, *Holland Sketches*, published by *Scribner's* in 1907. Another was a series of calendar illustrations, re-drawn in 1918 from the 1843 "Old Farmer's Almanack" for The Beck Engraving Company.

Penfield had a profound influence on American illustration through his own work, in his post as art director for *Harper's* magazine, and through his teaching at the Art Students League. He was president of the Society of Illustrators in 1921 and 1922.

"The Morning Stroll," Collier's; *cover, November 10, 1906.*

"Brother Sim's Mistake," published in The Century *magazine, July, 1899. Collection of Illustration House.*

E. Potthast

EDWARD HENRY POTTHAST, N.A. (1857-1927) is an important figure in American Impressionist painting, noted especially for his brilliantly colorful beach scenes with bathers. The latter part of his life was involved with painting for exhibition and he was elected to full membership in the National Academy in 1906. However, he earlier had a distinguished career as an illustrator; many of his subjects were Blacks, which he did with great sympathy and integrity.

C. S. Reinhart

CHARLES STANLEY REINHART, A.N.A. (1844-1896) was one of the select group of young artists under the tutelage of Charles Parsons, head of the art department of Harper Brothers in the 1870's, who were to launch the Golden Age of American Illustration. The group included Edwin Austin Abbey, Robert Blum, A. B. Frost and Howard Pyle. Reinhart was the senior member of the group, having begun his association as early as 1871 after his art studies in Paris and Munich. He was an expert draftsman in pen and ink, employing fine lines in modeling forms. His gouache illustrations suffered from the translation to wood engravings but indicate his good control of values. Reinhart was also an active exhibitor, winning a medal at the Paris Exposition in 1889, and the Temple Gold Medal, Pennsylvania Academy of the Fine Arts in 1888.

"The Serenade," from "Spanish Vistas," one of a series of illustrations made by Reinhart during a trip to Spain with a writer for Harper's Monthly; *published in April, 1882. Collection of Mort Künstler.*

"The Snow Trail," published in Collier's, *January 21, 1911.*

"There'll Be a Hot Time in the Old Town Tonight My Baby!"

FREDERIC REMINGTON

FREDERIC SACKRIDER REMINGTON, A. N. A (1861-1909) was a huge, hearty man who loved adventure and hard work equally. After a brief period of training in art at Yale University, he departed with the romantic idea of striking it rich in the West of the 1880's.

Remington arrived on the scene during the final period of the old lawless West. Today, we are the richer for the record of those picturesque days in the prodigious outpouring of drawings, paintings and bronzes his vigorous talent has left with us.

If his earliest work was somewhat crude, and had to be re-drawn for publication by a staff artist for *Harper's* magazine, the vigor and authenticity of his subject matter won him immediate recognition; and as his technical ability improved, he was given assignments as a reporter-artist, not only in the West, but also in other parts of the world.

In 1898 he accompanied the Fifth Corps to Cuba as a war-correspondent during the war with Spain when he made many notable paintings and drawings of the action. His painting, "Charge of the Rough Riders at San Juan Hill," helped enhance Theodore Roosevelt's reputation as a soldier. They had become personal friends, and he later

"An Old Time Plains Fight." Reproduced courtesy of the Remington Art Memorial, Ogdensburg, New York.

illustrated several of T. R.'s books and magazine articles.

Remington loved horses. He made a lifelong study of horses and knew at first hand the several strains of the western broncos, their peculiarities and strengths. His article, "Horses of the Plain," was published by *Century* magazine in 1889. He well earned his own suggested epitaph: "He Knew the Horse."

After his death, a Remington Memorial Museum was established in his home town of Ogdensburg, New York. Here are to be found some of the finest of his paintings and bronzes. His Indian Collection, together with his studio effects, are preserved in the Whitney Gallery of Western Art in Cody, Wyoming. He was elected to the Society of Illustrators Hall of Fame in 1978.

The Old Stage Coach of the Plains. Collection of the Amon Carter Museum of Western Art, Fort Worth, Texas.

Spot illustration for "Ranch Life and the Hunting Trail" by Theodore Roosevelt, 1888.

WILLIAM ALLEN ROGERS (1854-1931) took over the political cartoon cover of *Harper's Weekly* after Thomas Nast, and for many years his pen was at the service of the editorial policy of that magazine. While his cartoons never quite approached Nast's in power, his ideas were strongly presented and his drawings somewhat more skillful.

Rogers was born in Springfield, Ohio, and by the age of fourteen was drawing cartoons for a midwestern newspaper. He soon gravitated to the East and began to work as an apprentice in the art department of *Harper's* under the supervision of Charles Parsons. There he developed the skills to take on every kind of assignment, eventually becoming a "special artist" for *Harper's Weekly.*

Rogers was a member of the Century Association and the Society of Illustrators. He wrote an autobiography, *A World Worthwhile,* which was published in 1922.

"An Intolerable Burden," Harper's Weekly *cover, July 15, 1898.*

Sincerity and good taste, as well as her technical excellence, make the illustrations of ALICE BARBER STEPHENS (1858-1932) a pleasure to look at. The early discipline of her work as a wood engraver for *Scribner's* was in some measure responsible for her fine draftsmanship. She was most successful in quiet settings, with humble subjects. Among her best is a series of pictures of old men and women, inmates of the Philadelphia almshouse.

She was trained at the Pennsylvania Academy of the Fine Arts and at the Philadelphia School of Design for Women, where she later taught portrait and life classes.

Among her many awards were the Mary Smith prize, Pennsylvania Academy of the Fine Arts, 1890; Bronze Medal, Atlanta Exposition, 1895; and a Gold Medal in London, 1902.

Illustration for The Marble Faun, *by Nathaniel Hawthorne, Houghton Mifflin, 1900. Collection of Illustration House.*

Hired man (watching artist at work): "Ha! Ha! That sure is a good joke on them cows."

T Sullivant.

THOMAS STARLING SULLIVANT (1854-1926) was not an illustrator of serious subjects, yet his humorous drawings were so skillfully done that no collection of American illustration would be complete without them. He was born in Columbus, Ohio, and studied at the Pennsylvania Academy of the Fine Arts. His work reveals him as a master draftsman even though he chose to distort the facts rather than to record them as they were.

Here, for instance, he delightfully parodies the landscape artist and repeats the swooping shapes of his handlebar moustache with the curves of the palette and the paint brush. Sullivant's drawings of animals of all kinds are a delightful combination of his intimate knowledge of anatomy with a calculated exaggeration.

Irving R. Wiles

IRVING RAMSEY WILES, N.A. (1862-1948) was taught by his artist father, Lemuel M. Wiles, attended classes at the Art Students League, and then went abroad to complete his studies at the Academie Julien in Paris.

When he returned to America, he found an immediate reception for his pictures. He was a painting virtuoso, particularly in transparent watercolor, which suited itself perfectly for reproduction in the magazines. He also entered New York exhibitions and won many prizes; he became a member of the American Watercolor Society, the Society of American Artists and was elected a full member of the National Academy in 1897. In the latter part of his life he concentrated on portraiture, but also painted genre and landscape subjects.

"Open Eyed Conspiracy," watercolor.
In the Sanford Low Memorial Collection of American Illustration, New Britain Museum of American Art.

ALBERT BECK WENZELL (1864-1917) was born in Detroit, Michigan, and was sent to study art first in Munich and then in Paris where he stayed for seven years. Upon his return to America, he became the acknowledged master of fashionable society and drawing room subjects. His paintings were done with much "technique," often in full color, although usually reproduced in black-and-white. If his preoccupation with the rendering of the sheen of a silk dress or a starched shirt sometimes lessens the message of his pictures, he did, nevertheless, leave us an historic record of the settings and costumes of fashionable society at the turn of the century.

He was awarded a Silver Medal at both the Pan-American Exposition at Buffalo in 1901 and the St. Louis Exposition in 1904.

Two volumes of his paintings were published at the turn of the century by P. F. Collier, *Vanity Fair* and *The Passing Show*. Wenzell was one of the Founders of the Society of Illustrators and became its second president in 1902.

Portrait of A. B. Wenzell, by himself.

1900
1910

drawing by James Montgomery Flagg

THE DECADE: 1900-1910
Harold Von Schmidt
(1893-1982)

Although this was a period of American illustration in which I did not directly participate, throughout my career as an illustrator I have felt a direct kinship with it, both in the Old West, as exemplified in the paintings of Frederic Remington and Charles Russell, and with the mainstream of American illustration as a pupil of Harvey Dunn who, in turn, taught the philosophy of Howard Pyle, "father of American illustration."

A magazine was thought of in those days as a purveyor of the finest in literature and art. Advertising was limited to the front and the back; any tailing-in of advertising material with editorial matter would have been unthinkable. This lofty standard was reflected in the work of some of America's greatest illustrators: Edwin Austin Abbey, Walter Appleton Clark, A. B. Frost, E. W. Kemble, Edward Penfield, Charles Dana Gibson; and men who later became famous as American painters: Winslow Homer, William Glackens, John Sloan, Ernest Blumenschein, Everett Shinn and others. From 1900 on, I clipped and filed reproductions of their work.

This was an illustrious company. Among them, Howard Pyle was preëminent and probably the greatest illustrator America has ever produced. His career had begun 24 years earlier, in 1876, when he first did illustrations for the old *Harper's* magazine. His work continued through the next 35 years until his death in 1911. During this time he both wrote and illustrated a prodigious amount of work.

As an artist, Pyle's greatest love and interest was in Americana. He eagerly sought all information available about early Colonial times and actually interviewed a survivor of the Revolutionary War. His illustrations, as a result, carry an authentic stamp not only because of the accuracy of detail, such as in buttons or ruffles, but also because of his ability to portray the spirit of a rough-hewn but forthright American pioneering period.

Pyle's influence, had it rested on his pictures alone, would have been great; as a teacher his talents were equally important and created an even more lasting influence. For some time Pyle taught at the Drexel Institute in Philadelphia, but his dissatisfaction with the limitations of conventional classroom teaching and his passionate desire to help deserving and talented young students led him to form his own school at Chadd's Ford, Pennsylvania. No tuition was charged, and Pyle gave generously of his valuable time to the development of his pupils. As N.C. Wyeth, one of his pupils at the time, wrote later: "Howard Pyle's extraordinary ability as a teacher lay primarily in his penetration. He could read beneath the crude lines on paper, detect therein our real inclinations and impulses; in short, unlock our personalities. This power was in no wise a superficial method handed out to those who might receive. We received in proportion to that which was fundamentally within us."
(Quoted from *"Howard Pyle, A Chronicle,"* by Charles D. Abbott, published by Harper & Bros. 1925)

As part of his teaching, Pyle made his students fully aware of the practical use to which their pictures would be put. Through his contacts with publishers and art directors, he arranged that the students work on actual commissions or that finished pictures be shown to art directors for possible use. As he taught, "When you are making pictures to be reproduced in print, you are then given no favor and your pictures must be good as pictures or else they are of no possible use . . ." As he described it, ". . . my final aim in teaching will not be essentially the production of illustrators of books but rather the production of painters of pictures, for I believe that the painters of true American art are yet to be produced."

Pyle's high purposes were more than justified. His pupils have gone on to achieve eminent names in their own right and, in turn, have continued to pass Pyle's spirit on to a third and fourth generation of illustrators. The total influence of his personality on the whole field can never be measured; but it is a privilege for me to pay this small tribute to him.

HAROLD VON SCHMIDT

JOHN WOLCOTT ADAMS
SYDNEY ADAMSON
STANLEY MASSEY ARTHURS
EDMUND M. ASHE
CLIFFORD WARREN ASHLEY
WILLIAM JAMES AYLWARD
ANNA WHELAN BETTS
ETHEL FRANKLIN BETTS (BAINS)
HAROLD MATTHEWS BRETT
JOSEPH CLEMENT COLL
FANNY YOUNG COREY (COONEY)
HARRY GRANT DART
HARVEY DUNN
THOMAS FOGARTY
WILLIAM J. GLACKENS
PHILIP R. GOODWIN
ELIZABETH SHIPPEN GREEN
THOMAS KING HANNA
CHARLOTTE HARDING
GEORGE HARDING
LUCIUS WOLCOTT HITCHCOCK
HENRY HUTT
ORSON LOWELL
THORNTON OAKLEY
VIOLET OAKLEY
MAXFIELD PARRISH

CLARA ELSENE PECK
HENRY JARVIS PECK
ERNEST CLIFFORD PEIXOTTO
HERMAN PFEIFER
HENRY REUTERDAHL
CHARLES MARION RUSSELL
CHARLES NICOLAS SARKA
FRANK EARLE SCHOONOVER
EVERETT SHINN
FLORENCE SCOVEL SHINN
JOHN SLOAN
DAN SMITH
HOWARD EVERETT SMITH
JESSIE WILLCOX SMITH
FREDERIC DORR STEELE
ALBERT E. STERNER
SARAH S. STILWELL WEBER
FRED STROTHMANN
FRANK WALTER TAYLOR
HARRY EVERETT TOWNSEND
JOHN SCOTT WILLIAMS
EDWARD ARTHUR WILSON
GEORGE HAND WRIGHT
NEWELL CONVERS WYETH
FREDERICK COFFAY YOHN

"The Night Watchman" from The American Historical Scene.
Published by the University of Pennsylvania Press, 1935. Collection of the Delaware Art Museum.

S. M. Arthurs

Early Steamboat Days — Midstream Passenger

STANLEY MASSEY ARTHURS (1877-1950) was a student of Howard Pyle and one who was very close to him personally. Arthurs devoted his career to depicting American historical subjects, painting a series of episodes from earliest Colonial times through the Civil War era.

After Pyle's death, Arthurs occupied his studio and set for himself the same high standards Pyle had taught. Every detail of his pictures was painstakingly researched, and he immersed himself as thoroughly as possible in the mood and character of his picture subjects.

Arthurs' use of color was rich and varied; he produced a valuable contribution to the Ameican historical record. Many of his pictures are reproduced in James Truslow Adams' *History of the United States,* in the 15-volume *Pageant of America* edited by Ralph H. Gabriel, and in *The American Historical Scene* published by the University of Pennsylvania Press in 1935.

Arthurs also painted a number of murals including the "Landing of DeVries" at Delaware College and "The Crusaders" at the State Capitol, Dover, Delaware.

"The Chase of the Bow-Head Whale," from The Century Magazine, *April, 1910.*

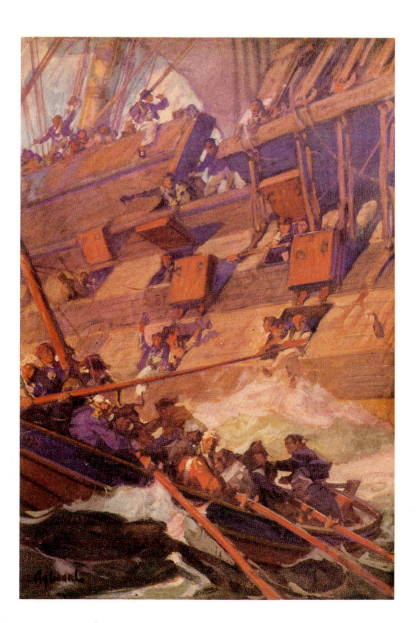

C W Ashley

CLIFFORD WARREN ASHLEY (1881-1947), who was also a student of Howard Pyle, came by his interest in the sea naturally. He was born in New Bedford, Massachusetts, the center of the early whaling industry, and specialized in illustrations of fishing and whaling subjects.

Ashley was also the author and illustrator of several books relating to seafaring, including the *Yankee Whaler* and *The Ashley Book of Knots,* an 11-year project, with some 7,000 drawings and diagrams, and the definitive work on the subject.

Ashley is represented by paintings in the Brooklyn Museum, The Whaling Museum in New Bedford, the Canajoharie (New York) Museum, Massachusetts Institute of Technology, the Delaware Art Museum in Wilmington, and the Mariner's Museum, Newport News, Virginia.

W. J. Aylward

WILLIAM JAMES AYLWARD (1875-1956) was born in Milwaukee, Wisconsin, but like Ashley, his greatest interest was in the sea and related nautical subjects. He, too, was a student of Howard Pyle.

Aylward's interest embraced more of the history of seafaring, however, and he both illustrated and wrote articles describing the earlier days of sailing. He also illustrated Jack London's *Sea Wolf,* Jules Verne's *Twenty Thousand Leagues under the Sea,* and other books on naval or marine subjects.

Aylward belonged to many art societies and exhibited widely, winning the Shaw purchase prize at the Salmagundi Club in 1911; the Beck prize, Philadelphia Watercolor Club in 1912; the Salmagundi prize for Illustration in 1914. He was also an official artist with the A.E.F. during World War I.

"Casting their officers adrift in a Boat," from "The Old Man-of-War's Man," written by the artist and published by Scribner's Magazine, *January, 1914.*

Decorative heading for House & Garden *magazine, March, 1916.*

John Wolcott Adams

JOHN WOLCOTT ADAMS (1874-1925) was born in Worcester, Massachusetts, a descendant of two illustrious United States presidents. He studied at the Art Museum in Boston, the Art Students League in New York, and with Howard Pyle.

His illustrations appeared in *Scribner's, Harper's, The Century, Delineator* and other magazines, usually as pen-and-ink drawings to accompany old songs, poetry and historical incidents.

Adams, who was also interested in the theatre, designed the stage settings for one of Walter Hampden's productions. He was a member of The Players and the Society of Illustrators.

This fine drawing is one of a series illustrating "The Hard Cider Campaign of 1840." From The Century Magazine, *September, 1912.*

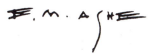

One of the earliest members of the Society of Illustrators (he joined in the first month), was EDMUND M. ASHE (1867-1941), a founder of the Silvermine Guild in Norwalk, Connecticut.

During Theodore Roosevelt's administration, Ashe was an artist-correspondent at the White House and was able to secure several scoops through his personal friendship with the President.

In addition to his illustrations for most of the magazines, he taught for many years. In the early 1900's he instructed at the Art Students League, later at Carnegie Institute of Technology from 1920 to 1939.

In this small vignette, Ashe reveals his complete mastery of the pen-and-ink medium.

SYDNEY ADAMSON was born in Dundee, Scotland, and received his art training in England. Active in English and Scottish art circles, he exhibited at the Royal Academy and in Edinburgh.

A world traveler, he wrote articles about his adventures accompanied by his own illustrations, which were published in American magazines, such as *The Century, Harper's Monthly, Scribner's* and *Success.*

His brother, also an illustrator, had a more popular public following under the name of Penrhyn Stanlaws.

Cover design for The Century Magazine, *which was also enlarged and reproduced as a poster.*

Harold Matthews Brett

HAROLD MATTHEWS BRETT (1880-1955) grew up in Brookline, Massachusetts, and studied at the School of the Museum of Fine Arts in Boston under Philip Hall and Frank Benson. Later he moved to New York to study at the Art Students League with Walter Appleton Clark, H. Siddons Mowbray and Kenyon Cox. By then a well-trained artist, Brett went to Wilmington, Delaware, in 1906, to study further under Howard Pyle.

He was soon thereafter able to make his professional debut in *Harper's Weekly,* and his work began to appear in most of the national magazines. Eventually, Brett moved back to Chatham on Cape Cod and for several years was associated with the Fenway School of Illustration in Boston. Brett particularly liked to do New England subjects with an historical setting; also did a series of portraits of Cape Cod sea captains. Eventually he specialized in portraiture, maintaining studios in New York City and Chatham.

"The Village Post Office — Her Letter," Harper's Weekly, *January 19, 1907.*

Anna Whelan Betts

ANNA WHELAN BETTS was born in Philadelphia and went to school there, studying at the Pennsylvania Academy of the Fine Arts under Robert Vannoh. She then attended Howard Pyle's classes, first at Drexel Institute and then in Wilmington, Delaware. Through Pyle she and several fellow students illustrated a serial story for *Collier's* magazine. After its publication, she found commissions from other magazines as well and over the years worked for *St. Nicholas, Harper's Monthly, The Ladies' Home Journal* and *The Century Magazine.* Her work was characterized by its great beauty and sensitivity.

In mid-career she developed eye trouble and had to give up illustrating to save her sight. Instead she became associated with the Solebury School in New Hope, Pennsylvania, as a director and as its art teacher, a post she held for another twenty years.

"The New Game," frontispiece for The Century Magazine, *August, 1904.*

ETHEL·FRANKLIN·BETTS·

ETHEL FRANKLIN BETTS (BAINS) was the sister of Anna Whelan Betts and, like her, studied with Howard Pyle at the Drexel School of Illustration in Philadelphia. After Pyle established his own classes in Wilmington, Delaware, she and her sister moved there to participate.

She soon found commissions for book illustrations which included several collections of poems by James Whitcomb Riley, "Favorite Nursery Rhymes," "The Complete Mother Goose," and "Fairy Tales from Grimm." She also illustrated stories, mostly child-oriented, for *St. Nicholas, McClure's* and *Collier's Weekly.* Miss Betts exhibited her paintings regularly in the Philadelphia area and won a Bronze Medal at the Panama-Pacific International Exposition in 1915.

"A Sudden Shower," from While Hearts Beat Young *by James Whitcomb Riley, The Bobbs-Merrill Company, 1906.*

FANNY YOUNG CORY (COONEY) (1877-1972) was
born in Waukegan, Illinois, and moved East to attend the
Art Students League and the Metropolitan School of Art.
Fanny was the niece of newspaper cartoonist, J. Campbell
Cory, who helped her make her professional debut.

As an illustrator her special forte was children. Her
drawings were generally in line or line and wash and
usually had a humorous tilt. Her work appeared in *The
Century Magazine*, *Harper's*, the *Bee* and *St. Nicholas*, as well
as a number of books including "The Memoirs of a Baby,"
by Josephine Daskam, and "Alice in Wonderland" by
Lewis Carroll.

HARRY GRANT DART (1869-1938) Unlike many
illustrators who graduated from newspaper art departments to the more lucrative magazine markets, Dart continued to work in both fields. Beginning with the *Boston
Herald*, he was sent to Cuba in 1898 by the *New York World* to
cover the Spanish-American War as an artist-
correspondent. Later he became art editor of the *World* with
a staff of artists under him.

However, he also carried on a simultaneous free-lance
career as an illustrator for *Harper's Weekly*, *Life*, *Judge* and
other magazines. He was especially intrigued by the future
of flight and concocted large, complex pictures of fanciful
flying machines and future cities all in perfect perspective
with convincing detail.

Dart was a member of the Players Club and the Society
of Illustrators.

"A Look into the Future," Harper's Weekly, *August 15, 1908.*

Illustration for "Telling Kate" by Juliet Wilbor Tompkins,
Harper's Bazaar, *1903.*

Illustration for one of a series of stories about "Galloping Dick," an English highwayman, by H. B. Marriott Watson. This was published by Associated Sunday Magazine, *December 27, 1914.*

"Sir Nigel" by Sir Arthur Conan Doyle, serialized in the Associated Sunday Magazine, *1905-1906.*

Coll

JOSEPH CLEMENT COLL (1881-1921) was perhaps America's greatest virtuoso in the use of pen and ink. He commanded an awesome technical dexterity. He employed his pen point as freely as a paint brush, showed it capable of the finest subtlety as well as the boldest slashes of black. As an illustrator, he also made masterful use of the white areas of his pictures, incorporating them to create a full spectrum of values.

His skill had been acquired through careful study of his predecessors, particularly Vierge, and the demanding pressure of deadlines in his earlier employment as a newspaper sketch-artist.

This technical skill was coupled with a vivid and unusual imagination which he displayed best in illustrations with exotic settings or for mystery stories by such authors as A. Conan Doyle and Sax Rohmer.

Coll illustrated several books and his work appeared in many periodicals, including *Associated Sunday Magazine, Collier's* and *Everybody's,* up to the time of his sudden death at the age of forty while his talents were still developing.

Original publication unknown; Half-title illustration for "The Magic Pen of Joseph Clement Coll" by Walt Reed; collection of Illustration House.

From "The Lost World," serialized novel by Sir Arthur Conan Doyle, published in Associated Sunday Magazine, *1912.*

"No Rain Fell" for *"The Face on the Waters,"* The Ladies' Home Journal, *May, 1925. Collection of Illustration House.*

"The Tea Party," The Ladies' Home Journal, *September, 1916. Collection of Les Mansfield.*

"Buffalo Bones Plowed Under," one of two versions. This example was a gift from the artist to Harold Von Schmidt. The other version is now part of the Dunn collection at the So. Dakota State University Memorial Art Center, Brookings, S.D.

HARVEY DUNN

HARVEY DUNN, N.A. (1884-1952) was a large, powerful man who paid for his art schooling by "sod-busting," plowing under the thick, virgin, prairie grass for his homesteading neighbors of the Red Stone Valley of South Dakota.

From the Art Institute in Chicago, he was invited by Howard Pyle to study at Chadd's Ford. Of all Pyle's students, Dunn was perhaps most deeply imbued with his philosophy, and as a teacher passed it along together with his own straightforward honesty and intolerance of pretense. Among his students were Dean Cornwell, Harold Von Schmidt, Amos Sewell, Lee Gustavson, Mario Cooper, Mead Schaeffer, Saul Tepper, and many others.

Dunn's pictures, like the man, were forceful, yet combined great sensitivity with brilliant use of color. During World War I, Dunn was commissioned a Captain as an official war artist with the A.E.F. He lived in the trenches, shared their dangers, and went over the top with the men. These experiences produced many striking documentary drawings and paintings, now part of the archives of the Smithsonian Institution in Washington, D.C.

From notes taken during one of his classroom criticisms, the following* fittingly describes his credo:

"Art is a universal language, and it is so because it is the expression of the feelings of man. Any man can look at a true work of art and feel kin to it and with him who made it — for he has the same number of heartbeats a minute, comes into the world to face the same joys, sorrows, and anticipations, the same hopes and fears. A vastly different vision may arise in the consciousness at the mention of a word, but our feelings are the same. By this you may know that the Brotherhood of Man *is.*"

Cover, The American Legion Magazine, *September, 1928.*

quoted from "An Evening in the Classroom," notes taken by Miss Taylor in one of Dunn's painting classes and printed at the suggestion of Mario Cooper in 1934.

"The Gunsmith" from Adventures in Friendship *by David Grayson, published by Doubleday, Page & Company, 1910.*

"In Town it's Different," from "An Urban Harbinger,"
Scribner's Magazine, *August, 1899.*

THOMAS FOGARTY

THOMAS FOGARTY (1873-1938) has imbued this pen and ink illustration with his own nostalgia for an earlier era when hand craftsmen ran their own small shops and youngsters could watch from a safe distance.

Fogarty did much illustration in many media but was at his best with simple homespun subjects in pen and ink or wash and crayon as exemplified by his interpretive pictures for the David Grayson books.

For many years he was a famous teacher at the Art Students League; among his pupils were Walter Biggs, McClelland Barclay and Norman Rockwell.

W. Glackens

WILLIAM J. GLACKENS, N.A. (1870-1938) began his career as a newspaper artist in Philadelphia. John Sloan, Frederic R. Gruger, and Everett Shinn were his co-workers and together they covered fires, riots, parades, and public ceremonies. Glackens' rapid facility made him the expert in sketching crowds.

McClure's magazine sent him to Cuba as an artist-correspondent during the War with Spain, but even before the success of these drawings he had entered the field of magazine illustration.

Hard work preceded the apparent ease of his drawings. He would sketch an action or pose of a figure over and over until he knew it thoroughly. Then discarding the sketches, he would be able to put down the essence of the pose with a deceptive economy of means.

Glackens had been early attracted to the work of Manet and Renoir and had adopted the Impressionist approach in his own work. Gradually, his interest shifted entirely to painting. He became one of The Eight, that famous and controversial group of painters who exhibited independently of the National Academy in 1908, and who gave a new impetus and direction to American art.

Philip R. Goodwin—

PHILIP R. GOODWIN (1882-1935) of Norwich, Connecticut, was a student at the Rhode Island School of Design and the Art Students League in New York. He also studied with Howard Pyle. His work exhibits much of Pyle's earnestness and discipline but is restricted almost entirely to subjects of hunting and fishing. In this limited area, however, he produced many notable pictures, the subject matter always convincing, dramatic in color.

Goodwin's pictures were published in *Harper's Monthly* and *Weekly, Outing, Scribner's* and *Everybody's* magazines in addition to calendar subjects for Brown & Bigelow and advertising for Winchester Arms and the Marlin Firearms Company. He also illustrated *African Game Trails* for Theodore Roosevelt.

"The Watcher of the Trail," 1905.

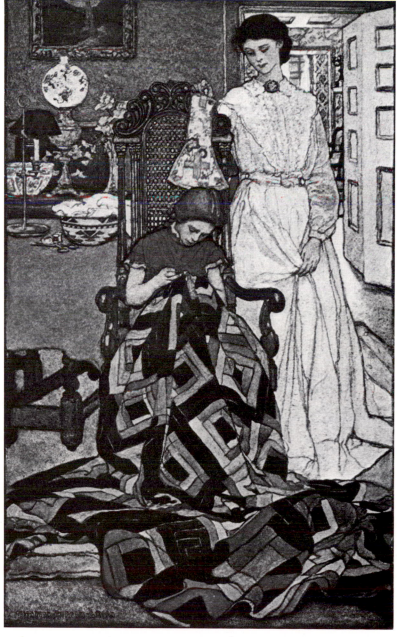

ELIZABETH SHIPPEN GREEN

ELIZABETH SHIPPEN GREEN (1871-1954), later Mrs. Huger Elliott, was born in Philadelphia and studied at the Pennsylvania Academy of the Fine Arts with Robert Vonnoh and Thomas Eakins. She also studied with Howard Pyle at the Drexel Institute where she met Jessie Willcox Smith and Violet Oakley. The three became close friends and shared studios for many years.

Although Elizabeth did some early illustration for *The Ladies' Home Journal* and *The Saturday Evening Post,* as well as a number of books, for many years she was under an exclusive contract with *Harper's* magazines. Her work is essentially decorative, especially in her brilliant use of color, similar in treatment to that of stained glass windows. In a time when the magazines used color very sparingly, a large percentage of her illustrations were reproduced in full color. Because she worked with a bold outline, her pictures reproduced equally well in color or in black and white.

From "The Thousand Quilt," published by Harper's Monthly, *December, 1904.*

C. Harding. 00.

CHARLOTTE HARDING (1873-1951), later Mrs. James A. Brown, was a student at the Philadelphia School of Design for Women, Pennsylvania Academy of the Fine Arts, and of Howard Pyle at the Drexel Institute. She also received encouragement and help from Alice Barber Stephens who shared a studio with her in Philadelphia.

Pyle's influence in her compositions is clearly apparent, but she had her own strong decorative sense as shown in her use of linear shapes and flattened tonal areas. Her work evinces her special sympathy and understanding of children who were her favorite subjects.

Charlotte Harding was awarded a Silver Medal at the St. Louis Exposition in 1904 and at the Panama Pacific Exposition at San Francisco in 1915.

"Their First Thanksgiving, 1846," published by Harper's Bazaar, *November, 1903.*

GEORGE HARDING

GEORGE MATTHEWS HARDING, N.A. (1882-1959) was the younger brother of Charlotte Harding and through her work became interested in illustration. With her influence, he was admitted to Howard Pyle's illustration classes in Wilmington. He later spent several months studying and sketching the life of Newfoundland fishing families. With this background, he returned home to find a market for his work with *The Saturday Evening Post* and other major magazines.

He was one of eight official artists sent overseas with the A.E.F. during World War I, with roving assignments to document the war in drawings and paintings. In his drawings he was concerned more with the effect of war on the men themselves than with portraying panoramic scenes of battlefields or ruins. These are now part of the permanent collection of the Smithsonian Institution in Washington, D.C.

A world traveler, Harding was sent with writer Norman Duncan on a trip through the Middle East, Southwest Asia, Australia and China to do a series of illustrated stories about their travels.

Harding subsequently taught illustration at the Pennsylvania Academy of the Fine Arts; he exhibited widely and painted many murals.

"South Sea Traders." Collection of the Society of Illustrators Museum of American Illustration.

LUCIUS WOLCOTT HITCHCOCK

LUCIUS WOLCOTT HITCHCOCK (1868-1942) painted in the academic tradition of the Laurens and Colarossi School of Paris where he studied with Lefebvre and Constant. His pictures were extremely well painted, and he was especially effective in presenting the social elite. His work appeared in most of the major magazines, including *Scribner's, Harper's Monthly* and *Woman's Home Companion.*

He was one of the early members of the Society of Illustrators; also joined the Salmagundi Club and the New Rochelle Art Association. His awards were many, including a Silver Medal for Illustration in Paris in 1900; Silver Medal for Illustration, and a Bronze for Painting at the St. Louis Exposition in 1904.

Illustration for "The Conquest of Canaan" by Booth Tarkington, Harper's Monthly, *June, 1905.*

T K HANNA

The illustrations of THOMAS KING HANNA (1872-1951) are strong and straightforward, yet very skillful. He does not rely on a stylish "technique," as did some of his contemporaries to cover weaknesses in drawing or composition. He was at home with both historical costume subjects and contemporary scenes, such as the one reproduced here.

Born in Kansas City, Missouri, Hanna studied at Yale University and at the Art Students League in New York under Kenyon Cox and C. S. Reinhart.

After a long career in illustration for magazines such as *Harper's, Scribner's, Life, American, Liberty, The Saturday Evening Post* and *Woman's Home Companion,* he turned to painting and exhibited widely. One of his paintings is in the collection of the National Art Gallery in Sydney, Australia.

"Quarreling Couple," Associated Sunday Magazine, *1907. Collection of Illustration House.*

HENRY · HUTT ·

In a day when the illustrators set the fashion, no artist was more influential in depicting the stylish, up-to-date female than HENRY HUTT (1875-1950). In spite of the differences of silhouette and time, the subtle detail and good taste of Hutt's illustrations are still apparent.

Hutt was born in Chicago, Illinois, and studied at the Chicago Art Institute. He sold his first picture to the old *Life* magazine at the age of sixteen and thereafter illustrated for most of the magazines of his day.

The *Henry Hutt Picture Book,* a volume containing more than eighty of his illustrations, published by the Century Company, was a popular gift book in 1908.

"A Conversation," Collection of the Delaware Art Museum.

ORSON BYRON LOWELL (1871-1956) was the son of the landscape painter, Milton H. Lowell, and his father encouraged his early efforts by expecting him to draw *something* every day. He entered the Art Institute of Chicago classes in 1887, remaining as a student and an instructor until 1893 when he moved to New York to enter the illustration field.

He found immediate success there and worked for most of the top magazines including *The Century, Scribner's, McClure's,* the Harper publications, *Collier's* and the Curtis magazines in Philadelphia. He also illustrated many books. In 1907 he became a member of the *Life* staff and was a prolific contributor for many years.

Lowell maintained a studio in New York and in New Rochelle and was a member of the Society of Illustrators, the Players, Dutch Treat Club, MacDowell (N.Y.), Cliff Dwellers (Chicago), and the New Rochelle Art Association.

Although accompanied with a long dialog when published by Life, *this drawing needs no caption.*

T Oakley -

This illustration by THORNTON OAKLEY (1881-1955) is typical of the artist's strong, carefully composed pictures. His style was particularly appropriate for industrial subjects and the theme of men at work with heavy machinery. He both wrote and illustrated for many magazines, including *Century, Collier's, Scribner's,* and *Harper's Monthly.*

Oakley studied architecture at the University of Pennsylvania; he also studied illustration with Howard Pyle. Throughout his career, he both illustrated and painted for exhibition. His work is represented in many major museums in the United States and abroad. During World War II he painted a series of forty-eight paintings of "American Industries Geared For War," and related subjects, for *National Geographic* magazine, published in 1942, '43 and '45.

He also taught and lectured about art; for some twenty years he served as head of the Department of Illustration at the Philadelphia Museum School of Industrial Art.

"The Turntable," one of a series of four illustrations for "In the Railway Yard," published by Century *magazine, January, 1907.*

V. Oakley

VIOLET OAKLEY (1874-1961) came from a family of artists; two grandfathers were members of the National Academy, and she was always encouraged in her own artistic efforts. She attended some classes at the Art Students League and spent several months in England and France where she was a pupil of Edmund Aman-Jean. She returned to the States to enroll in the Pennsylvania Academy of the Fine Arts, studying under Cecilia Beaux, then switched to the Drexel Institute to study with Howard Pyle. While Pyle helped her to gain illustration assignments, because of her strong color sense, he encouraged her to work in stained glass and at a larger, decorative scale.

This impetus was the beginning of her long career as a designer of stained glass windows and murals. Her largest commission was for the murals in the Governor's Reception Room in the new Capitol building in Harrisburg, Pennsylvania. Edwin Austin Abbey, who was painting another, larger portion of the mural decorations, died in 1911. Oakley completed them as well, taking another nineteen years to finish the assignment.

When the League of Nations was being formed in 1927, Miss Oakley spent several months in Geneva, Switzerland, recording the sessions and making portraits of the participants. Her work won her many awards and an honorary degree of Doctor of Laws from the Drexel Institute in 1948.

Lenten Cover, Collier's Weekly, *1899. Collection of Mr. and Mrs. Benjamin Eisenstat.*

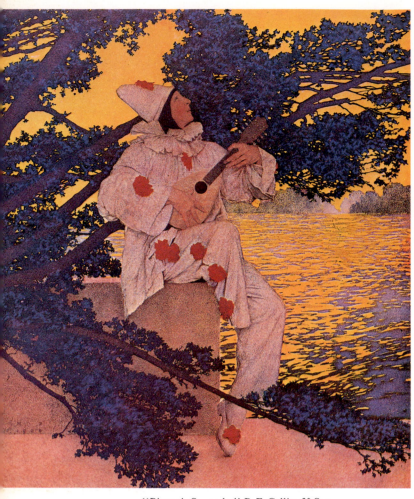

"Pierrot's Serenade," P. F. Collier & Son.

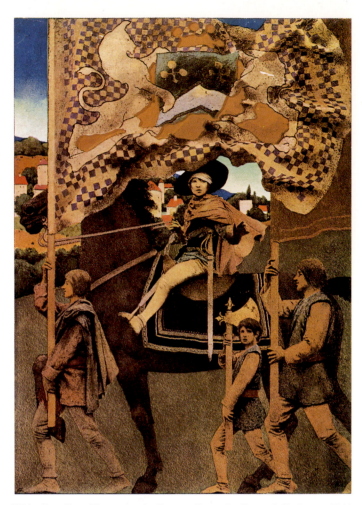

"Dies Irae," an illustration for Dream Days *by Kenneth Grahame, 1902.*

"Two Pastry Cooks" from The Knave of Hearts *by Louise Saunders, Charles Scribner's Sons, 1925.*

"A Florentine Fete," mural painting for the Curtis Publishing Company, 1916.

M . P

MAXFIELD PARRISH, N.A. (1870-1966) throughout his long lifetime created and painted a world of his own. As a child he made careful drawings of figures, cutting around their outlines and mounting the silhouetted shapes. This flat, almost two-dimensional treatment was later carried over into his mural decorations, in which the figures were superimposed against highly detailed backgrounds.

Parrish's subject matter, too, seemed to have originated with his childhood interests in fairy tales, giants, castles and other make-believe. His most successful illustrations were made for such books as Eugene Field's *Poems of Childhood* and Kenneth Grahame's *Golden Age* and *Dream Days*. He used the same kind of material for his mural subjects. His 30-foot wall decoration depicting "Old King Cole" was painted for the old Knickerbocker Hotel, later reinstalled in the St. Regis Hotel in New York. Other subjects included "The Pied Piper," for the Sheraton-Palace Hotel in San Francisco and "Sing a Song of Sixpence," in the Hotel Sherman in Chicago.

He was a sumptuous, rich colorist, noted especially for his luminous "Maxfield Parrish blue." Reproductions of his cover designs or illustrations were saved and framed by tens of thousands of families. One of the most popular of all his pictures was "The Dinkey Bird," originally for Field's *Poems of Childhood.* This mass appeal also made Parrish a favorite calendar illustrator for several subsequent decades.

From Mother Goose in Prose *by L. Frank Baum, Way & Williams publishers, 1897.*

"High Street, Lincoln," illustration for "Oliver Cromwell" by Theodore Roosevelt, published in Scribner's Monthly, *February, 1900. Collection of the Library of Congress.*

ERNEST CLIFFORD PEIXOTTO, A.N.A. (1869-1940) was born in San Francisco and received his art education in Paris as a student of Benjamin-Constant, Lefebvre and Coucet. Peixotto exhibited and won awards at the Paris Salon in 1895 and the World's Columbian Exposition in 1893. He was also a writer and world traveler. His articles, combined with his illustrations, were published in *Harper's Monthly, Scribner's Magazine* and other periodicals.

He also painted several murals, including "La Morte d'Arthur," for the Cleveland Public Library. During World War I, Peixotto was one of the group of eight artists sent to the Front with the Allied Expeditionary Force, and he became an expert in the design and use of camouflage. Much of his war reportage is in the collection of The Smithsonian in Washington, D.C.

HERMAN PFEIFER (1874-1931) was a pupil of Howard Pyle, studying with him in Wilmington in 1903 and 1904. His illustrations are marked by their unembellished, straightforward presentations, making them entirely believable, with but little of the romantic drama of Pyle's approach.

Pfeifer was a regular contributor to most of the national magazines, including *The Ladies' Home Journal, Woman's Home Companion, American Magazine, Redbook, Scribner's Monthly* and *Associated Sunday Magazine.* He also did some advertising illustration for various clients, such as Procter and Gamble's Ivory Soap.

"Frontier Wedding." Collection of the Society of Illustrators Museum of American Illustration.

Clara Elsene Peck

CLARA ELSENE PECK, (1883-unknown), as an illustrator, specialized in drawing women and children. Her pictures are decorative in composition, sensitive in rendering. They were particularly appropriate to articles she illustrated in the women's magazines on such subjects as education, child psychology, and the expectant mother. She also illustrated fiction in magazines and books, did advertising campaigns for Procter & Gamble, Aeolian Company, Metropolitan Life and others.

For a time, she was married to John L. Scott Williams and their styles were very similar during that time, permitting their occasional collaboration on pictures which they signed jointly.

Miss Peck was born in Allegan, Michigan, acquired her art education at the Minneapolis School of Fine Arts, the Philadelphia Academy of the Fine Arts and with William M. Chase, the painter. She was a member of the American Watercolor Society, exhibited extensively and won many awards.

Illustration for In the Border Country, *by Josephine Daskam Bacon, published by Doubleday, Page and Company, 1909.*

Henry J Peck

HENRY JARVIS PECK (1880-1964) grew up in Warren, Rhode Island, and studied at the Rhode Island School of Design, as well as the Eric Pape Art School in Boston. In 1901, Peck became a student of Howard Pyle in Wilmington and after three years began his career as an illustrator. He was particularly good at rural and New England marine subjects and occasionally wrote articles and short stories accompanied by his own illustrations. His work was published in *The Saturday Evening Post, Harper's Weekly, Outing, The Century, Scribner's Monthly, Collier's, Redbook, Pearson's* and other magazines.

"Birds of a Feather," Scribner's Monthly, February, 1913.

"Battle Practice, Division Firing," from *"With the Navy."* Reproduced by Scribner's Monthly, *March, 1914.*

ReuTerdahL.

HENRY REUTERDAHL (1871-1925) was a master painter of ships and the sea. His early pictures were literal and factually accurate, but in his later pictures his knowledgeability allowed him a more impressionistic approach in the manipulation of sea and ships, with a brilliance of color in keeping with his ageless subject.

During the Spanish-American War, he served as an artist-correspondent. He also accompanied the American Fleet on several voyages including one through the Straits of Magellan in 1907, and another to the Mediterranean in 1913. As a Lieutenant Commander during World War I, he was artistic adviser to the United States Navy Recruiting Bureau in New York and made paintings for many of the Navy's most effective and dramatic posters.

He is represented in the collections of the National Museum in Washington, D. C., the Naval Academy at Annapolis, Maryland, the Naval War College in Newport and in the Toledo Museum.

SARKA

CHARLES NICOLAS SARKA (1879-1960) had a chronic wanderlust which, if it interfered with the volume of work he might have done, nevertheless gave him a first-hand knowledge of the exotic subjects of his pictures.

He traveled to many remote areas, from Tahiti and the South Seas to North Africa and the hill tribes of Morocco, paying his expenses on the way with his brush. Thomas "Pop" Hart was one of his traveling companions. His credo was: "This was my art school: to travel and paint; to paint and travel."

Sarka first did illustration for newspapers in Chicago, San Francisco and New York. By 1904, he was illustrating for *Judge* and *Cosmopolitan* and later added to these most of the other major magazines.

He was a fluent watercolorist and a life member of the American Watercolor Society. But his early work was in line, and the mastery of his pen-and-ink drawings is brilliant, full of tonal subtleties, rich in texture.

"The Song of the Nile," published by Judge *magazine. Collection of Illustration House.*

"Taking Toll" — Indians stop the trail herd and Chief makes demand for beef, *"for eating up my grass."*
Reproduced as a special supplement for the February, 1927, number of Country Life.

The life and career of CHARLES MARION RUSSELL (1864-1926) has a number of singular parallels with that of Frederic Remington. They were both largely self-taught; both spent their early years living the rugged frontier life of the West; they both recorded in drawings, paintings, and sculpture, the panorama of a vanishing era. Yet they pursued their goals separately. Remington had early success but died young. Russell had several years of struggle before gaining a national reputation and had a relatively long career.

Russell was the more compassionate observer of the Indians' side of the "civilizing" of the West. His open-hearted, direct manner led the Indians to trust him instinctively. He lived with the Blackfeet in Alberta for several months, learning the language and making many drawings and paintings. For a while he even seriously considered becoming a squaw man himself.

Most of Russell's early pictures were made for himself or to give away to friends, until the economic necessities of marriage forced his wife to find a market for them. Within a few years, Russell's paintings and bronzes commanded high prices, and today his original works are eagerly sought by collectors and museums. Among the museums with good collections of his pictures are the Historical Society of Montana in Helena and the Trigg-Russell Gallery at Great Falls. One of his finest paintings is a mural, 24'9" by 11'7½", entitled "Lewis and Clark meeting the Flathead Indians at Ross's Hole," in the Montana State Capitol.

Illustration for "Finger-that-Kills Wins his Squaw," a story written and illustrated by Russell for Outing *magazine, April, 1908.*

71

"Cabs on the Fifth Avenue side of Madison Square," one of a series of four midwinter scenes in pastels for The Century magazine, *February, 1901.*

EVERETT SHINN

As one of The Eight EVERETT SHINN, N.A. (1876-1953) greatly influenced American art both in the gallery and on the printed page.

His milieu was New York, Broadway, the theatre, and colorful public gatherings. His immense technical facility is evident here, developed in his early career as a newspaper illustrator which demanded rapid, on-the-spot drawings for immediate deadlines. An individual of great enthusiasms and many interests, Shinn was also an accomplished inventor, playwright, and actor.

A mural, done for the residence of his friend, Clyde Fitch, led to a large number of other such projects, including those of the Belasco Theatre and a large 22-x44-foot mural for the Trenton, New Jersey City Hall.

Shinn is represented in many collections and museums, including the Metropolitan Museum of Art, Whitney Museum of American Art, and the Phillips Memorial Gallery in Washington, D. C.

Florence Scovel Shinn

FLORENCE SCOVEL SHINN (1869-1940) was a successful illustrator in her own right, before her marriage to Everett Shinn. They had met as classmates at the Pennsylvania Academy of the Fine Arts. Their marriage lasted fourteen years, and although divorced because of his philandering, they remained friends.

Her illustrations, usually in pen-and-ink and with a humorous, light touch, were used in *The Century Magazine* to accompany a regular feature, the "Editor's Drawer." She also worked for *Harper's Bazaar* and did a number of book commissions, including *Mrs. Wiggs of the Cabbage Patch* and the sequel, *Lovey Mary*, by Alice Hegan Rice.

In the latter part of her life she wrote a number of books having a religious and philosophical outlook and lectured on the subject at Carnegie Hall and the New York Unity Society.

*Illustration for "Our Prosperity is Based on Lobsters and Borders," *The Century Magazine, *October, 1902. Courtesy of the Brandywine River Museum, The Jane Collette Wilcox Collection.*

"The Convalescent" dated 1890, Harper's Monthly *magazine.*

Albert Sterner

ALBERT E. STERNER, N.A. (1863-1946) was a versatile performer in many media including pen-and-ink, watercolor, oils, lithography, pastels, etching, monotypes, crayon, red chalk and charcoal.

Born in London, Sterner studied on a scholarship at the Birmingham Art Institute. He came to America at 17 to start his career working as a scene painter, then went on to lithography and drawing for engravers on wood blocks.

By 1885 Sterner had moved to New York and begun illustrating for the old *Life, St. Nicholas,* and *Harper's* magazines. He later taught at the Art Students League, the school of the National Academy of Design, and the New York School of Applied Design for Women. During his long career he also received commissions to paint portraits of members of socially prominent families including the Vanderbilts, Lamonts, and Whitneys.

Sterner was president of the Society of Illustrators in 1907 and 1908 and was elected a full member of the National Academy of Design in 1934.

Strothmann.

FRED STROTHMANN (1879-1958) originally wanted to be a portrait painter. He was a pupil of Carl Hecker, studied in New York, Berlin and Paris. However, his natural inclinations were more for humor, and he gradually shifted to illustration with a decidedly comic slant. As he put it, "It was at the suggestion of those whose portraits I tried to paint that I went in for funny pictures."

Strothmann was a regular contributor to *Harper's Monthly, The Century, Hearst's International,* and other magazines, as well as illustrator for many books by authors such as Ellis Parker Butler, Mark Twain, and Carolyn Wells.

Illustration for Extracts from Adam's Diary *by Mark Twain.*

Illustration for "The Man who Chased a Ghost," American Boy, 1921. Collection of Mr. and Mrs. Irving Diton.

Frank E Schoonover

FRANK EARLE SCHOONOVER (1877-1972) owed much to Howard Pyle's belief that an illustrator should thoroughly immerse himself in his subjects, painting those things he knows best. After studying with Pyle, both at The Drexel Institute and at Chadds Ford, Pennsylvania, Schoonover began to receive assignments to do Indian and frontier subjects. In order to qualify himself properly, he made two trips to the Hudson Bay country in 1903, by snowshoe and dog team, and in 1911 by canoe, observing there the life and customs of the Indians. Over the years he did a great number of excellent, authentic illustrations based on these expeditions.

Similarly, he made field trips to other locations, such as the Mississippi Bayou country for a book which he both wrote and illustrated, *Lafitte, the Pirate of the Gulf.*

Over his long and productive life, he illustrated for many magazines and books, designed stained glass windows, taught at the John Herron Art Institute and at his own studio, and painted many landscapes of the neighboring Brandywine and Delaware River valleys.

Maria Awa-Sheesh, daughter of Tommo Awa-Sheesh, 1904. Published in Scribner's *magazine, April, 1905; also included in* Sled Trails and White Waters, *Penn Publishing Company, 1929.*

Collection of the Glenbow Museum, Calgary, Alberta, Canada.

S.S.SW

SARAH S. STILWELL WEBER (1878-1939) was fortunate as a student to attend the Drexel Institute in Philadelphia at the time Howard Pyle conducted his illustration class there (1894-1900). She also attended his summer classes at Chadds Ford, Pennsylvania.

Although Pyle's influence is evident in her work, her point of view was often highly imaginative and exotic; she did story illustrations about or for children particularly well. Her pictures were well adapted to books, and in addition to such magazines as *Harper's Bazaar, Collier's Weekly, St. Nicholas* and *The Saturday Evening Post,* she also illustrated a number of children's books; wrote and illustrated a song book, *The Musical Tree.*

Illustration for "The Princess Pourquoi," by Margaret Sherwood, published by Scribner's *magazine, November, 1902.*

JESSIE WILLCOX SMITH

JESSIE WILLCOX SMITH (1863-1935) never married but throughout her long career specialized in drawing and painting mothers, babies and children. Her training was acquired at the School of Design for Women, the Pennsylvania Academy of the Fine Arts with Thomas Eakins and at the Drexel Institute under Howard Pyle.

She had first planned to be a kindergarten teacher but turned to an art career with the stimulus and assistance of Howard Pyle. Some of her best-known illustrations were for books: *Little Women, Heidi, A Book of Old Stories* and Robert Louis Stevenson's *A Child's Garden of Verses.* She also painted a great many illustrations for magazines, such as *McClure's,* and did nearly 200 covers for *Good Housekeeping.*

She painted and exhibited widely, receiving many awards, including a Silver Medal at the 1915 Panama-Pacific Exposition in San Francisco. She also painted many commissioned portraits of children.

"The First Lesson," cover painting for The Ladies' Home Journal, *December, 1904.*

HOWARD SMITH '06

HOWARD SMITH

HOWARD EVERETT SMITH (1885-1970) was a New Englander, born in West Windham, New Hampshire. After attending the Art Students League in New York with classes under George Bridgman, he transferred to the Howard Pyle School in Wilmington, Delaware.

He was very soon able to have his work published, making early appearances in *Harper's Weekly* and *Harper's Monthly*. His illustrations were also published in *Scribner's Monthly* and *The Ladies' Home Journal*, as well as a number of books including *The Children's Longfellow* and *The Beginning of the American People*.

He was especially interested in rural subject matter and landscapes. Eventually Smith followed these interests by studying under Edmund Tarbell at the Boston Museum of Fine Arts School. In addition to landscapes, he also painted a number of portraits and was involved with lithography.

"Man and Horse," illustration for Harper's Weekly, *February 2, 1907.*

DAN SMITH (1865-1934) was born of Danish parentage in Ivigtut, Greenland. He came to America as a child; later went to Copenhagen where he studied at the Public Arts Institute. Eventually, he returned to the United States and studied further at the Pennsylvania Academy of the Fine Arts.

Smith's first work was done as a member of the art staff of *Leslie's Weekly;* and at the time of the Spanish-American War, he joined the Hearst organization.

Through drawing for newspapers, Smith developed a remarkable dry-brush technique that made him the star attraction for many years in the Sunday supplement of the old *New York World*. His drawings were syndicated and distributed throughout the country. During this time he also illustrated for the national magazines and exhibited his etchings and oils.

Illustration for Everybody's *magazine demonstrating Dan Smith's masterful control of dry brush.*

"Camouflaging the Tank," one of Townsend's documentary drawings made at the Front during World War I.

Townsend

Although HARRY EVERETT TOWNSEND (1879-1941) painted and exhibited in full-color oils, some of his best work was done in black and white, including his drawings in line for the old *Adventure* magazine.

Townsend was born in Camp Grove, Illinois, and attended school at the Art Institute of Chicago. In 1900 he was invited to study with Howard Pyle in Wilmington, Delaware, staying there until 1904. Moving to New York, he was soon illustrating for the leading magazines.

In 1917, Townsend, with seven other artists, was commissioned as a Captain with the A.E.F. and assigned to record the war. These drawings and paintings are now in the War College and in the Smithsonian Institution in Washington, D.C.

Active in art circles, Townsend was a member of the Society of Illustrators, Allied Artists' Association, Salmagundi Club, Architectural League of New York, Brooklyn Society of Etchers, Westport Artists, Darien Guild of Seven Arts, Silvermine Guild, and others. He was awarded the Shaw prize for illustration at the Salmagundi Club in 1920.

Spot illustration for Adventure *magazine. During the 'teens, Townsend made hundreds of these exquisite drawings as story headings, often adding the lettering as well.*

·J· Scott Williams·

JOHN SCOTT WILLIAMS, N.A. (1877-1976) was born in England, studied composition with Fred Richardson at the Art Institute of Chicago. His first illustrations were done as early as 1905 for *The Saturday Evening Post*. In subsequent years he did work for more than 20 different American magazines (of these only six are now being published). From 1927 to 1934, he contributed covers regularly for the magazine section of the *New York Herald Tribune*.

Williams later became a designer and painter of mural decorations including those for the Indiana State Library and Historical Building, Johns Hopkins University and a huge 72-by-28 foot ferro-porcelain enamel mural in the main concourse of the Union Terminal in Cleveland, Ohio.

Illustration for the story, "Campbell Corot," from Scribner's *magazine in 1907. Over the original pen-and-ink drawing in black, a yellow-ochre second color was printed, with both solid and benday tint blocks as specified by the artist.*

"Thorgunna, The Waif Woman," from the story by Robert Louis
Stevenson. Published by Scribner's *magazine, December, 1914.
Collection of Les Mansfield.

"The Battle at Glens Falls," from The Last of the Mohicans *by
James Fenimore Cooper, Charles Scribner's Sons, 1919.*

"Miles Standish" for The Courtship of Miles Standish *by Henry Wadsworth
Longfellow, Houghton Mifflin Company, 1920. Collection of Mort Künstler.*

"Cutting Out," illustrated for "A Day with the Round-up," for Scribner's *magazine, March, 1906.*
Collection of Buffalo Bill Historical Center, Cody, Wyoming.

N.C. WYETH

NEWELL CONVERS WYETH, N.A. (1882-1945) had a huge zest for life. He carried this enthusiasm through a tremendous number of paintings, more than 3,000 illustrations, numerous vast murals, and a great many still life and landscape paintings.

Howard Pyle was his teacher and idol. Wyeth emulated Pyle's approach as nearly as possible, painting much of the same kind of subject matter — medieval life, pirates, Americana. To this he added his own dramatic picture concepts and rich, decorative color. Outstanding in this phase of his work were the more than twenty-five books he illustrated for Charles Scribner's Sons' Classics series. The popularity of these books is such that, even after decades, most of them are still in print.

After painting in oils for many years, Wyeth turned to the egg tempera medium and also began to paint more for exhibitions. He encouraged an interest in the arts in his children, giving them every opportunity for self-expression. His daughters, Henriette and Caroline, are both accomplished painters; Ann, a composer, and his son, Andrew, is famous as a painter. His grandson, Jamie, is also an excellent painter in his own right. The October, 1965, issue of *American Heritage* contains an excellent article by Henry C. Pitz about the career of Wyeth and his family.

At the time of his tragic death in a railway crossing accident, N. C. Wyeth was one of America's best loved illustrators.

"A Mug of Ale at McSorley's," published in Harper's Weekly, *October 25, 1913.*
This is quite similar to his painting of the same subject, "McSorley's Bar," in 1912.

John Sloan

JOHN SLOAN, (1871-1951) worked for the *Philadelphia Press* as a young, newspaper artist, together with William Glackens, George Luks and Everett Shinn, all of whom studied at the Pennsylvania Academy of the Fine Arts. They subsequently became members of The Eight, but for some years continued to paint for exhibitions and, at the same time, to do illustration for the magazines.

Sloan came to New York in 1905 and became interested in recording city life and the social upheaval as he saw it around him. He became famous for his illustrations on this subject for that short-lived magazine, *The Masses.* He also contributed to *McClure's.*

He later devoted himself exclusively to painting, etching, and lithography and is represented in many major collections and museums, including the Museum of Fine Arts, Boston; and The Metropolitan Museum of Art in New York City.

For several years Sloan taught at the Art Students League in New York. He summarized much of his painting philosophy in his book, *Gist of Art,* published by American Artists Group in 1939.

Collier's
Household Number for January

THE ADVENTURE
of the
ABBEY GRANGE

Vol XXXIV No 14   DECEMBER 31 1904   PRICE 10 CENTS

EDWARD ARTHUR WILSON, A.N.A. (1886-1970) was elected to the Society of Illustrators' Hall of Fame in 1962 in recognition of his long and distinguished career as an illustrator. He was born in Glasgow, Scotland; spent his childhood in Rotterdam, Holland, and later came to America where he studied at the Chicago Art Institute and with Howard Pyle in Wilmington, Delaware.

Wilson's first commissions were for advertising, and he was most active in this field for many years. During this time he won many awards and honorable mentions in annual exhibitions of the Art Directors Club in New York. Notable among the campaigns he contributed to were: La Salle, Cadillac, Coral Gables Corporation and Victrola. He also illustrated for most of the major magazines during this period.

His first book illustrations were done as woodcuts for a collection of sea chanteys entitled *Iron Men and Wooden Ships.* It was a labor of love, as well as a great artistic success. He'd always been most interested in nautical subjects and this book established his reputation as an authority. Over the next several years he illustrated *Fall and By,* a collection of drinking songs, *The Pirate's Treasure,* which he also wrote, *Robinson Crusoe, Two Years before the Mast, Treasure Island* — altogether well over sixty books, many of them for the Limited Editions Club and The Heritage Press.

Poster design for the book. Published by Doubleday Doran and Company.

FRANK WALTER TAYLOR (1874-1921) worked almost exclusively with charcoal which he employed with a full tonal range from white to rich blacks.

Taylor was born in Philadelphia and studied at the Pennsylvania Academy of the Fine Arts. There he was awarded a traveling scholarship which enabled him to study in Paris. Upon his return to America, he worked as an illustrator for numerous magazines and also contributed a number of his own short stories. He was awarded a Medal of Honor for Illustration at the Panama Pacific International Exposition in 1915.

Cover design for Collier's Weekly, *February 9, 1907.* ▶

FREDERIC DORR STEELE (1873-1944) was a prolific illustrator for *Century, McClure's, Scribner's* and other publications, but he is best remembered for his portrayal of Arthur Conan Doyle's Sherlock Holmes, as depicted on this cover design in *Collier's* magazine. Steele's drawings were almost always made in line, with either a pencil on a textured paper or in dry brush. Benday screens were sometimes used for tonal effects in these illustrations.

Steele illustrated the works of many other famous authors, including Mark Twain, Richard Harding Davis, F. R. Stockton, Rudyard Kipling, Booth Tarkington, O. Henry, Joseph Conrad and Arnold Bennett.

Born in a lumber camp near Marquette, Michigan, Steele studied at the National Academy of Design and at the Art Students League in New York where he also later taught illustration.

He became a member of the Society of Illustrators in 1902, and was awarded a Bronze Medal at the St. Louis Exposition in 1904.

◀ *"Sherlock Holmes" cover illustration* Collier's *magazine, December 31, 1904.*

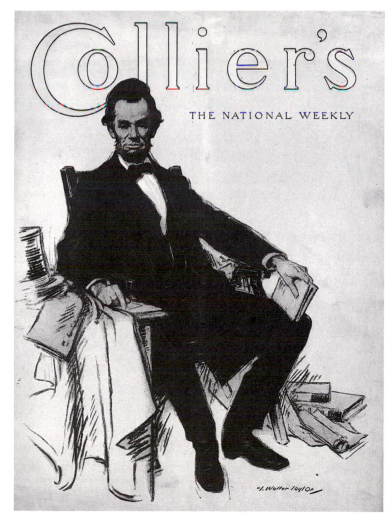

Illustration for "The Tides of Barnegat," published by Scribner's Monthly, *April, 1906.*

J. Wright

The son of a blacksmith, GEORGE HAND WRIGHT, N.A. (1873-1951) always retained a sympathy for rustic subjects and working people in his illustrations for *The Century, Scribner's, Harper's, The Saturday Evening Post* and other publications. He researched his pictorial material as a reporter, filling innumerable sketch books and making his finished illustrations from these on-the-spot drawings. In fact, many of his sketches were reproduced directly in the magazines as reportorial coverage for accompanying articles. He made no distinction in approach between these commissioned illustrations and the fine arts prints, etchings or pastels to which he restricted himself in his later years.

Wright studied at the Spring Garden Institute and the Academy of the Fine Arts in Philadelphia. He was a member and past president of the Society of Illustrators, the Westport Artists and The Salmagundi Club; also a member of the Dutch Treat Club and the Society of American Etchers.

F. C. YOHN

FREDERICK COFFAY YOHN (1875-1933) is most noted for his illustrations of historical and battle subjects. He did many reportorial paintings of the War with Spain in 1898, of both the Cuban and Philippine phases of the conflict. He also painted a fine series of historical illustrations to accompany Henry Cabot Lodge's *The Story of the Revolution,* published by *Scribner's* magazine.

Yohn was born in Indianapolis, attended the Indianapolis Art School and the Art Students League in New York where he studied under H. Siddons Mowbray. At nineteen, he made his first illustrations for *Harper's* periodicals. This was followed by a long career in illustration with most of the major magazine and book publishers.

A permanent collection of his work is in the Cabinet of American Illustration at the Library of Congress in Washington, D.C. and he is one of the Founders of the Society of Illustrators.

"Washington at Valley Forge," illustration for Scribner's Monthly.

82

1910
1920

drawing by Al Parker

THE DECADE: 1910-1920
Arthur William Brown
(1881-1966)

The year 1910 continued what we now think of as the Golden Era with Pyle, Abbey, Penfield, Parrish, Remington, Wenzell, Glackens and many other notables carrying on the fine tradition of illustration.

If you were lucky enough to work for the Big Four: *Century, Harper's, McClure's and Scribner's,* you had arrived. Other fine magazines were: *American, Everybody's,* the women's *Good Housekeeping, Woman's Home Companion, The Ladies' Home Journal, Delineator* and *Pictorial Review.* There were others, too — *Collier's* and *The Saturday Evening Post, Youth's Companion, St. Nicholas, Smith's, Success, Circle,* and many smaller ones. Finally there were the humorous weeklies: *Life, Puck,* and *Judge.* The market for art was large. Most of the magazines were a great help financially to the illustrator. When your drawings were accepted you went to the cashier and got your money at once in cash or by check.

Compared to today, reproductions of drawings were small. One magazine required that the head of a character be no more than one-and-one-quarter inches in height. Most work was in black and white; color was seldom used and then only sparingly.

Art editors were men of education, taste, and culture but few of them had been artists; however they knew the artist's ability and showed their confidence by giving him a free hand. They rarely asked for sketches or layouts; you were simply told how many illustrations to make for most illustrators had their own style and stuck to it consistently.

As a rule, illustrators drew from live models; anyone using photographs was frowned on; he was prostituting his art — a far cry from the present where camera is king. No mechanical gadgets like balopticons. Models' fees were low, whereas today, top models earn as much as many illustrators did then. This is a fact. Many models we used then, later became stars of stage and screen — Frederic March, Norma Shearer, Neil Hamilton, Joan Blondell, to name a few.

Artists who illustrated stories by popular authors became well known to readers who often were attracted by their pictures. With no radio and TV, illustrations created styles according to fan mail received. As an example, girls would write to say they liked a hat or dress in a drawing and would have it copied by a local milliner or seamstress. There was also what we called the Mistake-Finders' Society. They loved to write to the editor when catching the artist in a mistake; he hadn't followed the story and they pointed out details that were wrong. These letters were sent to us to answer; it was a command.

There were no artists' representatives then, and illustrators' contact with editors, art editors, and authors was on a warm personal basis. We enjoyed a certain prestige and dignity seldom found today. Illustrator and author often teamed up to talk over picture situations and continued to collaborate, sometimes for years. A case in point was the Ephraim Tutt series by Arthur Train, started in 1919 in *The Saturday Evening Post* and continuing regularly until 1944 when the author died.

Most young illustrators followed the work of the top men. Frederic R. Gruger was one who began a new trend. Starting as a newspaper artist on a Philadelphia paper, his work appeared in the first issue of *The Saturday Evening Post.* His compositions were monumental even in miniature. His characters were part of the story and believable. To Henry Raleigh, H. J. Mowat, and me — all close friends — Gruger was our hero.

When the United States entered World War I in 1917, many illustrators were in the Armed Forces, but those at home did everything possible to help the war effort and sell Liberty Bonds. A division of Pictorial Publicity of the Committee on Public Information was formed with Charles Dana Gibson as chairman. We met weekly at Keen's Chop House on West 36th Street in New York City where we received assignments for art work; anything from a newspaper spot to posters and billboards. James Montgomery Flagg created his famous poster of Uncle Sam pointing "I WANT YOU" and he posed for it himself. To help sell Liberty Bonds, Flagg and I did billboards in front of the New York Public Library. He did the figures, and I smeared in the background. We used live models and, with a girl wrapped in the Stars and Stripes, we did one on a scaffold high up in Times Square. The wind was strong; the street below looked safe and inviting. When traveling to Washington and other cities painting these billboards, we always attracted large crowds.

In January 1918 a number of illustrators were commissioned as official war artists and were sent overseas as Captains in the Engineers' Reserve Corps. These men often lived at the Front with the troops; in some cases, went over the top with them. Notable artwork resulted. These vivid drawings and paintings by Wallace Morgan, Jack Duncan, Harry Townsend, Harvey Dunn and others are part of the permanent collection in the Smithsonian Institution in Washington, D.C.

As this era ended, many of us went on to the next. Even with the War it was a great and glorious ten years for American Illustration.

ARTHUR WILLIAM BROWN —

ILLUSTRATORS 1910-1920

VICTOR C. ANDERSON
WLADSLAW THEODOR BENDA
WALTER BIGGS
ERNEST LEONARD BLUMENSCHEIN
FRANKLIN BOOTH
PAUL BRANSOM
GEORGE BREHM
WORTH BREHM
ARTHUR WILLIAM BROWN
CHARLES LIVINGSTON BULL
CHARLES SHEPARD CHAPMAN
HOWARD CHANDLER CHRISTY
WALTER JACK DUNCAN
WILLIAM HERBERT DUNTON
CHARLES BUCKLES FALLS
HARRISON FISHER
JAMES MONTGOMERY FLAGG
FREDERIC RODRIGO GRUGER

ARTHUR IGNATIUS KELLER
FRANK XAVIER LEYENDECKER
JOSEPH CHRISTIAN LEYENDECKER
WALT LOUDERBACK
ANGUS PETER MacDONALL
CHARLES DAVIS MITCHELL
WALLACE MORGAN
HAROLD JAMES MOWAT
ROSE CECIL O'NEILL (WILSON)
LUCILE PATTERSON (MARSH)
COLES PHILLIPS
WILLIAM ANDREW (WILLY) POGÁNY
NORMAN MILLS PRICE
HENRY PATRICK RALEIGH
PENRHYN STANLAWS (ADAMSON)
ADOLPH TREIDLER
JOHN ALONZO WILLIAMS

THE NEW~YEAR'S
LADIES' HOME JOURNAL

VICTOR C ANDERSON

VICTOR C ANDERSON

VICTOR C. ANDERSON (1882-1937) was the son of the Hudson River School painter, Frank Anderson. Although his father died when he was only eight, Victor drew and painted from an early age and by the time he attended Pratt Institute in Brooklyn, he was advanced enough to go directly into Life class. In the summer he studied with Birge Harrison in Woodstock, New York.

His illustrations appeared early in the old *Life* magazine, usually of homespun, rural subjects, and he was a contributor of covers and double center spreads for many years. He also appeared in *Woman's Home Companion, The Ladies' Home Journal, American, Collier's Weekly, Country Gentlemen, Woman's World* and many other magazines.

During these same years, Anderson was painting landscapes for exhibition, showing at the National Academy, The Salmagundi Club and the Grand Central Galleries in New York, winning numerous awards.

"The Moon Boy." This cover was framed or pinned up on the walls of countless homes after its publication on the cover of The Ladies' Home Journal *in 1908.*

W.T Benda

WLADYSLAW THEODOR BENDA (1873-1948) is remembered today primarily because of his beautiful theatrical masks. These creations, uniquely his, occupied the latter part of his career and were used in theatre and dance performances around the world.

Benda himself had an international background. He was born in Poznan, Poland, and drew from his earliest years. After a false start in civil engineering at the Krakow College of Technology, he switched to the Academy of Art. Following further studies in Vienna, he came to the United States and began his career as an illustrator.

It was the era of the pretty girl, and the "Benda Girl" joined the rest, but she stood out as intriguingly exotic among the American types. Her success kept Benda busy working for most of the magazines for many years.

Benda became an American citizen but was always proud of his Polish heritage and contributed several poster designs for recruiting Polish patriots during World War I.

Cover design for Hearst's International, *January, 1924.*

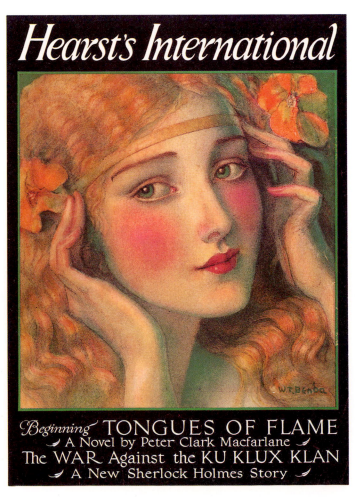

Hearst's International

Beginning TONGUES OF FLAME
⤙ A Novel by Peter Clark Macfarlane ⤚
The WAR Against the KU KLUX KLAN
⤙ A New Sherlock Holmes Story ⤚

Illustration for The Ladies' Home Journal, *May, 1936.*

W Biggs

WALTER BIGGS, N.A. (1886-1968) represents the South at its best, both as a gentleman and as an artist who painted the South with sensitive artistry and poetic nostalgia.

Biggs was born in Elliston, Virginia, and spent his boyhood there. He arrived in New York to study art at the Chase School, later renamed the New York School of Art. Among his teachers were Edward Penfield, Lucius Hitchcock and Robert Henri. Henri was an especially inspiring teacher who instilled in the students a real desire to work. Biggs was in an unusual class which included Clifton Webb, Eugene Speicher, Edward Hopper, George Bellows, Guy Pène Dubois, Rockwell Kent and W. T. Benda, all of whom became famous in their respective ways.

Biggs himself became a famous illustrator and teacher at the Art Students League and the Grand Central School of Art in New York. His illustrations over the years appeared in *Harper's, Scribner's, The Century, The Ladies' Home Journal, Woman's Home Companion, Good Housekeeping, McCall's, Cosmopolitan* and others.

He exhibited regularly at the National Academy, Salmagundi Club, American Watercolor Society and Philadelphia Watercolor Society, winning many awards. In 1963, the Society of Illustrators elected him to the Hall of Fame, "For distinguished achievement in the art of illustration."

Story illustration for Woman's Home Companion, *May, 1922.*

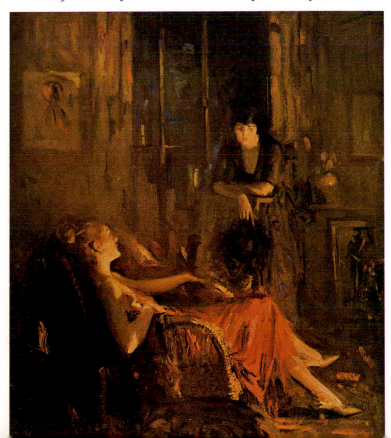

"Attacked by a wounded wolf," illustration for McClure's *Magazine, December, 1906.*

E · L · BLUMENSCHEIN ·

ERNEST LEONARD BLUMENSCHEIN, N.A. (1874-1960) was among the group of artists who settled early in or near Taos, New Mexico, attracted by the Indian life and pictorial color. Blumenschein painted many award-winning pictures there and is represented in several museum collections by his Indian subjects.

This Taos period came comparatively late in his life, however; earlier he had had an active career as an illustrator in the East. Born in Pittsburgh, Pennsylvania, he had attended the Cincinnati Art Academy and the Art Students League in New York. Later he studied with Joseph Benjamin Constant, Laurens and Collin in Paris. He was a very versatile and competent painter with a fresh, unusual viewpoint. Although he worked realistically, there was always strong design underlying his pictures.

For many years Blumenschein divided his time between New York and New Mexico, eventually settling permanently in Taos.

ARTHUR WILLIAM BROWN —

ARTHUR WILLIAM BROWN (1881-1966) had one of the longest and most prolific careers of any American illustrator. Born in Canada, he landed his first job as a chalk-plate artist on the local Hamilton, Ontario, *Spectator* at the age of fifteen. After four years of this, he saved enough money to go to New York where he studied at the Art Students League under Walter Appleton Clark.

Brown's first chance at magazine illustration came when a friend was assigned to write a circus article for *The Saturday Evening Post.* "Brownie" took a chance that he could make acceptable accompanying drawings and spent six weeks traveling with the circus. The *Post* was pleased with the result and the published illustrations became the first of a long and busy association which lasted over forty years.

During this time he had the opportunity to collaborate with many famous authors, including O. Henry, F. Scott Fitzgerald, Booth Tarkington, and Sinclair Lewis. In the early stages of their careers, Frederic March, John Barrymore and Joan Blondell all posed for him.

Brown was always an active member of the Society of Illustrators. He was its president from 1944 to 1947, and in 1964 he was unanimously voted to the Illustrators' Hall of Fame.

Illustration for Booth Tarkington's "Seventeen," the Metropolitan Magazine, *February, 1915.*

"The Little House," illustration for poem, Good Housekeeping *magazine.*

Franklin Booth

As a farm boy near Carmel, Indiana, FRANKLIN BOOTH (1874-1948) wanted to be an artist and so studied pictures in all of the books and magazines available. Most of the reproductions at that time were printed from steel or wood engravings. Mistakenly, believing the drawings were made with pen and ink, he painstakingly copied their character, line by line. This was eventually to become the basis for his unique line technique.

Booth described his working methods in the *Professional Art Quarterly* in 1934, "... In doing a drawing it has been my custom first, of course, to lay in my entire conception with the pencil. This penciled sketch is not a completed thing, but a generalization. Parts of this I then draw in more fully and follow immediately with the pen. My drawings are usually somewhat involved and a completed pencil drawing to begin with would, in places, become smudged and lost in the process of inking in other parts. So I proceed and complete a part or section at a time and follow through, in this way, to the outer edges of my drawing. At times in the making of my drawings, in one section or more, a completed picture will be seen in the midst of white paper and penciled suggestions.

By this method, also, the general relationship of values of the whole drawing, at the start, can be established in one small part. This becomes the guide. The point, therefore, of the beginning of a picture will usually be a place where a section of the darkest dark, the grays and the highest whites appear together."

If this method of rendering was a laborious one, it does not appear to have restricted Booth's picture concepts. All of his compositions are characterized by a feeling of space and lofty grandeur. Many of his pictures were used to accompany poetry or to decorate editorial articles. This same sense of beauty and taste was carried over into his advertising assignments. In an introduction to a book of 60 drawings by Franklin Booth, published by Robert Frank in 1925, Earnest Elmo Calkins wrote:

"Mr. Booth has done more than almost any one man to break down the barrier between the pure art of decoration as applied to the book or magazine page and the same art applied to the advertising page. Anything undertaken by him is approached in the same creative spirit and executed with the same sure touch ... His two great qualities are his dexterity with his pen and his imagination. His work appeals to the spirit. It has an uplifting effect. It suggests something just beyond, an ideal almost realized. His fine craftsmanship never becomes mere dexterity. It remains always as it should be, the instrument for expressing a fine creative imagination."

-G-BREHM-

Both GEORGE BREHM (1878-1966) and his younger brother, Worth, had the ability to illustrate stories about children, particularly boys, sympathetically and convincingly. Perhaps this insight developed from their small town, Hoosier upbringing.

George studied at the Art Students League in New York with Twachtman, DuMond, and Bridgman, but did his first illustration for the *Reader's* magazine, published by Bobbs-Merrill Company near his home in Indianapolis. On the strength of this work, he obtained an assignment from *Delineator* in New York, and his career was launched. Over the years he illustrated for most of the magazines; his most memorable pictures were done for *The Saturday Evening Post* for story series by Booth Tarkington, Octavius Roy Cohen and M. G. Chute.

"Cowboy and Indian." Collection of Morris Weiss.

WORTH
BREHM

WORTH BREHM (1883-1928) became interested in art through his brother. He prepared a series of sample drawings in Indiana, brought them to New York, and *Outing* magazine bought them all. Publication of these pictures led *Harper's* to commission him to illustrate *The Adventures of Tom Sawyer* and *Huckleberry Finn*.

He later did general illustrations for many magazines; the best known were for the *Penrod* stories by Booth Tarkington in *Cosmopolitan;* the M. G. Chute boyhood stories in *Good Housekeeping* magazine, and the Irvin S. Cobb stories of the Mississippi in *Cosmopolitan*. His work was always in demand from both magazines and advertisers up to the time of his death at the age of 44.

"Does a boy get a chance to whitewash a fence every day?"
Illustration for The Adventures of Tom Sawyer
by Mark Twain, Harper & Brothers, 1910.

THE SATURDAY EVENING POST

Volume 203, Number 32

Feb. 7, '31   5 cts.

10c. in Canada

Harry B. Smith—Stewart Edward White—Sophie Kerr—Arthur Train
Maude Radford Warren—Juliet Wilbor Tompkins—Stuart N. Lake

PAUL BRANSOM

PAUL BRANSOM (1885-1979) began drawing animals from early childhood. He was born in Washington, D.C. and, after leaving school at thirteen, became an apprentice-draftsman assisting with mechanical drawings for patents. This rigorous discipline in drawing, combined with his free-time sketching at the National Zoo, developed in him the habit of making a careful analysis and recording of the individual characteristics of each of the animals he drew. His work later led him to New York — and the chance to take over a vacancy at the *New York Evening Journal* doing a comic strip, "The Latest News from Bugville." He credited Walt Kuhn and T. S. Sullivant (both of whom did animal cartoon subjects then) with having most influenced his career, and " . . . of course, the greatest of all animal illustrators, Charles Livingston Bull."

During this time he haunted the Bronx Zoo to such a degree that he was permitted to set up a studio at the Lion House. His goal was to draw and paint animals for the magazines. The work in his portfolio so impressed the editor of *The Saturday Evening Post* that he bought, on the spot, four pictures for covers and several smaller drawings.

Paul Bransom had a long and distinguished career. He illustrated nearly fifty books on wildlife subjects, including Jack London's *Call of the Wild,* and hundreds of stories and articles for almost all of the major magazines. He also painted for exhibition and taught summer classes at an outdoor art school at Jackson Hole, Wyoming.

Cover illustration for The Saturday Evening Post, © 1931, *1959 by The Curtis Publishing Company.*

CHARLES LIVINGSTON BULL

CHARLES LIVINGSTON BULL (1874-1932) learned about animals almost literally from the inside out. His first job, at sixteen, at Ward's Museum in Rochester, New York, consisted of scraping out the inner linings of animal pelts preparatory to their being mounted. Later, he became an accomplished taxidermist and worked for the National Museum in Washington, D.C., as an expert on the anatomy of birds and animals.

He studied at the Philadelphia Art School and drew and painted his subjects in the course of his work, soon becoming one of our foremost animal illustrators. Both his taxidermy and paintings were greatly admired by President Theodore Roosevelt for whom he mounted many specimens now in the National Museum.

For many years Bull lived directly opposite the Bronx Zoo in New York in order to be able to sketch from living models. A lover of the outdoors, he also made numerous field trips into Mexico and Central and South America where he studied wildlife in its natural habitat. His book, *Under the Roof of the Jungle,* is a collection of illustrations and short stories of animal life in the Guiana wilds based on his explorations there. Bull was active in bird-banding for the United States Biological Survey and particularly interested in the plight of the American eagle. To arouse public interest in their preservation, he made many drawings and posters for pictorial publicity.

"Puma and Prey," illustration for Under the Roof of the Jungle. *Collection of Illustration House.*

"Voices of the Four Winds;" published by The Ladies' Home Journal, *December, 1920.*

Charles S. Chapman N.A.

CHARLES SHEPARD CHAPMAN, N.A. (1879-1962) was an illustrator and painter whose compositions convey a feeling of spaciousness and dignity. Part of the effect is achieved through his use of scale, but his subject matter also contributed. He was interested in the beauty of nature, especially in forest subjects, painted with much imagination and experimentation in textural effects.

Chapman was born in Morristown, New York, attended the New York School of Art, studying under William Merritt Chase and Walter Appleton Clark. He and Harvey Dunn conducted a school of illustration in Leonia, New Jersey, for several years. He also taught at the Art Students League, exhibited regularly and won many awards. His painting, "In the Deep Wood," was purchased by The Metropolitan Museum of Art in New York.

W J Duncan

WALTER JACK DUNCAN (1881-1941) came from Indianapolis to study at the Art Students League in New York. His first work was for *The Century* magazine in 1903. *Scribner's* sent him on assignment to England in 1905, and he subsequently worked for *McClure's, Harper's* and the other major publishers. In 1917, he was one of the artists, commissioned as officers in the Engineer Corps, who went overseas with the A.E.F.

Duncan specialized in pen-and-ink which he employed with great directness and skill. The directness resulted from his very careful and thoroughly worked out preliminary studies. He had been attracted to line because of its harmony with the text of the printed page and his interest in both books and writing. Most of his best friends were writers, among them Christopher Morley, for whom he illustrated several books, including *Tales from a Roll-top Desk, Pipefuls,* and *Plum Pudding.* Duncan himself wrote and illustrated a scholarly book entitled, *First Aid to Pictorial Composition,* published in 1939 by Harper's.

Some of his finest work was done for the late Henry B. Quinlan, art director of the Woman's Home Companion. *This example was one of a series of illustrations for "Mary Todd Lincoln" by Carl Sandburg, September, 1932.*

W. Herbert Dunton

WILLIAM HERBERT DUNTON (1878-1936) who was born in Augusta, Maine, studied at the Cowles Art School in Boston and the Art Students League of New York under Andreas M. Anderson, Joseph De Camp, Frank Vincent DuMond, William Ladd Taylor, E. L. Blumenschein, and Leon Gaspard. This thorough training is evident in his accomplished and well-composed illustrations for *Harper's, Scribner's, Everybody's,* and other magazines. His subject matter was spirited, usually of the West or other outdoor scenes, his use of color effectively keyed to the mood.

Dunton settled permanently in Taos, New Mexico, in 1921. In addition to his illustrations, he also painted and exhibited widely, received a Gold Medal in Nashville, Tennessee, in 1927, and won many other awards. He is represented in the collections of the Peoria Society of Applied Arts (Illinois), the Witte Memorial Museum, San Antonio, Texas, the Museum of New Mexico in Santa Fe, and by murals in the Missouri State Capitol, Jefferson City, and in the White House, Washington, D.C.

Falls

CHARLES BUCKLES FALLS (1874-1960) approached illustration primarily as a designer. Realism in his pictures was always tempered by a strong sense of decoration. This quality was first exemplified in the fine posters he made for many of the old vaudeville theatres in New York, now collectors' items.

In 1918 he designed a famous "Books Wanted" poster for the Armed Forces which provoked an enthusiastic flow of books to the training camps and gained an international reputation for Falls.

His pictures were ideally suited for books. As a personal project, he did an ABC book for his daughter, then three years old, comprised of colored woodcuts. This book has become a classic of its kind.

The long career of C. B. Falls included much illustration for advertising, magazine covers and editorial art for fiction and articles. In addition, he taught at the Art Students League in New York and produced his own woodcuts and paintings. He executed numerous mural commissions, among them a series of historical portraits for the ceiling of the New York State Office Building at Albany.

"The 'Breed' Trapper, 1830." Reproduced from Scribner's *magazine, July, 1914.*

Falls made two trips to Haiti where he found the native culture a great stimulus for woodcuts, drawings and paintings, as represented here. Collection of Illustration House.

Howard Chandler Christy

HOWARD CHANDLER CHRISTY (1873-1952) had a long, colorful and varied career. He had made his early reputation in accompanying the United States troops to Cuba during the Spanish-American War when articles illustrated by his drawings and paintings were published by *Scribner's* and *Leslie's Weekly.* The famous Christy Girl resulted from his picture, the "Soldier's Dream," in *Scribner's.* From then on he did beautiful girl pictures, for *McClure's* and other magazines, almost entirely.

Christy's painting technique was sumptuous, and he was in great demand as a portraitist. Among the notables he painted were Mrs. Calvin Coolidge, Secretary of State Charles Evans Hughes, Amelia Earhart, Lawrence Tibbett, and Mrs. William Randolph Hearst.

He was also a popular teacher and at various times instructed at Cooper Union, the Chase School, New York School of Art and the Art Students League.

In later years, Christy painted several murals, including his well-known decorations for the Café des Artistes in New York. His most famous mural, however, is a 20 by 30-foot canvas, "The Signing of the Constitution," which hangs in the rotunda of the Capitol in Washington, D. C. He was elected to the Society of Illustrators Hall of Fame in 1980.

"When Johnny comes Marching Home," illustration for Liberty Belles, *published by the Bobbs-Merrill Company, 1912.*

HARRISON FISHER (1875-1934) showed an early interest in drawing and from the age of six was instructed by his father, Hugh Antoine Fisher, a landscape painter. When his family moved from Brooklyn to San Francisco, Harrison studied there at the Mark Hopkins Institute of Art. At sixteen, Fisher had begun to make drawings for the *San Francisco Call* and later for the *Examiner.*

Soon after returning to New York, Fisher sold two sketches to *Puck* magazine which also hired him as a staff artist. He became noted for his ability to draw beautiful women, and his Fisher Girl became a rival to those of Gibson and Christy. The American Girl was a favorite theme for the magazines then, and Fisher did cover illustrations for most of them. For many years he was under an exclusive contract to do covers for *Cosmopolitan,* but eventually he restricted himself to painting portraits.

"The Girl I Like Best," cover illustration for American Belles, *Dodd, Mead and Co., 1910. Courtesy Judy and Alan Goffman.*

Portrait sketch of his friend, the actor William Powell. Collection of Illustration House.

Dean Cornwell (who was left handed) at work in his studio. Watercolor by Flagg. Collection of Illustration House.

Flagg was his own model for Uncle Sam and enjoyed posing for the role in many other illustrations and posters.

"Nervy Nat" epitomized Flagg's own irreverence for pompous authority.

"An Amusing Yarn," cover illustration for Judge, *November 27, 1920.*

JAMES MONTGOMERY FLAGG

JAMES MONTGOMERY FLAGG (1877-1960) lived with gusto. He epitomized the public concept of the handsome, bohemian artist, surrounded by beautiful models, dashing off pictures with sheer exuberance of talent. In Flagg's case, this was nearly true. He worked rapidly and easily in all media and with any subject matter. Humor and satire were his special forte. Early in his career he did a cartoon feature entitled, "Nervy Nat," and for many years he illustrated the zany characters of the P. G. Wodehouse stories and created the archetypical interpretation of the valet, "Jeeves." His rapid portrait studies and incisive caricatures were prized by many prominent sitters.

For over thirty years he turned out an immense amount of work, including many posters during World War I. Probably his best known illustration was the famous "I Want You" Uncle Sam recruiting poster. Over four million copies of this were printed and distributed throughout the country.

Flagg was a painter of serious portraits, too. He exhibited in the Paris salon of 1900, at the National Academy of Design and the New York Watercolor Club. He was elected to the Society of Illustrators Hall of Fame in 1980.

Illustration for "The Foolscap Rose" by Joseph Hergesheimer. Published in The Saturday Evening Post. © *1933, 1961 by The Curtis Publishing Company.*

"A Toast to Napoleon," from "The Thunderer," Harper's Bazaar, *September, 1926.*

"The Witch Doctor of Rosey Ridge." Reprinted from The Saturday Evening Post; © *1939, 1967 by The Curtis Publishing Company.*

Illustration for "Sunrise" by Alice Duer Miller, from The Saturday Evening Post, *April 10, 1926.*

FREDERIC RODRIGO GRUGER (1871-1953) wrote on the subject of Illustration for the Encyclopedia Britannica, describing the illustrator's role as follows:
"... Illustration may become a great art, but to become a great art, it must be creative. It cannot hope to compete with the camera in the reporting of facts. It has no business with the outer shell of things at all. It deals with the spirit. Dealing with the psychological aspects is a great opportunity and a serious handicap. Presupposing a pictorial presentation of the relations of people, the telling of a story is inevitable. A great and simple story, akin to truth, or a poor and trivial one, akin to meagre facts, may be told by the same incident — depending upon the insight, the vision of the artist. The nature of the story portrayed is the measure of the artist who portrays it ... ".

Gruger demonstrated this insight and vision in his work. His pictures were always concerned with the larger themes, and although the original drawings were actually quite small, they appear monumental in scale.

He worked in a medium developed out of his earlier work for the *Philadelphia Ledger*. The drawing was made with Wolff pencil, rubbed with a stump or eraser, oftentimes over an underlying wash, which produced a full range of values, particularly a rich, velvety black. The board itself was an inexpensive cardboard used by newspapers for mounting silver prints. It had a receptive, soft surface and has since become known as "Gruger board."

Gruger got his start with the old *Century* magazine and worked subsequently for many other publishers and advertisers, but was most closely identified through his long career with *The Saturday Evening Post*.

F. X. Leyendecker

FRANK X. LEYENDECKER (1877-1924), born in Germany, was always overshadowed by his older brother. His work was more sensitive but though very competent, never matched the assurance and dramatic poster quality of Joseph's. He, too, did illustrations and cover designs for leading publications and, later, also designed stained-glass windows.

The two brothers, neither ever married, worked together in a large studio estate in New Rochelle. The fascinating story of their personal lives is related in Norman Rockwell's *My Adventures as an Illustrator*.

"On the Road to Mandalay," cover design for Collier's *magazine. Collection of Illustration House.*

JOSEPH CHRISTIAN LEYENDECKER (1874-1951) was born in Montabaur, Germany, and came to America at the age of eight. Showing an early interest in painting, he got his first job at 16 in a Chicago engraving house on the strength of some large pictures he had painted on kitchen oilcloth. In the evenings after work he studied under Vanderpoel at the Chicago Art Institute, and saved for five years to be able to go to France to attend the Académie Julian in Paris.

Upon his return, as a thoroughly trained artist with immense technical facility, Leyendecker had no difficulty in obtaining top commissions for advertising illustrations and cover designs for the leading publications. His first *Post* cover was done in 1899, and he did well over 300 more during the next 40 years. Among the most famous of these was the annual New Year baby series.

His advertising illustrations made his clients famous. The Arrow Collar man was a byword for the debonair, handsome male, and women wrote thousands of love letters to him care of Cluett Peabody & Company. His illustrations for Hart, Schaffner & Marx were equally successful in promoting an image of suited elegance. He was elected to the Society of Illustrators Hall of Fame in 1977.

Illustration for Kuppenheimer clothing catalog. Collection of Illustration House.

Study for Karo Syrup advertisement. Collection of Illustration House.

Collier's *Cover, April 27, 1907. Collection of Les Mansfield.*

Cover painting for The Saturday Evening Post, *June 17, 1916.*

Poster design for World War I. Collection of Illustration House.

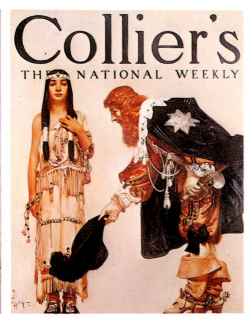

"The Conference," for the story, *"His Name was Jonah,"* The Ladies' Home Journal. *Collection of Mr. and Mrs. Charles H. Matz.*

Perhaps the first reaction to the work of ARTHUR IGNATIUS KELLER (1866-1924) is one of admiration for the brilliant facility of his technique. His preliminary studies, especially, show a mastery of drawing itself, the result of his long training both at the National Academy of Design and with Loefftz in Munich. The studies are not a stolid assimilation of facts, however, but rather a poetic exploration of the forms, freely and directly made from the model, for his own use in the finished illustrations.

This feeling of interpretation and poetry is carried further in his compositions, often crowded with figures, but controlled through passages of light or accents of carefully placed tones rendered with an impression of great spontaneity.

Illustration for "The Creators," published by The Century Magazine, *1910. Collection of Illustration House.*

Walt Louderback

The work of WALT LOUDERBACK (1887-1941) is broad and direct, with few subtleties. Yet for all his sledge hammer technique, romanticism permeates his pictures. His characters and their emotions seem heroic, larger than life. For the reader, the vicarious thrill of participating in the adventure is heightened as well.

Louderback was born in Valparaiso, Indiana, and studied at the Art Institute of Chicago. He lived in Europe for some time in the 'twenties, delivering his pictures by ship. A painter, as well as an illustrator, he was awarded the Daughters of Indiana Purchase prize and a special honorable mention at the Hoosier Salon in 1933.

"Pirates Plundering a Galleon," 1913. *Courtesy of Guy Rabut.*

"Yellow Bird," illustration for Cosmopolitan *Magazine.*

Spot illustration, Pen-and-Ink.

THE SATURDAY EVENING POST

An Illustrated W...
Founded A°. D! 1728 by B... ...nklin

OCTOBER 8, 1921

5c. THE COPY
10c. in Canada

In This Number: HAL G. EVARTS — KENNETT HARRIS — GEORGE WESTON
JOHN TAINTOR FOOTE — RICHARD CONNELL — LOWELL OTUS REESE

ANGUS MAC DONALL

ANGUS PETER MacDONALL (1876-1927), who came from St. Louis, was one of the early group of artists who settled in Westport, Connecticut, to make it a famous art colony. MacDonall was especially popular with fellow-illustrators because of his three beautiful daughters who were in great demand as models.

MacDonall illustrated for most of the magazines including *Scribner's*, *Harper's*, *American*, and *The Ladies' Home Journal*. For several years he did a regular double-spread illustration of human interest or social commentary for the old *Life* magazine.

Cover illustration for The Saturday Evening Post.

CHARLES D. MITCHELL

CHARLES DAVIS MITCHELL (1887-1940) had great drawing facility, and most of his illustrations were done in a technique somewhat similar to that of his friends, Arthur William Brown and Hal Mowat.

Mitchell drew very attractive young females, successfully adapting their changes in style and taste over three decades. His work appeared regularly in *McCall's*, *Redbook*, *Good Housekeeping*, *Cosmopolitan*, *Pictorial Review*, *Delineator*, *The Saturday Evening Post*, *The Ladies' Home Journal* and other magazines.

Originally from Wilmington, Delaware, Mitchell had his studio in Philadelphia and was a member of the Artists Guild, New York, and the Art Club in Philadelphia.

Illustration for ''The Heart Pirate,'' Cosmopolitan *magazine.*

WIMORGAN —

WALLACE MORGAN, N.A. (1873-1948), at the turn of the century, went through the tough school of the newspaper artist as did his friends and fellow-artists, Glackens, Shinn and Sloan. Forced to draw a constant variety of subjects under pressure, on the spot or from memory, he emerged with such facility that he never needed models in his later work. His finished renderings were attempted directly, without preliminary sketches. If difficulties arose, he'd abandon the drawing for a new try. This was the secret of that inimitable spontaneity.

Wallace Morgan viewed the human comedy with warmth, wisdom and humor, laced with irony. He traveled across the country with Julian Street, sketching, while Street wrote *Abroad at Home.* This ran serially in *Collier's,* and was published in 1914 by The Century Company.

Morgan was one of the official artists assigned to the A.E.F. during World War I. His quick sketching was especially useful for documentary recording of life in the trenches, as it was for his swift, salty portraits of top brass. This special flavor made his style a natural for illustrating the P. G. Wodehouse stories which ran in *The Saturday Evening Post* and in other magazines.

Morgan taught at the Art Students League, at intervals, from 1905 to 1929. He was made an honorary member of the League, a rare honor reserved for such greats as Bellows, Pyle, Henri, DuMond and others. He was elected a full member of the National Academy in 1947; received an award from the National Institute of Arts & Letters.

Morgan's clubs included The Players, Century, Dutch Treat; he was president of the Society of Illustrators from 1929 to 1936. In January, 1949, a memorial exhibition of Wallace's drawings was given at the Society of Illustrators, of which he was honorary president at the time of his death.

Illustration for "Four is Too Many" by Dorothy Walworth Carmen, published in The Woman's Home Companion.

MOWAT.

HAROLD JAMES MOWAT (1879-1949) always preferred to work in black and white, obscuring many of the details, highlighting others out of an overall tonality. In this method he shared the approach of a number of fellow artists: Henry Raleigh, Arthur William Brown, and especially Frederic R. Gruger.

Mowat was born in Montreal, Canada, and received his art education at the New York School of Art. His first illustrations were made for the *American* magazine. He lavished so much time and expense in models' fees on his work that he barely broke even. This kind of conscientiousness made him a relatively slow worker throughout his career, and he never became as popular with the public as did many of his more facile co-workers. However, other illustrators paid him the compliment of great respect and acknowledged his preëminence. He illustrated for most of the top publications, including *The Saturday Evening Post, The Ladies' Home Journal, McCall's, Woman's Home Companion,* and *Redbook.*

Describing his work, Mowat said, "My medium is a piece of white paper and a black pencil. Sometimes a bit of dirt from the floor. When at work, I'm at it from early morning until far into the night. I haven't known the meaning of true peace of mind for years, but I infinitely prefer the uncertainties and struggles of the illustrator to any other game on earth."

Illustration for "The Sightseers," Woman's Home Companion, *February, 1922.*

Kewpie Book cover, 1911. JLK

Illustration for Pictorial Review, *June 17, 1909. Collection of Illustration House.*

The familiar and pleasing legacy of ROSE CECIL O'NEILL(WILSON)(1875-1944) is the Kewpie doll. The dolls were patterned after her drawings of Kewpies — fanciful, elf-like babies who solved all sorts of problems in a bumbling, good natured way. Her drawings and stories were immensely popular for over two decades, appearing as a special feature in *Good Housekeeping* magazine and *The* *Ladies' Home Journal.* The dolls were sold all over the world.

A self-trained artist, Rose O'Neill became nationally known as an illustrator at nineteen. Her pictures appeared in *Puck, Truth,* the old *Life, McClure's,* and *Harper's.* She was also a novelist and poet, a member of the Societe des Beaux Arts in Paris and the Society of Illustrators in New York.

Lucile Patterson.

LUCILE PATTERSON (MARSH) (1890-unknown) was born in Rapid City, South Dakota. She studied at the Art Institute of Chicago and was awarded an American Traveling Scholarship by the Institute in 1913. She then migrated from Chicago to the Village in New York City to pursue a career of depicting children for covers of many national magazines and advertisers of child-related products. She also illustrated books, including the Gates *School Reader.*

Her work is marked by a strong sense of design and imaginative poster shapes, in contrast to that of many of her more conventional contemporaries.

Cover design for Every Week *magazine, 1916.*

Willy Pogány

WILLIAM ANDREW (WILLY) POGÁNY (1882-1955) was a native of Hungary and his first studies in Budapest and Paris were in engineering. Success in caricaturing led him to pursue an art career, first in London and then in America. His influences were the Oriental artists and illuminated books, and a great part of his career was devoted to book illustration.

Among his many successes were *The Rubaiyat, Hungarian Fairy Book* and *Gulliver's Travels*. He also painted murals, stage settings, exhibited widely and illustrated for most of the major magazines over his long career.

Penrhyn Stanlaws

PENRHYN STANLAWS (PENRHYN STANLEY ADAMSON) (1877-1957) was the younger brother of illustrator Sydney Adamson and changed his name to avoid a confusion of identity. Actually their work was too dissimilar to have caused any problem. Penrhyn was completely absorbed in the presentation of pretty girls and did so with great success. Their beautiful faces appeared on most of the magazines, including *The Saturday Evening Post, Associated Sunday Magazine, Hearst's International,* and *Metropolitan* magazine.

His other contribution to the arts was the construction of a studio building, the Hotel des Artistes, at 1 West 67th Street in New York, which is now a famous landmark for having housed so many prominent artists over the intervening years.

Cover illustration for Metropolitan *magazine.*

Illustration for "The Miracle" by Maude Radford Warren; Associated Sunday Magazine, *February 21, 1915.*

"The Fadeaway Girl" advertises Community Plate, Oneida Ltd., Silversmiths, 1924.

"The Fadeaway Girl" in A Young Man's Fancy, *published by Bobbs-Merrill, 1912.*

COLES PHILLIPS

The Fadeaway Girl was the particular hallmark of COLES PHILLIPS (1880-1927). Phillips pictured fashionably beautiful young women, using the device of tying the figure into the background by either color, value or pattern. This approach produced an intriguing poster-like effect of great simplicity; yet actually it was based on the most careful preliminary planning of shapes to carry out the illusion of the full figure.

Phillips was born in Springfield, Ohio, and had his first pictures reproduced as a student contributor to the *Kenyon College Monthly* magazine. Upon graduation he tackled a New York career, first as a solicitor for an advertising agency. Later he formed his own studio of artists. After further study at the Chase Art School, he decided to launch his art career. His first effort was sold to the old *Life* magazine as a double-page spread. When *Life* began to use color on its covers, the Fadeaway Girl made her initial appearance and was an instant success. For many years thereafter she appeared in a variety of guises, but was always the patrician beauty.

Phillips prided himself on being a good businessman-artist. His pictures, both for covers and for advertising campaigns, such as Holeproof Hosiery and Community Plate Silverware, were the product of a meticulous, cerebral craftsman.

One of a long series of advertising illustrations for Holeproof Hosiery. This appeared in 1921.

In this typical Raleigh illustration, the artist has freely used colored inks, colored pencils, Wolff pencil and opaque watercolor. Date and place of publication not known. Collection of Illustration House.

RALEIGH

HENRY PATRICK RALEIGH (1880-1944) was one of the most prolific of all our illustrators. In spite of this, he maintained a consistent high quality and good taste in all his work. His renderings in line, line and wash, colored inks or other combinations were ideally suited to the printed page.

In his illustrations he was able to translate the mood and setting of the story with easy versatility. His pictures look as though they flowed from pen or brush. He was probably at his best with society subjects and for many years depicted the ultimate in fashionable society for the Maxwell House Coffee advertisements.

Raleigh was born in Portland, Oregon; later moved to San Francisco. He left school at 12 to help support his mother and sisters. Befriended by the head of the coffee firm for which he worked as a clerk, Raleigh was sent to Hopkins Academy, a San Francisco art school, for two years.

At 17 he got a job in the art department of the *San Francisco Bulletin* where he learned to make drawings for the chalk-plate process. As a reporter-artist, he was later sent on assignments to sketch newsworthy subjects, such as fires, floods, or corpses at the city morgue.

By the age of 19 he was working for the *San Francisco Examiner* as one of its highest paid artists. His work attracted the attention of William Randolph Hearst, who sent him to New York to work for the *Journal.* He next went to the *New York World,* doing special features three days a week. This experience served as a base for his entry into the magazine field.

Raleigh was also a serious etcher and produced many fine plates, but these were seldom exhibited. Among his many awards were the Shaw Prize for Illustration at the Salmagundi Club in 1916 and the Gold Medal for Advertising Art in America in 1926. He was elected to the Society of Illustrators Hall of Fame in 1982.

"Mary Reed, Pirate" by Robert W. Chambers, *published by* Liberty *magazine. Collection of Morris Weiss.*

"Courtship," unpublished. Collection of Illustration House.

The hanging of Captain Blue-Jaws.

Illustration for "Love and the Lieutenant," Woman's Home Companion, 1934. Collection of the Society of Illustrators Museum of American Illustration.

Norman Price

NORMAN MILLS PRICE (1877-1951) never fully received the popular recognition that his work deserved. Because he was so intently interested in historical subjects, he restricted his work to these almost exclusively.

However, the dedication and artistry he brought to his work was especially appreciated and respected by a select group — his fellow-illustrators. His painstaking research into every detail made each picture an authentic documentary, but the detail was never allowed to detract from the dramatic concept of the illustration itself. Although Price made effective use of tone and color, his pen-and-ink drawings were especially effective, exhibiting a full range of values and textural effects.

Price was born in Canada, studied art there and in London and Paris. By 1912 he had established himself in New York and had begun to work for American publications. Some of his most successful illustrations were done for a series of historical novels by Robert W. Chambers. He was a charter member of the Guild of Free-Lance Artists, and honorary president of the Society of Illustrators at the time of his death.

Illustration for "Operator 13" by Robert W. Chambers, Cosmopolitan Magazine, 1933.

Collier's
THE NATIONAL WEEKLY

ADOLPH
TREIDLER

ADOLPH TREIDLER (1886-1981) was born in Westcliffe, Colorado, studied at the California School of Design in San Francisco and with Robert Henri in New York. He first illustrated for *McClure's* magazine in 1908, then made pictures or cover designs for *Harper's, Century, Scribner's, Collier's, The Saturday Evening Post, Woman's Home Companion* and many national advertisers.

Posters were his particular forte. During World War I he designed numerous Liberty Loan and recruiting posters and was Chairman of the Pictorial Publicity Committee for the Society of Illustrators during World War II.

His travel subjects were especially effective. For many years he painted posters for the Bermuda Tourist Offices, the Furness Bermuda and French Lines, and through these associations traveled the world over.

Treidler was a member of the Art Directors Club, Charter Member of the Artists Guild, and life member of the Society of Illustrators.

Cover design for Collier's Weekly, *February 10th, 1912.*

John Alonzo Williams

JOHN ALONZO WILLIAMS, N.A. (1869-1951) painted in watercolor throughout his career. Since most illustrations were reproduced in black and white in his era, a large portion of his work was done in wash, usually transparent. This example in color was published later in his career but is typical of his style.

Williams studied at the Art Students League and the Metropolitan Museum of Art school. During the same years he was illustrating, he also exhibited regularly. In addition to his membership in the Society of Illustrators, he was also a member of the Artists Guild, the Salmagundi Club, the American Watercolor Society and the New York Watercolor Club. He was elected a full member of the National Academy in 1947.

"The Auction," illustration for "Home Sweet Home" by Sophie Kerr, published in the Woman's Home Companion.

1920
1930

drawing by Dean Cornwell

THE DECADE: 1920-1930
Norman Rockwell
(1894-1978)

I am not sure that I should be writing about this decade. As a student at the Art Students League, my idols were of an earlier day — Abbey and Howard Pyle. As a matter of fact, after all these years, they still are. However, I guess that my own career did sort of blossom out in the 'twenties.

A lot of the old timers were still going strong then. James Montgomery Flagg was riding high. Coles Phillips was doing the most fashionable and elegant young females of the day. The Leyendecker brothers were working from the seclusion of their château in New Rochelle. Howard Chandler Christy was still capturing the headlines with his Christy Girl and was a judge of feminine pulchritude at the Miss America contests at Atlantic City.

The 'twenties were years of extravagance and experimentation; all the emphasis was on trying something different. Jazz was discovered; the sax and the uke were newly popular. Prohibition created the speakeasy and the hip flask. John Held, Jr. caught the essence of the times with his short-skirted flappers and frat men with their bell-bottom trousers.

Paris became the gravitational center for many artists. Not only were Picasso and the Cubists leading the avant garde, but French artists — Drian, Brissaud, Cassandre and Bernard Boutet De Monvel — were influencing a new look in American publications.

Dean Cornwell was coming into his own as the leading exponent of the Pyle school. He'd studied under Harvey Dunn, who was a student of Howard Pyle, and then with the English mural painter, Frank Brangwyn. Dean did the swashbuckling romantic costume stories that were popular then, but probably the best pictures he ever made were done for *Good Housekeeping,* a series on the Life of Christ and of the Holy Land made after a painting and sketching trip to the Middle East.

Walter Biggs was using color in a brilliant and poetic way. Charles Chambers, too, was a good influence; his pictures were in the Academy tradition, soundly painted, with good taste and sensitive characterization.

A new patron for the illustrator became a powerful influence in the field at this time — the advertising agency. Its influence was a mixed blessing. To many illustrators, including myself, I feel that it was a corrupting one. The temptation of their big budgets took away the kind of integrity that earlier artists like Howard Pyle had brought to their work. One could easily become too busy or too dependent on the income from painting for one product after another to afford to take on more worthy projects, such as a mural or an important book.

On the other hand, many artists (and art directors) had the ability to translate a commercial theme into more lofty concepts and their work was and is still, important. Franklin Booth and Harvey Dunn were such examples. The agencies also provided a whole new school for the development of talent; almost every illustrator of note from that time on has done advertising illustration.

So many influences, both old and new, were part of the development of illustration in the 'twenties that it is hard to pick a predominating one. Because it was a boom period and the economy of America was expanding in all directions, there seemed to be room for all of them — including mine.

If I were to try to summarize the decade, I'd say it was generally a healthy one — a lot of new ideas were tried and a lot of good pictures painted. If some of them look a little dated, well, look at today's pictures 40 years from now!

Norman Rockwell

ILLUSTRATORS 1920-1930

SAMUEL NELSON ABBOTT
ROLF ARMSTRONG
MAGINEL WRIGHT (ENRIGHT) BARNEY
RALPH BARTON
ARTHUR ERNST BECHER
MAURICE BOWER
CHARLES EDWARD CHAMBERS
RENÉ CLARKE
THOMAS MAITLAND CLELAND
DEAN CORNWELL
HAROLD THOMAS DENISON
WALTER H. EVERETT
MAUD TOUSEY FANGEL
CLARK FAY
NANCY FAY
LAURENCE FELLOWS
ANTON OTTO FISCHER
JOHN RICHARD FLANAGAN
ERNEST FUHR
ARTHUR D. FULLER
GORDON HOPE GRANT
WILLIAM HEASLIP
JOHN HELD, JR.
ALBIN HENNING
GUY HOFF
FRANK B. HOFFMAN

LYNN BOGUE HUNT
LYLE JUSTIS
WILLIAM HENRY DETHLEF KOERNER
ROBERT L. LAMBDIN
WILLIAM ANDREW LOOMIS
NEYSA MORAN McMEIN
HARRY MORSE MEYERS
WILLIAM OBERHARDT
RUSSELL PATTERSON
HERBERT PAUS
JAMES MOORE PRESTON
MAY WILSON PRESTON
WILLIAM MEADE PRINCE
ELLEN BERNARD THOMPSON (PYLE)
GRANT TYSON REYNARD
NORMAN ROCKWELL
TONY SARG
JOHN E. SHERIDAN
FRANK STREET
DONALD TEAGUE
EARLE GRANTHAM TEALE
SAUL TEPPER
RAEBURN L. VAN BUREN
LORAN FREDERICK WILFORD
CHARLES DAVID WILLIAMS

Cover illustration for The Ladies' Home Journal, *May, 1925. Collection of Illustration House.*

S·N·ABBOTT

The life and work of SAMUEL NELSON ABBOTT (1874-1953) would be better remembered today except for the artist's own extreme modesty and sense of loyalty. Born in Illinois, he had saved up enough to study in Paris under Laurens and Constant. Upon his return to the United States, he was given his first assignment to do the cover design and fashion illustrations of a catalog for Hart, Schaffner and Marx, clothing manufacturers. This began a collaboration that lasted for the next twenty-five years. These booklets, in full color, were greatly admired and collected by other illustrators, designers and agencies. Abbott rejected offers for any other commercial illustration assignments out of intense loyalty to his first employer, although he did some editorial illustration and cover paintings for *The Ladies' Home Journal, The Saturday Evening Post* and *Collier's.* His fine sense of design and color deserve recognition here.

Catalog cover for Hart, Schaffner & Marx during World War I.

The flamboyant signature of ROLF ARMSTRONG (1890-1960) has accompanied hundreds of equally spectacular portrayals of beautiful models and movie stars, glamorized to the ultimate degree. For many years his covers appeared on *Photoplay, College Humor* and *Metropolitan Magazine;* his girls advertised products, such as hosiery, underwear, lipstick and phonograph machines. But his greatest success was in the calendar field; Brown and Bigelow printed his subjects in the millions for many years.

Armstrong's success was based on solid training — three years under John Vanderpoel at the Art Institute of Chicago and further study under Robert Henri in New York. To pay for his education, he gave boxing and baseball lessons — he was a good athlete — and worked at many other odd jobs.

Early on, Armstrong discovered pastel and learned to exploit its special qualities in depicting flesh under complex lighting arrangements which contributed an exotic flavor to his beauties.

Typical Rolf Armstrong Girl. Collection of Beverly and Ray Sacks.

MAGINEL WRIGHT BARNEY

MAGINEL WRIGHT ENRIGHT — later BARNEY — (1881-1966) was the youngest of three children; the eldest, Frank Lloyd Wright, always encouraged his sister's talent for drawing and painting. When her school days were over, she attended the Chicago Art Institute. Then she worked for several years at an advertising agency before her marriage to Walter J. Enright, another young artist. They soon came to New York where, eventually, both became successful illustrators.

Maginel's earliest efforts were pictures for some fantasies by one Laura L. Bancroft, later unveiled as that *Wizard of Oz,* L. Frank Baum. Maginel illustrated young classics — *Heidi, Hans Brinker of the Silver Skates* — and innumerable fairy tales. She was largely responsible for revolutionizing the quality of illustration in children's readers ('til then fairly deadly) and over the years painted cover designs for many magazines, as well as illustrations in *McClure's, Everybody's Woman's Home Companion, The Ladies' Home Journal, Woman's World* and others.

When work became scarce during the Depression, she took up "painting in wool," landscapes and flower pictures. There were two exhibitions of these at the Marie Sterner Gallery and one, as recently as 1962, at the Sagittarius Gallery, in New York.

This design, "Christmas Frolics," painted in·1928, is still in print, having been contributed to the United Nation's Children's Fund (UNICEF) and used for a greeting card.

· ARTHUR · E · · BECHER ·

ARTHUR ERNST BECHER (1877-1960), who was born in Germany, was brought by his parents to Milwaukee at the age of eight. After high school, he worked for a lithography firm and studied art with local teachers. He also joined a local sketch club whose members included Carl Sandburg, Herman Pfeifer, William Aylward and Edward Steichen, under the tutelege of Louis Mayer. Becher, Aylward and Pfeifer all later became students of Howard Pyle; Becher was enrolled in the Wilmington school in 1902.

Soon thereafter he began to illustrate for magazines such as *The Ladies' Home Journal, Scribner's, McCall's* and *Pictorial Review,* many of his pictures having an allegorical theme or accompanying poetry. Although much of his work was done in black-and-white with carbon or charcoal pencil, he was a good colorist and worked in oils at a large scale. He also painted landscapes and exhibited occasionally — was a member of the Society of Illustrators, the Artists Guild and the Salmagundi Club.

"The Lady and the Frontiersman," illustration for the "Black Hunter" by James Oliver Curwood, published in 1925. Collection of Illustration House.

RALPH BARTON (1891-1931) was multitalented: an artist, cartoonist and drama critic. Born in Kansas City, Missouri, he was drawn to the sophisticated New York City scene and after studying art in Paris, made Manhattan his artistic base. His early work appeared in *Judge* and *Puck* magazines, follqwed by *Cosmopolitan, Vanity Fair, Smart Set* and the old *Life* magazine for which he also served as drama editor.

Barton had a very stylized and decorative approach, usually satiric, drawn in line and flat tone or color. This was an ideal technique for books, and he illustrated for many authors such as Anita Loos' *Gentlemen Prefer Blondes* (1925) and *But Gentlemen Marry Brunettes* (1928), Heywood Broun's *Nonsensorship* and Balzac's *Droll Stories.* At the height of his powers he took his own life over an unrequited love affair.

"Le Succube," illustration for Droll Stories *by Honoré de Balzac. Published by Boni & Liveright Co., 1925. Courtesy of the Graham Gallery.*

Stalking Indians, McCall's *magazine. Collection of Illustration House.*

MAURICE BOWER (1889-1980) was born in Ohio and like most youngsters who become artists, began to draw at a very early age. His family moved to Philadelphia, and Bower went through high school there and for a year at Penn State. Learning about the classes being taught by Pyle alumnus Walter Everett, he switched to the School of Industrial Art in Philadelphia. While still a student in school, he began to get work published in *St. Nicholas* magazine. Contracts totaling four years' work for the Hearst Syndicate followed.

Bower had always wanted to live and work in Paris, and when offered the opportunity by the McCall Corporation to do so, he accepted at once — with six months in Paris in the spring and summer and six months in Philadelphia in the fall and winter, for five years; a wonderful life that ended with the stock market crash. He continued to work for most of the magazines and painted several *Saturday Evening Post* covers in the 'thirties. In his early work Bower worked in charcoal, often on toned paper with chalk highlights. Later his pictures became more realistic and literal as he switched to oils.

Illustration for "Keeping the Peace" by Gouverneur Morris; Cosmopolitan *magazine, 1924.*

"A Conversation" from "Valley of the Giants" by Peter B. Kyne;
Redbook, 1918. Collection of Illustration House.

Departing from Liner — 1918.
Courtesy of the Brandywine River Museum,
The Jane Collette Wilcox Collection.

Illustration for "Never the Twain Shall Meet," Cosmopolitan Magazine, 1923. Collection of Morris Weiss.

"Christ and the Woman at the Well," reproduced in Good Housekeeping *and* Man of Galilee, *Cosmopolitan Book Corporation, 1928.*

DEAN CORNWELL

DEAN CORNWELL, N.A. (1892-1960) was a brilliant, left-handed painter who dominated the illustration field for many years. As a student of Harvey Dunn, he inherited much of the teachings of Howard Pyle and later studied under Frank Brangwyn, the British muralist. To these influences Cornwell added his own monumental style, almost rococo in manner.

Cornwell was an untiring worker who made a great many preliminary studies and compositions before attempting a final painting, usually in oils. These drawings have great interest in themselves for the beauty of their draftsmanship.

Prolific, and in great demand, he illustrated for a wide variety of magazines and advertisers, but found time as well to paint several important murals. Notable among them were those for the Los Angeles Public Library, The Lincoln Memorial in Redlands, California, The Tennessee State Office Building, Eastern Airlines in Rockefeller Center, and the Raleigh Room at the Hotel Warwick in New York City.

Dean was president of the Society of Illustrators from 1922-1926 and was elected to its Hall of Fame in 1959. He taught illustration at the Art Students League in New York, and by example created a whole new "Cornwell School."

"Strato-Flak," advertising illustration for General Motors Corporation during World War II. Collection of Les Mansfield.

C. E. Chambers

CHARLES EDWARD CHAMBERS (1883-1941) was born in Ottumwa, Iowa, studied at the Chicago Art Institute and later at the Art Students League in New York with George Bridgman.

His illustrations were extremely competent, marked by subtlety of value and color. He early learned to adapt his method of painting for the best possible reproduction and to insure fidelity of printing; he often followed the assignments through to the hands of the platemaker.

Chambers divided his time almost equally between editorial and advertising assignments. Among his advertising commissions was an outstanding series of portraits of musicians for Steinway & Sons. He also did a great number of distinctive illustrations for twenty-four-sheet outdoor posters, notably for Chesterfield and Palmolive Soap which set high standards for that field.

He illustrated stories in most of the major magazines, for such authors as Pearl Buck, Louis Bromfield, Faith Baldwin and W. Somerset Maugham; worked under exclusive contract for *Cosmopolitan* magazine for many years.

Among his numerous awards was the second Altman Prize at the National Academy of Design Exhibition in 1931, for his portrait of watercolorist and fellow-illustrator, John Alonzo Williams.

Illustration for "The High Cost of Conscience," Harper's Monthly *magazine.*

R.C.

RENÉ CLARKE (1886-1969) began life in Eustis, Florida, as James Alfred Clarke. He grew up in Springfield, Massachusetts, studied art briefly at the Connecticut League of Art Students in Hartford, Connecticut. While working on a number of printing and advertising jobs, he came under the influence of a fellow-artist, the French illustrator René Vincent. Later, he joined the advertising firm of Calkins & Holden, Inc., where he talked so much about his friend that the name René became transferred to him, and remained.

Although Clarke did some editorial illustration for *Woman's Home Companion, Collier's, McCall's,* and *Judge,* the greater part of his work was concerned with advertising. His drawings and high-key watercolor renderings for such clients as Wesson Oil, Snowdrift, Crane Paper Company and the Hartford Fire Insurance Company, were distinguished by artful simplicity and taste.

His work was awarded four gold medals and numerous other awards from 1920 to 1950 in annual Art Directors Club exhibits.

As art director, and later president, of Calkins & Holden he had a considerable and constructive influence in maintaining high artistic standards in the field of advertising art.

"Rags for the Crane Mill unloading at Troy," advertising illustration for Crane & Co.

THOMAS MAITLAND CLELAND (1880-1964)

"achieved three or four distinct reputations. He is known to large groups of people as the foremost decorative designer in America; to others, as a great printer; to still others as a great typographer . . . T. M. Cleland is not only an illustrator, he is a master in the world of graphic arts. When he accepts a commission every detail of it bears the touch of his genius." This was said of Cleland by George Macy, his host at a dinner given in his honor at the Grolier Club.

At 16, Cleland became a printer's apprentice; at 20, he had designed a typeface with ornaments and gone into the printing business for himself. For two years prior to World War I, he was art director of *McClure's* magazine.

Combining printing with designing and illustrating, Cleland was one of the first to invest institutional advertising with the mantle of fine art. His clients included Locomobile, Cadillac and Rolls-Royce. One notable project was the "Grammar of Color" which he wrote, designed and printed for the Strathmore Paper Company.

His sojourns in Paris confirmed his preoccupation with 18th-century subjects. His first commission for the Limited Editions Club was a two-volume *Tristram Shandy.* He spent three years on more than 62 color drawings for a masterful interpretation of the times. Two Fielding books followed — *Jonathan Wilde* and *Tom Jones,* relating text and illustrations in the finest tradition of the art of printing.

Cleland was a member of The Players, Century and the Coffee House Club; also of the Architectural League of New York and the American Institute of Graphic Arts.

"The Broadside," illustration for the West Virginia Pulp & Paper Company, 1926.

HAROLD DENISON

HAROLD THOMAS DENISON (1887-1940) came from Richmond, Michigan, studied at the Chicago Academy of Fine Arts and the Art Students League in New York. His illustrations, often in line with a color over-printed, are strong and straightforward and appeared regularly in most of the major periodicals for many years, beginning with the old *Life* magazine.

An enthusiastic etcher, as well as illustrator, Denison was a member of the Society of Illustrators, the Salmagundi Club and the Philadelphia Society of Etchers. His work is represented at the University of Nebraska in Lincoln and at the M. H. DeYoung Memorial Museum in San Francisco, California.

Illustration for the Country Gentleman *magazine.* © 1937, 1965 by The Curtis Publishing Company.

121

Illustration for The Ladies' Home Journal, *1909. Collection of Illustration House.*

zuty.everett

WALTER H. EVERETT (1880-unknown) lived on a farm in southern New Jersey and, as an art student, used to bicycle from home to the Wilmington ferry, cross the Delaware, and ride up to Howard Pyle's composition class on Franklin Street. He also worked his way through the School of Industrial Arts in Philadelphia where he later taught illustration for many years.

Everett developed a highly personal approach to illustration. His paintings were almost like posters, with flattened shapes and unmodeled forms, relying largely on color and value changes to delineate the objects. Unfortunately, most of his pictures were reproduced only in black and white, but those which did appear in color, particularly in *The Ladies' Home Journal,* were brilliant and impressionistic.

CLARK FAY (1894-1956) traveled East from Denver, Colorado, and studied illustration with N. C. Wyeth and Harvey Dunn. Most influenced by Dunn, Fay's work is bold and direct, with emphasis placed on the broad picture concept.

Fay's success came early. He illustrated for *The Saturday Evening Post, Delineator* and other major publications for several years, then moved abroad to the village of Chamant, outside Paris; later he lived in London, where he continued to pursue his career in illustration.

Illustration for "The Tiger God comes Home" by Emma Lindsay Squire. Published in The Country Gentleman, *July, 1928.* ▶

MAUD TOUSEY FANGEL had a special knack of drawing and painting babies that was both artistic and extremely appealing. Because she always insisted on drawing directly from life, her pictures reveal an extra insight and understanding of baby characteristics that could only have been gained in this way. Much of her work was done in pastels, appropriate to her subjects in range of color and softness of texture.

For many years she was very productive as a cover designer for *The Ladies' Home Journal, McCall's, Woman's Home Companion* and many other magazines, as well as illustrator for national advertising of the Cream of Wheat Corporation, Swift & Company, Squibbs Cod Liver Oil and other products for babies.

Born in Boston, Mrs. Fangel attended the Massachusetts Normal Art School, Cooper Union and the Art Students League in New York. She also did many portraits in addition to her illustrations.

Cover illustration for The Ladies' Home Journal, *July, 1921.*

NANCY FAY

NANCY FAY (1893-1930) was the wife of Clark Fay and enjoyed a successful career along with her husband while raising two children. Her work, humorous and spirited, was freely drawn with compressed carbon pencil and watercolor washes; it appeared regularly in *The Ladies' Home Journal, Woman's Home Companion* and other women's magazines in the twenties.

Illustration for "The Truth about the Pied Piper" by Sarah Addington, The Ladies' Home Journal, *March, 1922.* ▶

Early illustration for Kelly-Springfield Tires.

L·FELLQ⋀/.

LAURENCE FELLOWS (1885-1964) is probably best remembered for his outstanding series of illustrations for Kelly-Springfield Tire advertisements in the 'twenties. The drawings were in black and white with large areas of white space and an economy of line, combined with good taste and a restrained sense of humor.

Fellows was a native of Ardmore, Pennsylvania, and studied at the Philadelphia Academy of the Fine Arts. This was followed by a stay in England and France where he continued his studies. By the 'twenties he had returned to America and did a great many humorous drawings for *Judge* and the old *Life* magazine.

His technique was ideally suited to fashion illustration; his work also appeared regularly in *Vanity Fair, Apparel Arts,* and *Esquire.*

JOHN RICHARD FLANAGAN (1895-1964) carried on the tradition of Joseph Clement Coll in his pen-and-ink technique. For many years, he was associated with the same kind of subject matter in illustrating the "Dr. Fu Manchu" stories by Sax Rohmer for *Collier's* magazine. His renderings were much more "controlled" than Coll's but, as demonstrated here, he employed a richly varied pattern of textures and values.

Flanagan was born in Sydney, Australia, and apprenticed to a lithographer at the age of 12. At the same time he enrolled in art school. When he completed his art training, he came to the United States where he obtained his first illustration assignment from *Every Week* magazine to do a story concerning a Chinese episode. This and subsequent stories established him as an authority on the Orient, although he did not visit there until many years later on an assignment for the French Line.

Actually, Flanagan did a wide variety of illustration, in full color as well as with pen and ink or scratch board. In later years he designed stained-glass windows and also served as an instructor at the York Academy of Arts in York, Pennsylvania, from 1954 until the time of his death.

Advertising illustration for Amrad Radio, 1930.

Illustration for "The Yucca Bird" by William J. Neidig for The Saturday Evening Post, *September 8, 1923.*

E. Fuhr

ERNEST FUHR (1874-1933), a pupil of William Chase, also studied in Paris, but was most influenced by the point of view of Frederic R. Gruger.

The majority of Fuhr's illustrations were in black and white, and although he depicted a wide range of story backgrounds, he was at his best with small-town or rural subjects. His characters were never glamorous or fashionable; they were ordinary people presented plainly, and, therefore, most convincingly.

He began his career as a newspaper artist for the *New York Herald* and the *New York World* and for many years was associated with *The Saturday Evening Post*. His work also appeared in numerous other publications, including the juvenile magazines, *Youth's Companion,* and *American Boy.*

Arthur D. Fuller

ARTHUR D. FULLER (1889-1966), an ardent sportsman all his life, was identified with hunting and fishing pictures for the major part of his career. The accuracy of detail in his covers and story illustrations for *Field and Stream* won him a large following among sharp-eyed and critical readers for many years.

Earlier in his career, Fuller had illustrated more general subject matter for nearly all of the major magazines, including *Greenbook,* where he started, *Redbook, The Saturday Evening Post, Collier's, The Ladies' Home Journal, Cosmopolitan, The American Legion* and *McCall's.*

Fuller was born in Exeter, New Hampshire, and educated at Harvard, the Fenway School of Illustration in Boston and the Chicago Academy of Fine Arts. He also studied with Harvey Dunn. He was a member of the Animal Artists Society, the Salmagundi Club, the Westport Artists, and the Society of Illustrators in New York.

Illustration for The Saturday Evening Post, *October 9, 1920.*

125

ANTON OTTO FISCHER

The marine paintings by ANTON OTTO FISCHER (1882-1962) are as authentic as only a working sailor could make them. Born in Munich, Germany, but orphaned as a boy, Fischer ran away to sea at 16 and spent eight years before the mast on a variety of sailing ships. Paid off in New York, he stayed to apply for American citizenship and to teach seamanship on the school ship, "St. Mary's." He later served as a hand on racing yachts on Long Island Sound and worked as a model and handyman for the illustrator, A. B. Frost.

When he had saved enough money, he spent two years at the Académie Julian in Paris under Jean Paul Laurens.

Returning to the United States, Fischer sold his first picture to *Harper's Weekly*, and its success led to more commissions. *Everybody's* magazine sent him the first of several Jack London stories. In 1910, he began a 48-year association with *The Saturday Evening Post* which included illustrating for such story series as Peter B. Kyne's "Cappy Ricks," Norman Reilly Raines' "Tugboat Annie," Guy Gilpatrick's "Glencannon," as well as serials for Kenneth Roberts and Nordoff and Hall.

In 1942 he was given the rank of Lieutenant Commander as "Artist Laureate" for the United States Coast Guard and was assigned North Atlantic convoy duty on the Coast Guard cutter "Campbell" during the winter of 1943. The "Campbell" was disabled during a successful attack on a German U-boat, and Fischer's dramatic series of paintings of this experience was published by *Life* magazine. The pictures are now in the Coast Guard Academy at New London, Connecticut.

In 1947, Fischer wrote and illustrated a book about his earlier sailing years, entitled *Fo'c'sle Days,* published by Charles Scribner's Sons.

"U-Boat Kill," illustration for The Saturday Evening Post, *August 2, 1941. © 1941, 1969 by The Curtis Publishing Co.*

"The Derelict." Courtesy of Guy Rabut.

"Windjammer," Collection of Mr. and Mrs. Davies.

Gordon Grant

GORDON HOPE GRANT, N.A. (1875-1962) was born in San Francisco. His father sent him to school in Scotland in order to maintain ancestral ties. The voyage of four-and-a-half months, from San Francisco, was made around the Horn, in a full-rigged Glasgow sailing vessel. Grant's life-long interest in the sea began with this early experience. After graduation from school in Fifeshire, he studied art in London at the Heatherly and Lambeth Schools.

On his return to America, Grant served on the Mexican Border with the Seventh Regiment National Guard and, as a war correspondent, contributed pictures to newspapers in New York and San Francisco. Early in his career, he made illustrations of a great variety of subject matter but gradually, as his reputation grew, restricted himself to nautical subjects.

His painting of the "Constitution" was used by the Navy Department to raise funds for the preservation of "Old Ironsides." The picture is now in the President's office in the White House. Grant is represented in many collections, including The Metropolitan Museum of Art, the Library of Congress, Annapolis Naval Academy, International Business Machines, New Britain Museum of American Art. He also painted a mural for the Post Office in Kennebunkport, Maine.

Grant illustrated a number of books, was both author and illustrator of *Ships under Sail*, 1941; *The Secret Voyage*, in 1943; and other marine stories.

127

"Flying the Falls, 1911." Calendar illustration.

HEASLIP

WILLIAM HEASLIP (1898-1970) was born in Toronto, Canada. As a boy, he decided to become an artist. He was apprenticed to a lithographer at fifty cents a week (the amount to be raised fifty cents semi-annually for five years!)

World War I provided an opportunity for him to enlist in the Royal Flying Corps, and he became interested in flying and depicting aviation subjects from that time on.

After the war, Heaslip came to New York to study at the Art Students League and the National Academy of Design where he won the Suydam Medal. He soon thereafter broke into the magazines, and his illustrations appeared in *The Saturday Evening Post, Collier's, Boy's Life* and many other national publications.

Albin Henning

ALBIN HENNING (1886-1943) is best remembered for his spirited illustrations of World War I; after the war he researched the battlefields to confirm the authenticity of his work.

His special forte was adventure, and in addition to illustration for the major magazines he did many assignments for boys' stories, with subjects ranging from the French Foreign Legion to polar exploration, for *Boy's Life* and *American Boy.*

Henning was born in Oberdorla, Germany, but was reared in St. Paul, Minnesota. He studied at the Art Institute of Chicago and with Harvey Dunn at the Grand Central School of Art in New York.

"Stretcher Bearers," published in The Saturday Evening Post. © *1929, 1947 by The Curtis Publishing Company. Collection of the Society of Illustrators Museum of American Illustration.*

Cover for the old Life magazine, March 31, 1927.

"Bunkered," one of a series of a dozen watercolors related to golfing and its hazards.

John Held Jr

JOHN HELD, JR. (1889-1958), more than anyone else, expressed in his pictures the brash spirit of the 'twenties with his famous flappers and collegiate capers, bootleg gin, jazz bands, and necking parties. His drawings, highly stylized, are fragile and delicate, yet entirely appropriate to the artificiality of the era.

As a youth, Held had made a number of linoleum cuts styled after the early, crude, wood engravings. Harold Ross, the *New Yorker* editor, encouraged Held to develop this second approach; it became a very popular feature, usually as a vehicle for satirical parody of the Victorian era.

All of Held's work was tremendously successful throughout the 'twenties and appeared copiously in the old *Life, Judge, Liberty, College Humor, Cosmopolitan,* and the *New Yorker.*

With the onset of the Depression, such frivolity was no longer appropriate, and Held quietly turned to the more serious career of breeding and sculpting horses, working with ceramics and wrought iron. He was also artist in residence at Harvard in 1940 and at the University of Georgia in 1941.

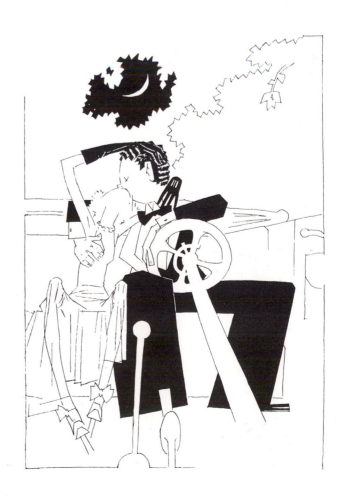

"I figure a little wrestling was the least I could do for her," from "Lochinvar" in The Flesh is Weak, *1931. Collection of Mrs. John Held, Jr.*

Illustration for "Green Pastures," published in The Ladies' Home Journal. *1927*

Hoffman

The father of FRANK B. HOFFMAN (1888-1958) raced horses in New Orleans, and young Frank spent all of his spare time working and sketching around the stables.

Through the interest of a family friend from Chicago who admired Frank's drawing of horses and other animals, he was given a job on the old *Chicago American* newspaper. There he had an opportunity to draw a great variety of subjects, from opera to prize-fights; he eventually became head of the art department. Meanwhile he acquired a more formal art training by studying privately with J. Wellington Reynolds for five years.

In 1916, having been rejected for military service because of an eye defect, Hoffman went West to paint, and eventually was drawn to the art colony in Taos, New Mexico. His bold, broad brush work and striking color attracted the attention of advertisers. He painted for national campaigns for many corporations, including Great Northern Railroad, General Motors, General Electric, and others. This was followed by illustrations for the leading national magazines for which he specialized in Western subjects. His ranch in New Mexico was convenient for keeping live models, not only of cow ponies and thoroughbred horses, but also longhorn steers, several breeds of dogs, eagles, a bear, and burros.

From 1940 on, Hoffman was under exclusive contract to Brown and Bigelow and painted over 150 canvases of the West which were used as calendar subjects.

Hoffman's dry-brush drawings, as typified by this vignette for Collier's *magazine, inspired countless imitators among pulp magazine illustrators who found the technique ideally suited to reproduction in line.*

"Moving the Herd," Collection of Buffalo Bill Historical Center, Cody, Wyoming.

W.H.D Koerner

WILLIAM HENRY DETHLEF KOERNER (1878-1938) came from Clinton, Iowa. His first art job, when he was 15, was with the *Chicago Tribune* where he later became assistant art editor. After a brief stint as the art editor of a Midwest magazine and an attempt to free-lance in New York, he realized his need for further study.

By this time Howard Pyle was no longer carrying on his school, but Koerner went to Wilmington where Pyle gave him special help. Pyle's pupils — Dunn, Wyeth, Arthurs, and Schoonover — were still in the area and provided much helpful criticism.

With this background Koerner was able to achieve his ambition to become an illustrator. He was identified with *The Saturday Evening Post* for most of his long career, specializing in Western and other outdoor subjects. He also illustrated a number of books including *Covered Wagon*, and *North of 36*, by Emerson Hough.

"In Search of Coups." A similar painting was the subject for a cover of The Saturday Evening Post, *March 3, 1934.*

Illustration for The Saturday Evening Post *story "Stage to Nowhere".* © *1929, 1957 by The Curtis Publishing Company.*

GUY HOFF

GUY HOFF (1889-1962). Born in Rochester, New York, Hoff was trained at the Art School of the Albright Gallery in Buffalo and the Art Students League in New York City.

His first commercial illustrations were done for the Niagara Lithograph Company in Buffalo. In New York, he did program covers for the Shubert Theatres and then sold his first magazine cover to *Smart Set,* which put him on the national scene. Over the years, in addition to work for *Smart Set, Pictorial Review, The Saturday Evening Post* and other magazines, he also did advertising illustrations for Procter and Gamble, Lux and Ivory soaps. His last commercial work was done in 1938 and after that he concentrated on pastels and paintings for exhibition.

Cover illustration for The Saturday Evening Post, *date not known.* © *The Curtis Publishing Company. Collection of Illustration House.*

LYNN BOGUE HUNT

LYNN BOGUE HUNT (1878-1960) painted pictures of wildlife almost exclusively. Although he occasionally included human figures in his illustrations, he felt more at home with the animals, fish or birds, which he painted with great authority and dramatic use of color.

Born in Honeoye Falls, New York, Hunt became interested in wildlife at an early age, studied the anatomy of birds and animals, and learned taxidermy. Some of Hunt's first illustrations were done for the old *Outing* magazine. He subsequently worked for a wide range of publications and manufacturers of arms and ammunition but for many years was closely identified with *Field and Stream* magazine.

"Mallards," illustration for an article by T. Gilbert Pearson, "Can We Save our Game Birds?" — one of a series of paintings related to the protection of threatened species.

R.L. LAMBDIN

ROBERT L. LAMBDIN (1886-1981) was one of the many illustrators who came out of the training school of the newspaper art departments. Born in Dighton, Kansas, he studied for a year at the Read Art School in Denver. His first job was with the *Rocky Mountain News;* he then worked for the *Denver-Republican,* and eventually the *Kansas City Star* where he became an illustrator of feature stories.

From this training ground he came to New York, in 1917, and obtained his first story manuscript from the old *Greenbook* magazine. In subsequent years he illustrated for nearly all the major magazines, did advertising commissions, and illustrated many books.

Much of Lambdin's early work was done in pen and ink; later as line went out of vogue, he worked in halftone washes and oils.

A member of the National Society of Mural Painters, he did a series of murals in New York City, the Post Office in Bridgeport, several schools and banks in other Connecticut locations.

Early illustration for the Kansas City Star. *Collection of Illustration House.*

LYLE JUSTIS

LYLE JUSTIS (1892-1960) displays in this lively illustration his unique approach to pen drawing. Self-taught, Justis evolved a method of developing his drawings and compositions by means of a series of warm-up work sheets, covered with exploratory characters and poses. They were done without preliminary penciling-in or any prior planning. With these drawings as a guide, he was able to retain much free informality and vigor in his finished renderings. As an illustrator, Justis was at his best with historical subjects crowded with figures, especially rough frontier types, his flexible pen line perfectly adapted to reproduce their roistering gusto.

Justis was born in Manchester, Virginia, and obtained his first art work doing music titles. Eventually he illustrated for many books, magazines, advertising campaigns and motion pictures. For many years he was an active member of the Sketch Club and the Pen and Pencil Club of Philadelphia; his pictures won several awards in exhibitions of the Philadelphia Art Directors Club.

One of a series of advertising illustrations for The Mead Paper Company.

ANDREW LOOMIS

As a youngster WILLIAM ANDREW LOOMIS (1892-1959) loved to draw pictures, but it was a visit to the nearby studio of Howard Chandler Christy that made him decide to seek for himself an artist's career.

Loomis was born in Syracuse, New York, and grew up in Zanesville, Ohio. At 19 he went to New York to attend the Art Students League where he studied under George Bridgman and Frank Vincent DuMond.

In 1915 he got a job in Chicago with the art organization of Charles Daniel Frey; he also attended classes at the Chicago Art Institute. This was interrupted in 1917 when he enlisted in the Army and served 20 months, half of them overseas, in France.

After the war, Loomis returned to Chicago to work at the Charles Everett Johnson Advertising Art Studio, then for Bertch and Cooper. He finally opened his own studio as a free-lance artist. Equally at home in either editorial or advertising illustration, Loomis had a long career in both and also painted many outdoor twenty-four-sheet posters.

This broad experience expecially qualified him as a teacher at the American Academy of Art in Chicago. Countless other art students who could not study with him personally have benefited from his several art books, including *Fun with a Pencil, Figure Drawing for All It's Worth,* and *Creative Illustration,* published by The Viking Press.

Cover painting for The Saturday Evening Post. © 1935, 1963 *by The Curtis Publishing Company.*

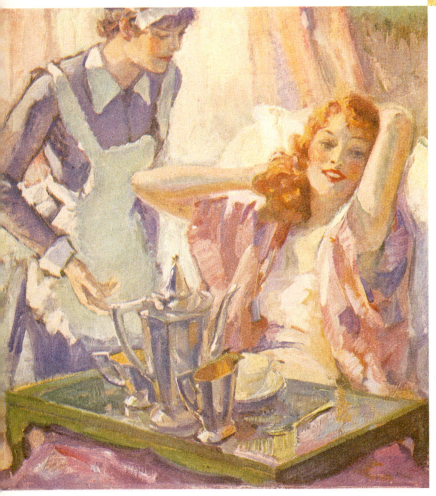

HARRY MORSE MEYERS.

HARRY MORSE MEYERS (1886-1961) was a collector of antique arms and armor which he displayed on two carved oak screens that had belonged to the curator of arms at the Tower of London. Since he illustrated many period stories, these authentic objects frequently served as props for his characters.

Meyers was from New Orleans, Louisiana; attended Tulane University there, followed by classes at the Art Students League in New York and further study with Harvey Dunn.

With a few years' interruption during World War I as an Army airplane pilot, he had a long and successful career as an illustrator for the Crowell-Collier publications, particularly *Collier's* magazine.

This advertising illustration for Wm. A. Rogers Silverware demonstrates Meyers' excellent use of color.

McMein

NEYSA MORAN McMEIN (1890-1949) — in private life Mrs. John Baragwanath — wanted, as a girl in Quincy, Illinois, to be a musician. Although she changed her mind and attended the Art Institute of Chicago, she paid her way through school by writing music and playing piano in a ten-cent store.

She painted her first *McCall's* magazine cover in 1923 and for many years made pastel portraits of beautiful or notable young women for *McCall's* monthly issues, as well as occasional covers for the *Woman's Home Companion* and *The Saturday Evening Post*. She also regularly contributed her drawings for the annual *New York Times'* "Hundred Neediest Cases."

Neysa was equally noted as a hostess and friend of such notables as Alexander Woollcott, Irving Berlin, Marc Connolly, Bea Lillie, Irene Castle, Richard Rodgers, Dorothy Parker, Jascha Heifetz and George Abbott, who visited at her studio or home. As young models, Kay Francis and Frederic March posed for her.

Eventually she turned to portraiture and painted most of the country's prominent women. The Whitney Museum of American Art has established a memorial fund in her honor, which is used to purchase work by living American artists.

She was elected into the Society of Illustrators Hall of Fame in 1984.

Cover illustration in pastel, McClure's *Magazine, January, 1920.*

Oberhardt

WILLIAM OBERHARDT, A.N.A. (1882-1958) early in his career as an illustrator found his greatest interest in delineating the human head. Over the years he developed a remarkable faculty for presenting the special qualities revealed by the sitter's character. An important factor in this ability came from his own warm personality which relaxed and charmed his subjects.

"Obie" would never draw from photographs but always insisted on working directly from the model, earning added respect from editors and his fellow-artists for his refusal to lean on the photograph for help in getting a likeness.

His sitters comprised a veritable *Who's Who*. He said that most of them were people he would have paid willingly for the privilege of portraying. Among these famous subjects were Presidents Taft, Harding, and Hoover; Thomas Edison, Sergei Rachmaninoff, Luther Burbank, Ezio Pinza, Cardinal Spellman, Bernard Baruch and Walter Lippmann.

During World War II, Oberhardt contributed a great number of portrait sketches at various centers and hospitals for men of the armed services from many nations.

Portrait of Luther Burbank, painted from life for an Elgin Watch Company advertisement, 1925.

"Helpful Janitor." Date and place of publication not known.
Collection of Mr. & Mrs. Ben Eisenstat.

Woman's Home
Companion

September 1929   Ten Cents

Russell Patterson [signature]

RUSSELL PATTERSON (1896-1977) was very influential not only as an illustrator (in the 'twenties his flappers were as famous as those of John Held, Jr.), but he was also equally successful in many areas outside illustration.

Patterson was born in Omaha. The family moved to Canada, where he spent one year studying architecture at McGill University. When financial reverses terminated that study, Patterson tried various newspaper jobs, finally doing a comic strip in French, "Pierre et Pierrette," for *La Patrie* in Montreal.

He next went to Chicago and attended the Chicago Art Institute and the Academy of Fine Arts. His early work was for department stores: Carson, Pirie, Scott & Company, and Marshall Field, where he became noted for his interior designs.

A year of painting landscapes in France followed. When he returned to America in 1921, the Jazz Age was just beginning. Patterson began to draw flappers, and they were an immediate success when they appeared in *College Humor*. With his flair for clothes, Patterson also became a pacemaker in setting styles. The raccoon coat and galoshes were among his contributions to collegiate garb; and his drawings were followed eagerly for what was *right* to wear.

Commissions for the theatre followed. Patterson did both the costumes and set designs for the Ziegfeld Follies of 1922 and a number of other Broadway shows, including George White's Scandals.

Patterson spent the 'thirties in Hollywood doing set and costume designs for the movies, mostly elaborate musicals, similar to his Broadway shows.

In the late 'thirties, he returned to New York again to the department store field. He designed coats for I. J. Fox, Christmas toy windows for Macy's and resumed with advertising illustrations.

During World War II, he designed the Women's Army Corps uniforms, train interiors, did a comic strip; also designed hotel lobbies and restaurant interiors. No one, including Patterson himself, knew quite what he would be doing next.

PAUS

HERBERT PAUS (1880-1946) was a native of Minneapolis and got his first job as a cartoonist for the St. Paul *Pioneer Press*. Ambitious to become an illustrator, he enrolled in the Fine Arts School there, later found employment in a Chicago art studio.

Eventually he moved to New York where he became a free-lance illustrator. Paus had a strong sense of design, ideally suited to the many effective posters he painted during World War I. This approach, combined with a striking use of color, was carried over into his magazine illustrations and cover designs.

Paus painted for such advertisers as Victor Records, Hart, Schaffner & Marx, and for several years was under exclusive contract to do all of the covers for *Popular Science* monthly.

"The Celebrity," cover illustration for Woman's Home Companion, *September, 1929.*

Wm Meade Prince

WILLIAM MEADE PRINCE (1893-1951) was born in Roanoke, Virginia, and grew up in Chapel Hill, North Carolina. He could not choose between West Point and architecture at Georgia Institute of Technology, settled it by going North to study art at the New York School of Fine and Applied Arts.

After five years of advertising work in Chicago, he settled in Westport, Connecticut, where he could combine his illustration work for the magazines in New York with his interest in riding and maintaining fine Arabian horses. When Westport eventually became too urban for riding, Prince returned to Chapel Hill, where he built his own studio and stables and continued to do illustration. He was particularly noted for his spirited and sympathetic interpretations of Roark Bradford's Black stories for *Collier's* magazine.

For several years Prince also taught illustration and figure drawing at the University of North Carolina and was head of the Art Department there from 1943-1946.

Cover painting for The Country Gentleman, *June, 1928.*

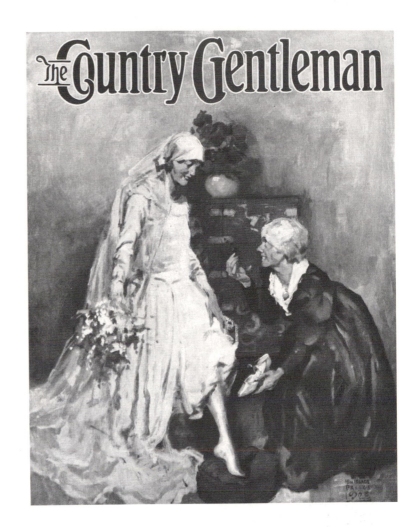

Reynard

GRANT TYSON REYNARD, N.A. (1887-1968) attended the Chicago Art Institute and the Chicago Academy of Fine Arts, paying his own way by doing odd jobs, including piano playing for sheet music sales, in his home town of Grand Island, Nebraska.

His first job was as art editor of *Redbook* magazine, then in Chicago. There he met and worked with many of the top writers and illustrators and had his first opportunity to do his own illustrations.

After three years Reynard decided to come East to study further with Harvey Dunn in Leonia, New Jersey, with the hope of working for the larger magazines. Within a year he had made it and had begun illustrating for *The Saturday Evening Post, Harper's Bazaar, Cosmopolitan, Good Housekeeping* and *Collier's*. During this time most of his illustrations were done in charcoal with a full range of values.

He began experimenting with other media for exhibition pictures and gradually turned to an independent career as painter and etcher. Study with Mahonri Young and Harry Wickey, with a year of travel and sketching in Europe, furthered this ambition. Reynard's pictures and prints now hang in many major museums including The Metropolitan Museum of Art, Addison Gallery of American Art, Fogg Museum in Boston, Newark Museum and the Library of Congress. He also won a number of prizes.

Over the years, Reynard taught at various art schools and universities and lectured widely.

"Set a Thief," illustration in charcoal for Cosmopolitan *magazine, 1921.*

"Abstract and Concrete," original oil painting for The Saturday Evening Post. © *1962 by The Curtis Publishing Company.*

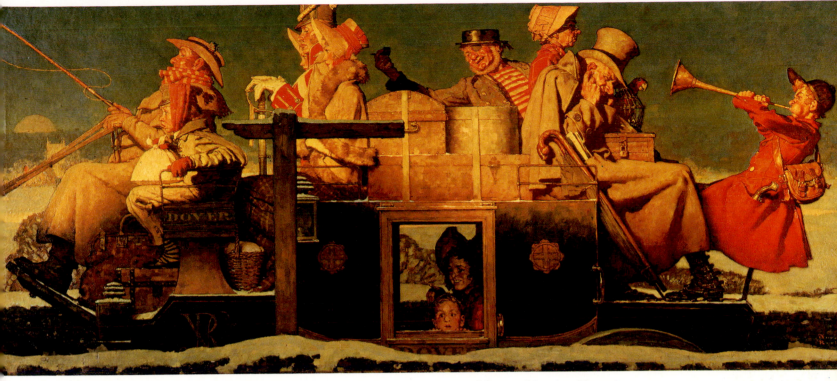

"The Dover Coach," Collection of the Society of Illustrators Museum of American Illustration.

Norman Rockwell

The pictures of NORMAN ROCKWELL (1894-1978) were recognized and loved by almost everybody in America. The cover of *The Saturday Evening Post* was his showcase for over forty years, giving him an audience larger than that of any other artist in history. Over the years he depicted there a unique collection of Americana, a series of vignettes of remarkable warmth and humor. In addition, he painted a great number of pictures for story illustrations, advertising campaigns, posters, calendars, and books.

As his personal contribution during World War II, Rockwell painted the famous "Four Freedoms" posters, symbolizing for millions the war aims as described by President Franklin Roosevelt. One version of his "Freedom of Speech" painting is in the collection of The Metropolitan Museum of Art.

Rockwell left high school to attend classes at the National Academy of Design and later studied under Thomas Fogarty and George Bridgman at the Art Students League in New York. His early illustrations were done for *St. Nicholas* magazine and other juvenile publications. He sold his first cover painting to the *Post* in 1916 and ended up doing over 300 more. Presidents Eisenhower, Kennedy, and Johnson sat for him for portraits, and he painted other world figures, including Nassar of Egypt and Nehru of India.

In 1957 the United States Chamber of Commerce in Washington cited him as a Great Living American, saying that ... "Through the magic of your talent, the folks next door — their gentle sorrows, their modest joys — have enriched our own lives and given us new insight into our countrymen."

A museum has been established in Stockbridge, Massachusetts, where he maintained his studio. Thousands of visitors continue to visit there each year to see a large collection of his original paintings.

"Gary Cooper as the Texan," cover painting for The Saturday Evening Post, *May 24, 1930. © 1930, 1958 by The Curtis Publishing Company. Collection of Judy and Alan Goffman.*

Illustration for Woman's Home Companion, *January, 1931.*

Advertising illustration for Eaton's Highland Linen, 1923.

Jam Preston.

JAMES MOORE PRESTON (1873-1962) studied at
the Philadelphia Academy with fellow students Henri,
Luks, Sloan, and Shinn, and then went to Paris to complete
his training. There he met May Wilson; they were married
in 1903 upon their return to the United States. The success
of their union can be seen in the similarity of styles,
reflecting their influence on each other.

For many years both were active contributors to nearly
all of the major magazines.

May Wilson Preston

MAY WILSON PRESTON (1873-1949) came to New
York to attend the Art Students League after graduating
from Oberlin. This was followed by study in Paris with
Whistler at the World's Art center. She first came to the
master's notice when he discovered black on her palette.
"There is no such color ... scrape it off!" Such was
Whistler's prestige that other students eagerly offered him
their lace handkerchiefs for his use as a paint rag — to be
treasured later as momentos.

May Wilson's first magazine illustrations were published by *Harper's Bazaar* as early as 1901. For the next thirty
years she illustrated stories for *McClure's, Scribner's,* and
particularly *The Saturday Evening Post,* including a number
of serials by Mary Roberts Rinehart. A prolific painter, her
illustrations were airy and witty, reflecting her own energy
and good humor.

THE SATURDAY EVENING POST

OCT. 8, 1927   5 cts.

Arthur Conan Doyle – F. Scott Fitzgerald – Horatio Winslow – Hal G. Evarts
Nunnally Johnson – Henry L. Stimson – Thomas Beer – Ben Ames Williams

Ellen Pyle

ELLEN BERNARD THOMPSON (PYLE) (1876-1936) was one of the original ten students in Howard Pyle's illustration class at Drexel Institute to be invited by him to attend his first summer school at Chadds Ford in 1898. Under his tutelege, she was soon able to obtain illustration assignments. Her first, with several other Pyle students, was to illustrate the novel, *Janice Meredith*.

In 1904, she married Pyle's younger brother, Walter, and interrupted her career to raise four children. After her husband's death in 1919, she returned to illustrating as a livelihood, finding a market doing covers for *The Saturday Evening Post*. She did young people very sympathetically, often using as models her own children or youngsters she knew. Her paintings were done in a broad poster manner with strong color which was very effective for cover design, and she continued with the *Post* for the rest of her career.

Typical cover painting for The Saturday Evening Post.

Tony Sarg

The interests of TONY SARG (1882-1942) were as diversified as his background. Sarg was born in Guatemala, sent to school in Germany. With no formal art training, he did his first professional work in London for *Sketch* magazine and also did advertising drawings.

In London he became fascinated with marionette performances by the great Holden and for months followed the troupe from one engagement to another to learn the secrets of the craft.

When Sarg came to America in 1914, he successfully organized his own marionette workshop and also experimented with early animated cartoons.

Among Sarg's first illustration assignments was one for Irvin Cobb's "Speaking of Operations" in *The Saturday Evening Post*. The humor of his drawings matched Cobb's delightfully. He eventually illustrated for a great number of publications and advertisers. Sarg also wrote and illustrated several books for children; designed textiles, wallpapers, boxes, rugs, glass and pottery, toys, and the monster balloons for the annual Macy parades on Thanksgiving Day in New York City.

"The Mad Artists Ball," cover design for Vanity Fair, *November, 1923.*

VANITY FAIR

November · 1923   The Condé Nast Publications Inc   35 cts · 3.50 a year

"Waiting for Trouble," awarded the Gold Medal for watercolor, Cowboy Artists of America exhibition, 1972.

DONALD TEAGUE

DONALD TEAGUE, N.A. (1897-   ) is respected by his fellow-illustrators as a thorough craftsman whose pictures are composed and painted with great professional competence.

Teague begins a picture with many thumbnail sketches in black-and-white, followed by small full-color studies of the most promising approaches. After a composition has been evolved, models are posed for further sketching and photographing (for factual information). Photostats, reduced in scale from the rather large figure studies, are then projected and traced on watercolor paper, free from any corrections or erasures, ready to render in watercolor or gouache.

Research, for authenticating every detail, is equally important in his picture-making. Teague, who lives in California near the motion picture studios, has had the advantage of using their props for Westerns. He can obtain cowboy actors, a stage coach complete with horses, and even use the Western Town movie sets. The Pacific Ocean is equally accessible for his sea illustrations. Air express has made it possible for him to keep deadlines with publishers in the East.

Teague was born in Brooklyn, New York, studied at the Art Students League in New York under Bridgman and DuMond. After serving in the Navy during World War I, he went to England and studied under Norman Wilkinson, P.R.I. Back in America, he found Dean Cornwell most helpful while he was getting started as an illustrator.

Besides his work for publications, Teague has exhibited regularly. His prizes and awards, too numerous to list, include the Gold Medal of Honor, American Watercolor Society in 1953 and the S. F. B. Morse Gold Medal, National Academy, 1962. He is also represented in many museums and private collections, including the Virginia Museum of Fine Arts in Richmond; Frye Museum, Seattle, Washington; and Collection of the State of California in Sacramento.

Vignette for a Collier's *story, "Tavern at Powell's Ferry," under the pseudonym of Edwin Dawes. Because of rivalry between the two publications, Teague used his own name for* The Saturday Evening Post; *"Dawes" at* Collier's.

SAUL TEPPER (1899-   ) was born on the lower East side of New York City and has remained a New Yorker all his life.

As a youngster, Tepper won a correspondence course in the Landon School of Art. He also studied at Cooper Union, the Art Students League and at the Grand Central School of Art, under Harvey Dunn.

He worked as a letterer in a fashion catalog studio before establishing himself as an illustrator. Tepper has since illustrated almost equally for fiction and advertising assignments for most of the magazines and for many national accounts, such as Mobil Oil, Texaco, Packard, General Motors and Coca-Cola.

Among his many honors are the Harvard Award (1929), the Newspaper Award (1936), Annual Advertising Award (1940) and the Laskinlamb Institute Award (1943).

For many years, Tepper has also been an active teacher and lecturer at Pratt Institute, Cooper Union, the New York Art Directors Club and the Society of Illustrators.

Music has been a parallel interest with him. Saul has written many popular songs which have been recorded by Nat ("King") Cole, Ella Fitzgerald, Ezio Pinza, Glenn Miller, Harry James and others. He is a member of ASCAP and AGAC and has written sketches, lyrics and music for fifteen annual Society of Illustrators' Shows. He is a life member of the Society of Illustrators and was elected to its Hall of Fame in 1980.

"The New Boss Lady". The influence of Harvey Dunn's teaching is apparent in this strong illustration for the American *magazine, May, 1932. Collection of Les Mansfield.*

"Exodus from Theatre," American *magazine, July, 1933. Collection of Joseph Mendola.*

5
Sheridan

JOHN E. SHERIDAN (1880-1948) was at his best as a poster and cover artist, as exemplified in his paintings for *The Ladies' Home Journal, The Saturday Evening Post, American, Collier's* and in the posters he made for the Bureau of Public Information during World War I. He was also noted for his advertising illustrations for Hart, Schaffner & Marx and the Bosch Magneto Company.

Sheridan was born in Tomah, Wisconsin, and earned his tuition for Georgetown University in Washington, D.C. by painting posters for sports events. He also spent a year at the Colorossi School in Paris. He next became art editor of the *Washington Times* and later helped to produce the first Sunday supplement in color for the *San Francisco Chronicle.*

He was an active member of the Society of Illustrators, The Players, Dutch Treat Club, and taught at the School of Visual Arts in New York from 1945-48.

Cover illustration for the American Magazine, *March, 1931.*

FRANK STREET

FRANK STREET (1893-1944) came from Kansas City, Missouri, to study at the Art Students League in New York and at the Charles Chapman-Harvey Dunn School of Illustration in Leonia, New Jersey.

Dunn, who carried on the Pyle tradition, was the dominant influence in Street's work. He also helped him to obtain his first illustration commission from Walter Dower, then art editor of *The Saturday Evening Post.* Street had a long career of illustration with the *Post* and with many other publications, including *The Ladies' Home Journal, Cosmopolitan, Collier's,* and *The American Legion* magazines.

Although he did not exhibit them formally, Street painted many landscapes and portraits, between illustration commissions, and also conducted private classes in his own studio for the last five or six years of his life.

Illustration for The Ladies' Home Journal, *March, 1925.*

R. Van Buren

RAEBURN L. VAN BUREN (1891-   ) who was born in Pueblo, Colorado, learned his craft in the best of training schools — as a newspaper sketch artist. In his case, he was fortunate to work on the *Kansas City Star* under an excellent art editor, H. Wood. Out of that same bull-pen came Robert Lambdin, Tony Balcom and Loran Wilford — all of whom went on to careers as illustrators in New York. Van Buren spent three-and-a-half years in Kansas City and at the age of twenty-one felt he was ready for the big time.

His newspaper friends, already in New York, introduced him to a number of art editors, and he was soon working alongside them. After his first assignment for Street & Smith, he went on to *The Saturday Evening Post, Liberty, Redbook, Cosmopolitan, Collier's, Esquire, The New Yorker* and other magazines.

In 1937, the late Al Capp offered to collaborate with him on a comic strip and "Abbie and Slats" was born, with Capp doing the writing and Van Buren the drawings. This kept Van Buren on a treadmill of deadlines for many years but built him a loyal and large following until the strip finally folded in 1971. Van Buren was named "Best Cartoonist" in 1958 and elected to the National Cartoonist Society Hall of Fame in 1979.

"Bill Collector," illustration for The Saturday Evening Post.

Teale

EARLE GRANTHAM TEALE (1886-1919) was tragically killed while standing in the darkened interior of a garage when a driver coming in from the bright sunlight failed to see him in time.

At the time of his death he was one of the country's foremost automobile artists, having painted a brilliant series of advertisements for the White Motor Car Company. Also memorable was an illustrated catalog for the Canadian Pacific Railway Company's Transatlantic Steamship Service, lavishly printed in full color. Teale's style was decorative and influenced by both his admiration for Japanese prints and his interest in murals.

He had attended the Art Students League in New York and later studied architectural design at Stanford University as a preparation for mural painting. His death occurred when he was just reaching his prime as an artist, cutting off a career that deserved to have far greater influence and recognition.

"The Limousine," advertising illustration in Vogue *magazine for the White Motor Car Company, October 15, 1919.*

Dry-brush illustration for The Ladies' Home Journal, *March, 1928.* © *by The Curtis Publishing Company.*

LORAN FREDERICK WILFORD (1893-1972) taught at the Ringling School of Art in Sarasota, Florida, prior to his teaching at the Grand Central School of Art in New York City, following a long career of painting for exhibition and illustrating for newspapers and magazines.

Born in Wamego, Kansas, Wilford studied at the Kansas City Art Institute and was soon doing feature illustrations for the *Kansas City Star.*

Ambitious, he gravitated to the East for further study with Jonas Lie and George Pearce Ennis. Soon he began a career working for such publications as *Cosmopolitan, Everybody's, McCall's,* and *Hearst's International.* His early illustrations were done in dry-brush; later he became very much interested in watercolors which he soon began to exhibit.

He went on to become an outstanding watercolorist and won many honors for both his watercolors and oils. He painted several murals and is represented in the permanent collection of the Toledo Museum of Fine Art, the High Museum of Atlanta, Georgia, and in many private collections.

CHARLES DAVID WILLIAMS (1875-1954) worked in pen-and-ink in the early part of his career; especially notable were his sensitive line drawings for Booth Tarkington's *Monsieur Beaucaire.* He later worked in charcoal and in pastels with great control and subtlety in this difficult medium.

Williams, who was from Pittsburgh, had had a brief career in the 'nineties, as a professional lightweight boxer.

Gregarious and hard-working, he spent much of his time on behalf of the programs of the Society of Illustrators and served as its president from 1927 to 1929.

Illustration for the cover of Every Week *magazine, June 25, 1917.*

1930
1940

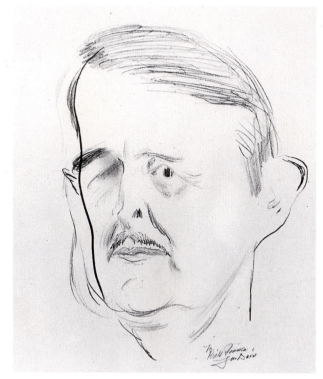

Self portrait

THE DECADE: 1930-1940
Floyd Davis
(1896-1966)

We thought of ourselves not merely as illustrators but also as fine artists and took our work very seriously. We believed that the field of illustration was eminently worth-while and that our goal was to paint the best pictures we knew how. Of course, we were subject to the particular limitations of the subject matter, the policy of the publication, the mechanics of working for good reproduction, and so forth. However, these restrictions, if different, were perhaps no greater than those placed on the painters of pictures in the past by awkward architectural settings, poor lighting, or dogmatic interpretation of religious subjects by church officials.

A good illustration should be able to stand on its own as a picture. If it has merely been a "photograph" of an incident in a story, its usefulness will be as transient as the sentences it illustrates. However, if it is a picture true to human behavior or motivation as revealed by the manuscript — and done with artistry and integrity — it has a chance of being worth-while. To make a great picture requires a combination of many qualities, plus good luck. It is rare good fortune to feel, even once in a lifetime, that you are joining hands with Rembrandt.

Good art directors, too, had their share in making illustration important. The best of them, men like Bill Chessman of *Collier's,* Pete Martin of *The Saturday Evening Post,* and Henry Quinan of the *Woman's Home Companion,* brought out the best in us with their stimulation and encouragement. We were challenged to try new approaches in our own individual ways, without the restraint of contrived layouts or predetermined situations in the manuscript. Whenever possible, we were allowed to take the extra time necessary to interpret the assigned story creatively.

There were a great many talented and dedicated men in the illustration field in the 'thirties: John Gannam, Henry Raleigh, Frank Hoffman, Harold Von Schmidt, Albert Dorne, Rockwell Kent, Lynd Ward, Edward A. Wilson, Wallace Morgan, Eric and many others. Some are still active. I admire the work of all the good ones. These artists raised the position of American illustration to international preëminence, both in technical excellence and in the scope of their influence.

The Depression had some effect on the illustration field then, but since we were in our busy, productive years as artists, we didn't feel the economic pinch as much as did many of the easel and mural painters, some of whom needed the relief assistance of the Federal Government to survive at all as artists.

Denys Wortman, in his syndicated "Metropolitan Movies," "Mopey Dick and the Duke," and "Mrs. Rumpel's Boarding House," made poignant and wry commentary on this period in his humorous newspaper drawings. The pulp magazine, inexpensive and printed on cheap, uncoated paper, became very popular during this time. The covers were generally lurid in color and subject, although some, such as *Adventure* magazine and *Bluebook,* were "quality" pulps which showed better taste and better art. Inside illustrations were almost invariably done in a drybrush technique which reproduced inexpensively in line, often styled after Frank Hoffman's earlier, sparkling black-and-white drawings. Devoted to special subjects, such as Westerns, detectives, and aviation, the pulps provided an excellent market for upcoming authors and young illustrators. Amos Sewell, John Clymer, Walter Baumhofer, John Falter and Tom Lovell were among those who were active in this field and later graduated to eminence in the slicks. (The quality magazines were printed on coated, or slick, paper.)

By the end of the 'thirties, the Depression was over and, with it, an era. As war came to Europe in 1939, great changes were taking place in the United States, too. The effects of war mobilization were felt throughout the economy, including the art field. The insular hill-billy disappeared, and subsequently we all became involved with the war effort.

F. M. Davis

ILLUSTRATORS 1930-1940

CONSTANTIN ALAJÁLOV
JAMES EDWARD ALLEN
HAROLD N. ANDERSON
BORIS ARTZYBASHEFF
ERNEST HAMLIN BAKER
LOWELL LEROY BALCOM
McCLELLAND BARCLAY
CECIL CALVERT BEALL
HARRY BECKHOFF
FRANK C. BENSING
EARL BLOSSOM
VLADIMIR BOBRITSKY (BOBRI)
E. MELBOURNE BRINDLE
ELMORE J. BROWN
PAUL BROWN
PRUETT A. CARTER
FREDERICK TRENCH CHAPMAN
BENTON CLARK
MATT CLARK
RALPH PALLEN COLEMAN
GRATTAN CONDON
DAN CONTENT
MARIO RUBEN COOPER
BRADSHAW CRANDELL
WILLIAM GALBRAITH CRAWFORD
DOUGLASS CROCKWELL
JOHN HENRY CROSMAN
ROBERT W. CROWTHER
FLOYD MacMILLAN DAVIS
WILLIAM JAMES DUFAULT
NICK EGGENHOFER
CARL OSCAR AUGUST ERICKSON (ERIC)
JOHN RUSSELL FULTON
EDWIN A. GEORGI
FRANK GODWIN
JULES GOTLIEB
RUTH SIGRID GRAFSTROM
ROY FREDERIC HEINRICH
WILMOT EMERTON HEITLAND
C. PETER HELCK

DAVID HENDRICKSON
EDWIN HENRY
E. EVERETT HENRY
R. JOHN HOLMGREN
GEORGE HOWE
FRANCES TIPTON HUNTER
ELBERT McGRAN JACKSON
ROCKWELL KENT
STEVEN R. KIDD
WALTER CHARLES KLETT
CLAYTON KNIGHT
LARRY B. KRITCHER
JOHN LaGATTA
CHARLES LOUIS LaSALLE
MANNING DeVILLENEUVE LEE
PHILIP LYFORD
ORISON MacPHERSON
RONALD NORMAN McLEOD
FREDERIC KIMBALL MIZEN
IRVING NURICK
ROBERT PATTERSON
GARRETT PRICE
WILLIAM REUSSWIG
MARTHA SAWYERS
MEAD SCHAEFFER
OSCAR FREDERICK SCHMIDT
JAMES W. SCHUCKER
HOWARD SCOTT
HENRY J. SOULEN
ROY FREDERIC SPRETER
HERBERT MORTON STOOPS
KATHERINE STURGES (KNIGHT)
HADDON HUBBARD SUNDBLOM
DAN SWEENEY
HARRY LAVERNE TIMMINS
RICO TOMASO
EDMUND F. WARD
WILLIAM P. WELSH
JAMES W. WILLIAMSON
DENYS WORTMAN

J.E. ALLEN

JAMES EDWARD ALLEN (1894-1964) was a student and serious experimenter all his life. Born in Louisiana, Missouri, he attended the Art Academy in Chicago, the Art Students League, the Grand Central Art School and the Hans Hoffman School in New York. He also studied in Paris and London.

Among his instructors were Frank Stick, Joseph Pennell, Robert Brackman, Robert Philipp, William Auerbach-Levy, Arshile Gorky, Sigurd Skou and Harvey Dunn.

He began illustrating for the *People's Popular Monthly* in 1913. Assignments from nearly all of the major magazines followed. Most of his pictures were painted in oils, but he was also interested in lithographs and etchings which have been exhibited widely in the United States and abroad.

Allen was a member of the Salmagundi Club, the Society of Etchers, the Chicago Society of Etchers, the Philadelphia Society of Etchers and the New Rochelle Art Association. His work won many awards and is represented in several collections, including the Brooklyn Museum, the Cincinnati Museum, Cleveland Museum of Art, Seattle Art Museum, Philadelphia Museum of Art and the Library of Congress.

Cover illustration for Motor Boating *magazine, March, 1925.*

HAROLD ANDERSON

HAROLD N. ANDERSON (1894-1973) studied at the Fenway Art School in his native Boston. Among his instructors were Chase Emerson, Harold Brett, and Arthur Spear.

His first illustrations were made for *Boy's Life* in 1919 and were followed by work for most of the leading publications, many national advertising campaigns and twenty-four-sheet billboard posters.

He won numerous poster awards and exhibited in Art Directors Club shows in 1937, 1940, 1942, 1946, 1950 and 1951. Anderson was a member of the Society of Illustrators, The Old Greenwich Art Society, the Artists Guild and the Westport Artists. He had a one-man show at the Society of Illustrators in 1942.

Cover illustration for The Saturday Evening Post. © *1933, 1961 by The Curtis Publishing Company.*

Artzybasheff

BORIS ARTZYBASHEFF (1899-1965) combined a spirit of fantasy with wry humor in his incomparable ability to give human qualities to machines; a meticulous rendering made his most imaginative creations entirely convincing. His designs were always carefully planned — there is not an accidental stroke in them — and he mastered every technical problem by thoughtful preliminary studies.

Artzybasheff was born in Kharkov, Russia, and was graduated from the Prince Tenisheff School in St. Petersburg. After the Revolution he escaped the country on a freighter. When he arrived in America in 1919, he had only a few Turkish coins, the equivalent of 14 cents.

Befriended by a Russian Orthodox priest, he found work in an engraving shop doing lettering, borders and ornamental details. He first gained a reputation as an artist by illustrating over 40 books, several of which he also wrote or edited. The best known of these, perhaps, are his *Aesop's Fables, Seven Simeons,* and *Balzac's Droll Stories.* Advertising and cover painting assignments followed. He was a regular contributor of incisive and penetrating cover portraits for *Time* magazine for 24 years, painting over 200 covers. His work was also well known abroad; he did commissions for firms overseas as well as many advertising campaigns for leading companies in the United States.

During World War II Artzybasheff served as an expert adviser to the U.S. Department of State, Psychological Warfare Branch.

During his long career, he was the recipient of many awards, including the Newberry Medal and citations from the American Institute of Graphic Arts.

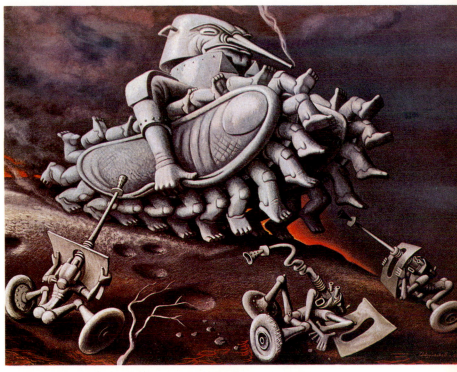

"Imperturbable tank and anti-tank guns," one of a series of illustrations that appeared in Life *magazine, November 3, 1941.*

alajálov

CONSTANTIN ALAJÁLOV (1900-   ) sold his first cover to *The New Yorker* magazine in 1926 and has since painted a long and colorful series of satirical vignettes of American life for *The New Yorker* and *The Saturday Evening Post.*

Alajálov was born in the Russian town of Rostov-on-the-Don. The Revolution came when he was seventeen and a student at the University of Petrograd. He survived this period by working as a government artist, painting huge propaganda pictures and portraits, and eventually made his way, in 1921, to Constantinople, which was an international refugee haven.

Although largely self-taught as an artist, Alajálov earned a precarious living by sketching portraits in bars or painting sidewalk advertisements for movie houses. He eventually progressed to doing murals for night clubs, taking mostly food as payment. After two years of this, he saved enough to pay his passage to America.

Once here, Alajálov resumed painting murals, in Russian night clubs, and within three years had sold that *New Yorker* cover. He has continued to give us a candid and refreshing look at our foibles ever since.

Drawing by Alajálov; © 1930, 1958 by The New Yorker Magazine, Inc. Collection of the Museum of the City of New York.

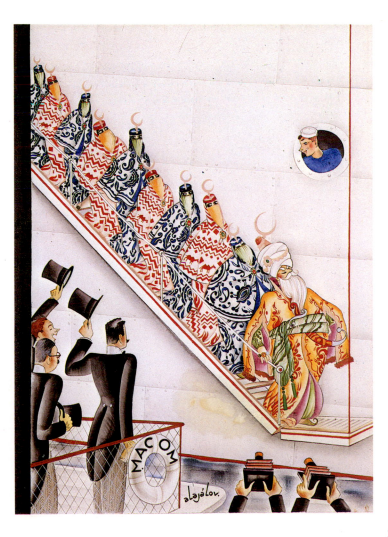

Ernest Hamlin Baker

ERNEST HAMLIN BAKER (1889-1975) was a self-taught artist who evolved his own personal, and painstakingly intricate, approach as typified by the nearly 400 cover portraits he painted for *Time* magazine.

The portraits were painted from photographs of the subjects taken from all possible angles, with different light sources, and then studied minutely — even with a magnifying glass — to give him a knowledge of the whole face and head.

Baker then made a highly detailed preliminary pencil study or "facial guide-map." Every wen, wart, indentation or vein was factually and honestly depicted. It was from a careful analysis of these "facts" and their relationship to each other that a faithful likeness emerged, a likeness that revealed character.

His painting process was equally detailed, beginning with a tracing from the pencil drawing on illustration board. The portrait was gradually built up with repeated strokes of diluted tempera color, allowing the drawing beneath to show through. From time to time this pencil drawing was reinforced to retain it clearly. Values were thus built up from light to dark with minute strokes, even for the large areas (never broad, flat washes), each stroke successively blotted to remove any excess of color. This unique process, laborious as it was, gave the artist complete control of the painting right up to the final stroke.

Cover portrait painting of Chief of Staff, George C. Marshall. Ernest Hamlin Baker for Time *magazine.* © *1942 by Time, Inc.*

BALCOM

LOWELL LEROY BALCOM (1887-1938) was born in Kansas City, Missouri, and got his start there. He studied privately with John D. Patrick and at the Kansas City Art Institute with Charles Wilimovsky. His first job was as an artist for the *Kansas City Star.* In the Army, during World War I, his duties consisted largely of drawing and painting portraits of officers.

After the war, Balcom visited the Virgin Islands to paint in watercolors and oils. He made his first experiments there with linoleum cuts which he was later to develop as his own personal medium.

Balcom's first break came when he did a series of illustrations for the U. S. Shipping Board which also provided him an opportunity to travel to the Orient and the Mediterranean. Subsequently, he did illustrations for numerous magazines such as *The American Legion* and *Hearst's International* and for advertisers including Exide Batteries and Bridgeport Brass.

He was a member of the Artists Guild in New York and active in the Silvermine Guild in Norwalk, Connecticut, up to the time of his death.

Unpublished variation of the cover illustration for the December, 1930, issue of The American Legion *magazine, linoleum block.*

C.C. Beall

CECIL CALVERT BEALL (1892-1967) traveled a long way from his birthplace of Saratoga, Wyoming. He studied at the Art Students League under George Bridgman and at Pratt Institute. His early illustrations were done in bold poster style in watercolor marked by a strong pattern of light and shadow, favored by a number of illustrators of the *Collier's* "school."

In 1936 Beall did a composite portrait of President Franklin D. Roosevelt for a *Collier's* cover which so pleased the President that he appointed Beall art director for the National Democratic Committee.

During World War II, Beall painted the portraits of a number of decorated heroes as covers for *Collier's* magazine. At the close of the war, Beall was one of the privileged few to witness the surrender ceremony aboard the U.S.S. Missouri. His painting of the event was made the official one by President Harry S. Truman.

Beall was a member of the Society of Illustrators; won their Award of Excellence in the 1961 exhibition; also belonged to the American Watercolor Society, the Overseas Press Club, the Hudson Valley Art Association and the Salmagundi Club.

His pictures are included in many collections, including the Air Force Academy Museum in Colorado Springs, Colorado, and the Marine Museum at Quantico, Virginia.

Story illustration for Collier's *magazine, May 13, 1939.*

FRANK BENSING

FRANK C. BENSING (1893-1983) was born in Chicago, Illinois, and received his art training there at the Art Institute. Among his teachers were DeForrest Schook, Wellington Reynolds, Charles Schroeder and Walter Biggs.

Bensing's first illustrations were made in 1926 for *Redbook,* an association which continued for many years. He also worked for *McCall's, Country Gentleman, The Saturday Evening Post, American, Pictorial Review, The American Legion* and *This Week* magazines.

Bensing combined his illustration for periodicals with exhibitions of his oils and watercolors at the National Academy of Design, the American Watercolor Society, Allied Artists and others. In later years he turned increasingly to portraiture.

Bensing was a member of the Dutch Treat Club, Artists and Writers, Allied Artists, Salmagundi Club, the American Watercolor Society and the Society of Illustrators.

Illustration for Redbook *magazine.*

153

McClelland Barclay

McCLELLAND BARCLAY (1891-1943) was appointed a Lieutenant Commander, U.S.N.R., during World War II and contributed many posters, illustrations and officer portraits for the Navy before being reported missing in action, in the Pacific Theatre, aboard an L.S.T. which was torpedoed.

Before the war, Barclay was most noted for his ability to paint strikingly beautiful women, as best exemplified by his series for General Motors illustrating the slogan, "Body by Fisher."

Born in St. Louis, Missouri, Barclay was a student of H. C. Ives, George Bridgman and Thomas Fogarty. He was a member of the Artists Guild, the Art Students League of New York and the Society of Illustrators.

In 1946, on the third anniversary of his death, a foundation was established in his name, The McClelland Barclay Fund for Art, "to aid the thousands of American artists who have never had a fair opportunity."

One of a series of illustrations for Fisher Body which appeared in the late 'twenties and early 'thirties.

Here Barclay updated the Coles Phillips "Fadeaway Girl" idea in this black on black cover for The New Movie Magazine *in 1933.*

This illustration by Barclay for an advertisement for the Koppers Company was awarded The Art Directors Club Medal posthumously in 1944, "in recognition of his long and distinguished record in editorial illustration and advertising art and in honor of his devotion and meritorious service to his country as a commissioned officer of the United States Navy, which lists him as missing in action in the South Pacific."

Here is a typical, odd assortment of Beckhoff types for the Collier's *story, "The Senator was Indiscreet."*

BECKHOFF

HARRY BECKHOFF (1901-1979) began his pictorial compositions with small sketches that were almost literally thumbnail in size. These tiny drawings contained all of the information needed for the final rendering — even down to facial expressions. He then pantographed the drawing, about five times larger, and inked in the outlines. The tone or color areas were painted in with flat washes.

Beckhoff described his work as having been influenced by the French illustrators Martin, Brissaud and Marty. He also cited his teachers, George Bridgman, Dean Cornwell and Harvey Dunn for their encouragement and training.

Country Gentlemen published his first magazine illustrations in 1929. He subsequently worked for many of the other periodicals, but Beckhoff was most closely associated with the wonderful Broadway characters he drew to illustrate Damon Runyon's famous stories which ran for many years in *Collier's* magazine.

Earl Blossom —

EARL BLOSSOM (1891-1970) had no formal art instruction but received his training in the practical school of advertising. Some of his early work included drawings for men's fashions, newspaper illustration for the *Chicago American* and a stint as a bull-pen artist in the old Charles Daniel Frey studio in Chicago.

Many of today's largest advertising agencies were getting started in the 'twenties and Blossom worked at one time or another for most of them. He also spent some time promoting the land boom in Florida — wrote and illustrated full-page advertisements for Boca Raton.

Blossom had known Pete Martin earlier in Chicago and under his art direction at *The Saturday Evening Post,* Blossom began to do fiction illustration. He was not entirely happy at the *Post,* however, where "everyone was supposed to imitate Arthur William Brown," and when Martin left the *Post,* Blossom switched to *Collier's* magazine.

William Chessman, who was art director at *Collier's,* encouraged Earl to develop his own humorous bent. Said Chessman, "He is a masterful artist. You never have to tell him what to do. Just give him a good story and let him alone." Blossom responded with a wonderful blend of comedy and realism that became his specialty.

Illustration for Collier's *"Ill Wind," by Frank Condon.*

Illustration for Saks Fifth Avenue advertisement which appeared in Vogue *magazine, 1934.*

bobri

VLADIMIR BOBRITSKY (BOBRI) (1898-) was a student at the Kharkov Imperial Art School in the Ukraine before the Revolution and had begun to design sets for the Great Dramatic Theatre of Kharkov.

Swept up in the conflict, he fought in several armies on both sides and eventually, with a passport he forged himself, managed to escape to Constantinople.

Several years of varied art activities followed — painting Greek icons and playing guitar in a gypsy chorus before Bobri was able to come to America.

His experiences here were no less varied, ranging from the operation of a textile printing business, to art direction for Saks Fifth Avenue. His newspaper and magazine layouts represented a fresh departure. Bobri soon found himself with enough clients to embark on a free-lance art career, largely for advertising illustration, and strongly influenced by his background of classical training and theatrical designing.

He continued his serious study of the guitar both as composer and performer; is president of the Society of the Classic Guitar in New York and serves as editor and art director of the *Guitar Review.* He has also illustrated a great many children's books.

Melbourne Brindle

E. MELBOURNE BRINDLE (1906-), who was named for his birthplace in Australia, has made a reputation for himself in the United States with his precise and fastidious illustrations.

With no formal training, Brindle progressed through a number of jobs in the San Francisco area, from show card writing to a department store art department, to affiliation with a large advertising agency.

Although now at home in every medium, he first developed a brilliant black-and-white technique which won him medals in the New York Art Directors Club's annual shows in 1935 and 1938.

Brindle began to do editorial illustration for *Woman's Home Companion* in 1940, followed thereafter by commissions from most of the other national magazines. He is especially expert in depicting antique automobiles since he collects and restores them as a hobby. He also researched and fully illustrated with his own paintings a beautiful book, titled *Twenty Silver Ghosts,* on historical Rolls-Royce cars, published by McGraw-Hill in 1971.

Cover painting for The Saturday Evening Post. © *1946, 1974 by The Curtis Publishing Company. Collection of Mr. and Mrs. Robert Wale.*

Elmor Brown

ELMORE J. BROWN (1899-1968) illustrated Ernest Hemingway's first published short story, "A Matter of Color," in the *Tabula,* an annual for the Oak Park (Illinois) High School where both were students in 1916.

Brown went on to study at the Chicago Art Institute and the Art Students League in New York. Among his instructors were John Norton, George Bellows, Leopold Seyffert, Leon Kroll and Eugene Speicher.

His first major illustrations, done for *The Ladies' Home Journal* in 1931, were soon followed by work for most of the other magazines. However, his work appeared most regularly in *Collier's* magazine from 1933 to 1949.

Brown, who was a keen student of the technical problems of painting once, determined that to obtain Munsell's neutral #5 gray requires .01 of an ounce of black and .3904 of an ounce of white! He worked from light to dark in accord with his own scientific analysis of the problems of painting.

He was a member of the Artists and Writers Association and a life member of the Society of Illustrators.

Collier's illustration for the story, "The Hunters" by Mary Hastings Bradley.

Paul Brown

PAUL BROWN (1893-1958) began to draw horses at the age of six; they continued to be his favorite subject to the end of his life. During this time, he wrote thirty-three books of his own and illustrated over 100 more by other authors.

Brown's knowledge of horses was acquired through continuous study and sketching at polo matches and races until he became so familiar with them that he could draw entirely without models. His specialty was painting horses in sports or in violent action.

He began drawing catalog and sporting illustrations for Brooks Brothers in 1920, continuing with them for nearly forty years. He also illustrated for many of the major magazines, including *Cosmopolitan, Collier's, Spur, Polo, Harper's Bazaar, Liberty, The Elks* and *The American Legion.*

Cover illustration for The American Legion, *June, 1937. Collection of Mr. and Mrs. William Kerr.*

Illustration for The Ladies' Home Journal, © *1933, 1961 by The Curtis Publishing Co. Collection of Norman Rudolph.*

"Ballerina," McCall's, *October, 1929. Collection of the Society of Illustrators Museum of American Illustration.*

PRUETT CARTER

PRUETT A. CARTER (1891-1955) once described the role of the illustrator in this manner:

"The illustrator may be likened to the director of a motion picture, or a spoken stage-play. He must know his characters — their emotions and desires — he must set the stage and direct the arrangement and action and conflict of drama. He must live the part of each actor. He must do the scenery, design the costumes and handle the lighting effects. His illustration must be deeper than a poster, for he must make his characters live and breathe and react to each other as the author intended."

For nearly 40 years, Carter fulfilled this role in his work for the leading magazines. Especially, he had the ability to paint women sympathetically; his heroines were noted for their gentle, patrician beauty. Walter Biggs had taught him the use of color; Pruett used his palette with brilliance and taste.

Carter was born in Lexington, Missouri, and was reared on an Indian reservation in Wyoming where his father ran a trading post and his mother taught school. The family moved on to California so that Pruett could go to high school there. Upon graduation Carter was encouraged in his art ambitions by James Swinnerton, the cartoonist, creator of "Little Jimmy."

Carter went to the Los Angeles Art School and got his first job on the Hearst *New York American,* was later transferred to the *Atlanta Georgian.*

As a step toward his ambition to become a magazine illustrator, Carter next became art editor for *Good Housekeeping* magazine and, eventually, was able to assign one of the story manuscripts to himself. From then on he worked as a free-lance illustrator.

A vacation trip to California in 1930 became a permanent move. Taking along an assignment from Henry Quinan, art editor of *Woman's Home Companion,* Carter air-mailed the pictures back. He found this to be a practical arrangement, with the addition of long distance telephone conferences.

Carter taught many of today's illustrators, some at the Grand Central School of Art in New York, others at the Chouinard Art Institute in Los Angeles, where he headed the Illustration Department for several years. He is remembered with great affection and respect by all of them.

"Southern Belle," Good Housekeeping *magazine, October, 1927. Collection of Mr. and Mrs. Mort Künstler.*

RALPH
PALLEN
COLEMAN

Over his long career, RALPH PALLEN COLEMAN (1892-1968) illustrated stories by many famous authors including Somerset Maugham, Rex Beach, F. Scott Fitzgerald, Louis Bromfield and Clarence Budington Kelland, his work appearing in most of the major magazines.

Coleman, who was educated at the Philadelphia Museum School of Industrial Art, sold his first illustration to *The Saturday Evening Post* in 1919. His work appeared regularly thereafter in the *Post* and other magazines for over twenty years. He also found time in his busy career to paint many portraits and a number of murals in churches in Jenkintown, Lancaster and Montoursville, Pennsylvania and in Wilmington, Delaware. In addition, he did a series of paintings depicting the Life of Christ for the George Washington Memorial Park in White Marsh, Pennsylvania.

"The Narrow Corner," illustration for W. Somerset Maugham's story in Cosmopolitan *magazine, 1932.*

FREDERICK TRENCH CHAPMAN (1887-1983) had a strong sense of line and pattern which logically led to his concentration in the field of book illustration. He was an acknowledged master of the figure in action and specialized in period costume subjects for which he could utilize his love of historical research.

Notable examples of this talent are seen in his illustrations for the *History of America,* published by D.C. Heath and Company; *Virginia: History, Government, Geography,* published by Charles Scribner's Sons; plates drawn for *The Quarterly, The Company of Military Collectors & Historians* and the many historical juvenile novels he illustrated for various publishers.

Chapman was a Californian who studied at the Art Students League of New York with George Bridgman. Some of his early artwork was done in collaboration with the Czech artist, Vojtech Preissig, who was an expert printmaker and exponent of the use of the linoleum block.

For a number of years Chapman illustrated for magazines such as *Everybody's, Harper's Bazaar, Collier's, Liberty* and *Woman's Home Companion,* but it was the success of his first book, *Voyages to Vinland,* published by Alfred A. Knopf, in 1942, that led to his eventual specialization as an illustrator of books.

"Exploring the Catacombs," illustration for a story by Alice Duer Miller in Woman's Home Companion, *January, 1929.*

Cover for The Saturday Evening Post, *December 11, 1937.* ©
1937, 1965 by The Curtis Publishing Company. Collection of
Illustration House.

OUGLASS
ROCKWELL

The illustrations of DOUGLASS CROCKWELL (1904-
1968) were often simply signed "Douglass" to avoid confusion with the signature of Norman Rockwell, particularly
since their work was being published on the covers of *The
Saturday Evening Post* during the same period. Necessary
too, because Crockwell also worked very realistically, and
like Rockwell, was particularly good with children.

   Their backgrounds, however, were entirely different.
Crockwell was born in Columbus, Ohio, and took his
degree in Science at Washington University, followed by
study at the Academy of Fine Arts in Chicago and the St.
Louis School of Fine Arts. He received his first commission
for a cover for *The Saturday Evening Post* in 1933 and this was
followed by many more, as well as work for other periodicals and a long list of national advertisers.

   During the 'thirties he also completed Post Office murals
in Vermont, New York State and Mississippi, and began to
work on experimental animated films. The films, and
inventing a "pan-stereo" viewing camera to produce
them, occupied the rest of his life although he also continued to do some twenty to forty illustrations a year.

   His work won Art Directors Club medals in 1943, 1945
and 1946, and his films are in the Museum of Modern Art
Film Library.

Advertising illustration for Republic Steel, 1944.

"The Parley," illustration for the story "Free Land" by Rose Wilder Lane, published in The Saturday Evening Post.
© *1938 , 1966 by The Curtis Publishing Company.*

Benton Clark

BENTON CLARK (1895-1964) owed much, as have all subsequent painters of the Old West, to Frederic Remington and his original recording of the period. Benton also greatly admired Harvey Dunn and Frank Hoffman for their work in this locale.

Clark's own contribution is in dramatically synthesizing the era in a robust and colorful way. His illustrations make the past alive and convincing; the picture reproduced here exemplifies his work at its best.

Benton was trained at the Art Institute of Chicago and the art school of the National Academy of Design in New York. His early work was in the art department for M.G.M. in Culver City, California; for the Stevens, Sundblom Studio and the Kling Studio, both in Chicago.

He first illustrated for *Liberty* magazine in 1927, subsequently for most of the other major magazines, including *The Saturday Evening Post, McCall's, Cosmopolitan* and *Good Housekeeping.*

"Wagon Train," illustration for "You Ever Fought an Injun?" by M. G. Chute published by The Saturday Evening Post.
© *1940 , 1968 by The Curtis Publishing Company.*

MATT CLARK

MATT CLARK (1903-1972), like his older brother, Benton, was born in Coshocton, Ohio. He, too, attended the National Academy Art School in New York and was also an expert in depicting the Old West, particularly horses and their accoutrements, harnesses and buggies. Matt's subjects were in no way restricted to the Old West, however; he was equally at home with contemporary subjects from the farm to urban society.

Although Benton worked almost exclusively in oils, Matt was noted for his masterful use of dry-brush, often combined with watercolor. This medium, because of the underlying black-ink drawing, reproduced exceptionally well, whether in full color or in black-and-white.

His first illustrations were published by *College Humor* in 1929; he, too, added nearly all of the other magazines to his list of clients.

Illustration for story in the American Boy-Youth's Companion, *February, 1931.*

GRATTAN CONDON

GRATTAN CONDON (1887-1966) is perhaps best known for his illustrations of stories of World War I although he could draw other subjects equally well. Many of his illustrations were rendered in charcoal and have a freely drawn effect as though done directly at the scene; it is this quality that makes his war subjects so convincing. Among other leading publications, he was a regular contributor to *The Saturday Evening Post* and *The Ladies' Home Journal*.

Condon was born in Eugene, Oregon, and studied at both the Los Angeles School of Art and Design and the Art Students League of Los Angeles; his teachers included Walter Biggs and Lewis Daniel.

An illustrator, painter and educator, Condon was a member of the Society of Illustrators and the Salmagundi Club in New York City.

DAN CONTENT

The illustrations of DAN CONTENT (1902-   ) retain the strong stamp of his teacher, Dean Cornwell. A precocious student, Content also studied at Pratt Institute and the Art Students League of New York. He sold his first illustration at the age of twenty-one to *McCall's* magazine.

Stories of high adventure predominate among his illustrations for such magazines as *Cosmopolitan, Good Housekeeping, Liberty, The Ladies' Home Journal, Collier's, Woman's Home Companion.*

Content taught at the Work Shop School of Art in 1947-48 and in recent years has been affiliated with an advertising marketing firm in New York City.

"Ladies at Leisure," date and place of publication unknown. Courtesy, the Graham Gallery.

MARIO COOPER

MARIO RUBEN COOPER, N.A. (1905-) has had several careers in the field of art, each pursued with great enthusiasm and marked by excellence.

Born in Mexico City of Mexican-American parentage, he was reared in Los Angeles and received his education there at the Otis Art Institute and Chouinard Art Institute. He later attended the Grand Central School of Art and Columbia University in New York. Among his teachers were Pruett Carter and Harvey Dunn — Dunn especially influencing his philosophy and point of view.

Cooper was at various times employed in an engraving house, and as a visualizer for Batten, Barton, Durstine and Osborne; as art director for Lord and Taylor, and as an expert layout man and letterer, before finally obtaining his first commission for an illustration from *Collier's* magazine.

An an illustrator, Cooper is noted for the dramatic concepts of his pictures combined with a meticulous rendering, usually in colored inks on illustration board. His work has appeared in many national magazines but was closely identified with *Collier's* and other Crowell-Collier publications.

Cooper himself has taught illustration at the Grand Central School of Art, Columbia University, National Academy, Art Students League, City College of New York, and a class for returned veterans after World War II at the Society of Illustrators.

He has also been an active watercolorist, President of the American Watercolor Society and is the author of several books on watercolor painting techniques.

A parallel interest has been sculpture. He studied under Oronzio Maldarelli and has executed a number of commissions for churches and other institutions.

A long-time member of the Society of Illustrators and National Sculpture Society, he is also a past president of the Audubon Artists.

Two illustrations for "The Patriotic Murders," serialized novel by Agatha Christie, published in Collier's *magazine.*

165

The Nativity in a Hillbilly setting; illustration for The Saturday Evening Post.

"Yellow Shoes" by James Street, published by the American *magazine, June, 1943. Collection of Illustration House.*

FLOYD MACMILLAN DAVIS (1896-1966) gave much of the credit for the success of his pictures to the critical judgment of his wife, painter Gladys Rockmore Davis. Floyd Davis' point of view, however, was uniquely his own. His visual world was peopled by a gallery of wonderful characters depicted with poetic realism and warm humor. The wealth of detail in his pictures would seem to have required much study from models or photos of them. In fact, Davis did not use models at all but relied instead on his remarkably retentive memory and lively imagination.

In his early years he did a lot of advertising illustration notable for the fragile beauty and lofty hauteur of the society types he drew.

In the 'thirties, however, Davis began to illustrate stories of humbler subjects. His pictures of southern rural and hill people for such authors as William Faulkner, Sigman Byrd, Glenn Allan and MacKinlay Kantor became immensely popular. He loved these assignments and filled the pictures

not only with a fascinating cast of individuals, but added the special Davis touches, a cat crouched in the corner ready to leap out at a rival, a fly on an old man's head, a small lizard hiding behind a tree. None of these details intruded on the picture story itself — they are there for the perceptive viewer to discover. Readers responded enthusiastically; his pictures were admired as much as the stories themselves.

With the outbreak of World War II, Davis was selected as a correspondent-artist for the War Department and painted in various war theatres. Many of these distinguished paintings were reproduced by *Life* magazine as part of a pictorial record of the war and now hang in the Pentagon building in Washington, D.C.

Over the years, Davis won several Art Directors Club medals and other awards, but more important than this, his work had the admiration of his whole profession. Floyd Davis was one of the great figures of American illustration.

167

Bradshaw Crandell

BRADSHAW CRANDELL (1896-1966) took over the *Cosmopolitan* cover where Harrison Fisher left off. For a period of twelve years, in the 'thirties and 'forties, he did a continuing series of beautiful girls' heads in pastels for their monthly covers. Many top Hollywood stars and young starlets of that time were his models.

Crandell was born in Glens Falls, New York, educated at Wesleyan University and the Chicago Art Institute. He sold his first cover to *Judge* magazine in 1921 and from then on concentrated on cover designs for such other publications as *Collier's, Redbook, American, The Ladies' Home Journal* and *The Saturday Evening Post.*

In later years he confined his work to portraiture, painted the governors of various states and many prominent society figures.

He was a member of the Society of Ilustrators, the Artists and Writers Association and the Dutch Treat Club.

Carole Lombard. Cover design in full-color pastels for Cosmopolitan *magazine, November, 1935.*

J. H. Crosman

JOHN HENRY CROSMAN (1897-1970) began his career in illustration in the 'twenties as a brilliant performer in pen-and-ink. In the 'thirties, however, tastes in illustration changed considerably, and the pen-and-ink medium was no longer popular with the magazine reading public. Crosman then successfully changed his technique to half-tone, working occasionally in watercolor or wash, but usually with Russian charcoal.

For over twenty years Crosman illustrated for most of the major publications, including *Collier's, Woman's Home Companion, The Ladies' Home Journal, The Saturday Evening Post, American* and *Good Housekeeping,* but later confined his work to portraiture.

Born in Swampscott, Massachusetts, he attended the Massachusetts Normal Art School in Boston studying under Richard Andrew and Ernest Major. He also did some teaching and was a member of the Guild of Boston Artists.

Illustration in charcoal, published in The Ladies' Home Journal. © *1934, 1962 by The Curtis Publishing Company.*

Robt. W. Crowther

ROBERT W. CROWTHER (1902-1978) worked in charcoal from which he obtained a full range of values from rich blacks to crisp whites. This insured good reproduction and made for strong, dramatic pictures.

Crowther was born in Philadelphia and attended both the Pennsylvania Museum School of Industrial Art and the Pennsylvania Academy of the Fine Arts, then also studied under Thornton Oakley. He taught at the Pennsylvania Museum School of Industrial Art from 1926-28.

Illustration for a Joseph Hergesheimer story in The Saturday Evening Post. © *1936 , 1964 by The Curtis Publishing Company.*

His first illustrations appeared in the *Lutheran Young Folks* magazine in 1924; eventually he worked for most of the major publications, including *The Saturday Evening Post, Country Gentleman, Farm Journal, Liberty, Cosmopolitan, Pictorial Review, McCall's* and *Good Housekeeping.*

N. EGGENHOFER

NICK EGGENHOFER (1897-   ) was born in Gauting, Bavaria. As a young boy he was fascinated by stories of Buffalo Bill and other heroes of the American Wild West. He also greatly admired the drawings and paintings of Frederic Remington and Charles Russell which were reproduced in German publications.

By the time he arrived in the United States at the age of sixteen, he had decided to become a Western artist himself. He studied nights at Cooper Union and thoroughly immersed himself in the subject by making exact scale models of wagons, stagecoaches, harnesses and other authentic props.

In *Western Story,* pulp magazine of Street & Smith, he found a ready and voracious market for all the drawings he could produce for years. He illustrated for other magazines, also, and many books to which his dry-brush black-and-white drawings are ideally suited. He wrote and illustrated *Wagons, Mules and Men,* published by Hastings House in 1961, and his autobiography, *Horses, Horses, Always Horses,* printed by Sage Publishing Company in 1981.

Eggenhofer now makes his home in Wyoming and paints Western subjects which have been exhibited widely in the West and in the Kennedy Galleries in New York.

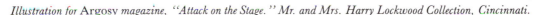

Illustration for Argosy *magazine, "Attack on the Stage." Mr. and Mrs. Harry Lockwood Collection, Cincinnati.*

Eric

CARL OSCAR AUGUST ERICKSON (ERIC) (1891-1958) dominated the field of fashion illustration for over thirty-five years. His virtuosity of line and tone was combined with innate elegance and taste. Eric's work looks deceptively effortless, but dozens of preliminary attempts often were discarded before a final direct and spontaneous effect was ready for his signature.

Eric's birthplace was Joliet, Illinois; his formal art training was limited to two years at the Chicago Academy of Fine Arts. This was followed by work for Marshall Field, Lord & Thomas, and other advertising accounts in Chicago until 1914, when he moved to New York City.

In New York, he continued doing advertising illustration, and did his first fashion drawings for the *Dry Goods Economist*. In 1920, Eric made his initial trip to Paris where he felt in total rapport; for the next twenty years it was his second home. During that period he illustrated for French publications, and did society portraits. Beginning in 1923, he became a staff illustrator for *Vogue* magazine. In 1940 he returned to America, continuing his work for Condé Nast, and began illustrating for American, rather than French, advertisers.

Himself the personification of his elegant world, Eric wore a bowler and carried a walking stick, and he directly participated in the fashionable life of the international set. His drawings and paintings are authentic because he knew his subjects and their world; his taste and beautiful draftsmanship reveal him to be an artist of permanent importance.

The Brooklyn Museum held a retrospective show of his drawings in 1959 shortly after his death.

Marlene Dietrich in her role in Alexander Korda's film, "Knight without Armour." Published in Vogue *magazine, October 15, 1936. © 1936, 1964 by The Condé Nast Publications, Inc.*

Cover illustration for Vogue *magazine, October 1, 1932. © 1932, 1960 by The Condé Nast Publications, Inc.*

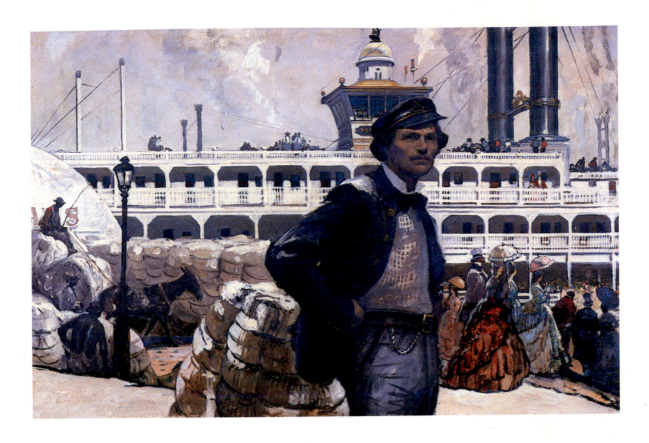

JOHN RUSSELL FULTON was a studio artist who did advertising illustrations for several years but is best remembered for his association with two periodicals, *Redbook* and *Blue Book.*

His *Redbook* illustrations in oils were in the manner of Harvey Dunn, strong and well composed, but it was in *Blue Book* that he developed his own individual approach. *Blue Book's* masculine, swashbuckling subject matter gave Fulton an opportunity to use dramatic action and a much freer technique. He developed a dry-brush method of working in black over white and vice-versa on a rough white ground which allowed good reproduction in line, yet produced a rich halftone quality. Oftentimes he used a second color, also in line, to heighten the dramatic effect.

WILLIAM GALBRAITH CRAWFORD (1894-unknown) is best known for the humor and drawings of his widely syndicated panel cartoon, "Side Glances," which he drew for twenty-three years. A prolific and facile draftsman who signed his work "Galbraith," he had had extensive experience prior to this as an illustrator for such publications as *The Saturday Evening Post, Vanity Fair, The New Yorker, Harper's Bazaar, Cosmopolitan,* and *Delineator* magazines.

Crawford was born in Salt Lake City, Utah, and attended Brigham Young University for two years. This was followed by instruction at the New York Art Students League, the Los Angeles School of Art and Design and the University of Mexico. Among his teachers were Mahonri Young, Thomas Fogarty, Edward Dufner and Henry Wolf.

FRANK GODWIN

FRANK (FRANCIS) GODWIN (1889-1959) divided his career between cartooning and illustration, moving from one field to the other with basically the same approach. A self-taught artist, he became a master of pen-and-ink. When the medium went out of vogue for illustration, he adapted it to cartoon strips, notably "Connie" and "Rusty Riley," but also many others, sometimes under other by-lines. To make his characters realistic and consistent, Godwin, who had also worked in the studio of sculptor Gutzon Borglum, modelled busts of them in clay so they became perpetual models he could turn to for variations in position and lighting.

Godwin, the son of the city editor of the *Washington Star*, was born in Washington, D.C. and started his art career as an apprentice on that paper. Later study at the Art Students League and the helping hand of James Montgomery Flagg got him his first work in New York, mostly for the humor magazines. Over the years, his work appeared in *Liberty, Cosmopolitan, Collier's* and many other periodicals; he also did advertising illustrations for clients such as Prince Albert Tobacco, Texaco, and Coca-Cola.

Illustration for Collier's, *"Behind the Mask," May 20, 1933. Collection of the Society of Illustrators Museum of American Illustration.*

Grafstrom

RUTH SIGRID GRAFSTROM (1905-   ) was born in Rock Island, Illinois, and studied at the Art Institute of Chicago and at the Colorossi Academy in Paris with Henri Morriset.

A fashion artist for *Vogue* magazine from 1930 to 1940 in the New York, Paris, and London offices, she has also done free-lance advertising illustrations for Saks Fifth Avenue, the Matson Line, and various fabric, cosmetic and clothing manufacturers.

This work led to fiction assignments for magazines such as *Delineator, Cosmopolitan* and *Woman's Home Companion,* involving fashionable people and backgrounds. Miss Grafstrom's work is marked by sophistication and good drawing which won her many awards and citations in annual exhibitions of the New York Art Directors Club. She has also been a member of the Society of Illustrators in New York.

Illustration for Vogue *magazine,* © *1938, 1966 by The Condé Nast Publications Inc.*

GOTLIEB

JULES GOTLIEB (1897-unknown) traveled in many out-of-the-way parts of the world, from North Africa to the jungles of Dutch Guiana, collecting background material for his illustrations. He also accumulated a library of over 2,000 volumes for reference in doing historical illustrations for nearly every national magazine, including *Collier's, Cosmopolitan, Redbook, American, Woman's Home Companion, Liberty, This Week, The Ladies' Home Journal* and for several books.

A native New Yorker, Gotlieb studied at the National Academy School of Fine Arts, the Pennsylvania Academy at Chester Springs and the Art Students League. Among his teachers were George Bridgman and Harvey Dunn. He later taught at the League himself from 1932 to 1934.

Illustration for Good Housekeeping *magazine, 1928.*

DAVID HENDRICKSON (1896-1973), born in St. Paul, Minnesota, won a scholarship there to attend the St. Paul Institute of Art. He later studied at the Ecole des Beaux-Arts at Toulouse, France, Grand Central School of Art, and the Art Students League of New York. Among his teachers were Harvey Dunn, Dean Cornwell and George Bridgman.

Beginning in 1913 with his first art job for the *St. Paul Dispatch and Pioneer Press,* Hendrickson had a long and varied career, illustrating for periodicals, advertisers, book publishers, and he exhibited widely.

Hendrickson's special ability was in portraying the rural American scene, sympathetically, truthfully and without artifice. His direct, vigorous pictures are basically in line, sometimes with washes of tone or color added.

He was a member of the Artists Guild, Society of American Etchers and Graphic Artists, Society of Illustrators, Phillips Mill Artists in New Hope, Pennsylvania, and the Palo Alto Art Club in California, where he also taught from 1948 to 1951.

"Country Auction," illustration for Country Gentleman, *1941.*

Illustration for The Mentor, *February, 1930.*

Illustration for a Saturday Evening Post *story, "A Man in Her Room" by Richard Stern, November 18, 1950.*
© *1950, 1978 by The Curtis Publishing Company.*

Georgi

EDWIN A. GEORGI (1896-1964) was studying civil engineering at Princeton when World War I broke out. He volunteered and served as a pilot in the U.S. Air Force.

After the war, Georgi took his first job doing paste-ups in an advertising agency art department and began his practical training as an artist.

His early illustrations were for advertisers. Over the years, he did a number of notable series for such clients as Hartford Fire Insurance, Crane Paper Co., Hockanum Woolens and Yardley & Co.

Georgi's ability to depict beautiful women and sumptuous settings also brought him story manuscripts; he was soon illustrating for most of the national magazines, including *Woman's Home Companion, Redbook, McCall's, Cosmopolitan, The Ladies' Home Journal* and *The Saturday Evening Post.* His use of color was lavish and dramatic, giving his pictures great impact on the printed page.

RFH

ROY FREDERIC HEINRICH (1881-1943) was best known for his series of Vermont historical illustrations and had completed exactly 100 of them at the time of his death. The drawings, made with litho-crayon, are noted for their authenticity of detail and spirit, as well as originality of concept.

Heinrich was born in Indiana, reared in New York State; studied at the Connecticut League of Art Students under Charles Noel Flagg. His first work was for a small Sunday newspaper. In 1910 he moved to Detroit, as one of the earliest automobile illustrators, where his clients included Graham-Paige, Packard, Ford, Chevrolet, Buick, Dodge, Chrysler and Cadillac. He also illustrated for many other advertising accounts.

Of all his assignments, however, Heinrich most enjoyed doing the pictures of early Vermont. These were exhibited widely in galleries in New York and New England, shown in the Vermont building at the New York World's Fair (1939-40). They were published in book form, of which several hundred thousand were furnished by the advertiser to fill requests from schools and individuals all over the country.

"African Drummers and Dancers." Date and place of publication unknown. Reproduced courtesy of Guy Rabut.

W EMERTON HEITLAND

WILMOT EMERTON HEITLAND, N.A. (1893-1969) was a master watercolorist — his paintings of Barbados, particularly, rival the directness and vigor of Winslow Homer. His illustrations also had the same quality of strength, the watercolor reinforced by a bold outline, with emphasis on composition and rich color.

Heitland was born in Superior, Wisconsin, studied at the Pennsylvania Academy of the Fine Arts, won the Cresson traveling scholarship in 1913, attended the Colarossi School in Paris and the Art Students League in New York. His teachers included Arthur Covey, Harvey Dunn and Walter Biggs.

He first illustrated for *Collier's Weekly* in 1922. This was followed by work for *Cosmopolitan, McCall's, Woman's Home Companion, Delineator* and other magazines. Both his illustrations and exhibition watercolors won many awards, and his work is represented in several museums, including the Brooklyn Museum, Art Institute of Chicago and Philadelphia Museum of Art. He also taught at the Art Students League, Pennsylvania Academy Summer School and the Philadelphia Museum School of Art.

This illustration for Woman's Home Companion *in 1936 shows Heitland's typical use of line and pattern.*

Edwin Henry

EDWIN HENRY was primarily an advertising illustrator, his career coinciding with the tremendous growth of advertising art in the 'twenties and 'thirties. As a partner in the Chicago advertising art service of Stevens, Sundblom and Henry, he did illustrations for many of the largest national accounts, including Studebaker, Packard, Procter & Gamble, Camel and Chesterfield cigarettes, Kohler of Kohler, Graybar Electric, Postum, Quaker Oats and others. He painted editorial illustrations for most of the major magazines as well, his work marked by sensitivity and very effective use of color.

Henry was born in Mt. Sterling, Kentucky, and studied at the National Academy of Design in New York. He later taught illustration at the Studio School and the American Academy in Chicago as well as at the Grand Central School of Art in New York. He was also a member of the Artists Guild and the Society of Illustrators.

Story illustration for American *Magazine.*

Everett Henry

E. EVERETT HENRY (1893-1961) was an advertising artist during much of his career, which began in the 'twenties, and illustrated for many advertising campaigns.

Henry brought to his work a thorough academic training through study at the Art Students League, the School of Fine and Applied Art, New York University and Columbia University. He also did some teaching at the School of Fine and Applied Art in New York.

In 1935 he painted murals for the Ford Company Building at the San Diego Fair. This led to many other mural commissions, several of which he executed in collaboration with Allen Saalburg and Louis Bouché. These included decorations for twelve clubcars for the Pennsylvania Railroad, designs in the Westinghouse Building, the U. S. Government Building and the Building Service Center at the New York World's Fair of 1939-40. He also painted both murals and easel pictures for private collectors, and is represented in the permanent collection of the Whitney Museum.

Cover illustration for The American Weekly, *1951.*

HOLM
GREN
1

The illustrations of R. JOHN HOLMGREN (1897-1963) were characterized by a fresh, youthful outlook and bright color. He managed, over a long span of years, to keep his fiction heroines looking contemporary, beginning with the pert flappers in his first cover illustrations for the old *Life* and *Judge* magazines in the 'twenties.

Holmgren was born in St. Paul, Minnesota, and studied at the St. Paul Art Institute before going to New York in 1919 to study at the Art Students League under C. O. Woodbury, George Bridgman, Robert Henri and Frederic R. Gruger.

His illustrations appeared in most of the national magazines and for many advertisers, including Chevrolet, Ford, Alcoa, White Rock and Cunard Lines.

A long-time member of the Society of Illustrators, Holmgren was its president from 1941 to 1944. He was also a member of the Dutch Treat and Artists and Writers Clubs.

"Widows Weeds." Courtesy of the Graham Gallery.

G H

GEORGE HOWE, originally HAUTHALER, (1896-1941) was born in Salzburg, Austria. He ran away from home at the age of fourteen, visited the United States, then went to France where he studied art for two years before returning to America to stay.

He had to work at all kinds of jobs, from dishwashing and chauffeuring to painting scenery for a motion picture studio, before he eventually realized his ambition of illustrating for the magazines.

Howe painted almost exclusively with watercolor, treated in a flat, poster style, similar to that of Ludwig Hohlwein of Munich, Germany. For many years his work was associated with the Crowell-Collier publications: *Collier's, American* and *Woman's Home Companion,* although he also illustrated for others, such as *Elks* and *Good Housekeeping.*

Illustration for "Go Down, Moses" by William Faulkner, published in Collier's *magazine, January 25, 1941. Collection of Illustration House.*

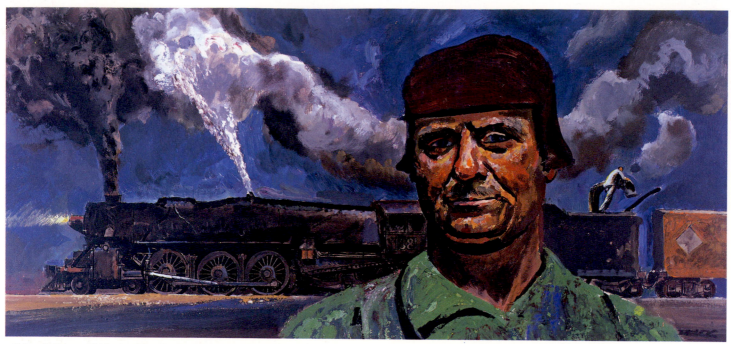

"Gandy Dancer." Featured here is Harm Melius, boss of the section gang of the once-active Harlem Division of the New York Central system. This painting evolved from much study of steam locomotives taking on water during the night hours at Millerton station; published in Esquire magazine.

"Frisco to New York Bike Race," published in True magazine, 1955. Collection of Les Mansfield.

"1908 Vanderbilt Cup Race." Collection of William C. Williams.

"Conducting Fracture Test" advertising illustration for National Steel.

"The Brighton 24-hour Race (Quick tire change for Al Poole's Simplex)," published by Esquire, *April, .1946. Collection of the National Art Museum of Sport.*

PETER HELCK

C. PETER HELCK, N.A. (1893-   ) has spent his life painting a record of man's work. He has made this basic theme a monumental one in his pictures, whether it be a giant foundry, an open pit mine, or a dramatic moment in an historic automobile race.

Peter came by his love for automobiles as a boy when he saw some of the early racing competitions. He eventually came to know many of the drivers and their giant racing cars intimately. These later became the inspiration for his illustrated book, *The Checkered Flag,* published in 1961. He himself owns a number of old automobiles, including "OLD 16," the famous Locomobile which won the Vanderbilt Cup Race in 1908. The second of his two books, *Great Auto Races,* was published in 1976.

Helck studied at the Art Students League of New York and privately with many distinguished teachers, including Frank Brangwyn in England. In addition to complete artistic competence, he has great capacity for hard work, as evidenced in the preliminary, thinking stages of his pictures. The nature of his subject matter demands a thorough mechanical knowledge, including the parts that do not appear in the picture itself. His working drawings which precede the finished paintings are completely worked out even down to the placement of bolts or rivets.

Helck's rare combination of artistry and factual know-how has for many years made him the dominant figure in this field. He has won many medals and awards in art director's exhibitions. He has illustrated for almost every national magazine; his advertising clients have been the industrial giants, General Electric, Chevrolet, Mack Trucks, National Steel Corporation and numerous others.

During the 1920-1940 period Helck traveled and painted extensively abroad. Subsequently, this work was given one-man shows in New York and shown in major Fine Art annuals in the East and Midwest. However, except for some favorable reviews and awards, the forty-year effort to breach the barrier separating Fine and Commercial Art proved unrewarding. It was natural for him to resume full time in the remunerative field of advertising and magazine illustration.

Says Helck, "*Esquire* offered the first real opportunity to produce subjects of intense interest to me, a series of eight spreads depicting early auto racing. Then followed my first book which initiated six one-man shows in as many states. Yes, all devoted to the heroic age of the sport." By good fortune, the shows seemed expertly timed with the advent of the antique car craze and the present avid interest in nostalgia. At age ninety, Helck is blessed with a clientele, affluent collectors of rare cars and automotive art.

Frances Tipton Hunter

FRANCES TIPTON HUNTER (1896-1957), like many other women illustrators, made children her specialty. Her own childhood was scarred by the death of her mother when she was only six years old, and she was raised by her aunt and uncle.

Her art talent appeared early in high school, and she graduated with honors from the Philadelphia Museum School of Industrial Arts. Further study at the Philadelphia Academy of the Fine Arts and the Fleisher Art Memorial prepared her for her debut as an illustrator.

Early work appeared in the *Woman's Home Companion* followed by illustrations for *Collier's, Liberty, Good Housekeeping,* and a long series of covers for *The Saturday Evening Post.* She also produced an extremely popular series of calendar paintings over a period of eleven years and many advertising illustrations for products, such as Listerine and Occident Flour. A book, *Frances Tipton Hunter's Paper Dolls* was published in 1943 by the Whitman Publishing Company.

Cover illustration for The Saturday Evening Post. ©*1938 , 1966 by The Curtis Publishing Company.*

Jackson

ELBERT McGRAN JACKSON (1896-unknown) as a child showed early interest in drawing and took Saturday morning lessons from the only art teacher in town, but went on to graduate as an architect from Georgia Tech.

He eventually realized that his real ambition was to be an illustrator and went back to study art at night. With the help of "arrived" illustrators, such as James Montgomery Flagg, he was able to sell his first pictures.

Jackson had a special flair for posing and painting women to make them seductively glamorous, and his architectural training made his picture settings a convincing background for them. Like most artists of that era, Jackson always painted from the posed model and that contributed much to the spontaneity of his technique. Although generally given manuscripts involving romance and high society, he was able to do a wide variety of subjects from murder mysteries to masculine adventure. In addition to the stories illustrated for most of the magazines, he also did covers for publications such as *Collier's, The Ladies' Home Journal* and *The Saturday Evening Post.*

Jackson's portrayal of fictional detective, Philo Vance for "The Casino Murder Case" by S.S. Van Dine in Cosmopolitan *magazine, July, 1934. Collection of Morris Weiss.*

"Two Ropes Sang," illustration for "Haven" by Hal Borland, published in The Ladies' Home Journal, *November, 1927.*

WILL JAMES

Vignette for same story.

WILLIAM JAMES DUFAULT (1892-1942) was born in Great Falls, Montana, of French-Canadian parentage. His mother died when he was a year old, and his father was killed by a rampaging steer three years later. Thus Will was orphaned at the age of four and was brought up by a Montana fur-trapper, who taught him to read and write. The trapper drowned when Will was 13 and from that time on he took care of himself, hiring out as a cowhand and rodeo rider.

Will James' introduction to art was quite by chance. Harold Von Schmidt was conducting a painting class at the California School of Fine Arts in San Francisco and advertised for a cowboy model. James, just then in the city with a shipment of cattle, answered it and was hired. During the course of posing sessions, Will brought in some of his own crude drawings, and Von Schmidt recognized in them an observation and knowledge of animal anatomy which showed great promise. Through the encouragement and criticism of both Von Schmidt and Maynard Dixon, another fine painter of the West who was a co-instructor, James was able to sell his first drawings to *Sunset* magazine.

A year later he sold a short story with his own illustrations to *Scribner's* magazine. The combination of true-to-life

Western story and drawings was an immediate success and was followed by several more. His first book appeared in 1924. He was awarded the Newberry medal by the American Library Association for his book, *Smoky.* Both *Smoky* and another book, *Lone Cowboy,* were made into films. Altogether he wrote and illustrated 20 books and many short stories.

"Homeport," woodcut illustration for the American Car and Foundry Company, 1931. Courtesy ACF Industries.

"The Ballad of Yukon Jake" in Vanity Fair, *November, 1923, with the signature "Hogarth, Jr."*

"The Memoirs of Jacques Casanova," privately printed in 1925.

Rockwell Kent

ROCKWELL KENT, (1882-1971) won fame outside of illustration as an engraver, lithographer, mural painter, writer and lecturer.

As an illustrator, Kent was equally noted for his own books, *Wilderness, Voyaging, N. by. E., Salamina, This is My Own,* and for those of others, such as *Candide, Moby Dick, Leaves of Grass* and *Canterbury Tales.*

Kent also made a great many distinguished illustrations for advertisers, among them Marcus & Company, Jewelers; Steinway & Sons; Rolls-Royce, and American Car and Foundry Company. Some of his advertising and humorous pictures are signed "Hogarth, Jr."

Born in Tarrytown Heights, New York, Kent studied art with Robert Henri, Abbott Thayer and William Chase. Much of his work was based on personal experiences in his travels to such remote areas as Greenland, Alaska, and Patagonia.

During his lifetime, Kent was a controversial political activist, and his open sympathies with leftist causes resulted in his blacklisting during the McCarthy era. In retaliation, Kent refused his title of National Academician when elected.

Christmas greeting design by Kent.

Klett.

WALTER CHARLES KLETT (1897-1966) specialized in painting glamorous women for the reason, as he put it, that Rubens, Velasquez, or Botticelli preferred to paint beautiful females rather than ugly ones. He painted portraits of many celebrated women, including Gladys Swarthout, Mrs. William Woodward, Mrs. Jansen Noyes, Alicia Markova, Vera Zorina and Bidu Sayao.

Klett, who had been a painter for both magazine illustration and for the galleries, brought a contemporary approach to each. His fiction illustrations appeared in most of the national magazines, and he designed and executed numerous campaigns for national advertisers. He also exhibited in many museums and galleries, including the Pennsylvania Academy, Farargil Gallery, Reinhardt Gallery, The Metropolitan Museum of Art, Grand Central Art Galleries, and at shows of the Art Directors Club of New York.

Born in St. Louis, Klett attended the St. Louis School of Fine Arts, Washington University, and made study trips to France, England, Italy, Switzerland and Germany. He was the author of a popular book, *Figure Painting,* published by Watson-Guptill, and taught portrait and figure painting for ten years at Pratt Institute in Brooklyn, New York.

Alicia Markova, reproduced from Collier's *magazine.*

KIDD

STEVEN R. KIDD (1911-) illustrated for the Sunday fiction page of the *New York News-Chicago Tribune* coast-to-coast syndicate for over thirty years. Despite their transitory life, Kidd lavished on those illustrations the same artistry and design that distinguishes his work for magazine and book publishers.

Kidd's versatile pen line can be decorative or realistic, bold or delicate. Over the years he has successfully coped with every possible pictorial subject and historical period, his conceptions always original and arresting.

Kidd was born in Chicago, Illinois, and attended the Chicago Art Institute there. Coming to New York, he studied at the Art Students League with George Bridgman and, for ten years, with Harvey Dunn at the Grand Central School of Art.

During World War II, he was an official Army war artist and covered the occupation of Korea for the Historical Section of the War Department. Many of these oil and watercolor paintings hang in the Pentagon. He has since painted illustrations for the Air Force Historical Museum.

Kidd is a member of the Society of Illustrators, taught for three years at the Newark School of Fine and Industrial Art in New Jersey and currently is in his twenty-second year of teaching at the Art Students League in New York.

A Christmas Carol *by Charles Dickens, newspaper illustration, Dec. 25, 1938, New York News Syndicate Co., Inc.*

CLAYTON KNIGHT

CLAYTON KNIGHT (1891-1969) brought a lifetime of knowledge and authority to his aviation illustrations. During World War I, he joined the U. S. Army Air Service which was attached to the Royal Flying Corps in France, was shot down and taken prisoner by the Germans, and spent many months in hospitals recovering from his wounds.

After the war, Knight returned to an illustration career for books and magazine stories or articles about flying. To keep pace with the rapid changes in aviation, he made frequent flying junkets of his own and was a guest of the Army and Navy during their annual maneuvers.

Prior to United States' entry into World War II, Knight headed a committee which assisted American flyers in joining the Canadian and Royal Air Force during the critical Battle of Britain. He himself was combat historian for the 8th, 11th and 20th Air Forces, covered the Aleutians, Alaska and the Pacific. He also attended the historic ceremony of Japan's surrender on the U.S.S. Missouri at the end of the war.

Knight was born in Rochester, New York, and studied at the Art Institute of Chicago. Among his teachers were Robert Henri and George Bellows. He was married to Katherine Sturges, a well known advertising artist; their son, Hilary Knight, is a contemporary illustrator of children's books.

"Attacking an Observation Balloon;" from Knight's book, Pilot's Luck, *published by David McKay Co., 1929. Collection of Illustration House.*

LARRY B. KRITCHER (1900-   ) spent eleven years on the editorial side of the desk as a *Saturday Evening Post* associate art director assigning manuscripts to other illustrators, only an occasional one to himself. In 1943, he turned to a full-time, free-lance illustration career and was subsequently kept busy by the *Post* and other publications.

Kritcher was born in McKeesport, Pennsylvania, studied at Carnegie Institute of Technology in Pittsburgh and the Pennsylvania Academy of the Fine Arts in Philadelphia where he was awarded a Cresson Scholarship to study and travel in Europe for two years.

Kritcher returned to America just in time for the 1929 stock market collapse and found that the art market had disappeared with it. Newly married, he and his wife tried to sit out the Depression in southern France, but after a year they returned to the United States, determined to find work, and in 1932 he joined the *Post* staff. This was valuable experience for gaining an insight into the requirements of illustration from the magazine's point of view; Kritcher's illustrations are always directly to the point, explicit and competent.

In 1963 Kritcher moved to Spain for his wife's health and there they stayed for the next fifteen years. He painted Spanish landscapes during that time; after her death he returned to stay permanently in the States.

Illustration for "The Mountain Maid" in The Saturday Evening Post. © 1939, 1967 *by The Curtis Publishing Company.*

CHARLES LASALLE

CHARLES LOUIS LaSALLE (1894-1958) was a classmate of Harold Anderson and Arthur Fuller at the Fenway Art School in Boston. He and Anderson later had studios together at the Beaux Arts Studio in New York and then in New Rochelle.

LaSalle, who was born in Wakefield, Massachusetts, first worked as a bull-pen artist in the Snow Advertising Agency in Boston. His early work, in emulation of F. R. Gruger and Henry Raleigh, was in Wolff pencil. He later began to use charcoal and developed a mastery of the medium in his own style. His first magazine illustrations were for *Boy's Life,* and he was soon working for *The Saturday Evening Post, Collier's, Redbook* and others. Advertising clients included Ford, General Motors and General Electric.

After many productive years, he moved to Arizona where he followed a new career, painting Western subjects for galleries and exhibitions, until the time of his death.

LYFORD

PHILIP LYFORD (1887-1950) painted one of the best known posters of World War I as an illustration for the poem, "In Flanders Fields." It was also used as a flyer for the fifth Victory Loan, and a reproduction of it, 150 feet high, was lighted in San Francisco Bay. The painting, made while he was a young artist in a Chicago studio, helped to launch his own career; he became one of Chicago's top advertising illustrators. He also illustrated for such publications as *Redbook, Collier's, College Humor, Country Gentleman* and *The Saturday Evening Post.*

Lyford was born in Worcester, Massachusetts, and studied for four years at the Boston Museum of Fine Arts under Frank Benson, Edmund C. Tarbell and Philip Hale.

Painted with the authority of the avid duck hunter that he was, LaSalle produced this subject for Outdoor Life *magazine, February, 1950.*

Illustration for "The Glad Son" by Zack Cartright; The Country Gentlemen, *February, 1930.*

Illustration for The Saturday Evening Post. © 1938 , 1966 by The Curtis Publishing Company.

Typical LaGatta painting in which the clothes reveal rather than conceal the figure. Collection of Illustration House.

Fashion illustration for The Ladies' Home Journal.

JOHN LaGATTA

JOHN LaGATTA (1894-1977) showed a full appreciation of the female figure in his illustrations. In even the most decorously dressed of his models, the clothes appeared to reveal the figure rather than to hide it. Millions of readers would have had it no other way. Probably no illustrator in the 'thirties was more popular or did a greater number of pictures, both for advertising and editorial assignments.

In spite of his emphasis on the figure, there is no overtone of suggestiveness in LaGatta's work. The women are painted in frank admiration of their beauty — colorful, curvaceous, vital — in the same spirit as Rubens' more buxom, but very female, nudes.

LaGatta was born in Naples, Italy, but received his education in America, studying under Kenneth Hayes Miller and Frank Alvah Parsons at the New York School of Fine and Applied Art. His first work was in advertising and much of his early work shows the influence of Drian, the famous French illustrator.

Later, as he developed his own personal style, LaGatta's work was in tremendous demand. He worked for nearly a decade to the limit of his capacities in supplying all the magazines that competed for his pictures. After the 'forties, LaGatta continued to do a curtailed amount of illustration but found a new career in his enthusiasm for teaching at the Art Center School in Los Angeles, California.

He was elected into the Society of Illustrators Hall of Fame in 1984.

"No Scarlet Woman," illustration for American magazine.

Illustration for "Gold" by Clarence Budington Kelland in The Saturday Evening Post. © *1931, 1959 by The Curtis Publishing Company.*

ORISON MACPHERSON

ORISON MacPHERSON (1898-1966) spoke with the Scottish accent of his Pictou, Nova Scotia, birthplace. His art education was acquired partly at the Ontario Art School in Toronto, and at the Art Students League in New York under John Sloan. He learned most, however, from the helpful advice of his friends, J. W. Schlaikjer, Franklin Booth, and the artist whose work he admired above all others, F. R. Gruger.

MacPherson got his start in the art field, after the usual odd jobs to keep alive, as an assistant to the art director of the old Hearst's *International* magazine. Within a short time he started his career in illustration with an assignment from the *Country Gentleman,* followed soon by others from *The Saturday Evening Post, Good Housekeeping,* and several Canadian publications, *MacLean's* magazine and *Chatelaine.* He also did a long series of advertising illustrations for the Jones and Laughlin Steel Corporation.

Frederic Mizen

FREDERIC KIMBALL MIZEN (1888-1965) was a dominant figure in the outdoor advertising field for several years, many of his paintings doubling as magazine advertisements. He also did fiction illustration for magazines, such as *Cosmopolitan* and *The Saturday Evening Post,* but is probably best known for his long and distinguished series of advertising paintings for the Coca-Cola Company in newspapers, magazines and billboards.

A Chicagoan, Mizen attended Smith's Art Academy from 1904-06 and obtained his first employment with the Gunning System, a predecessor to General Outdoor Advertising. Meanwhile, he continued to study in evening classes at the Art Institute of Chicago under John Vanderpoel, DeForrest Shook and Walter Marshall Clute.

He later conducted his own school, the Mizen Academy of Art, for several years, but eventually restricted himself to portraiture.

Cover illustration for The Saturday Evening Post.
© *1934, 1962 by The Curtis Publishing Company.*

THE SATURDAY EVENING POST

NRA An Illus... Founded A? D... ...lin

APRIL 7, 1934 Volume 206, Number 41 **5 cts. THE COPY** 10c. in Canada

BEGINNING A NEW SERIAL By E. PHILLIPS OPPENHEIM

Illustration for "Farewell to Valor" in 1938, published by the Country Gentleman.

M. de V. Lee

MANNING DeVILLENEUVE LEE's (1894-1980) art education was interrupted by two stints of Army duty. The first was on the Mexican border in Texas as a member of the Virginia Field Artillery in 1916. This was promptly followed by service in World War I as a Lieutenant at the front in France with the anti-aircraft artillery.

Following the war, Lee resumed his studies at the Pennsylvania Academy of the Fine Arts, won the Cresson Scholarship for travel in Europe in 1921. The following year he won the Second Toppan Prize at the Pennsylvania Academy and with this encouragement began his long career as a free-lance illustrator.

Over the years, Lee illustrated for a great many magazines and advertisers, and for more than 200 books for 27 publishers. He also made film strips and designed several series of postage stamps for the Republics of Liberia, Indonesia and Guinea.

IRVING NURICK

IRVING NURICK (1894-1963) took a trip to France in 1928 for a chance to study art and to make a change from the advertising drawing and layout work he had been doing in New York. He fell in love with Paris, and it became his second home.

His Paris paintings and sketches provided an entrée into the field of magazine illustrations. Mrs. Nurick showed them to various editors who were impressed and began sending him manuscripts.

Although Nurick did many pictures with Continental settings, he eventually became best known for his ability to depict young people sympathetically — teen-agers and sub-debs. The young responded with enthusiasm, wrote him for suggestions about clothes and hair styling; Irving Nurick fan clubs came into existence as far away as New Zealand and Australia.

Nurick also continued his painting for exhibition, had one-man shows in New York and Paris; won the Ranger Prize in 1957, and the Samuel Finley Breese Morse Medal in 1960, in exhibitions at the National Academy of Design.

Illustraton for "Spanish Omelet," published by Cosmopolitan *magazine, April, 1937.*

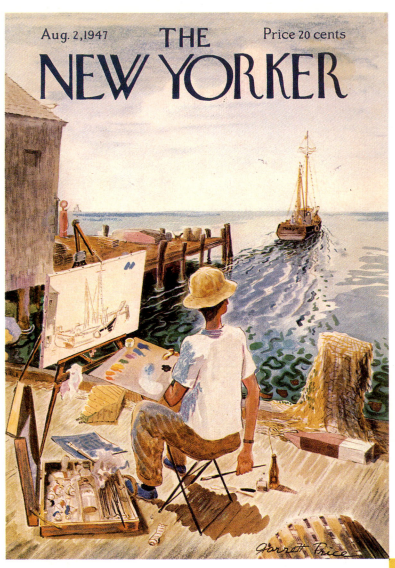

Aug. 2, 1947 **THE NEW YORKER** *Price 20 cents*

Garrett Price

GARRETT PRICE (1896-1979) made it a lifetime habit to carry a small sketch pad with him. Many of his best picture ideas were generated from these on-the-spot notes, sometimes coming to light years afterward.

Although Garrett had a long career as an illustrator, he was best known for the original humor and incisive renderings of his *New Yorker* covers.

Price was born in Bucyrus, Kansas, attended the University of Wyoming and the Art Institute of Chicago. His earliest art job was in 1916 with the Chicago Tribune where he first carried his sketchbook on assignments for news stories. Later he made the transition to illustrating for magazine stories for *College Humor,* the old *Life, Collier's, Scribner's* and other major magazines. A collection of his work titled *Drawing Room Only* was published by Coward-McCann, Inc., in 1946.

Garrett exhibited widely — at The Metropolitan Museum of Art, Philadelphia Academy of the Fine Arts, American Watercolor Society, Chicago Art Institute, and others. He was an active member of the Society of Illustrators in New York, the Westport Artists and the Mystic Art Association in Connecticut.

Price did over fifty covers for The New Yorker, *spanning twenty-five years. Editor Harold Ross called this "his favorite cover of all time." Drawing by Garrett Price.* © *1947, 1975 The New Yorker Magazine, Inc.*

RONALD McLEOD

RONALD NORMAN McLEOD (1897-1977) was born in St. Paul, Minnesota, and was educated at the University of Chicago. He never had formal art training but made up for it by arduous self-education and observation.

In the process, McLeod developed a bold poster style in transparent watercolor, an unusual use of a medium that is traditionallly somewhat muted.

Beginning in 1928, McLeod illustrated for *Collier's* regularly for twenty years; also worked for many other periodicals including *American, Cosmopolitan* and *Pictorial Review.* Over this same period, he did an immense amount of advertising and poster illustration, several times had his work included in "100 Best Posters of the Year."

Cover Illustration for Collier's *magazine.*

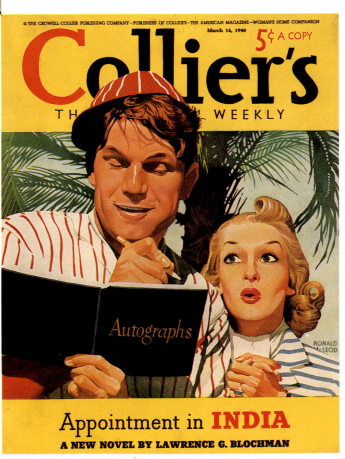

© THE CROWELL-COLLIER PUBLISHING COMPANY—PUBLISHERS OF COLLIER'S—THE AMERICAN MAGAZINE—WOMAN'S HOME COMPANION

March 16, 1940

Collier's 5¢ A COPY

THE NATIONAL WEEKLY

Autographs

Appointment in INDIA
A NEW NOVEL BY LAWRENCE G. BLOCHMAN

Reusswig [signature]

WILLIAM REUSSWIG (1902-1978) was a fine illustrator, and married to an equally fine one, Martha Sawyers (below). They traveled the world together and, in collaboration, wrote and illustrated two books about the Far East, published by Grosset & Dunlap. They worked in a New York apartment with two studios where each could pursue individual assignments.

William was born in Somerville, New Jersey, studied at Amherst College and the Art Students League in New York. He was only twenty-three when he made his first illustrations for *Collier's* magazine and then illustrated for most of the other publications, with masculine subjects of adventure and sports his special forte.

His painting for *True* magazine illustrated the westward ordeal of the Donner Party, nearly half of whom perished in the Sierra Nevadas during the winter of 1846-47.

Collection of E. Edward Cerullo.

Martha Sawyers [signature]

MARTHA SAWYERS (1902-   ) became an illustrator unintentionally. Her drawings and paintings of China and Indonesia were on exhibition at the Marie Sterner Gallery and happened to be seen by William Chessman, art editor of *Collier's*. Chessman offered her a manuscript with an Oriental setting, which she illustrated with the sensitivity and taste for which her work has since become famous.

Martha is from Cuero, Texas, studied at the Art Students League; has lived and painted in Paris, Bali, Peking, Nepal, and numerous other parts of the world.

During World War II, *Collier's* sent her as an artist-correspondent to the China-Burma-India area and published numerous illustrated articles by her about the armed forces personnel and the native populations. *Life* magazine published a series of her pastel protraits of Orientals in the British Merchant Navy. She also designed posters for China Relief. In addition, Miss Sawyers brought special insight to her illustrations for the writers of fiction, Mona Gardner and Pearl S. Buck.

Illustration for an article, "Dancing Lady," also written by Miss Sawyers, for Collier's *magazine, 1944.*

Robert Patterson

ROBERT PATTERSON (1898-1981) was born in Chicago and attended the Chicago Art Institute. Among his teachers there and later were Harvey Dunn, Walt Louderback, Ralph Barton, Pierre Brissaud, and Carl Ericson.

Patterson began his professional career in Chicago, and for some time, with his brother Loran, directed the Patterson studios there. In 1922 he came to New York and began doing fashion illustration.

Judge magazine sent him to France in 1924 to do a feature, "Betty Goes Abroad." When *Judge* failed in 1927, he managed to obtain a fashion illustration assignment from *Vogue* in Paris, where he stayed until 1934.

Upon his return to the United States, he began to do editorial illustrations for the major magazines, including *McCall's, Cosmopolitan, Good Housekeeping, The Ladies' Home Journal, Redbook, Collier's, Woman's Home Companion* and *American* magazine, as well as advertising assignments and book illustration.

O. F. Schmidt

OSCAR FREDERICK SCHMIDT (1892-1957) attended Pratt Institute in Brooklyn and won a scholarship to the Art Students League where he studied under George Bridgman.

During World War I he served in the artillery in France. Following his discharge, he went on an extended tour of the world, including North Africa and the Marquesas Islands, where he remained to carve a tombstone for the unmarked, weed-grown grave of Paul Gauguin.

Schmidt preferred to paint in gouache which he handled with great competence in illustrations for magazines such as *Redbook, Liberty* and *The Saturday Evening Post.*

He exhibited often and was a member of the Salmagundi Club and the Society of Illustrators in New York.

Design for twenty-four-sheet poster.   Collection of the Society of Illustrators Museum of American Illustration.

HOWARD SCOTT

HOWARD SCOTT (1902-1983) thought of his twenty-four-sheet poster designs as analogous to one-act plays. He acted as the director to set the scene, cast the characters, and direct the actors. The moral, or message, had to be immediately clear to the viewer, traveling 60 miles-per-hour along a highway.

Scott also added to his work a sparkling watercolor technique and an ability to obtain very realistic characterizations in a bold poster treatment.

As an artist, he was noted as a completely regulated and organized performer who kept his studio as neat and businesslike as a reception room.

Scott was long associated with Esso, Ford, Schlitz, Heinz, Servel and other national products but also did magazine cover designs, notably for *The Saturday Evening Post.*

Schucker

JAMES W. SCHUCKER (1903-   ) was born in Mt. Carmel, Illinois. He received his education at Carnegie Institute of Technology, The Art Institute of Chicago, and studied with Harvey Dunn at the Grand Central School of Art.

His first editorial illustrations were for *Redbook* magazine; over the years, his work appeared in most of the national periodicals. He also did campaigns for advertisers, notably Quaker State Motor Oil, Travelers Insurance Company, and Seagram Distillers Corporation.

An active painter, Schucker received an honorable mention at the Watercolor International show at the Chicago Art Institute, is a member of the Philadelphia Art Alliance, and teaches at his own school in Quakertown, Pennsylvania.

Story illustration for American *magazine, 1936.*

Illustration for "The Dragon Fly" in The Ladies' Home Journal, *February, 1925.*

H. J. Soulen

The work of HENRY J. SOULEN (1888-1965) is richly colored and strongly patterned. Each of his pictures is treated in a manner appropriate to the flat surfaces of a mural painting, and equally, to a magazine cover; he was given a Peabody Award for his magazine cover designs.

Soulen was born in Milwaukee, Wisconsin. He attended the Chicago Academy of Fine Arts and later studied with Howard Pyle. For many years his work appeared regularly in most of the quality magazines and usually in color — even when the use of color was restricted — because of the brilliance of his palette.

During World War II he gave free art lessons at the Valley Forge Military Hospital, a rehabilitation center for veterans.

Spreter

ROY FREDERIC SPRETER (1899-unknown) is another of a gifted group of painters who made advertising art their special province.

The work of Spreter, in particular, is distinguished for the subtlety of his color and values and the good taste which his art conveys to the advertiser's products. He was long associated with the campaigns of Camay, Campbell's Soups, and Bon Ami, and in demand as an artist for twenty-four-sheet posters, which require sure control, since the reproduction enlarges the original art from eight to ten times.

His fiction illustration, equally colorful and artistic, was mostly for the women's monthly magazines where his sensitive and beautiful heroines found much favor.

Spreter, a Chicagoan, had brief training at the Art Institute there, but learned most from Joseph Chenoweth, Philip Lyford, Leopold Seyffert and other members of the Palette and Chisel Club. He was a member of the Art Directors Club and Society of Illustrators in New York.

Illustration for Pictorial Review, *May, 1936.*

Katharine Sturges

KATHERINE STURGES (KNIGHT) (1890-1979), the wife of aviation artist Clayton Knight, was an accomplished illustrator in her own right. Born in Chicago, she attended the Art Institute there. She afterwards traveled to Japan to study Oriental art.

Her illustrations for an early children's book, *Little Pictures of Japan,* were inspired by the trip. Her work continued to reflect this Japanese influence throughout her career which included greeting card designing, illustrating other children's books, fashion drawing for *Harper's Bazaar* and award-winning advertising illustrations for clients such as McCallum Hosiery, Stehli Silks and Oneida Community Silver.

In 1956 Mrs. Knight designed a commemorative toile depicting the career of President Eisenhower which was used in Blair House. She also designed for Spode china, as well as jewelry and fabrics for Macy's based on Peruvian motifs.

In the 'forties and 'fifties, she also collaborated with her husband in doing several books on aviation subjects.

This advertising illustration for McCallum Silk Hosiery in 1924 displays the artist's homage to Japanese art both in subject and in her linear drawing with flattened color areas within a fan shape.

DAN SWEENEY

DAN SWEENEY (1880-1958), a native of Sacramento, California, began his long career as a newspaper illustrator for the *San Francisco Chronicle*.

Sweeney also painted posters for theatre lobbies which led to his doing travel posters. He began to specialize in this for various steamship lines and traveled around the world, to many out-of-the-way places, doing background research for unusual poster subjects. One of his most successful series of pictures was of pirate characters for the Grace Lines.

For many years, Sweeney was a steady contributor of fiction illustrations to *Collier's* magazine, particularly of sea and Western subjects rendered in wash or transparent watercolor.

Story illustration for Collier's, *April 22, 1939.*

"Lewis and Clark Expedition," cover illustration for Blue Book, *June, 1947. Collection of Mr. and Mrs. Davies.*

Advertising Illustration for
Graybar Electric Company, 1927.
Collection of Illustration House.

Dry-brush drawing for
"Kioga of the Wilderness,"
Blue Book *magazine.*

"Who Goes There?" Painted for World Peaceways.

HERBERT
MORTON
STOOPS

HERBERT MORTON STOOPS (1888-1948) was closely identified with *Blue Book* magazine during his long career in illustration. This periodical published adventure fiction. Its wide variety of subject matter gave Stoops an opportunity to display his expert knowledge of military subjects, the Old West — particularly Indians, animals, and human figures in violent action. Many of his black-and-white dry-brush illustrations were attributed to his pen name, Jeremy Canon. He also painted *Blue Book's* monthly cover illustrations regularly for over 13 years. At the time of his death, he had painted the 17th of a series of covers depicting historical episodes in each of the 48 states.

Stoops, a clergyman's son, was reared in Idaho, attended Utah State College, worked as a staff artist for newspapers in San Francisco and Chicago. In 1917 he enlisted and served as a First Lieutenant with the Sixth Field Artillery of the First Division in France.

After the war, Stoops began his illustration career and his association with *Blue Book*. He did not confine himself to *Blue Book* alone, however, illustrating for *Collier's, This Week, Cosmopolitan,* and many others, as well as painting for exhibition. His picture, "Anno Domini," won the Isador medal at the National Academy Exhibition in 1940.

Stoops served as president of the Artists Guild in New York, was a member of the Salmagundi Club, the Society of Illustrators, The American Artists Professional League, and prized highly his honorary membership in the New York Association of Veterans of the French Foreign Legion.

"Mardi Gras," illustration for The Counte of Monte Cristo, *published by Dodd, Mead & Company. Collection of Dr. Robert Denby.*

"Paratroopers," the first of the series of Post *covers illustrating branches of military service.* © *1942 , 1970 by The Curtis Publishing Company. Courtesy of Judy and Alan Goffman.*

Mead Schaeffer—

The work of MEAD SCHAEFFER (1898-1980) divides itself into two periods. The early one deals with romantic, swashbuckling and theatrical subjects. The second, although still strong and dramatic, is based on authentic, factual themes and is more reportorial.

Mead, who was born in Freedom Plains, New York, studied at Pratt Institute, and with Harvey Dunn and Dean Cornwell. A brilliant student, he was illustrating for the major magazines while still in his twenties and had begun a series of sixteen illustrated classics for Dodd, Mead, including *The Count of Monte Cristo, Les Miserables, Typee* and *Moby Dick.* Eventually, however, he became dissatisfied with romance and costume stories; he wanted to deal with contemporary subjects that he could personally observe and learn about.

With this in mind, Schaeffer began to paint covers for *The Saturday Evening Post,* which at that time was featuring Americana. The *Post's* artists traveled to various parts of the country to find regional material with national appeal. Schaeffer made an extended trip to the West with his friend and fellow-artist, Norman Rockwell. From this and other trips, many fine covers resulted.

During World War II, Mead painted a notable series of *Post* covers of American soldiers, representative of various branches of the service. The paintings were done with the full approval and cooperation of United States military authorities who provided all the facilities. In researching the pictures, Schaeffer rode aboard a submarine, Coast Guard patrol boat and various aircraft. Later, under the sponsorship of the *Post,* the paintings were exhibited in more than ninety cities in the United States and Canada in promoting the war effort.

In other exhibitions Schaeffer won the Salmagundi Shaw Prize in 1930 and Gold Medal at the Pennsylvania Academy in 1944.

"Blood Money," one of the colorful series of illustrations for the "Captain Blood" stories of Rafael Sabatini, published in American *magazine. Collection of Andrew Sordoni III.*

199

Timmins

HARRY LAVERNE TIMMINS (1887-1963) was an extremely versatile illustrator who was at home in every medium from dry-brush to gouache, with a wide variety of subject matter developed from a long advertising and editorial art career.

His pictures appeared in *The Ladies' Home Journal, Woman's Home Companion, Pictorial Review, Cosmopolitan, American, This Week, Collier's,* and in several Canadian publications. These and his national advertising illustrations won numerous awards over the years.

Timmins was born in Wilsonville, Nebraska, and studied at the Art Institute of Chicago. He was a co-founder of the American Academy of Art there, where he also taught for several years in the 'twenties. In the last years of his life he painted for galleries in Carmel, Hollywood, and San Francisco, California, and had several one-man shows.

He was a member of the Society of Illustrators, the American Federation of Arts and the Palette and Chisel Club of Chicago.

Advertising illustration, 1929.

Rico Tomaso

As a young man, RICO TOMASO (1898-   ) played piano in a small dance orchestra — wearing heavy, black woolen gloves as his trademark — (but also to be able to hit harder on the keys to compete with the drummer). The drummer was Dean Cornwell, then just starting his illustration career.

Tomaso, who was encouraged in his art ambitions by a family friend, John T. McCutcheon, the famous cartoonist for the *Chicago Tribune,* studied at the Chicago Art Institute. Among his teachers were Cornwell, Harvey Dunn, Robert Henri, and J. Wellington Reynolds. His work mostly resembled Cornwell's in concept and broad brush style. Tomaso was at his best illustrating mystery stories or those of high adventure in exotic locations as, for example, the Albert Richard Wetjen stories of the South Australian Mounted Police for *The Saturday Evening Post.* He is also known for a series of vigorous, full-color, portrait illustrations for Granger Pipe Tobacco.

For some years, after the Grand Central School of Art was dispossessed from Grand Central Terminal, Tomaso carried on Harvey Dunn's illustration class in Mamaroneck. He now paints for exhibition, has been represented by the Grand Central Art Galleries and by Jean Bohne, Inc., in New York.

Illustration for Erle Stanley Gardner's "The Case of the Lame Canary," for The Saturday Evening Post. © *1937, 1965 by The Curtis Publishing Company.*

WELSH

WILLIAM P. WELSH (1889-   ) developed his decorative painting approach through his study at the Julian and Delecluse Academies in Paris and at the Art Students League in New York.

Although Welsh did fiction illustration for numerous publications and advertisers, his poster style was best suited to the many magazine covers he painted, particularly for *Woman's Home Companion*. He also did several murals, many portraits, exhibited internationally and taught at the Chicago Art Institute. In 1945 and 1946, he made paintings in the Far East Theatre of Operations for the Historical Records of the United States Army Air Forces.

Among his numerous awards are: First Prize at the International Watercolor Exhibition in 1921; First and Third Prizes, Poster Competition for Chicago's World's Fair, and medals from the New York Art Directors Club's annual exhibitions of advertising art.

Welsh has been a member of the Tavern Club, Chicago, the Chicago Society of Arts and the Society of Illustrators in New York. He was elected a Fellow to the British Royal Society of Arts in 1950 and of the International Institute of Arts and Letters in 1962.

Cover painting for the Woman's Home Companion, *February, 1932.*

E F WARD

EDMUND F. WARD (1892-   ) made his first illustrations for *The Saturday Evening Post* before he was twenty. His early pictures were large, generally with a dark tonality, and serious, painted in oils. Over a period of time he gradually changed to more humorous subjects and began to work in wash and watercolor. For many years he illustrated the Alexander Botts and Assistant District Attorney Doowinkle stories for the *Post*.

Ward was born in White Plains, New York, and studied at the Art Students League in the same class with Norman Rockwell. Among his teachers were Edward Dufner, George Bridgman and Thomas Fogarty.

He has spent his professional illustration career in White Plains, where he also painted a mural for the Federal Building. He is a long-time member of the Salmagundi Club, the Guild of Free Lance Artists, and was a member of the Society of Illustrators.

Illustration for "The Girl who wanted a Fairy Prince" by Maude Radford Warren, November, 1921.

201

Full-color, full-page illustration for The Ladies' Home Journal.

Advertising illustration for Maxwell House Coffee, 1928.

SUNDBLOM

HADDON HUBBARD SUNDBLOM (1899-1976) dominated the art field in Chicago beginning in the 'twenties when he formed a studio partnership with Howard Stevens and Edwin Henry.

The studio, under the artistic direction and influence of Sundblom, attracted a great number of young artists who later, as alumni of the "Sundblom circle," went on to become name illustrators in their own right. Among those included in this book are Harry Anderson, Earl Blossom, Matt Clark, Edwin Henry, Walter Richards, James Schucker, Thornton Utz and Coby Whitmore. Sundblom acknowledged the influence on his own style of many painters, including John Singer Sargent, Anders Zorn, Robert Henri and Sorolla. As amalgamated by Sundblom, it was a brilliant and colorful technique, combined with his own good taste and *joie de vivre*.

These qualities kept his work in steady demand for nearly forty years for both magazine stories and advertis-

ing campaigns and won for him many medals and citations. His style became a hallmark for advertisers, such as Coca-Cola, Procter and Gamble, Palmolive, Peet & Company and Maxwell House Coffee. For over twenty years Sundblom painted a Santa Claus subject for Coca-Cola; its prominence on the back cover of many national magazines made it a famous feature. Sundblom used himself as the model in the latter years.

Sundblom, born in Muskegon, Michigan, left school to work at the age of thirteen when his mother died. For many years he attended school at night or took correspondence courses to make up his education. He also studied for four years at the Chicago Art Institute and three-and-a-half years at the American Academy of Art. His art apprenticeship was served at the Charles Everett Johnson Studio in Chicago and, in 1925, the partnership of Stevens, Sundblom and Henry was launched.

J. W. Williamson (signature)

JAMES W. WILLIAMSON (1899-   ) has made an immense number of advertising illustrations for such clients as Arrow Shirts, Clicquot Club Ginger Ale, Ford, Paul Jones and Yardley, all treated with circumspect restraint.

However, in his editorial illustration his sense of humor emerged and became his most engaging characteristic. Williamson distilled action and renderings down to their essentials; the poses of the figures told the story.

Williamson was born in Omaha, Nebraska; was a graduate of the 1923 class at Yale.

A self-taught artist, he sold his first work to the old *Life* magazine while still in college. This was followed by sales to *Judge, Vanity Fair, Delineator,* and nearly all of the rest of the major magazines, including *The Saturday Evening Post,* where his work appeared for over thirty years.

During those years, his work was exhibited regularly at Art Directors Club shows in New York and Los Angeles, winning many awards. Williamson also taught at the Art Students League for a year in 1933.

He was elected into the Society of Illustrators Hall of Fame in 1984.

Typical Williamson story illustration; date and place of its publication not known.

Wortman

DENYS WORTMAN, N.A. (1887-1958) was a social commentator of penetration and wit. He conveyed much good humor and sympathetic perception in his daily cartoon panel, "Metropolitan Movies." Although his drawings were predominantly concerned with New York characters: frowzy landladies, bums and hangers-on, the panel was syndicated in 45 newspapers as "Everyday Movies." The common touch and wealth of homely observation made it equally appreciated across the country. His characters, like "Mopey Dick and the Duke," managed to evoke smiles even through the somber period of the Depression.

Wortman was born in Saugerties, New York, educated at Stevens Institute of Technology, Rutgers University, and the New York School of Fine and Applied Art, under Kenneth Hayes Miller. His first artwork was done for the old *Herald Tribune,* and he illustrated for many magazines including *The New Yorker, The Saturday Evening Post,* and *Collier's,* but his longest association was with the old *New York World-Telegram and Sun.*

Wortman was equally interested in serious painting. He exhibited at the Armory Show, the National Academy, the Macbeth Galleries, and the Society of Illustrators where he served as president from 1936 to 1938.

His work is represented in the collections of the Metropolitan Museum of Art and the New York Public Library.

"Mopey Dick and The Duke," *reprinted by permission of the New York World-Telegram and Sun.*

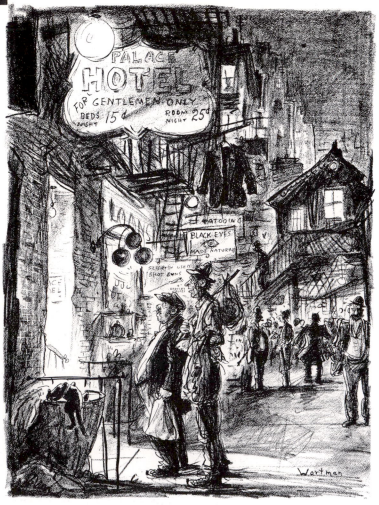

1940

1950

THE DECADE: 1940-1950
Al Parker

drawing by Robert Fawcett

"Too bizarre!" "Tinsel!" "Gimmicky!"

These were the critical cries heard when venturesome new art saw light of day in the popular women's magazines during the Depression of the 'thirties. The commercial value of this young talent, however, was observed only by a few astute art directors, who decided that here was something to nuture.

In those days, the success of a young artist depended greatly on the capacity of an art director to evoke it. Once evoked, the director expounded its merits to the editor-in-chief of the magazine, who usually asked for a watered-down version — pure innovation being mostly reserved for failing magazines in their dying gasps for attention.

Not until the crisis of World War II did the young artist fully realize his potentialities. It was then that acclaim from reader polls and art awards verified the fact that a minority of art directors had not facilitated a mere fad.

The magazines of the early 1940s concentrated on new formats for entertaining their most important reader: the young housewife and mother. This need was met in editorial art by depicting an idealized world, peopled with handsome men and gorgeous women, bedecked in their best in the most fashionable of settings. The young artist's ingenious execution of this policy established an astonishing rapport with the female reader — still unsurpassed.

Nevertheless, an overplus of taboos accompanied his rewards. He was permitted to paint sauteed mushrooms but not a steak (meat was rationed in World War II); a pair of snakeskin shoes with matching purse but not a snake (too frightening); the mood of a costume story but nary a costume (too old-fashioned); a garaged automobile but not one in motion (gasoline was rationed, too), and never, never, a trace of obesity.

While this hardly created a climate for discovery, the young artist gratified his creative impulse by concentrating on adornment, design and layout of pages. Further, the wartime shortage of art supplies became an asset by inducing him to experiment with substitute materials, adding unusual techniques to his endeavors.

Illustration had become a commodity. Chic accessories with which he peppered his pictures provided a sustained involvement for the reader. Each illustration that featured these props produced letters from near and far. A chair covered in needlepoint, placed in a compositon because of its interesting texture, brought inquiries about the availability of its pattern. A flowering epiphyllum incited requests for sources of rooted cuttings.

The dynamic simplicity that produced these fresh illustrations also affected reproductions, since the paper shortage had foisted inferior stock on the magazines. It was advantageous to employ clean, flat colors from a high-keyed palette, leaving plenty of white areas for vignetting the composition. Large close-ups of the hero's and heroine's heads eliminated unwanted clutter from the background.

Contrasty subject matter was *verboten,* as, for example, a prominently displayed zebra rug, for it was sure to stripe the art and text on the reverse side of the page. Thin paper held no secrets.

As these exercises flowed from the illustrator's brush he took time to join in the war effort. Planned trips of portrait sketching were arranged by the Red Cross and other organizations, for visits to veterans' hospitals around the country. The lifesize likeness brought joy to convalescing service men and women, and to their folks back home.

Some patients were encased in plaster casts. The variety of matte white shapes made ideal surfaces for the painting of whatever was deemed appropriate — a blonde, brunette or redhead. The hospital wards resembled galleries of Environmental Art as the proud patients, propped in bed, exhibited their decorative conversation pieces.

Meanwhile, the illustrators painted war posters and donated their original art work as prizes to entice buyers in war bond drives. Some illustrators enlisted in the armed forces. Others used their talents in designing war media, from instructional booklets to film animation. Many became artist-war-correspondents, armed with pencil and paper in combat areas.

Members of the Society of Illustrators in New York City had among their hospital sketching group some jazz musicians. By day they would sketch, then stay on after dinner to play request numbers. Sometimes the hospital rocked with a jam session while a patient augmented the band with his own instrument.

At the end of the war, the illustrator strutted amidst a pageant of plenty. Advertising budgets had skyrocketed and magazines bulged with fiction, providing work for all who painted in the style of the innovators. Subtle changes became apparent. Unheralded, the fine arts painter, so sparingly used in editorial and advertising art, was emerging as an innovator. Although too avant garde to be widely marketable, he gave evidence of being the forerunner of a new approach.

His intense, turbulent expressions, his avoidance of photographic realism, his wilful lack of polished craftsmanship, imparted an infinished look to his finished art. What appeared to be a rehearsal was the actual performance itself. Those functional little accessories that starred in other illustrations were absent in his works — the illustration being the star. The ferment of these drastic concepts and techniques developed as the major influence of today's illustrator.

Sports cars roared in from abroad; new country estates looked out on the suburban horizon. The illustrator partook of these luxuries and began to live the life he painted. The need to escape was already waning and, with it, escapist art. He had stretched the boundaries of editorial and advertising illustration; now came a call for new talent to explore the exposed areas.

John Gardner, in his book *Self-Renewal, The Individual and the Innovative Society,* published by Harper & Row, says:

"... The revolution in modern art succeeded magnificently in shattering the rigidities of traditional art. It also fastened on the field of painting a mystique of rebellion and innovation which has hung around its neck like an albatross ever since."

Today, the march of time brings an echo to our ears as the pros cry out at the new venturesome art:
"Greasy fingerpainting!" "Too bizarre!" "Gimmicky!"

ILLUSTRATORS 1940-1950

COURTNEY ALLEN
HARRY ANDERSON
LYMAN MATTHEW ANDERSON
JOHN ATHERTON
WARREN BAUMGARTNER
WALTER M. BAUMHOFER
LONIE BEE
ROBERT BENNEY
GEOFFREY BIGGS
GILBERT BUNDY
JOHN CLYMER
STEVAN DOHANOS
ALBERT DORNE
JOHN PHILIP FALTER
ROBERT FAWCETT
FRED FREEMAN
JOHN GANNAM
JOHN F. GOULD
HARDIE GRAMATKY
HAMILTON GREENE
GLEN GROHE
JOHN GROTH
LEALAND R. GUSTAVSON
ROBERT GEORGE HARRIS
GEORGE HUGHES
EARL OLIVER HURST
ROBERT F. KUHN

ROBERT E. LOUGHEED
TOM LOVELL
FRED LUDEKENS
ALFRED PARKER
PERRY PETERSON
JOHN PIKE
HENRY CLARENCE PITZ
BEN KIMBERLY PRINS
RAY PROHASKA
PAUL RABUT
FRANK JOSEPH REILLY
WALTER D. RICHARDS
ROBERT RIGGS
NICHOLAS F. RILEY
LESLIE SAALBURG
RICHARD SARGENT
BARBARA E. SCHWINN
AMOS SEWELL
EDWARD SHENTON
NOEL SICKLES
BENJAMIN ALBERT STAHL
FREDERIC VARADY
HAROLD VON SCHMIDT
LYND WARD
JACK W. WELCH
JON WHITCOMB
MORTIMER WILSON, JR.

LYMAN ANDERSON

LYMAN MATTHEW ANDERSON (1907-) got his big break when some spot illustrations he'd made for an insurance company advertisement were accepted for exhibition in the New York Art Directors Club's annual show. Unknown to the acceptance jury, the original paintings were very large and when hung, dominated the whole show. The pictures attracted much favorable attention and launched Lyman on the national scene as an illustrator.

Anderson had prepared himself well for the opportunity when it came. Born in Chicago, Illinois, he was a graduate of the Art Institute there, attended the Grand Central School of Art in New York City. Among his teachers were Pruett Carter, Walter Biggs, Harvey Dunn, Naum Los and Wayman Adams. In his early artwork he did a great deal of illustration for pulp magazines, also a syndicated comic strip for King Features.

During his career, his clients have included such advertisers as Pepsi-Cola, Vitalis, New York Life Insurance Company, and Pan-American; magazines such as *Woman's Home Companion, The Saturday Evening Post, Cosmopolitan* and *American*. He has been a long-time member of the Society of Illustrators and is an honorary life-member of the Joint Ethics Committee.

Illustration for Woman's Home Companion, *1940.*

COURTNEY ALLEN

COURTNEY ALLEN (1896-1969) sold his first drawing to his home-town newspaper in Norfolk, Virginia, at the age of eleven. Thus encouraged, he decided early on an art career; later studied at the National Academy, the Corcoran School of Art in Washington, D.C., and with Charles W. Hawthorne in Provincetown, Massachusetts. His study was interrupted by fifteen months spent in the American Army during World War I — twelve months in France, eight of them at the Front in the Camouflage Section.

In the following years, Allen divided his time between illustrating for books and magazines, painting for exhibitions and, from 1946-50, teaching at the Huguenot School of Art in New Rochelle, New York.

During World War II, he was a regular participant in sketching trips with other members of the New Rochelle Art Association to Halloran Hospital on Staten Island, making portrait drawings of convalescent servicemen.

He was an active member of the New Rochelle Art Association, where he won a Gold Medal for oil painting; also exhibited and won other awards at the Hudson Valley Art Association, Norfolk Museum of Arts and Sciences, National Academy, Allied Artists in New York, Chrysler Art Museum of Provincetown and the Provincetown Historical Museum.

Illustration for The Saturday Evening Post *serial, "Golden Portage."* © *1939, 1967 by The Curtis Publishing Company.*

"New York Welcomes President-elect George Washington in 1789." Illustration for Exxon in 1976.

Harry Anderson

HARRY ANDERSON, A.N.A. (1906-   ) became a watercolorist because of an allergy to oil paint. However, he employs tube opaque watercolors, or tempera, whose properties most resemble the qualities of oils. With them he has retained the malleability of oil and added the spontaneity of the water medium.

Anderson (no relation to Lyman Anderson) was born in Chicago, attended the University of Illinois, graduated from Syracuse University in 1930. He has had studios successively in New York, Chicago, Washington, D.C. and is at present in Ridgefield, Connecticut.

His illustrations have appeared in most of the major magazines, and he exhibits regularly. He is currently represented by Settlers West Gallery in Tucson, Arizona. A member of the American Watercolor Society, he won the Grumbacher Purchase Prize in the 1956 Exhibition.

Atherton

For JOHN ATHERTON (1900-1952) there was no line drawn between "fine" and "commercial" art. He painted pictures for advertisers, magazine covers, and galleries alike, all characterized by his strong sense of design, color, and good taste.

Atherton was born in Brainerd, Minnesota, studied at the College of the Pacific, and the California School of Fine Arts in San Francisco. He first worked in a number of West Coast art studios learning the basics of his craft. When he won a $500 first prize award in the annual exhibit of the Bohemian Club in 1929, it financed his move to New York.

There he began to do illustrations for advertisers, including General Motors, Container Corporation of America and Shell Oil, and covers for *Fortune, Holiday,* and *The Saturday Evening Post.*

His first one-man show was held in Manhattan in 1936; in the "Artists for Victory" show in 1943, his painting, "The Black Horse," won the $3,000 fourth prize from among 14,000 entries. It now hangs in the Metropolitan Museum of Art in New York. His work is also represented at the Whitney Museum, Museum of Modern Art, Chicago Art Institute, the Pennsylvania Academy of the Fine Arts, The Albright Art Gallery in Buffalo, and the Wadsworth Atheneum in Hartford.

Atherton's great avocation was fishing. He tied flies of original design expertly, was a member of the Anglers' Club and author of a book, *The Fly and the Fish.* His death occurred while he was on a salmon-fishing trip in New Brunswick, Canada.

This Saturday Evening Post *cover illustration appropriately depicts a successful catch.* © 1944, 1972 by The Curtis Publishing Company.

THE SATURDAY EVENING
POST
APRIL 15, 1944   10¢

THE MAGIC LIE DETECTOR
By ALVA JOHNSTON

THE BATTLE
WITHOUT A NAME
By CAPT. ROBERT W. BLAKE, USMCR

Baumgartner

WARREN BAUMGARTNER, N.A. (1894-1963) was born in Oakville, Missouri, and came by a lifetime love of fishing from his boyhood in the Ozarks. In the years following, he studied at the Art Institute of Chicago under Wellington J. Reynolds, the Grand Central School with Pruett Carter and with Walter Biggs.

A very fine watercolorist, Baumgartner painted pictures for both magazine illustrations and exhibitions, winning numerous awards in both fields.

He was a member of the Society of Illustrators, American Watercolor Society, National Academy of Design and the Salmagundi Club of New York.

Published in True *magazine.*

For years, WALTER M. BAUMHOFER (1904-   ) painted cover designs for the pulps, such as *Adventure* magazine, Street & Smith magazines and Popular Publications. A bold, dramatic approach has characterized his work ever since.

A versatile performer, Baumhofer has illustrated for publications as diverse as *The Ladies' Home Journal, Liberty, Outdoor Life, Cosmopolitan, True, Women's Day* and *Sports Afield*.

Baumhofer studied at Pratt Institute in Brooklyn, New York, and was a long-time member of the Society of Illustrators.

Illustration for "Love of My Life" by Belva Plain, McCall's *magazine. Reprinted by permission of the McCall Publishing Company.*

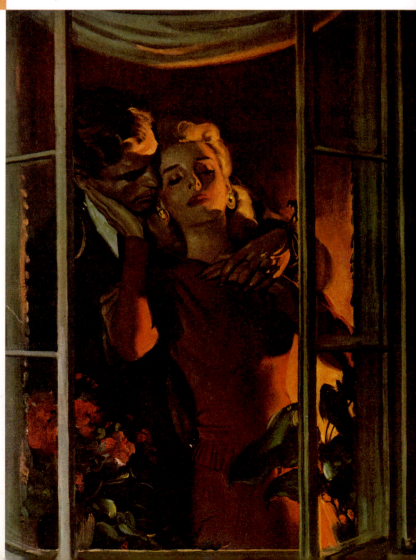

Lonie Bee

LONIE BEE (1902-   ) was born in Santa Rosa, California and has remained there as one of the "West Coast Artists."

After training at the University of California and the California School of Fine Arts and Crafts, he appeared on the national scene with his spirited illustrations for the magazines, *Collier's, American, Cosmopolitan, Woman's Home Companion, Woman's Day, Good Housekeeping* and *The Saturday Evening Post.* For all of these, he painted numerous covers. Over the years, he has also done advertising illustrations and painted designs for twenty-four-sheet posters, winning many awards and citations.

More recently Bee has turned to landscape painting and portraiture. He has exhibited at the Society of Illustrators in New York, The Bohemian Club and the Carmel Gallery in California.

Watercolor illustration for Faith Baldwin's serial in Cosmopolitan *magazine, 1945.*

ROBERT BENNEY

In his work, ROBERT BENNEY (1904-   ) ably combines the roles of painter and reporter. During World War II, he was a war correspondent under the Office of the Surgeon General, with assignments successively for the Navy and the Army in combat areas.

After the war, Benney began to specialize in producing art work for industry and agriculture, accepting commissions to record the operations of some of the nation's largest companies, including the American Sugar Refining Company, Standard Oil of New Jersey, American Tobacco, Chrysler Corporation, Shell Oil, Western Electric, General Foods and others.

Benney was born in New York, studied at the Cooper Union Art School, the Art Students League, National Academy School of Fine Arts and Grand Central School of Art. Among his teachers were George Bridgman, Walter Biggs, Harvey Dunn and Dean Cornwell. He himself has taught at the School of Visual Arts and at Pratt Institute.

His work has won many awards and is represented in several collections and museums. He has also been an active member of the Society of Illustrators, serving on committees for education, exhibitions and scholarships.

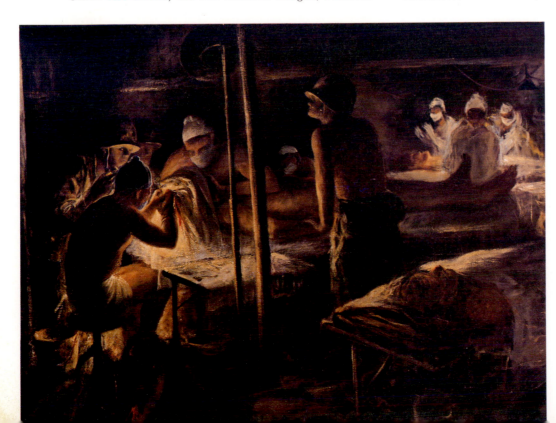

Flashlight Surgery in Saipan, WWII. U.S. Army Art Collection.

Gilbert Bundy

GILBERT BUNDY (1911-1955) was born in Centralia, Illinois, the son of an oil company scout. He was brought up in a succession of oil boom towns in Oklahoma. He eventually finished high school in Winfield, Kansas, and went to work for a Kansas City engraving company.

In 1929 Bundy headed for a career in New York and began to do cartoons for the old *Life* and *Judge* magazines.

In the early 'thirties he became associated with the fledgling *Esquire* magazine. His deftly drawn, risqué humor had much to do with the success of that magazine, which was also a valuable showcase for Bundy, and led to his spectacular popularity as an illustrator for most of the major magazines and many advertisers. These included campaigns for Cluett Peabody, Munsingwear and Sanka Coffee.

Bundy's pictures looked spontaneous but were the result of much careful research and study. He emulated the classic Chinese method of drawing from memory once he had made many preliminary studies from the model.

During World War II, Bundy covered the Pacific War Theatre as a combat artist for King Features. He went through a series of harrowing actions, including Tarawa, Iwo Jima and Okinawa; was the sole survivor of a direct hit on an Amtrak and spent a day and night in the water before being rescued.

Although he resumed his career in illustration after the war, Bundy never recovered from the severe shock of his experiences and took his own life in 1955.

"Please go away — I want to think."
Typical bawdy illustration for Esquire *magazine.*

GEOFFREY BIGGS

GEOFFREY BIGGS (1908-   ) was born in London, England, but went through high school in America and studied at the Grand Central School of Art. Among his teachers were Arthur Woeffle, Arshile Gorky and Harvey Dunn.

Biggs' work, which is highly detailed and realistic, was first published in *Collier's,* where it attracted wide attention, and was soon followed by commissions from most of the other periodicals, including *The Saturday Evening Post, True, Liberty, Woman's Home Companion, Coronet, Pic* and *Good Housekeeping,* as well as from many major and minor advertising agencies in New York.

In addition, Biggs has found time to exhibit at the Society of Illustrators and the Midtown Galleries in New York.

Illustration for "Return from Maracaibo," for Collier's *magazine, November 8, 1941.*

"Horse Farm," cover illustration for The Saturday Evening Post, *July 26, 1961.* © *1961 by The Curtis Publishing Company. Collection of the New Britain Museum of American Art.*

John Clymer

JOHN CLYMER, A.R.C.A. (1907-   ) was born in Ellensburg, Washington. His art education was acquired at the Vancouver School of Fine Art in Vancouver and the Ontario College of Art in Port Hope, Canada, as well as at the Wilmington Society of Fine Arts in Delaware and the Grand Central School of Art in New York. With this background, his loyalties have ever since been divided between the United States and Canada.

Clymer's first illustrations were made for Canadian publications, then the American pulps, followed by editorial assignments for most of the American magazines; numerous advertising campaigns; and an extensive series of paintings of historic episodes for the United States Marine Corps.

His paintings have been exhibited widely in both countries as well, with the North West Artists in Seattle, The Ontario Society of Artists, The Royal Canadian Academy in Toronto, Canada, The National Academy in New York, Salmagundi Club, Society of Animal Artists and Hudson Valley Artists. Clymer is an exhibiting member of The Cowboy Artists and the National Academy of Western Art, winning numerous awards. He was elected to the Society of Illustrators Hall of Fame in 1982.

Typical pulp illustration, an early stepping-stone in Clymer's career.

213

"Ice Cream Break," cover for The Saturday Evening Post, *Sept. 22, 1951.*
© *1951 , 1979 by The Curtis Publishing Company. Collection of Judy and Alan Goffman.*

"Heart Broken," story illustration for The Saturday Evening Post. © 1944, 1972 by The Curtis Publishing Company. *In the Sanford Low Memorial Collection of American Illustration, New Britain Museum of American Art.*

Stevan Dohanos

STEVAN DOHANOS (1907-   ) painted a series of pictures of fire plugs which reveals much about him as an artist. First, it is typical of him to have seen a picture possibility in such a commonplace subject. However, as a searching realist, he was not content merely to record the appearance of the hydrants but had to know all about how they worked, too. In the course of his investigation, he talked with town officials and hydraulic engineers, examined and made many sketches of various types of hydrants in other towns as well.

Dohanos studied nights at the Cleveland School of Art long enough to get a job as an apprentice letterer and, gradually, developed a solid studio background. A hard worker, he simultaneously did painting and engravings for national exhibitions.

In 1936 he painted an assignment for the Treasury Art Project in the Virgin Islands and, later, various mural commissions for federal buildings in Elkins, West Virginia; West Palm Beach, Florida; and Charlotte Amalie, Virgin Islands. His pictures are in the collections of the Cleveland Museum of Art, Whitney Museum, Pennsylvania Academy of Art, Avery Memorial of Hartford, New Britain Museum of American Art and of several private owners.

His illustrations have appeared in almost all of the major magazines; for several years he painted covers for *The Saturday Evening Post.* Twice a victim of tuberculosis himself, Dohanos has contributed Christmas seal designs to the National Tuberculosis Association and made many posters and designs for national and local charitable purposes. He has designed over forty stamps for the U. S. Postal Service. For several years he served on the Citizen Stamp Advisory Committee for the Postmaster General and as its Design Coordinator.

He is a member of the National Society of Mural Painters, Artists and Writers Club, Dutch Treat Club, served as president of the Society of Illustrators from 1961-63, was inducted into its Hall of Fame in 1971 and elected Honorary President in 1982.

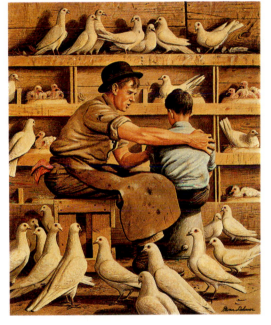

"Pigeon Loft." Published in The Saturday Evening Post, *Nov. 30, 1946.* © 1946, 1974 by The Curtis Publishing Company. Collection of Les Mansfield.

"Canada Goose Decoy," recent gallery painting which has been reproduced in a signed, limited edition.

"Duel of the Ironclads," illustration for Time-Life Books.
Collection of the Society of Illustrators Museum of American Illustration.

Fred Freeman

From logging to layout work in a large department store, FRED FREEMAN (1906-   ) has accumulated a diversity of experience which has contributed greatly to his artistic development. He was a Naval Reserve Lieutenant Commander during World War II, skippered three different ships, taking part in actions at Guadalcanal, New Zealand, the Solomon Islands, Saipan, Guam and the Aleutians. With this naval background, he was able to combine a technical knowledge with dramatic impact in his authoritative illustrations for *United States Submarine Operations in World War II.*

In his subsequent illustration career, Freeman has continued to combine this intricacy of documentary detail with strongly composed artistry. The burgeoning developments of space-age technology have been a special province for Freeman who has taken on many major illustration assignments for publications such as *Collier's, The Saturday Evening Post* and *Reader's Digest.*

John F. Gould

JOHN F. GOULD (1906-   ) estimates that he did about twelve thousand adventure and detective story illustrations for pulp magazines before tackling *The Saturday Evening Post.* To prepare himself for the *Post,* he spent a year-and-a-half picking a different story each week and redoing the illustrations in his own way. A representative group of these, shown to the *Post's* art editor, won Gould his first commission.

Since then he has illustrated for *Redbook, Collier's, The Saturday Evening Post* and numerous national advertising accounts.

Born in Worcester, Massachusetts, Gould studied at the Tiffany Foundation and was graduated from Pratt Institute where he then taught for twenty-two years. He has also taught at the Newark School of Fine and Industrial Art, as well as in classes at the Bethlehem Art Gallery near Newburgh, New York.

His expert watercolor paintings are represented in many private collections.

World War II Saturday Evening Post *illustration for "Where the Buffalo Roam" by Richard Sale.* © *1943, 1971 by The Curtis Publishing Company.*

"Tree-lined Street," typical of Gramatky's direct watercolor technique. Collection of the Society of Illustrators Museum of American Illustration.

HARDIE GRAMATKY —

As a boy, HARDIE GRAMATKY, N.A. (1907-1979) wanted to be a comic strip artist. He realized that ambition early, "ghosting" the Ella Cinders comic soon after completing his studies at Stanford University and the Chouinard Art Institute in Los Angeles. This preparation led to a job in Walt Disney's studio where, for six years, he worked his way up and finally became head animator.

In 1936, Gramatky came to New York to free-lance; some of his first assignments were reportorial paintings for *Fortune* magazine. He specialized in the watercolor medium, and his illustrations for fiction, articles and advertising appeared in virtually all the magazines.

As a result of painting tugboats, he became interested in doing a children's book. His story, *Little Toot,* has been a

perennial best seller ever since, was made into an animated film by Disney, is part of the CARE-UNESCO book program, and has been rated by the Library of Congress as one of the great children's books of all time. He subsequently wrote and illustrated many other books well known in the children's book field.

Gramatky also painted and exhibited all over the world, winning many top watercolor awards, including the Chicago International in 1942, the National Academy in 1952 and the American Watercolor Society in 1962. His paintings are in the permanent collections of the Brooklyn Museum, Springfield Museum of Art, Toledo Museum and many private collections.

HAMILTON GREENE

HAMILTON GREENE (1904-1966) produced a great quantity of competent illustrations, beginning with the pulp magazines, later for men's magazines — *Argosy, True, Cavalier, Elks* and for Dell publications.

Greene was appointed an overseas artist-correspondent for *The American Legion* magazine in 1944-45 and made many authentic, eyewitness drawings of fighting in the European theatre. While with a Ninth Army Patrol near Geilenkirchen, Germany, he was wounded in the stomach and lungs by sniper fire. According to an excerpt from a letter by the director of the Public Relations Division, Supreme Headquarters, A.E.F., "Mr. Greene was conspicuously forward in every operation in which he participated and was well known to the personnel of the units he accompanied because of his place in the forward assault where he sought opportunity to watch the reactions of the American soldiers in the attack . . ." In 1951 Greene again served, as a war correspondent in Korea, for *Blue Book* magazine. A large collection of his war illustrations is in the U. S. Army Center of Military History in Washington, D.C.

Illustration for Blue Book *magazine, "Holland Para-drop," September, 1949.*

217

"P.T. Barnum," colored ink advertising illustration. Courtesy of John Hancock Mutual Life Insurance Company.

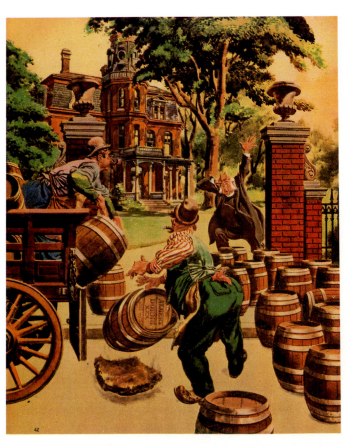

ALBERT DORNE

ALBERT DORNE (1904-1965), who was born and grew up on the lower East side of New York, had to leave school in the eighth grade to go to work. In 1963 he fittingly received the Horatio Alger Award for Achievement from the American Schools and Colleges Association, Inc.

In the intervening years, Dorne, through a combination of natural ability and strong drive, progressed successively from being an unpaid assistant to a commercial artist to one of New York's most successful advertising artists, while still in his early twenties. He went on to become a leading editorial illustrator, was elected president of the New York Society of Illustrators (1947-48), and in 1948 became the founder-director of the Famous Artists Schools in Westport, Connecticut.

These remarkably successful correspondence schools sprang originally from Dorne's interest in helping aspiring artists who continually came to him for advice.

Among his achievements, Dorne ranked high his being co-founder of the Code of Ethics and Fair Practices of the Profession of Commercial Art and Illustration. In 1953 he was awarded the first Gold Medal for a "distinguished career" by the New York Art Directors Club. Adelphi College conferred on him an honorary Doctor of Fine Arts degree in 1958.

"The Spiteful Nature of Gentlemen Joe," illustration for True magazine, June, 1946.

"*The New School Marm*" (1975) Collection of Ralph Kaschai.

JOHN FALTER

JOHN PHILIP FALTER (1910-1982) was born in Plattsmouth and reared in Falls City, Nebraska. He studied at the Kansas City Art Institute, at the Art Students League in New York on a scholarship, and at the Grand Central School of Art in New York. Among his teachers were Mahonri Young, George Wright and Monte Crews.

Falter began his career in illustration early, starting with the pulps, and at 20, sold his first slick illustration to *Liberty* magazine. Talented and prolific, he soon added most of the other magazines, and many advertising agencies, to his roster of clients.

His most important pictures were painted for the covers of *The Saturday Evening Post,* and he produced more than 200 of them. Many were based on the experiences of his Nebraska boyhood, in small town and country settings. He also painted a notable series of street scenes in cities across the United States. These grew out of a chance visit of a *Post* art editor to Falter's studio; there a picture caught his eye, a painting of Gramercy Park which Falter had painted for pleasure.

John served in the Navy as a Chief Boatswain's Mate during World War II; later, was commissioned a Lieutenant on special art assignments. Among other assignments after the war he illustrated over 40 books for *Reader's Digest* and completed many portrait commissions, including those of Admiral Halsey, Louis Armstrong, Olivia de Havilland, James Cagney, Mrs. Clark Clifford and John Charles Thomas. He also did an outstanding series of Bicentennial oil paintings of historical subjects for the 3M Company in 1976.

Falter was a member of the Society of Illustrators, The Players, and the Philadelphia Sketch Club. In 1976 he was elected to the Society of Illustrators Hall of Fame. Although he did not often exhibit, his paintings are represented in several museums and private collections.

"*Return from Vacation,*" *cover for* The Saturday Evening Post. © 1952, 1980 *by The Curtis Publishing Company. Courtesy of Judy and Alan Goffman.*

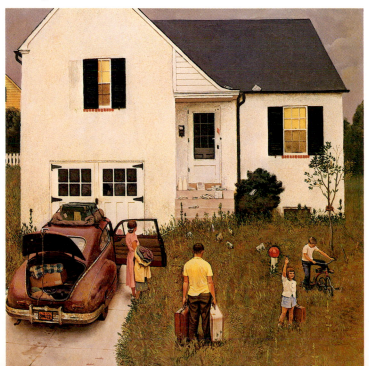

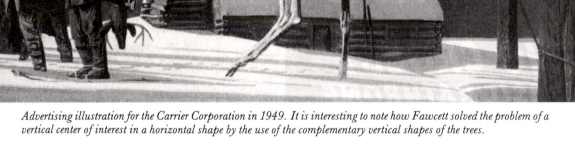

Advertising illustration for the Carrier Corporation in 1949. It is interesting to note how Fawcett solved the problem of a vertical center of interest in a horizontal shape by the use of the complementary vertical shapes of the trees.

ROBERT FAWCETT, A.N.A. (1903-1967), who was born in London, was given much encouragement in his early drawing efforts by his father, an amateur artist. Fawcett's family moved from England to Winnipeg, Canada, and later to New York City.

At nineteen, Fawcett returned to London, and for two years studied drawing under the rigorous discipline of the famous Slade School of London University. He came back to the United States in 1924 and began the long career in advertising and editorial illustration that brought him preëminence as "the illustrators' illustrator." Fawcett earned that reputation through his superb draftsmanship and mastery of composition as shown in a series of Sherlock Holmes stories he illustrated for *Collier's* magazine.

In later years he preferred to restrict his work to reportorial assignments, as, for example, the assignment on Oxford, Mississippi, for *Look* magazine. His book, *On the Art of Drawing,* was published in 1958; in 1960, he painted a series of murals for the Commonwealth Institute of London.

Fawcett was twice president of the Westport Artists and also a member of the founding faculty of the Famous Artists Schools in Westport, Connecticut.

He was elected to the Hall of Fame of the Society of Illustrators in 1967. A second book, *Drawing the Nude,* based on Fawcett's drawings and teaching, was written by his colleague and friend, Howard Munce, and published in 1980.

Figure study included in Drawing the Nude.

Sherlock Holmes story, "The Adventure of the Black Baronet," published in Collier's, *1953.*

A perfection seeking craftsman, Gannam made innumerable studies of his subjects on-the-spot, as for "First Snow" by Elizabeth Barton de Trevino in Cosmopolitan *magazine.*

JOHN GANNAM

JOHN GANNAM, A.N.A. (1907-1965) was an intense, dedicated artist. He worked almost exclusively in watercolor and was a lifelong student of the effects of light and color. Oftentimes a particular problem would preoccupy him for months as he tried out innumerable variations. He kept on until satisfied, finally, that he understood such effects as sunlight and under-water rocks on the surface of a mountain stream or the glow of a fire in the sky, and its reflection on wet pavement as firemen fought a blaze.

Gannam worked at his paintings almost vertically, very freely, his brush loaded with water. He was after the broad, but exact effect, little concerned with details or with corrections which could be made later, if needed, with opaque.

John, who was born in Lebanon, grew up in Chicago but was forced to leave school to work, at 14, when his father died. He went through a succession of menial jobs until he eventually became a messenger boy in an engraving house. Here he first found a purpose for himself — to become an artist like the men who did the layouts, lettering and drawings for engravings. Within a few years, by dint of close observation and a stiff schedule of self-education, he reached his goal, working for studios in Chicago and Detroit.

The next step was New York and, eventually, magazine illustration. He received his first manuscript from Henry Quinan of *Woman's Home Companion,* followed soon thereafter by work from most of the other magazines. Gannam always sought fresh, unstereotyped viewpoints which, with his excellent taste, kept him in constant demand by advertisers as well as publishers. His illustrations for campaigns of Pacific Mills, Ipana and St. Marys Blankets are particularly memorable.

Gannam also exhibited his watercolors, was an associate of the National Academy of Design, member of the American Artists' Professional League, the American Watercolor

Society, the Society of Illustrators, and appointed to the faculty and board of directors of the Danbury Academy of Arts. In 1981 he was elected to the Society of Illustrators Hall of Fame.

Gannam made a long series of illustrations for Pacific Mills which were immensely popular with the public. To his fellow illustrators each new painting was an inspiring event.

grohe

GLEN GROHE (1912-1956) was born in Chicago and worked his way through the Art Institute and the American Academy of Art there.
He obtained his first job with the Swan Studio in Chicago and in 1937 went to New York, joining the staff of an advertising magazine and later the Charles E. Cooper Studio.

He attracted the attention of magazine art editors through the originality and strong design of his advertising illustrations which he carried over into his work for periodicals, including *The Saturday Evening Post, This Week, Cosmopolitan* and *Good Housekeeping* magazines.

Among Grohe's many advertising clients were the Dow Chemical Company, Conoco and The Travelers Insurance Company. During World War II, he served as a consultant in the Graphics Division of the O.E.M. and did posters for the O.W.I.

Grohe was also interested in still and motion picture photography. He made a documentary film for the San Mateo County Recreational Department and had nearly finished a very imaginative film on the artwork of patients in a mental institution at the time of his death.

"Sieving the Baby," advertising illustration for *The Travelers Insurance Company in 1940.*

John Groth

JOHN GROTH, A.N.A. (1908-   ), as a hopeful young artist, was advised by an artist friend to make a hundred drawings a day. John took the advice literally and kept up the practice for years. This driving pace trained him as an artist and shaped his free, expressionistic style of drawing.

Impressed by the vigor of his work, *Esquire* magazine hired him as its first art director. He promptly assigned himself on travel junkets to draw and paint for the magazine in Mexico, Russia, France, England and Germany.

During World War II, as an artist-correspondent for the *Chicago Sun,* he was present at the liberation of Paris and the surrender of Berlin. He became a friend of Ernest Hemingway in France and out of this association came his assignment to illustrate Hemingway's *Men without Women;*

Hemingway also wrote the preface for Groth's own book of war drawings and experiences, *Studio: Europe.* Groth later covered the Korean War, wrote and illustrated another book, *Studio: Asia.*

In the years between wars Groth continued to travel, has carried out assignments for *Look, Fortune, Sports Illustrated, Town and Country,* and has illustrated several classics including *War and Peace* and *Grapes of Wrath.*

Groth teaches at the Art Students League and the National Academy of Design; he also paints and exhibits. His pictures are in several collections, including The Museum of Modern Art, Library of Congress and National Gallery of Art. He is a member of the Society of Illustrators.

"Marine Patrol, North of the Han," illustration from *Studio: Asia, written and illustrated by Groth; The World Publishing Company, 1952.*

GUSTAVSON

LEALAND R. GUSTAVSON (1899-1966) was born in the Swedish community of Moline, Illinois. He studied nights for several years at the Chicago Art Institute while working in printing houses, advertising agencies and art services. He later resumed night classes studying under Walter Biggs and Harvey Dunn after moving East.

Although he illustrated for *The Saturday Evening Post, Collier's, McCall's* and many other periodicals, Gustavson was one of the mainstays of *Blue Book* magazine for many years and in his illustrations for the blood and thunder stories managed to "kill a staggering number of people in all the diabolical ways an author can dream up . . ."

Along with his interest in art, he was an ardent sportsman. For several years he played tournament badminton throughout the East, holding a national championship title and several New England titles. He was just as interested in golf — as a player and in illustrating the fine points of the game for books and magazine articles.

He exhibited widely and won many awards, taught at the Chicago Art Institute and Ray Commercial Art School in Chicago, was a member of the Salmagundi Club, the American Watercolor Society and the Academic Artists Association.

Illustration for one of the David Lamson stories in The Saturday Evening Post. © *1941 , 1969 by The Curtis Publishing Company.*

ROBERT GEORGE HARRIS (1911-   ), from boyhood in Kansas City, Missouri, always knew he wanted to be an artist. After study with Monte Crews at the Kansas City Art Institute, he went East via motorcycle, attended classes at the Grand Central School of Art with Harvey Dunn and the Art Students League under George Bridgman.

His first published art work was for Street and Smith's Western story magazine covers before he eventually graduated to the slicks. Harris became noted for his highly finished and sympathetic renderings of children and young love, which made him a natural choice for art editors of the women's magazines, such as *The Ladies' Home Journal, Good Housekeeping* and *McCall's.* Many national advertising accounts followed.

At present he lives in Arizona where he is spending full time with portrait painting commissions. Harris is a life member of the Society of Illustrators and a member of the Phoenix Art Museum which has held a one-man show of his portraiture.

Illustration for "The Child No One Wanted," published by The Saturday Evening Post, *October 26, 1957.* © *1957 by The Curtis Publishing Company.*

"Culture at Silver City," illustration for Cosmopolitan *magazine.*

"The Essex," illustration for *"The Savage Sea"* by Dale Shaw, True *magazine.*

"Hand Warmer." This painting is in the collection of the Cowboy Hall of Fame.

Tom Lovell

TOM LOVELL (1909-   ) is an intense, serious artist who drives himself to the point of perfection he seeks in his documentary approach to illustration; no detail of research is too small to be verified. His settings are painted with a conviction based on many years of experience in painting from nature.

Tom was born in New York City and was graduated with a B.F.A. from Syracuse University where he studied with Hibbard V.B. Kline. While still in college, he did his first illustrations for the pulp magazines and continued on in this field to develop his technical facility.

With this solid apprenticeship, Lovell was a fully developed artist when he appeared in the major national magazines, and has since worked for nearly all of them.

During World War II, Lovell served as a staff sergeant in the U.S. Marine Corps Reserve. Many of his paintings of Corps history are now in the permanent collection of the Marine Corps. Other institutions holding his work are The National Geographic Society, The Explorers Club of New York City, and the Permian Basin Petroleum Museum in Midland, Texas.

He is a member of the American Watercolor Society, the Society of Illustrators — he won a Gold Medal in their 1964 annual exhibition and was elected into the Illustrators Hall of Fame in 1974.

Several years ago Lovell moved to Santa Fe, New Mexico, and he has been a regular exhibitor in the annual shows of Western artists held in Arizona, Texas and Oklahoma. He was the recipient of the *Prix de West* awarded by the National Academy of Western Art and the Gold Medal in Oil from the National Cowboy Hall of Fame. A member of the Cowboy Artists of America since 1975, he also has won silver and gold medals in their exhibitions.

 Hughes—

GEORGE HUGHES (1907-   ) conveys a feeling of realism and authenticity in his work by careful selection, and by emphasis on the essential characteristics of his subject matter.

Hughes is a native New Yorker and studied in New York at the Art Students League and at the National Academy of Design. Some of his early work included fashion drawing, and there was a stint as a special designer in the automobile field in Detroit. Back in the East, he now divides his year between Arlington, Vermont, and on Long Island in Wainscott, New York.

For many years Hughes was one of the most prolific painters of *Saturday Evening Post* covers; in addition, he has done many editorial illustrations for the *Post* and other publications, including *McCall's, Woman's Day, American, Reader's Digest* and *Cosmopolitan* magazines.

Also a painter, he has exhibited at the Pennsylvania Academy, The Detroit Museum and the Art Institute of Chicago. In recent years he has restricted his work to portraiture.

"Just Engaged," cover illustration for The Saturday Evening Post, *January 22, 1949.* © *1949, 1977 The Curtis Publishing Company. Collection of Judy and Alan Goffman.*

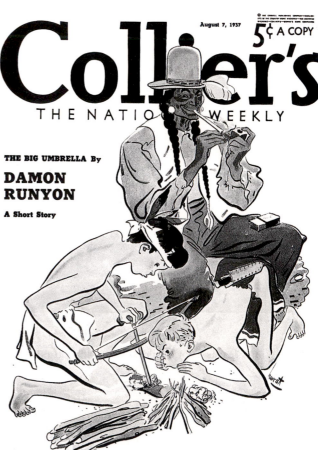

Hurst

Great good humor was the most characteristic trait of EARL OLIVER HURST (1895-1958), as an individual and in his illustration.

Hurst's illustrations look very facile and as though dashed off, in keeping with their spirit of fun. However, they are very soundly based on thorough preliminary preparation. In fact, for some time it was his practice to do every illustration twice to see how much more freedom and excitement he could add to the first rendition.

Hurst was born in Buffalo, New York, and attended the Albright Art School in Buffalo, the Cleveland School of Art, John Huntington School of Art; studied under Pruett Carter at the Grand Central School of Art and Boardman Robinson at the Art Students League in New York.

He exhibited often and his work received many awards. He wrote and illustrated several juvenile books and was a contributing editor of *American Artist* magazine, conducting a regular monthly column, "The Hurst Page," with information and interviews pertaining to commercial art and illustration.

Hurst's telegraphic style was ideal for cover designs, and he made them regularly for Collier's *for many years. This is a typical example, published in 1937.*

"A Fresh Kill." Collection of Mr. and Mrs. Fausto Yturria.

KUHN

ROBERT F. KUHN (1920-   ) is more interested in drawing and painting animals than any other subject and always has been. As a boy he sketched animals continuously, later frequenting zoos to draw them from life whenever possible. In his youth, Kuhn's idol and mentor was Paul Bransom, who offered him a great deal of personal encouragement and criticism.

Kuhn was born in Buffalo, New York, and studied at Pratt Institute in Brooklyn. Among the guest lecturers who especially influenced him there were Harold Von Schmidt and Paul Brown.

To further his study of animals under their natural conditions, Kuhn has traveled extensively in the wilderness areas of Newfoundland, Western Canada, Alaska and other parts of the United States, with several months in Africa.

His first illustrations appeared in *Field and Stream,* followed by publication in *True, Outdoor Life, Reader's Digest* and other magazines. He has also illustrated numerous books, painted for calendars and advertisements. His own book, *The Animal Art of Bob Kuhn,* was published by North Light in 1973.

Kuhn has also exhibited his wildlife paintings, winning several awards including First and Second prizes in the National Academy of Western Art annual shows and First prize, purchase award, at the Wildlife Art Show. His pictures are included in the collections of the National Cowboy Hall of Fame, the Wildlife World Museum in Monument, Colorado, the Genesee County Museum, Rochester, New York, and many private collections.

ROBERT E. LOUGHEED (1910-1982) was born on a farm in Ontario, Canada, and from childhood on his subjects were animals, all kinds of animals, but particularly horses.

His first art training came through a correspondence course in commercial design which he worked at assiduously during the long Canadian winters. With this start, he got a job in the art department of an engraving and printing firm in Toronto; later he worked for the *Toronto Star Weekly* doing news illustrations.

From there, Lougheed headed for New York, supported himself by doing cover paintings for the pulp magazines and studied at the Art Students League under Frank Vincent DuMond.

Lougheed then divided his time between illustrating for publishers such as *True, The National Geographic, Reader's Digest,* and Brown & Bigelow, and painting for exhibitions and galleries. He regularly painted animals in their natural habitats, traveling north of the Arctic Circle, throughout Canada, Alaska and other parts of the United States to observe them.

Lougheed was a member of the Animal Artists Society, the Salmagundi Club, The Cowboy Artists and the National Academy of Western Art where his art won many awards.

Pony Express Rider, "Deep in Buffalo Country." Collection of the Oklahoma City Chamber of Commerce.

In a prophetic story, "Murder in the Sky," by Frank Harvey, an unarmed plane is shot down by M.I.G. fighters. Published by The Saturday Evening Post; © *1955, 1983 by The Curtis Publishing Company.*

Opening illustration for the serialized novel, Ramrod, *by Luke Short in* The Saturday Evening Post, *March 27, 1943.* © *1943, 1971 by The Curtis Publishing Company.*

FRED LUDEKENS (1900-1982) was born in Huoneme and was a third generation Californian. He grew up in Victoria, British Columbia, and during those years made several trips to Alaska.

His only art training was a night class under Otis Shepard at the University of California Extension.

Ludekens worked for the Foster and Kleiser outdoor advertising agency in San Francisco, then free-lanced for a time, and later became art director for the San Francisco office of Lord and Thomas. This gave him an insight into advertising art from the business point of view which helped him eventually to become one of the best advertising illustrators in the country.

A commission to illustrate a book about his boyhood country, *Ghost Town,* led *The Saturday Evening Post* to assign him a Western serial story. The success of these pictures thus launched his second career as an editorial illustrator, and he pursued both, later adding another top position as co-creative director of Foote, Cone and Belding. He also, with Albert Dorne, founded the Famous Artists School in Westport, Connecticut, and was Chairman of the Board of Directors prior to his death.

The illustrations of PERRY PETERSON (1908-1958) were done with special flair and apparent spontaneity. Peterson took pride in creating this effect and worked hard in the preparatory stages to achieve it. Years of training in art studios gave him a complete technical command of the watercolor medium which he used with strong three-dimensional effect.

Peterson was born in Minneapolis, Minnesota, and his first art education was through the Federal Schools' correspondence course, followed by brief attendance in the evening at the Chicago Art Institute. His early art jobs included catalog illustration for Montgomery Ward in Chicago, automobile renderings in Detroit and advertising drawings for the Byron Musser Studio in New York.

Soon after his first illustrations for *Liberty* magazine, published in 1942, he received assignments for stories in *Good Housekeeping, Woman's Home Companion, Collier's, The Saturday Evening Post* and others, until his untimely death from burns received in an accidental fire in his New York studio.

Illustration for "Stolen Goods" by Clarence Budington Kelland in The Saturday Evening Post. © *1949, 1977 by The Curtis Publishing Company.*

Illustration involving Inspector Chafik of the Baghdad Police, in one of a series of stories for Collier's *magazine, published June 17, 1950.*

JOHN PIKE, N.A. (1911-1979) was a lifelong student of the watercolor medium despite some diversion along the way at such varied jobs as theatre designing, jewelry making, and as director of advertising for a Jamaican rum company.

Born in Winthrop, Massachusetts, Pike studied in Provincetown with Charles Hawthorne and Richard Miller. He next spent five years in Jamaica, W.I., before returning to this country where his one-man shows and illustration for magazines made a full-time art career possible. He illustrated not only for many magazines but also for advertising accounts, and exhibited widely.

In addition, Pike served in the Combat Art section, Corps of Engineers, heading a unit to record the United States occupation of Korea; also made paintings for the United States Air Force Historical Foundation in France, Germany, Greenland, South America, Formosa and Japan.

Pike's work is represented in many collections, public and private; he won numerous prizes, including the "Watercolor U.S.A." Award, and the National Academy Hallgarten Prize. He was a member of the American Watercolor Society, the Philadelphia Watercolor Club, the Salmagundi Club, Woodstock Art Association, Grand Central Art Galleries, the Society of Illustrators, and the National Academy of Design.

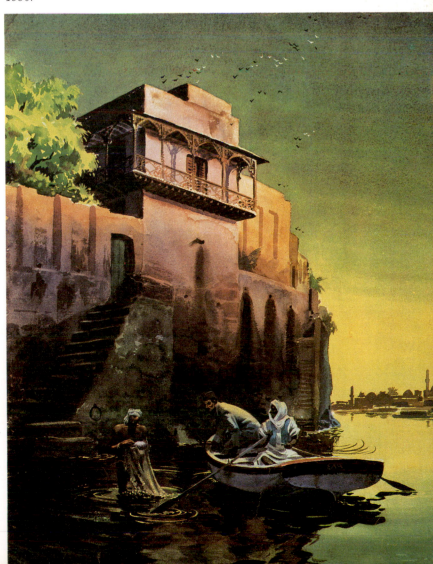

Prins

BEN KIMBERLY PRINS (1904-1980) was born in Leiden, Holland, but was brought to the United States at the age of one. Reared in Brooklyn, he was a graduate of Pratt Institute and also studied at the Art Students League and the Grand Central School of Art. His teachers included Arthur Guptill, Ernest Watson, George Bridgman and Dean Cornwell.

He began his career as an art director at Batten, Barton, Durstine & Osborn Inc., then worked at the Dorland International Agency, and Lennen & Mitchell. By 1939, he was free-lancing and his drawings for an *Illustrated History of the Railroad* won him a Gold Medal at the Art Directors Club show in 1940.

Prins soon thereafter began to do magazine illustration for publications such as *Collier's, Woman's Home Companion, Pictorial Review* and *The Saturday Evening Post* for which he also painted a number of covers.

Prins was a member of the Society of Illustrators, The Art Directors Club of New York and the Wilton Historical Society.

Illustration for The Saturday Evening Post *story,* "Unwanted," *by Kingsley Tufts.* © *1953,1981 by The Curtis Publishing Company.*

Ray Prohaska

RAY PROHASKA (1901-1981) was born in Mulo, Yugoslavia, and came to America at the age of eight. He studied at the California School of Fine Arts in San Francisco, and followed this with several years of commercial work on the West Coast and in Chicago.

He came to New York in 1929 and obtained his first illustration manuscripts from *Delineator* and *Woman's Home Companion.* Prohaska's contemporary style and careful characterizations soon won him a long list of other magazines as clients, and many advertising commissions as well.

Along with his illustration, he also painted for exhibition and won several prizes, including the Hallmark Award 1949, Audubon Medal 1954, John Marin Memorial Award 1962, M. Grumbacher First Prize 1958, and Society of Illustrators' Gold Medal 1963.

Prohaska served as president of the Society of Illustrators in 1959-60, taught at the Art Students League in 1961 followed by the post of Artist in Residence at Washington and Lee University in Lexington, Virginia. He also painted a large mural depicting the communications media for the Department of Journalism and Communications at the University.

His book, *A Basic Course in Design,* published by North Light Publications, has been in print for many years.

Illustration for "The Cat-Eyed Woman," *published by* The Saturday Evening Post. © *1953, 1981 by The Curtis Publishing Company.*

Henry C. Pitz

HENRY CLARENCE PITZ, A.N.A. (1895-1976) was
an outstanding performer in several fields, including illustrating for magazines and books, teaching and lecturing,
writing on art subjects, painting and exhibiting.

His talents appeared early; while still in high school in
Philadelphia he won a scholarship to study at the
Philadelphia Museum School of Art and then went on to
the Spring Garden Institute. Among his teachers were
Walter Everett and Maurice Bower.

Although Pitz experimented with, and worked in, almost every medium, he had a special affinity for line
drawing and book illustration. He illustrated more than
160 books as well as for a whole range of magazines from
The Saturday Evening Post to *St. Nicholas.*

Among his many popular art books were: *Pen, Brush and
Ink, The Practice of Illustration, Drawing Trees, Ink Drawing
Techniques* and *Illustrating Children's Books.*

Pitz exhibited nationally and internationally, winning
awards too numerous to list here. His work is represented
in many public collections, including the Library of
Congress in Washington, D.C. and the Philadelphia
Museum of Art.

Pitz also served as Director of the illustration course,
Philadelphia Museum College of Art, Visiting Lecturer
and Instructor, and Contributing Editor of *American Artist*
magazine.

*Illustration for one of the legends of Charlemagne, date of publication
not known. Collection of Bernard Hrico.*

PAUL RABUT

PAUL RABUT (1914-1983) characteristically immersed
himself so thoroughly in research for his illustrations that
he became an authority on the subject matter of his assignments. This led to his long-time interest in United States
history, in logging, in Northwest Indian culture and artifacts, as well as other primitive art: Oceanic, pre-
Columbian, and especially African wood-carvings and
masks. He was a consultant for collectors and galleries on
the subject of primitive art and had one of the finest private
collections in the country.

Rabut attended the College of the City of New York, the
Art School of the National Academy of Design, the Grand
Central Art School and the Art Students League; his
teachers included Jules Gotlieb, Harvey Dunn, Ivan
Olinsky and Lewis Daniel.

His first break came when one of his early story illustrations for *American Girl* magazine won the Art Directors
Club Medal in their annual exhibition in 1942. This led
directly to commissions from *The Saurday Evening Post* and
other major magazines. Subsequently he won several additional Art Directors Club awards for both editorial and
advertising illustrations, and his work was selected for the
State Department advertising-art traveling exhibition to
Europe and South America in 1952. He exhibited widely
and is represented in the permanent collection of the U.S.
Medical Museum, Washington, D.C.

Illustration for The Saturday Evening Post. © *1945,1973
by The Curtis Publishing Company.*

Props play a large role in Parker's illustrations, not only supporting the period and setting of the story, but sometimes dictating the composition as in his use here of the antique sketching easel and potted plant to tie the figures together. Illustrated for "The Rich Woman," The Ladies' Home Journal. © 1947, 1975 by The Curtis Publishing Company. Collection of Mr. and Mrs. Benjamin Eisenstat.

The work of ALFRED PARKER (1906-   ) is so varied and inventive that it is difficult in this space to choose pictures that represent him fully or summarize his career.

From the time of his arrival in New York from St. Louis in the mid-'thirties, Parker's illustrations excited and beguiled public and publishers alike. As his popularity grew, so did the number of his imitators, and the Al Parker approach became the dominant one in the magazines. What set his work apart from his imitators, however, was not only his impeccable taste, but the originality of his thinking. Other artists were always one step behind him.

Each of Parker's pictures is unique in composition and color. He has used all of the media, and combinations of them, from children's crayons to acrylics. His versatility is such that he once illustrated a whole issue of *Cosmopolitan* magazine by himself using a different name and style for each story.

In 1939 Parker did a mother-daughter cover for *The Ladies' Home Journal* which was immensely successful, creating the demand for a long series that followed and setting a whole new style for mother-daughter fashions.

A jazz buff, Parker had played saxophone in a band on a Mississippi river boat and participated in many combination jam sessions and sketching trips to service hospitals during World War II.

Over the years he has won more than twenty-five gold medals and awards of excellence in Art Directors Club and Society of Illustrators' shows. He is a past president of the Westport Artists and was elected to the Society of Illustrators Hall of Fame in 1965.

Parker now lives in Carmel, California, and with the demise of many of the magazines, his output of illustrations is curtailed. However, he has continued to do occasional assignments for publications, such as *Sports Illustrated* and *Boy's Life.* One such commission was a series of paintings of the Grand Prix auto race of Europe for *Sports Illustrated.*

"Ben Franklin, First Postmaster General, Handing Mail to Postrider, Philadelphia, 1775." Painted as an advertising illustration for the Continental Distilling Corporation, Philadelphia, Pennsylvania.

FRANK REILLY

FRANK JOSEPH REILLY, A.N.A. (1906-1967) was a great teacher. In addition to the qualities which made him an outstanding illustrator, Reilly had a scientist's sense of order and analytical acumen combined with a missionary's enthusiasm for his subject. Reilly was Bridgman's successor at the Art Students League in New York and for over twenty-nine years, his classes were the largest there. He then founded his own school in New York City, the Frank Reilly School of Art.

Frank received his own instruction at the League under George Bridgman and Frank Vincent DuMond. He later worked as Dean Cornwell's assistant on several mural projects, and it was Cornwell who influenced him most, both as an artist and teacher.

Reilly illustrated for many editorial and advertising assignments. Outstanding were those for Pennsylvania Railroad and Continental Distilling Corporation. He also designed a 63-foot mosaic mural for the Bronx High School of Science.

He was an associate member of the National Academy of Design, painter-member of the Art Commission of New York City, member of American Artists' Professional League, Allied Artists, Century Association, National Society of Mural Painters, Salmagundi Club, Artists and Writers Guild, Art Students League and the Society of Illustrators.

Walter Richards

WALTER DuBOIS RICHARDS (1907-   ) worked in black-and-white for many years as an advertising artist; his illustrations are characterized by a mastery of values whether in monochrome or full color.

Richards was born in Penfield, Ohio, and was graduated from the Cleveland School of Art. He first worked in the famous Sundblom studio in Chicago, later for the Tranquillini studio in Cleveland where he met and worked with Stevan Dohanos. Next, Richards moved to New York where he joined the Charles E. Cooper studio and then free-lanced as an illustrator for most of the magazines and many national advertising accounts.

Through the years he has continued to experiment and to paint for national and international shows in watercolor and print-making. He is an active member of the American Watercolor Society, Society of Illustrators, Connecticut Watercolor Society, Westport Artists, and the Fairfield Watercolor Group. His work has won many awards, including four consecutive first prizes in lithography at the Cleveland Museum of Art, 1935-38.

Advertising illustration for Pontiac Motor Division, General Motors Corporation, published in 1945.

Nicholas F. Riley

NICHOLAS F. RILEY (1900-1944) taught many hundreds of students of illustration in his years as a teacher at Pratt Institute. His thorough grasp of fundamentals and his gentle courtesy in presenting them won the respect of his classes and conveyed to many a lasting sense of idealism for the art of painting and illustration.

Riley was born in Brooklyn and was graduated from Pratt Institute. This was followed by two years of study with M. Scott in Paris. One of his portrait paintings was selected and hung in the Paris Grand Salon in 1925.

He began his teaching career at Pratt in 1927, soon after his return to America, and continued there until the time of his death. In the meantime, he also contributed many illustrations to *The Saturday Evening Post, Woman's Home Companion, Good Housekeeping, Redbook* and other magazines.

He was a member of the Salmagundi Club, the Lotus Club and the Society of Illustrators.

Illustration for The Saturday Evening Post *story, "Don't Tell Your Mother" by Kenneth Payson Kempton.* © *1940, 1968 by The Curtis Publishing Company.*

DICK SARGENT

RICHARD SARGENT (1911-1978) did many cover paintings for *The Saturday Evening Post.* As in the example here, they are characterized by their good humor and insight into human frailties. He also illustrated for *Fortune, Woman's Day, American, Photoplay* and *Collier's* magazines.

Sargent, who was born in Moline, Illinois, received his art education at the Corcoran School of Art and Phillips Memorial Gallery in Washington, D.C. He also worked with Ben Shahn.

His pictures were exhibited in many parts of the United States, including New York City, Washington, D.C. and San Francisco, California, as well as abroad. He was a member of the Society of Illustrators in New York, and for many years lived and painted in Spain.

"A Mother's Day Greeting," presented by Sargent as a distinctly mixed blessing in this colorful cover, The Saturday Evening Post. © *1957 by The Curtis Publishing Company.*

"Slave Ship," painted for Life *magazine, September 3, 1956. Collection of Les Mansfield.*

Robert Riggs

ROBERT RIGGS, N.A. (1896-1970) was a painter and lithographer of monumental compositions, yet achieved his effects through meticulous means. In lithography, he worked from black to white, picking out detail with a scraper blade. For color, he used dry tempera mixed with mastic varnish and alcohol, a medium that dried immediately and allowed him to paint over successive layers if necessary.

Riggs was born in Decatur, Illinois, and studied for two years at James Milliken University in Illinois. He followed this with a year of study at the Art Students League in New York, terminated by two years in the Army during World War I. Following the armistice, he stayed overseas for several months to study at the Académie Julian in Paris.

After his return to the United States, Riggs spent several years sketching for the N.W. Ayer & Son advertising agency, and produced many excellent advertising illustrations. Over the years, he was a consistent prize-winner in the annual Art Directors Club shows.

His simultaneous efforts in fine arts contributed to his success in both fields. His favorite lithographic subjects were the circus and prize fighting; many of his prints are in museum collections, including the Brooklyn Museum, Library of Congress and the Dallas Museum of Fine Arts.

Riggs collected a great many primitive artifacts during extended trips to Europe, North Africa, India and Thailand, and part of his studio and living quarters constituted a personal museum.

"Clown Alley," a typical Riggs lithograph of one of his favorite subjects.

Les li Saalburg

LESLIE SAALBURG (1897-1974) was temperamentally of the old school. He admired the elegance of fine old interiors, correct attire, good manners and the fine craftsmanship of artisans unhurried by modern pressures of mass production.

Saalburg's work beautifully recreated this air of the genteel past in his renderings of spacious drawing rooms, restaurant interiors; antique and classic automobiles.

In his approach to picture making, Saalburg also preferred the classic method of sketching directly from the objects or settings, independent of photography for facts unless absolutely necessary. His first sketches were, in effect, shorthand notes with additional details drawn to indicate a section of paneling, a color of fabric or design of a rug. These were then the factual basis for a full-scale working drawing in which perspective was completely determined, and all details carefully constructed. This working drawing was then traced onto drawing paper for final rendering. The scale of the illustrations was small, usually as near to the printed size as practical, with the result that most of the richness of the original was retained in reproduction.

Saalburg had only three months of instruction at the Art Students League but rebelled against it, preferring to learn to draw and paint by continuously practicing by himself. He also learned much through employment in various art studios until experienced enough to become a free-lance illustrator. He was associated longest with *Esquire* magazine for whom he painted several "portfolios" of special subjects, but also worked for *Collier's, Vogue, Town and Country, Vanity Fair, Holiday* and many publications abroad.

Illustration for Esquire *magazine depicting the former interior of the famous Delmonico's Restaurant in New York City.*

schwinn

BARBARA E. SCHWINN (1907-   ), later Mrs. F. Bertram Jordan, wanted to be a fashion designer from the time she was twelve, when she first cut out and made her own dresses. To prepare for this, she studied at the Parsons School of Design in New York and at its branch in Paris.

Her first work after graduation was making accessory and fashion drawings for department stores; in a short time she was able to obtain top assignments from Lord & Taylor, Macy's and Best & Co. This was followed by a period of drawing for continuity strips and, later, cover designs and magazine illustrations for such publications as *Collier's, Cosmopolitan, American, The Saturday Evening Post* and *The Ladies' Home Journal.* Many of her illustrations have also appeared in European periodicals.

She has recently turned to portraiture, with an international clientele, including Queen Sirikit of Thailand, Princess Grace of Monaco, Deborah Kerr, Conrad Hilton and Maurice Pate, former Director of UNICEF. She also completed a painting of Princess Margaret of Britain, who had not previously posed for an American artist.

Illustration for the story, "Stowaway," in Cosmopolitan *magazine, July, 1953. It is interesting to note her use of the Coles Phillips' "Fadeaway" technique here.*

This illustration was one of a series of Sickles' visualizations of the Crete Invasion by the Germans during World War II for Life *magazine.* © *1940, 1968 Time, Inc.*

Western illustration for Reader's Digest. *Collection of Illustration House.*

"Remember the Alamo" by Sigman Byrd was illustrated by Sickles in a basic line and tone technique with color washes added; published by The Saturday Evening Post. © 1948, 1976 by The Curtis Publishing Company.

Noel Sickles

NOEL SICKLES (1911-1982) was a master in the use of line. His brush work was direct and spare, each stroke reduced to the most expressive minimum. Although he used color very effectively, it was usually subordinate to the drawing — often applied in thin washes over the basic black-and-white brush rendering.

Sickles' approach grew logically from his early career as a newspaper artist and cartoonist. He established a whole new style of cartooning in his adventure strip, "Scorchy Smith," by indicating full light and shade in his black-and-white drawings.

Seeking to develop further as an illustrator, Sickles abandoned the strip and began to accept advertising and editorial commissions. Among these was a notable series of World War II drawings for *Life* magazine. These resulted in his being placed under contract by both the War and Navy

Departments in Washington to do similar illustrations for instruction in the Armed Services, much of his work highly confidential.

After the war, Sickles resumed his free-lance illustration career with special emphasis on his interest in American historical subjects. He made many outstanding illustrations for *The Saturday Evening Post, Life, This Week* and the Reader's Digest condensed books.

Sickles was elected to the Society of Illustrators Hall of Fame in 1983.

One of Sickles' expressive illustrations from the Life *magazine publication of Ernest Hemingway's* The Old Man and the Sea. *The strength and dignity of the drawings in line and halftone are a perfect complement to the spirit of the manuscript. Noel Sickles for* Life *magazine,* © *1952, 1980 Time, Inc.*
Collection of the Society of Illustrators
Museum of American Illustration.

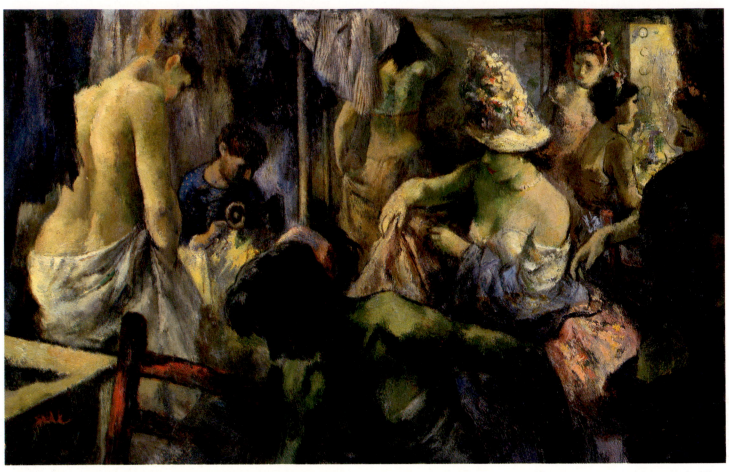

"Backstage." This illustration for Esquire *magazine in December, 1951, "A Show They Never Forgot," clearly reflects the influence of Degas on Stahl's work at that time. Collection of Beverly and Ray Sacks.*

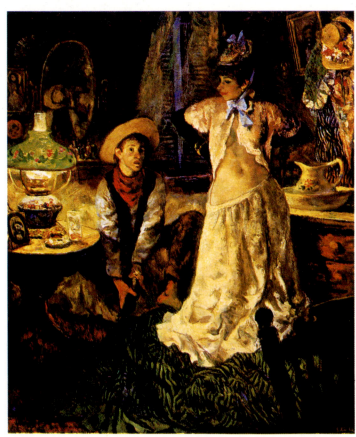

"The Green Lamp," recent painting on a Western theme.

"Lace Hat," early Stahl illustration for Woman's Home Companion.

Stahl illustrated several serials relating to the fictional English Naval Commodore Hornblower. Published by The Saturday Evening Post.
© *1946, 1974 by The Curtis Publishing Company.*

Stahl

BENJAMIN ALBERT STAHL (1910-   ) as a boy, was encouraged to become an artist by his grandmother who took him to visit the Chicago Art Institute and the Marshall Field Art Galleries. At seventeen, he got a job as an errand boy and apprentice in an art studio, and within five years had landed a job as an artist with one of the top studios in Chicago.

In 1937, *The Saturday Evening Post* editors saw one of his advertising paintings of a seascape and invited him to illustrate a sea story. This was the beginning of his career in illustration, in which he worked for nearly all of the magazines and for many national advertising campaigns.

Stahl's many other activities have included a series of illustrations for the Bible; a book he has written and illustrated, *Blackbeard's Ghost,* published by Houghton, Mifflin and later made into a movie by the Disney Studios with Peter Ustinov as Blackbeard. Several years ago, Stahl built a Museum of the Cross in Sarasota, Florida. He designed the building and painted the large mural-size Stations of the Cross around the museum walls. At the height of its fame, the entire collection of paintings was stolen and never recovered.

The artist also created an educational TV series on the art of painting called "Journey into Art with Ben Stahl." It consisted of twenty-six half-hours of painting demonstrations and lectures by the artist. Aired by hundreds of ETV stations both here and abroad, it is still available through the South Carolina ETV Network which produced the series, and on Home Box Office.

Stahl has lived for protracted lengths of time abroad, including three years in southern Spain. Currently he lives in Mexico. This Mexican influence has resulted in a renewed interest in the Old West and much of his current work is on that theme. Recently, he exhibited in the invitational Cowboy Hall of Fame show and the Settlers West Gallery.

Stahl has taught at the Chicago Academy of Fine Arts and at the American Academy of Art in Chicago. He also was one of the founding faculty members of the Famous Artists Schools in Westport, Connecticut.

In 1979 he was elected to the Society of Illustrators Hall of Fame.

Cover illustration for The Saturday Evening Post. © *1962 by The Curtis Publishing Company.*

Vignette in charcoal for The Saturday Evening Post *illustration.* © *1939 , 1967 by The Curtis Publishing Company.*

AMOS SEWELL (1901-1983) had a special empathy for children and also particularly enjoyed doing homespun, rural subjects. These special gifts were ideally combined in the illustrations he made for a series of stories about Babe, Little Joe, Big Joe, and Uncle Pete by R. Ross Annett that ran for over twenty years in *The Saturday Evening Post.*

Sewell was born in San Francisco and studied nights at the California School of Fine Arts, working days in a bank. After some years of this he decided to try his luck as an illustrator in the East. To get there, he shipped out as a working hand on a lumber boat going by way of the Panama Canal.

In New York he studied at the Art Students League and at the Grand Central School of Art. Among his teachers were Guy Pène DuBois, Julian Levi and Harvey Dunn. At the same time he bagan to do black-and-white dry-brush illustrations for the pulp magazines.

His first major manuscript was illustrated for the *Country Gentleman* in 1937; next came *The Saturday Evening Post,* for which he subsequently also painted many covers. This led to commissions from the other national magazines. Sewell also illustrated for many major advertisers, and his work won awards from the Art Directors Clubs of New York and Cleveland, were exhibited at the Society of Illustrators and in traveling exhibits both here and abroad.

The Saturday Evening Post *story,* "Limbs is a Flourish Word" *by Lucretia Penny.* © *1940,1968 by The Curtis Publishing Company.*

Edward Shenton

EDWARD SHENTON (1895-1977) specialized in black-and-white illustration and managed to exploit a great variety of value and textures from the line medium. His drawings, although quite realistic, are also stylized and decorative as shown here.

Shenton was born in Pottstown, Pennsylvania, studied at the Pennsylvania Museum School of Industrial Art and the Pennsylvania Academy of the Fine Arts, where his teachers included Thornton Oakley, George Harding and Henry McCarter. He won the Lee Prize in 1922, and the Cresson Traveling Scholarships in 1923-24 which enabled him to study further in Paris.

Although Shenton's work appeared in *The Saturday Evening Post, Collier's* and *Reader's Digest,* his line technique was ideally suited for books, and he illustrated for many book publishers including Scribner's, Doubleday, Random House, Harcourt Brace and W.W. Norton.

In addition, Shenton had an active career in editing and writing. One of his earliest jobs was as an editor for the Penn Publishing Company, and he also served as a part-time editor for Macrae Smith. His short stories have appeared in *The Saturday Evening Post, Collier's, Scribner's* and *Cosmopolitan,* and he wrote and illustrated several books. His wife, Barbara Webster, also wrote a number of books about Pennsylvania Country life, which he illustrated charmingly.

His mural projects included a wall of the Chester County Court House in West Chester, Pennsylvania, and two large facing panels in the Chapel of the War Memorial Cemetery at Saint-James in Brittany, France.

In addition to all of these assignments, Shenton also taught classes at the Moore College of Art in Philadelphia and at the Pennsylvania Academy of the Fine Arts.

Illustration for "The Bear" by William Faulkner, published by The Saturday Evening Post. © *1942, 1970 by The Curtis Publishing Company.*

Varady

FREDRIC VARADY (1908-   ) was born in Budapest and attended the Royal Hungarian Academy of Art there. Upon graduation he began to do movie posters, worked on theatre set designs and made fashion drawings.

He left Hungary in 1927 and worked at a succession of art jobs from painting lampshades to murals in private houses in Istanbul. He did fashion drawing and suit designing in Paris and in Berlin, before coming to the United States to establish himself as a free-lance fashion artist.

Varady's dramatic flair for drawing and his meticulous rendering made a very favorable impression on magazine art editors, and he obtained his first manuscript to illustrate from *American* magazine in 1939. This was soon followed by commissions from most of the major magazines, including *Cosmopolitan, Good Housekeeping, McCall's, Collier's, Redbook, Today's Woman* and *The Saturday Evening Post.*

Varady now does some men's fashion illustration, but spends more time painting large abstractions for exhibition.

Illustration for a Cosmopolitan *magazine story.*

Poster for Community War Fund (W.W. II).

"Slayer in the Night," illustration for The Saturday Evening Post. © 1943, 1971 *The Curtis Publishing Company.*

"Rounding the Horn," painted for John Morrell & Co. Collection of the State of California.

"Horse Race," illustration for Cosmopolitan *magazine, 1933. Collection of the Society of Illustrators Museum of American Illustration.*

HAROLD VON SCHMIDT

HAROLD VON SCHMIDT (1893-1982) grew up in the West a generation after Remington and Russell, but had a close kinship with them and the old West throughout his painting career. A native Californian, Von Schmidt was orphaned at five and reared by his grandfather who had been a Forty-niner. His grandfather's stories, together with his own experiences as a construction worker, lumberjack and cowhand gave him an authentic insight into the earlier era.

He studied at the San Francisco Art Institute and the California College of Arts and Crafts, also with Worth Ryder and Maynard Dixon. His first art work was as an art director for Foster & Kleiser, followed by illustrating for *Sunset* magazine.

In 1924 Von Schmidt came East to study further with Harvey Dunn. He acknowledged the tremendous effect that Dunn's teaching had on his career. It was Dunn who taught him to paint the epic rather than the incident, and he always kept to this high standard.

He was an ardent athlete all his life, was a member of the American Olympic Rugby Football team at Antwerp, Belgium, in 1920. He also played baseball, hockey, and coached the local High School football team. Feeling that an artist should also be active in civic affairs, he served as a Selectman, Town of Westport, Connecticut, for eight years, on the Board of Finance, Police Commission and Public Library Board.

During World War I, Von Schmidt did posters for the U.S. Navy; during World War II he was an invited artist-correspondent for the U.S. Air Force, European Theatre of Operations, and artist-correspondent for King Features Syndicate in the Pacific Theatre of Operations.

Twelve of his paintings depicting the westward trek and the Gold Rush of 1849 hang in the Governor's office in Sacramento, California; five Civil War paintings are in the permanent collection of the United States Military Academy at West Point, and many others are in private collections.

Von Schmidt was a life trustee of the Artists Guild, New York; president of the Society of Illustrators, 1938-41; member and officer of the American Indian Defense Association; president of the Westport Artists, 1950-51; and a founding member of the Famous Artists Schools in Westport, Connecticut. He was awarded the first Gold Medal by the trustees of the National Cowboy Hall of Fame in 1968 and was elected to the Society of Illustrators Hall of Fame in 1959.

247

LYND WARD

LYND WARD, A.N.A. (1905-   ) first came to prominence as an artist for his woodcut novel, *God's Man*. He eventually produced five others, including *Mad Man's Drum, Song without Words,* and *Vertigo.* (In 1974, these six novels were republished in one volume by Harry Abrams, Inc., titled *Story Teller without Words.*) These books established Ward as an original talent; magazine and book publishers kept him busy until his retirement in 1975.

Much of his work has been in wood engraving, but to keep his outlook fresh, he experimented with lithography, pen or brush and ink, watercolors, oils, casein and other media.

Ward had prepared for his career thoroughly, with four years at Columbia University studying theory of design, art history and teaching methods. This was followed by a year as a special student at the State Academy for Graphic Arts in Leipzig, Germany, where his instructors were Hans Mueller, Alois Kolp and George Mathey.

He has illustrated many of the classics for the Limited Editions and Heritage Book Clubs; also collaborated with his author-wife, May McNeer, and produced some of his finest illustrations. A member of the Society of Illustrators and the Society of American Graphic Arts, he has won many awards, including the Caldecott Medal, John Taylor Arms Memorial Prize, Library of Congress Award and Limited Editions Club Silver Medal.

Illustration for Collier's *magazine.*

Welch

JACK WELCH (1905-   ) is a tall Texan from Cleburne. He went through public schools in Temple, Texas, took the W.L. Evans correspondence course in cartooning, and did a short turn at Southern Methodist University illustrating yearbooks. This was enough to launch him as a newspaper artist; he worked for papers in Texas, California, Seattle, Chicago, Philadelphia and New York.

The next logical step was as an advertising agency sketch man; he spent several years doing sketches and comprehensive drawings for advertising layouts. His sense of humor and feeling for action, freely rendered, made him a natural for drawing children, and he began to do the "finishes" for advertisers such as Keds, Jell-O, Pullman, and Traveler's Insurance.

These illustrations, in turn, brought his work to the attention of *The Saturday Evening Post* for which he did a number of memorable covers; then other magazines, including *Family Circle* and *Woman's Day.*

His work has brought Welch several awards in annual New York Art Directors Club shows and for outdoor advertising art.

The Saturday Evening Post *cover, needing no caption.*
© 1953, 1981 by The Curtis Publishing Company.

Illustration for Redbook *magazine, October, 1956.*

"A Girl to Marry," published in Redbook *magazine, December, 1958.*

JON WHITCOMB (1906-   ) has made his name synonymous with pictures of young love and glamorous, beautiful women. During World War II, a series of illustrations for advertisements he created on the theme, "Back Home for Keeps," became a pin-up fad for women deprived of their husbands or sweethearts.

Jon was born in Weatherford, Oklahoma, and reared in Manitowoc, Wisconsin. He attended Ohio Wesleyan University and was graduated from Ohio State where he did pictures for the school publications and worked during the summer painting posters for a theatre in Cleveland.

This was excellent training ground for Whitcomb. Although he had majored in English with an ambition to write, Jon switched to art classes. After graduation he was able to obtain work in a series of studios doing travel and theatre posters, as well as general advertising illustrations.

In 1934, he moved on to New York to combine studio work with free-lance illustration. His first illustrations were for *Collier's,* followed by *Good Housekeeping,* and then the others in succession as Whitcomb's pretty girls began to attract enthusiastic readership.

His career was interrupted by World War II when he was commissioned a Lieutenant, j.g. in the Navy. His assignments varied from mine-sweeping duty off the East coast, to the Public Relations Department in Washington, to the Pacific as a combat artist with the invasions of Tinian, Saipan, and Peleliu. After hospitalization for tropical infec-

Cover portrait of Mrs. John F. Kennedy for Cosmopolitan *magazine, April, 1961.*

tions, he was discharged in 1945 and resumed his art career.

Whitcomb's writing ability became useful when he began to do a monthly series of sketches and articles about motion picture stars for *Cosmopolitan,* called "On Location with Jon Whitcomb." He has also written several short stories, two children's books about poodles, *Coco,* and *Pom Pom's Christmas,* and a book about feminine glamour, *All About Girls.*

Illustration for Cosmopolitan *magazine, "Before the Crime." Collection of Mr. and Mrs. Mark Baron.*

Mortimer Wilson Jr

Illustration for American *magazine.*

MORTIMER WILSON, Jr. (1906-   ) from Lincoln, Nebraska, has a rich, sumptuous style of painting, based in part on his training as a portraitist. His father, conductor of the Atlanta Symphony and a composer, had wanted his son to follow a musical career, but both violin and piano were discarded when Mortimer showed a genuine interest in drawing and painting.

Wilson studied painting at the Art Students League in New York, continued studying on his own and painted a few portraits. He also became involved in summer theatre work as a director while teaching painting on the side.

The need for earning enough money to marry prodded him into trying story illustration. The combination of his dramatic experience with the painter's craft produced a fresh approach, and Wilson soon became a popular illustrator for *American* magazine, *The Saturday Evening Post* and *Woman's Home Companion,* as well as for advertisers including Maxwell House Coffee and Woodbury Facial Soap.

In 1956, he moved to Arizona and has exhibited his portraits, still lifes, and genre paintings widely in the West.

1950
1960

THE DECADE: 1950-1960
Austin Briggs
(1909-1973)

It was during the 'fifties that a healthy revolt against the slick, photograph-oriented illustration then in vogue really began to gather adherents. This revolution was accelerated by the demise of several national periodicals in a losing competition with television for presentation of fictional escapism. Other floundering publications sought salvation in acquiring a new image — anything different and strident enough to retain the attention of a wavering public.

These conditions produced an opportunity for the illustrator to be truly creative with a freedom from the restraints of the past never before experienced. Yet, despite the present ferment in both illustration and the so-called fine arts, there is hardly enough genius to go around. A neighbor of mine remarked, after glancing through the latest Illustrators Annual, "All the pictures appear to have been done by the same five or six people!"

In the meantime, the illustrators of the past have fallen into the grip of the same stultifying watchfulness that infects the fine art establishment. Each appearance of a novelty compels the established illustrator to take inventory of his resources and to decide whether it is to his advantage to embrace the novelty or to fight it — I am now quoting Harold Rosenberg from his book, *The Anxious Object*. He continues, speaking of the gallery painter — but it is the same for us — "Must the artist weight the advisability of a new move against the likelihood that the style with which he is identified will continue to arouse interest? — Has the time come to unload and take on something new, and if so, whose judgment ought one to follow, one's own? or some current loud noise?"

It has been my contention that illustration has lived mainly on ideas from the avant garde, and to quote a speaker from the last Aspen Conference, "The calamity threatening us now is what happens when the avant garde has no formal thought to pass down to the professional level?"

Let's remind ourselves that last year's fresh idea is today's cliché. The field we love and live on is infected with thieves and peddlers. No new brush stroke can appear in any publication but some skillful craftsman in a studio can master it by the following noon. I am not opposed to these people because of their mastery of technique, but rather because they are not provoked to perform out of an observation of humanity ... Really it's because they have observed and coveted the success of another. Should they ever look at the public, whom we must actually see in order to communicate, they would see nothing at all. A Japanese poet once wrote, "When you look in a mirror, you do not see your reflection: Your reflection sees you!"

Because our reading habits have changed so drastically, the printed picture carries a greater responsibility than ever before to function literally as copy ... as text ... I have been fortunate enough during a long career to invent and abandon a whole series of technical innovations, and these techniques have had much to do with the length of that career; but today we are awash in a veritable sea of Liquitex. Technique without the merest shadow of content is our "Stencilled Brillo Box." We must make our pictures easier to read and identify with than the written or spoken word, I am certainly not opposed to innovation. I do not suggest that we, like Christopher Isherwood, become cameras with the shutter left open, but we are goofing a great opportunity through a kind of simple inertia. Even the

drawing by Bernie Fuchs

good, new artists are less interested in solving the problem than in "doing what they want."

The artist's traditional role is to lead, but we seem to have lost the necessary virility with which to do it. Everyone knows that we see things as we are, and not as they are, so why copy artists as fallible as ourselves? Let's stop feeling threatened by truly new ideas and have some of our own.

The past has always seemed a pendulum ... what was in would surely go out, and what was out, in! But now, with the pendulum eager to swing in our direction ... nobody swings!

Excerpt from a talk before the Minneapolis-St. Paul Association of Professional Artists, 1965.

JAMES S. AVATI
JAMES ELLIOTT BAMA
ISA BARNETT
JAMES R. BINGHAM
BRUCE BOMBERGER
JOSEPH BOWLER
WARD BRACKETT
AUSTIN BRIGGS
McCAULEY CONNER
BERNARD D'ANDREA
JOE DE MERS
STANLEY W. GALLI
DENVER GILLEN
LOUIS S. GLANZMAN
ALBERT GOLD
ROBERT TOMPKINS HANDVILLE
RAYMOND F. HOULIHAN
BILL JOHNSON
ROBERT JONES
MORGAN KANE
ROBERT LAVIN

JAMES LEWICKI
MIKE LUDLOW
DAVID STONE MARTIN
ROBERT THEODORE McCALL
JOHN R. McDERMOTT
FRANKLIN McMAHON
STANLEY MELTZOFF
AL MUENCHEN
PAUL NONNAST
GEORGE EDWARD PORTER
ROBERT RIGER
KEN RILEY
MORTON ROBERTS
ALEX ROSS
JOHN SCOTT
WILLIAM ARTHUR SMITH
TRACY SUGARMAN
ROBERT A. THOM
THORNTON UTZ
M. COBURN WHITMORE

JAMES S. AVATI (1912-   ) is probably the best representative of a new group of illustrators who successfully faced the challenge of a declining illustration market in the traditional magazines in the 'sixties by gravitating to the field of paperback cover art.

Previously, as a wartime outgrowth of the pulp magazines, the early paperback covers were especially lurid in concept. Although Avati did do some magazine illustration beginning in 1949 for *Collier's, American* magazine, *McCall's, Atlantic Monthly* and others, it was in the paperback field that he found his special niche and where he brought new distinction to that art.

Avati's approach was honest and realistic, but he painted with an artistry that won readership for the books and a score of imitators who tried to emulate the "Avati look." In self-defense Avati has gone through successive stylistic changes, and he remains a major force in the field. This influence is the more remarkable for his having had no formal art training. His is a graduate of Princeton University, but self-taught in art. In the 'seventies, Avati started teaching in his own small school. He also exhibits occasionally and is a member of the Society of Illustrators where his work has won several awards.

Cover illustration for Tobacco Road *by Erskine Caldwell; published by the New American Library in the 1950s.*

JAMES ELLIOTT BAMA (1926-   ) currently lives and works in a Wyoming studio on his ranch, twenty miles from the nearest town. Having been born and lived in New York City for his first forty-two years, he prefers it that way.

Bama studied at the High School of Music and Art in New York and at the Art Students League. His early illustration work included many of the men's magazines, as well as *The Saturday Evening Post* and other major magazines, but his style matured through his many covers for paperback publishers. He also became affiliated with the New York Giants football team as their official artist, and worked for the Baseball Hall of Fame.

Through the Society of Illustrators he traveled extensively on assignments for the U.S. Air Force; his art is in the Air Force Academy collection.

The decision to move West and to paint western subjects grew out of a vacation trip to a friend's ranch. Once made, it resulted in a whole new painting career for Bama. His first showing was a complete success, and he has continued to build a clientele of collectors, which has given him freedom from publishers' deadlines and the opportunity to paint subjects of his own choice. Many of his western works are in musuem collections, such as the Whitney Museum of Western Art, The Calgary Foundation, the Klamath Falls (Oregon) Museum of Art and the Cowboy Hall of Fame in Oklahoma.

"Portrait of Tony Martin, Hunting Guide," which also doubled as a cover for the paperback, The Killers, *published by Bantam Books, 1976.*

Illustration for "Someone in the Kitchen," published by McCall's *magazine, June, 1966. Reprinted by permission of The McCall Publishing Company.*

JOSEPH BOWLER (1928-   ) knew early in his career that he wanted to be an illustrator and accomplished it by making his first sale to *Cosmopolitan* magazine at the age of nineteen. He has since become one of the top performers, and for many years his romantic illustrations appeared regularly in *McCall's, Good Housekeeping, Redbook, The Ladies' Home Journal* and other publications.

Born in Forest Hills, New York, Bowler studied at the Art Students League under Frank Reilly, Robert Hale and Howard Trafton. In 1948 he joined the staff of the Charles E. Cooper Studio, noted for developing talented young artists, and from there launched his illustration career.

Among his other activities, he has made recruiting posters for the Air Force and is represented in the perma-

nent collection of the Air Force Academy in Colorado Springs. He has also appeared as a guest lecturer at the Parsons School of Design in New York. In 1958 Bowler was almost completely paralyzed by polio but through determination and long and intensive physiotherapy was eventually able to resume his career.

In recent years, Bowler has devoted himself almost exclusively to portraiture, working in his studio on Hilton Head Island, South Carolina; his sitters have included members of the Eisenhower and Kennedy families and other notables.

His work has won many awards in various annual exhibitions of the New York Art Directors Club and Society of Illustrators, and he was named Artist of the Year by the Artists Guild of New York.

ISA BARNETT (1924-   ) was born in Carbondale, Pennsylvania. He studied at the Philadelphia Museum School of Industrial Art and the Barnes Foundation. Among his teachers were Henry Pitz, Robert Riggs and later Robert Fawcett, who gave him special instruction.

His art career was postponed by World War II — he was a much-decorated United States paratrooper — but by 1946 he had sold his first illustration to *Argosy* magazine. This was soon followed by assignments from *American Weekly, Life, True, The Saturday Evening Post, Cosmopolitan, Outdoor Life, American Heritage, This Week* and many others.

Barnett has exhibited at the Art Alliance in Philadelphia, won Gold Medals in Cleveland and at Philadelphia Art Directors Club Shows.

He has also taught at the Philadelphia Museum School, the Moore Institute, and at the Philadelphia College of Art.

"England's Surrender at Yorktown," one of a series of historical illustrations for This Week *magazine, July 4, 1965.*

Bingham

JAMES R. BINGHAM (1917-1971) was born in Pittsburgh, Pennsylvania and studied at the Carnegie Institute of Technology. During World War II, he put in a stint animating Army Air Force films and received an appointment as a Naval officer attached to the Office of Research and Invention.

Following the war, the heroics and adventure in his life was confined to the usual subject matter of his illustrations, such as a long series of pictures for the Erle Stanley Gardner "Perry Mason" serials and other mystery stories

in *The Saturday Evening Post*. He also illustrated the "Tugboat Annie" series for the same publication.

In addition to editorial work, Bingham did a great deal of advertising illustration for clients such as Philadelphia Whiskey, Gulf Oil Corporation, Air Transport Association, the Caterpillar Tractor Company and won numerous awards, including Art Directors Club Medals in New York, Philadelphia, Chicago and Miami.

Illustration for "The Immortal Harpy" in The Saturday Evening Post. © *1944, 1972 by The Curtis Publishing Company.*

Bruce Bomberger

BRUCE BOMBERGER (1918-1980) was a native Californian who, except for a year in New York, made his career there as one of the "West Coast Artists." He had a varied background of experience, from art service, to Lord & Thomas, to free-lancing, to a partnership in an art service, and finally back to free-lancing again.

Bomberger, who was a past president of the San Francisco Society of Illustrators, did a wide variety of advertising illustration in addition to editorial drawings and paintings for *True, The Saturday Evening Post, Cosmopolitan, Good Housekeeping, This Week* and other publications.

Outstanding among his pictures were the wildlife paintings he did for the Weyerhaeuser Timber Company advertising series.

"The Secret of Sidewinder Gulch," illustration for The Saturday Evening Post. © 1960 by The Curtis Publishing Company.

Illustration for "The Way of a Man" by Andrina Iverson. Reprinted by permission of Good Housekeeping *magazine,* © 1960 by the Hearst Corporation.

Ward Brackett

WARD BRACKETT (1914-   ) is a sound painter who developed his abilities through many years as a studio artist. He was born in Milwaukee, Wisconsin, and studied at the Layton School of Art there. At the age of twenty, he was fortunate to be taken on at the Stevens, Sundblom and Stultz studio in Chicago. From there he went to the Grauman Studios in 1938 and to the Charles E. Cooper Studio in New York in 1940.

During World War II, Brackett was attached to the Quartermaster School where his duties involved producing a large volume of visual aids and training posters.

Following the war, he free-lanced for the Crowell-Collier magazines, *McCall's, Good Housekeeping, Parents, Redbook, Reader's Digest, Cosmopolitan* and others.

In 1953 he traveled with a USO troupe to Japan and Korea, doing portrait sketches of Army and Marine personnel in hospitals and rest centers, and artillery emplacements. In 1964 he toured the United States Air Force bases in Spain, with other illustrators, to make reportorial drawings and paintings. This work is represented in the Air Force Academy art collection.

Brackett returned to school in mid-career to study painting with Reuben Tam at the Brooklyn Museum. His time now is devoted almost entirely to painting, especially landscapes, with some figure work and portraiture. He currently exhibits in Naples and Sarasota, Florida (where he has a winter studio), and in Wilton and Southport, Connecticut and as a member of the Silvermine Guild in Connecticut. His comprehensive instruction book, *When You Paint,* published by North Light, contains much of his personal philosophy and painting techniques. Brackett has also designed eight U.S. postage stamps.

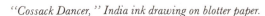
"Cossack Dancer," India ink drawing on blotter paper.

"The Ultra Intellectual." This drawing was one of an advertising series for T V Guide. *To get more strength in the reproductions, Briggs separated the drawing, made in line, from the tonal wash which was painted as an overlay. The engraver made a "combination" plate from the line and halftone negatives. Reprinted courtesy of Triangle Publications, Inc.*

AUSTIN BRIGGS (1909-1973) did some of his early illustrations for *Blue Book* magazine on the textured surface of white window shade cloth. It was his answer to obtaining a halftone effect for a magazine restricted to line reproductions.

Such resourcefulness and experimental enterprise characterized Briggs' entire career. Once he mastered a particular medium or method of working, he was never long satisfied with either. In the process, he left his many imitators behind and, for over thirty years, kept his work fresh and contemporary.

Briggs was born in a private railway car on a siding near Humboldt, Minnesota. His father was an electrical engineer employed in installing telegraphic equipment, and his family traveled along. Austin grew up in Detroit, Michigan, and was awarded a scholarship to the Wicker Art School. After a brief stay there, followed by a semester at the City College of Detroit, he had an opportunity to become assistant to an automobile illustrator, doing figures to set off the automobile.

Ambitious to do story illustration, he made some drawings for the *Dearborn Independent*. With these as samples, he tackled New York where he obtained work from *Collier's*, *McClure's* and *Pictorial Review*. He also continued to study and enrolled in classes at the Art Students League under George Bridgman and Jack Duncan.

This auspicious beginning was blighted by the Depression as the magazines retrenched. Briggs, who had not yet developed his own individual style, was expendable. For the next several years, he did a variety of art work, from movie posters to ghosting the drawings for the comic strip, "Flash Gordon." He also began to do pulp illustration for Don Kennicott of *Blue Book* magazine. *Blue Book* became a new training ground; the care that Briggs lavished on these assignments began to bring out in him a more individual point of view. He attracted the attention of *Redbook*, then *Cosmopolitan*, *The Saturday Evening Post* and others. From that period on, Briggs became a dominant force in illustration. In 1969 he was elected to the Hall of Fame of the Society of Illustrators.

"Lonely Stop in the Black Belt," from "The Fast Changing South," Look *Magazine, Nov. 16, 1965. © 1965 Cowles Communications.*

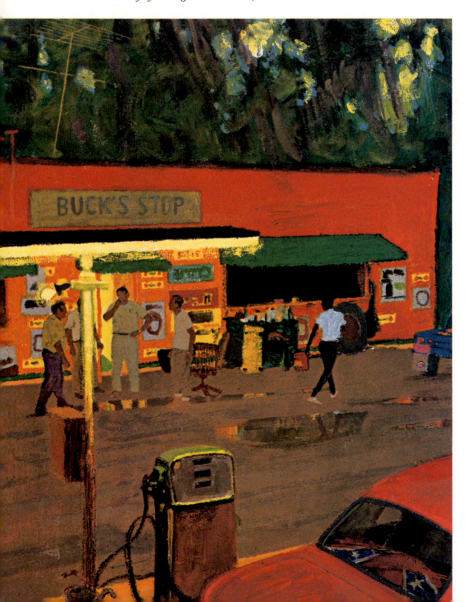

"The Model," illustration for *"Murder for Millions"* by Nancy Rutledge *in* The Saturday Evening Post.
© *1948, 1976 by The Curtis Publishing Company.*

"Fashion Photographer," date and place of publication unknown. Courtesy of Guy Rabut.

Conner

McCAULEY (MAC) CONNER (1913-) sold his first covers to *The Saturday Evening Post* while still an art student. He studied at the Philadelphia Museum School with Henry Pitz and at the Grand Central School of Art in New York under Harvey Dunn.

Service in the Navy interrupted his career for several years, after which he joined with William Neeley to form an art agency, Neeley Associates.

Conner has also had an active free-lance career as an illustrator for the *Post, McCall's, Cosmopolitan, Redbook, Woman's Day, Argosy, Woman's Home Companion, The Ladies' Home Journal* and other magazines.

Conner is a member of the Society of Illustrators, has exhibited at the Palm Beach Galleries and the Country Art Gallery in Westbury, Long Island. His work won the Philadelphia Art Directors Award in 1959.

D'Andrea

BERNARD D'ANDREA (1923-), illustrator, painter, teacher, has had an active career, always searching for new artistic horizons.

Born in Buffalo, New York, D'Andrea's illustration career started in 1950 in New York City, as an illustrator represented by the eminent Charles E. Cooper Studio, after four years as a U.S. Army artist. Launched on a long and successful career that has spanned the decades of the middle 1950s, '60s, '70s, and into the '80s, he continues to appear in national and international publications. Over the years he has been the recipient of many awards and distinctive honors for his work.

Most recent prominent assignments have been a series of paintings illustrating a major atlas, "People and Places of the Past," for the National Geographic Society of Washington, D.C. He continues also to illustrate for the Hearst Corporation and others.

In May, 1983, D'Andrea had a successful "sold out" exhibition of landscape paintings at the Red Piano Gallery of Hilton Head Island in South Carolina. He has also had a major exhibition of landscape painting for the Contemporary Gallery of the Hunter Museum of Chattanooga, Tennessee.

D'Andrea was married to the late Lorraine Fox, the illustrious Hall of Fame artist who died in 1976. He is now remarried to Jean Reist Stark, a prominent goldsmith, teacher and painter, represented in museum and private collections. They live and work in their respective studios in western New Jersey.

Illustration for "Peoples and Places of the Past." © *1983 by the National Geographic Society.*

260

Illustration for "Granpa and the Trolley Car" in the January, 1961 issue of the Reader's Digest. © 1961 Reader's Digest Assn., Inc.

DENVER GILLEN (1914-unknown) was born in Vancouver, British Columbia, Canada, the son of a sea captain.

Gillen had no intention of becoming an artist until, at seventeen, a protracted illness kept him in a hospital bed for several months. As therapy, the doctor, who was an amateur artist, interested his patient in drawing. When Denver was well again, he obtained a beginner's job in the art department of the Hudson's Bay Company. He also studied with Frederick Varley during this time and began to go on outdoor painting expeditions.

Later he progressed from studios in Toronto and Chicago (including a stint for Montgomery Ward's art department making catalog drawings) to a variety of free-lance assignments on every possible subject. In the process, he was evolving his own personal style, strongly linear, and began to obtain manuscripts to illustrate from *Collier's, True, Outdoor Life,* and many other magazines including a long stint at the *Reader's Digest.*

In addition to magazine and advertising assignments, Gillen continued to do independent paintings, exhibiting at the Toronto Museum, the Chicago Art Institute, the Society of Illustrators in New York, and the Oehlschlaeger Gallery in Chicago. He also completed a series of mural paintings for the Missouri Pacific Railroad.

"Hex Sign Painter," illustration for Sunday Bulletin *magazine, Philadelphia.* © 1962, Bulletin Company. Collection of Illustration House.

In this day of specialization, ALBERT GOLD (1916-   ) is a rarity — the complete artist. He is a realist but does not try to see photographically; a painter-reporter for the printed page as well as for exhibition walls; a social commentator in his choice of subject and a gifted teacher.

Gold was born in Philadelphia and attended the Philadelphia Museum College of Art, studying under Earl Horter and Henry Pitz.

During World War II, he contributed to *Yank* magazine and spent three years as an artist-correspondent in Europe. The rigorous training of that on-the-spot selection and drawing has shaped his work since.

Much of his postwar commissioned work for publications such as *Ford Times, Argosy, What's New* (Abbott Laboratories), *Lincoln-Mercury Times, Holiday, The Lamp, Bulletin* magazine and others, has been of a reportorial nature.

Gold has also exhibited regularly in the major shows, has won two Tiffany Foundation grants, the Prix de Rome (1942), the Sesnan Gold Medal from the Pennsylvania Academy of the Fine Arts and numerous other awards. His work is represented in many collections, including the Philadelphia Museum of Art, the Smithsonian and Library of Congress in Washington, D.C., the New York Public Library, and the New Britain Museum of American Art.

During this period, from 1946 to the present, he has also found time to teach at the Philadelphia Museum College of Art, and is Associate Director of the Graphics Department.

Joe De Mers

JOE DE MERS (1910-1984) specialized in that most transitory and ephemeral area of illustration, depicting the modern American girl. He did them, not as stereotypes, but as a diverse array of dazzling females — sweet, predatory or sophisticated. To dress them, he enlisted the fashion expertise of his wife, Janice, for styles that would not become dated in the six months between painting and publication.

De Mers was born in San Diego, California, and attended the Chouinard Art School in Los Angeles. Among his teachers were Pruett Carter, Lawrence Murphy and later, Rueben Tam at the Brooklyn Museum Art School. De Mers spent about ten years as a production illustrator and designer for motion pictures, mostly for Warner Brothers Studios.

His first illustration assignment was for *Fortune* magazine in 1937, followed by assignments from *Esquire,* and then from most of the other major magazines in the United States and Europe. He was one of several illustrators who found a steady market for second rights to pictures for publishers in England and on the Continent.

De Mers exhibited at the New York Museum of Modern Art, Corcoran Museum of Art, the Los Angeles County Museum, various Art Directors Club shows, and at the Society of Illustrators in New York. He taught at the Chouinard Art School from 1934-37 and later at the Parsons School of Design in New York. He was a resident of Hilton Head Island in South Carolina for several years and the proprietor of an art gallery there.

Typical De Mers illustration with emphasis on shape and color. Published by McCall's *December, 1956. Collection of Illustration House.*

"The First Fast Gun," illustration for story by Williams Forrest in The Saturday Evening Post, *January 7, 1961.*
© *1961 by The Curtis Publishing Company.*

STANLEY W. GALLI (1912–   ) was born in San Francisco and spent seven of his formative years between high school and art school doing many odd jobs. The Depression was on, and he worked successively as a roust-about and ranch hand near Reno, Nevada, an apprentice in a Reno bakery, a longshoreman in San Francisco and, as a member of the Teamsters' Union, went through all the violence of a coastal strike.

Galli finally saved enough to enroll at the California School of Fine Arts in San Francisco (now the San Francisco Institute of Art). Hired out of school by a San Francisco art service, he became a partner in the firm just before World War II. He was then called into special service by the Navy Department to work at structuring educational programs and materials. After the war, he returned to his art service partnership but found the business aspects of this too demanding and decided to return to drawing and painting as a free-lance illustrator.

He eventually received assignments from most of the major publications, including *The Saturday Evening Post, True* magazine, *McCall's, Today's Woman* and the *Reader's Digest.*

Galli also played a key role in developing an advertising campaign for the Weyerhauser Company based on themes of conservation, making over fifty paintings himself and enlisting other artists to illustrate the wildlife scenes. On the same theme, Galli has designed twenty-six stamps for the U.S. Postal Service, mostly commemoratives for wild-life conservation; several have won important prizes.

In 1981, Galli was elected to the Hall of Fame of the Society of Illustrators. His time is now divided between his studios in California and in Tuscany, Italy, where he spends several months each year.

LOUIS S. GLANZMAN (1922-   ) had no formal art training but, from childhood on, a strong urge to draw impelled him to train himself. He accomplished this largely through study of the George Bridgman anatomy textbooks, *Art Instruction* magazine (predecessor of *American Artist*), an out-dated set of an art correspondence course, and the on-the-job training of drawing for comic books.

The Army gave Glanzman his first acquaintance with art on a professional level when he was attached to the *Air Force* magazine art department in New York. There he was able to fill in many of the gaps in his art background and by the time of his discharge was ready for a career as a freelance illustrator.

True magazine bought his first pictures in 1948. Later he sketched court trials for *Life* magazine, illustrated for *Collier's* and *The Saturday Evening Post, Cosmopolitan, Redbook* and *Woman's Day*. During this same period he illustrated many children's books, along with advertising work. *Life* magazine assigned him subjects for their Civil War and Presidential series. For *Time* magazine, he did over forty portraits of prominent people, as well as Neil Armstrong's landing on the moon. He has done many paintings for the National Parks Department and *National Geographic* has commissioned him for articles in their magazine and several of their books.

He has won awards from the Society of Illustrators, New York Art Directors Club and the Salmagundi Club. His paintings are in many collections, including the Smithsonian, U.S. Air Force Historical Art Collection; Museum of the City of New York and the Civil War Museum at Fredricksburg, Virginia.

Portrait of Robert F. Kennedy for Time *magazine, June 14, 1968.* © *1968 Time, Inc. All rights reserved.*

ROBERT TOMPKINS HANDVILLE, A.N.A (1924-   ), born in Paterson, New Jersey, studied at Pratt Institute and the Brooklyn Museum Art School under Reuben Tam. He is a member of the Society of Illustrators, the American Watercolor Society, and was elected to the National Academy as an associate in 1981. He currently is a member of the faculty of The Fashion Institute of Technology.

Handville has exhibited throughout the country and has won many awards. Among them are the Ranger Fund Purchase Prize, the 21st and 27th Annual New England Exhibition awards for painting, the National Academy of Design's Speyer Prize, 1982, American Watercolor Society's Mary Pleissner Memorial Award, 1981, and the Mario Cooper Award, 1983.

The artist is the designer of the Yellowstone National Park Commemorative Postal Stamp and The Alfred Verville Commemorative Air Mail Stamp.

Handville has been a contributing, commissioned artist-reporter for *Sports Illustrated* since 1962. Also, he was Chairman of the Society of Illustrators "Artists in the Parks" program for the National Park Service, Department of the Interior.

Collections and exhibitions include the Metropolitan Museum of Art's "200 Years of American Watercolor Paintings;" the National Portrait Gallery show, "Champions, Heroes of American Sport," in 1981-82; The President John F. Kennedy White House Collection; United Nations; Time, Inc.; U.S. Air Force Historical Art Collection, and Syracuse, Denver, and Oklahoma Universities' collections as well as the Royal Society of Watercolour Painters, London, England, by invitation.

Cover illustration for Sports Illustrated *magazine. Robert Handville for* Sports Illustrated; © *1964 Time, Inc.*

"Richard Burton — King of Adventure." Illustration for Coronet, *May, 1955.*

Ray Houlihan

RAYMOND F. HOULIHAN (1923-   ) started out by doing cartoons for his hometown newspaper in Worcester, Massachusetts. This short career as a cartoonist was interrupted by World War II.

Houlihan was assigned as a combat soldier to an armored division in Europe. There, during his spare time, he helped to start a battalion newspaper. Gradually his duties were shifted to allow him time for special map-making projects and to make sketchbook drawings of terrain and inhabitants. He believes that this training was extremely valuable in his artistic development.

After the war he returned to the *Worcester Telegram* but found himself increasingly interested in becoming an illustrator. Through the G.I. Bill, he was able to go to the Art Students League in New York where he attended classes under Reginald Marsh, John Groth and Jon Corbino.

Soon afterward he began to obtain work from *Blue Book, Pic, Coronet* and then from many other magazines and book publishers. His pictures are all distinctly linear in nature — even in halftone — and lend themselves ideally to the historical subject matter he enjoys. Some of his most distinguished work has been in black-and-white for American Heritage.

Bill Johnson

BILL JOHNSON (1929-   ) paints adventure and dramatic action subjects.

Following World War II, there was a spectacular growth in magazines oriented to men, and Johnson's work appeared in most of them, including *True, Argosy, Outdoor Life, Saga* and *Cavalier.*

Another almost parallel growth has been the paperback book with illustrated covers, selling millions of copies. This, too, has been a natural field for Johnson who has painted cover designs for many of the major publishers, including Bantam, Gold Medal, Crest and Avon Books.

Johnson, who was born in Seattle, Washington, attended the Cornish and Burnley Art Schools in Seattle. He was awarded a full scholarship to the Chicago Art Institute and also studied at the Chicago Academy of Fine Arts.

His work has been exhibited at the Northwest Painters in Seattle, the Westport Artists in Connecticut and the Society of Illustrators in New York.

Illustration for "My Cold War with the Reds," published by Argosy *magazine, October, 1962.*

265

MORGAN KANE

MORGAN KANE (1916-   ) adopted a very effective practice which contributed much to his growth as an illustrator. Between assignments, he spent his time trying out new approaches for hypothetical stories. Art directors were so impressed by these samples that, in several instances, they bought the picture to hold for an appropriate story. In one case, a story was specially commissioned to fit the picture.

Kane was born in Wilmington, Delaware, and won a scholarship to the Cleveland Art Institute. This was followed by three-and-a-half years in the Air Force during World War II. After the war, he got a job doing advertising illustrations in Chicago and obtained his first story manuscript for *Extension* magazine. Eventually, he has illustrated for nearly all of the major periodicals.

Morgan is also an expert photographer and in the early 'sixties left illustration for full-time photography. However, he resumed painting in the mid-'seventies, with clients for advertising, paperback covers and movie posters for Paramount Pictures, United Artists, Universal Studios and Warner Brothers.

Kane is also painting and exhibiting in several galleries in the West.

Movie poster for "On Golden Pond." Not published.

ROBERT JONES (1926-   ) became an illustrator by way of cartooning. Born in Los Angeles, he was doing animation drawings for Warner Brothers while he was still in high school.

After high school, Jones became a gunner and aviation radio operator in the Navy. He next attended the University of Southern California for two years, followed by another two-and-a-half years at the Art Center School in Los Angeles.

He was still interested in humorous illustration when he joined the Charles E. Cooper Studio in New York, and his early fiction assignments in *The Saturday Evening Post* were on whimsical subjects. He has gradually expanded his range, however, and now illustrates a wide variety of subject matter for many national publications, including art for paperback covers.

"Too Many Brides," illustration for a Saturday Evening Post *story. © 1960 by The Curtis Publishing Company. Collection of Robert Wale.*

266

McCall

ROBERT THEODORE McCALL (1919-   ) is from
Columbus, Ohio. He studied at the Columbus Fine Arts
School and the Art Institute of Chicago. Following his
military service, he worked as an illustrator with Bielefelt
Studios in Chicago for three years and then joined the
Charles E. Cooper studio in New York.

He is well qualified to do aviation and aerospace illustration; during World War II, he was an Army Air Corps
bombardier instructor. Since the war, he has traveled
around the world with special trips to Europe, Africa, the
Far East, Japan, India and the Middle East, as a guest of
the United States Air Force, for various documentary
painting projects and contributions to the U.S.A.F. art
collection in Washington, D.C. and Colorado Springs,
Colorado.

In 1976, McCall completed a huge mural project for the
Space Museum in Washington, D.C. In 1983 he finished
another large mural painting, "The Prologue and the
Promise," at the Disney EPCOT Center in Florida. Mc-
Call has also served as consultant on several movies,
including "Star Trek," and "The Black Hole," for which
he was given screen credit as art director.

Two of his books on space have been published: *Our World
in Space* in 1973 and *A Vision of the Future — the Art of Robert
McCall*, published by Abrams in 1982. He also has designed fourteen commemorative U.S. postage stamps.

McCall is a member of the Aviation Writers Association
and the Society of Illustrators in New York.

*Master study for one of the elements of McCall's space mural,
"Cosmic View," National Air and Space Museum, Washington,
D.C.*

*New Method of Making Steel with Basic Oxygen Furnace. Painted
for National Steel Corporation, 1978.*

Lavin

ROBERT LAVIN (1919-   ) ably combines drama and
fact in his paintings of industrial and mechanical subjects.
This has made him a successful illustrator for such accounts
as General Electric, National Steel and United Engineers,
as well as fictional subjects involving planes and ships for
*The Saturday Evening Post, Reader's Digest, American Weekly,
Argosy, Newsweek,* and others.

Lavin was born in New York City and obtained his B.A.
at the College of the City of New York. He also studied at
the National Academy of Art School under Ivan Olinsky.

He is an active painter and exhibitor, won second prize
in the Long Island Annual Art Show in 1962, and is a
member of the Society of Illustrators and the American
Watercolor Society. He also taught at the College of the
City of New York from 1957 to 1966.

Lavin now lives in Austin, Texas, and specializes in
industrial painting for corporate offices, publications, annual reports and public relations.

LEWICKI

JAMES LEWICKI (1917-1980) was a scholar as well as an artist; many of his painting projects came from ideas suggested by research. He was probably best known for his several major series for *Life* magazine, including "The Folklore of America," a five-part series consisting of sixty-six paintings, (later expanded into a book, *The Life Treasury of American Folklore),* the "Pageant of Life," on evolution, "The Origin of Christmas," "Christmas Legends" and others. His paintings are all distinguished by their originality of concept, their authenticity and their brilliant color.

Lewicki was born in Buffalo, New York, and majored in art at the Buffalo Technical High School. He attended the Albright Art School there, won a scholarship to the Detroit Society of Arts and Crafts School, was graduated from Pratt Institute in 1939, and also studied at New York University.

His first assignment while still at Pratt was a book, *New York from Village to Metropolis,* published in 1939. From then on Lewicki had commissions from nearly every magazine and from many book publishers.

He also exhibited widely, won many awards, traveled extensively to do research, served as Chairman, Fine Arts Committee of the Long Island Arts Center, taught design at the Evening School of Pratt Institute from 1946-52. He was Professor of Art and Chairman of the Visual Arts Department at C.W. Post College, Long Island, New York, at the time of his death.

Cover design for the American Druggist *magazine, August, 1951.*

MIKE LUDLOW (1921-   ) combines a light touch with the ability to depict beautiful girls. This made *Esquire* magazine a logical market, and he painted a great many female subjects for them. He has also completed more decorous subjects for *Family Circle, Good Housekeeping, Collier's, Woman's Home Companion, American, Today's Woman, Coronet, The Saturday Evening Post,* and others, as well as national advertising assignments.

Ludlow was born in Buffalo, New York, and attended classes in illustration, composition and life drawing at the Art Students League under William C. McNulty.

His first illustrations were made for the Sunday supplement of the *Journal American* in 1948, and he has been a prolific painter since.

Illustration for Esquire *magazine, January,1955.*

David Stone Martin

DAVID STONE MARTIN (1913-   ) had no formal art training beyond high school in Chicago and began his career as a graphic designer. He has designed many publications and is an expert calligrapher. Among his major projects were designs and murals for the "Century of Progress" Chicago World's Fair, and he worked variously as a supervisor of a Federal Arts project for the Elgin State Hospital in Illinois, art director of the Tennessee Valley Authority for six years and, as assistant to Ben Shahn, doing murals. He was artist-correspondent for Abbott Laboratories and for *Life* magazine during World War II. He also worked for the O.S.S. and was an art director in the Office of War Information in 1942-43. Since the war he has followed a free-lance career, participating in many advertising illustration projects for clients such as the Disc Company of America and CBS Television.

Martin uses a calligraphic line that has been widely imitated. No one else, however, has matched his ability to present the essence and mood of a subject in that very personal way.

His advertising and editorial illustrations have received a great many citations and awards, and examples of his work are included in numerous Art Directors Club Annuals.

He has also found time to teach — at the Brooklyn Museum School of Art in 1948-49, and at the Workshop School of Advertising and Editorial Art in New York in 1950.

"The Non-Stop Piano Player," illustration for The Saturday Evening Post. © *1963 by The Curtis Publishing Company.*

McMahon

FRANKLIN McMAHON (1921-   ) is a Chicagoan by birth and education. He attended the Art Institute, the Harrison Commercial Art Institute, and the Institute of Design there. Among his many teachers were Francis Chapin, Paul Weighardt, E.W. Ball, Emerson Woeffler and Richard Fillopowski.

A B-17 navigator during World War II, McMahon was shot down over Mannheim, Germany, and spent the last three months of the war in German P.O.W. camps.

After the war, he re-established his studio in Chicago and began to do free-lance illustration for advertising, magazines and books. In addition, he has pursued an active career in painting and has won many awards.

McMahon is essentially a reportorial artist with an especially strong sense of line. He also has an innate feel for composition — he can begin a drawing at a given point without prior planning or blocking in, and carry it through to a finish. This gives his work a look of on-the-spot authenticity which a more finished rendering based on photographic information would not provide. He does, in fact, work directly from his subjects whenever possible, and his assignments have taken him to many parts of the world for most of the leading publications. Many of his assignments, such as his coverage of the Ecumenical Council and Vatican II are self-generated and sold to the appropriate publications after completion. In recognition of McMahon's many talents, the Artists Guild of New York chose him as "Artist of the Year" in 1963.

This illustration for Look *magazine was part of the artist's coverage of the Democratic Convention which nominated John Kennedy as its presidential candidate.*

MCD

JOHN R. McDERMOTT (1919-1977) was born in
Pueblo, Colorado. After finishing high school in
Hollywood, he went to work for the Disney Studios as an
animator. This ended at the outbreak of World War II, and
McDermott became a Marine in the Pacific Theatre.
During part of this time, he served as a combat artist and
made drawings for the Corps' records of actions in the
Solomons, Guadalcanal, Guam and Okinawa.

At the end of the war some of these drawings were seen
by *Blue Book,* and this began McDermott's illustration
career, establishing him as expert in military subjects and
depiction of action.

A few years later, with a group of his illustrator friends,
McDermott made a home movie, "Dawn Patrol," as a
parody on all World War I movies. The project became so
interesting that John decided to use the motion picture
camera as a serious art medium and with his friends as
volunteer actors produced a memorable documentary film
on the Civil War, "Pickett's Charge," which was shown
twice in 1957 by C B S Television. In 1964 he received a
Ford Foundation Grant for further film experimentation
and made a film of the Marines at the Battle of Belleau
Wood in 1918, again with his group of amateur actors.

McDermott was the author of four novels; one, *The Rat
Factory,* was an unsympathetic version of his Disney experi-
ences. Another book became the movie, "Loving," with
George Segal and Eva Marie-Saint.

Illustration for This Week *magazine.*

SM

STANLEY MELTZOFF (1917-   ), who was born in
New York City, earned a B.S. from the College of the City
of New York and an M.F.A. from the Institute of Fine Arts,
New York University. His pre-war teaching was interrupted by four years in the Army during World War II,
during which he eventually became art editor of *Stars and
Stripes* in Africa and Italy. After the war he resumed
teaching, first at C.C.N.Y. and then at Pratt Institute,
continuing his own painting and learning to be an
illustrator.

His first major opportunity was an assignment to do
covers for the reborn *Scientific American,* more than sixty of
which were eventually painted. These were largely sym-
bolic still lifes in the guise of realism. His most notable
advertising assignments were new chemical products for
Rohm and Haas, and a long series of industrial subjects for
United Engineers. Illustrations and covers were made for
The Saturday Evening Post, Argosy, Field and Stream, and above
all, *Life.* Subjects ranged in history from prehistoric masto-
don hunts, ancient Greece, the American Civil War, and
political history, to present-day high steel workers.

Having been a diver by avocation for most of his adult
life, Meltzoff was assigned to paint fish underwater for
Dick Gangel at *Sports Illustrated.* Finding himself almost
alone in this field, he became a specialized painter of
submersive subjects for *Sports Illustrated* and later *National
Geographic.* He has completed an extended series on ten big
salt water game fish. In the process, his market gradually
shifted to art galleries and large limited edition prints. At
present he is engaged in finishing the last of the six species
of billfish, on a long Pacific trip.

"In the company of stingrays and a sand shark . . ." Sports
Illustrated, *September 4, 1967. Courtesy of the Garcia
Corporation.*

Antarctica painting for U.S.A.F. Documentary Art Program.

Al Muenchen

AL MUENCHEN (1917-1975) painted this picture of the aftermath of a dramatic Air Force C-130 plane landing during a ''whiteout'' at McMurdo's Williams Field in Antarctica. Blinded by a blizzard, the plane was guided down by G.C.A. into soft snow. After the storm, the Seabees welded together a special sled which was dragged to the plane and managed to tow it undamaged back to its runway.

Muenchen's painting was done in connection with his trip to Antarctica for the Air Force to record the life and work of personnel based there. It is part of the Air Force Permanent Art Collection.

He was born in Cincinnati, Ohio, and attended the Chicago Art Institute and Carnegie Institute of Technology, Pittsburgh, Pennsylvania. He first worked for Pittsburgh Studios in 1937 and did a considerable amount of advertising illustration prior to his fiction assignments, which appeared in *The Saturday Evening Post, Cosmopolitan, Collier's, American, True* and other magazines.

Muenchen was an active member of the Society of Illustrators, serving on the Exhibition committee and the Joint Ethics Committee for the Graphic Arts.

nonnast

PAUL NONNAST (1918-   ) chose an artist's career because of a heart condition in his youth, but he has been working at it strenuously ever since.

He was born in Carlisle, Pennsylvania, and was graduated from the Philadelphia Museum School of Art in 1940. Nonnast worked first for the McCandlish Lithograph Corporation and the *Philadelphia Record,* followed by free-lance advertising illustrating for many national accounts, including Armco, Bell Telephone, Chevrolet, Masonite, Dole Pineapple and United Air Lines.

The Saturday Evening Post gave him his first illustration assignment in 1947; he has since contributed to the *Post, Cosmopolitan, Field and Stream, Argosy, Reader's Digest* and others.

Nonnast has won two Gold Medals in Philadelphia Art Directors shows and served as head of the Advertising and Illustration department of the Moore Institute of Art in Philadelphia from 1943 to 1946.

A serious photographer as well, he has traveled widely in the United States, Canada and Europe to take pictures.

Illustration for ''Seventeen Stories Up,'' in The Saturday Evening Post. © 1961 by The Curtis Publishing Company.

George Porter

GEORGE EDWARD PORTER (1916-) was born in Perry, Florida. He studied at the Ringling School of Art in Sarasota and the Phoenix Art Institute in New York under a distinguished group of teachers, including Lucille Blanche, Thomas Fogarty, Sr., Franklin Booth, Lauros Phoenix and later with Reuben Tam at the Brooklyn Museum.

During the war years of 1944-45, he did historical and combat art for the Fifth Air Force in the Far East and for the Navy. Under the auspices of Dr. Charles Mayo, and the American Red Cross, he had a one-man show in the hospital at NADZAB, a base in New Guinea.

Since the war, Porter has done both advertising and editorial illustrations appearing in *Good Housekeeping, McCall's, Redbook, The Saturday Evening Post, Woman's Day, Parents,* and *The Ladies' Home Journal.*

Porter is a member of the Society of Illustrators and has exhibited in its annual shows as well as at those of the Art Directors Clubs of New York and Baltimore.

Illustration for "After the Kids have Gone," by Steve McNeil, in The Saturday Evening Post. ©1962 by The Curtis Publishing Company.

Robert Riger

ROBERT RIGER (1924-) is a student of sports who draws, paints, photographs, analyzes and writes expertly about the outstanding performers.

Riger was born in New York City where he studied at the High School of Music and Art and at Pratt Institute. His early ambition was to become a teacher, but he switched to advertising design while at Pratt. After graduation he worked as a layout artist for *The Saturday Evening Post.* This was followed by art and advertising agency work until he got the chance to combine his love of sports with drawing for the newly launched *Sports Illustrated* magazine.

He was one of the first illustrators to use a sequence of action drawings in revealing the key to championship form in baseball, boxing, football and other major sports. To research these, Riger had to become an expert photographer, taking endless shots, in order to analyze and select the significant details for his drawings.

More recently Riger has become associated with television coverage of outstanding sports events, combining drawing with personal commentary. His book, the *ABC Wide World of Sports,* featuring his drawings and photographs of some of these competitions, was published by the American Broadcasting Company in 1965. He also published a book in collaboration with Branch Rickey, *The American Diamond.*

"Portrait of Bud Werner," dedicatory drawing for the book, ABC Wide World of Sports, *by Robert Riger.* © Sports Programs, Inc., 1965.

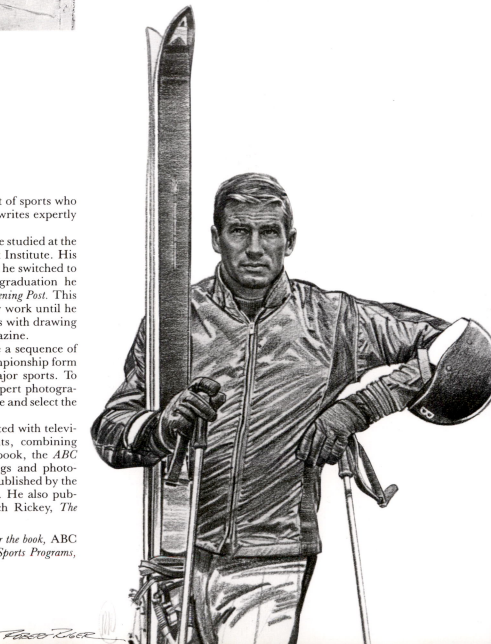

THE Elks MAGAZINE
MARCH 1962

SPRING FISHING ISSUE

John Scott

JOHN SCOTT (1907-   ) developed his strong, sound approach to illustration by the simple expedient of hard work.

His first art assignments were for the Western pulp magazines during the 'thirties until the outbreak of World War II.

During the war, Scott was overseas as a staff artist on *Yank* and covered the war in Europe as artist-correspondent.

After returning home, John began to work for the general magazines such as *This Week, Woman's Day* and the Canadian publications, *Chatelaine* and *Toronto Star*. He gradually gravitated to the men's magazines, however, including *True, The Elks, Argosy* and *Sports Afield*. He particularly enjoys the hunting and fishing assignments, which give him an opportunity to go on location in the wilderness to write and paint. Further such assignments were carried out for the Winchester Arms Company and the Garcia Corporation. These led to a series of paintings on the early days of oil drilling in Texas for the Permian Basin Petroleum Museum in Midland. Several years were then spent on very large 12 by 32 foot murals for buildings in Washington, D.C. and Salt Lake City for the Mormon Church. At the present time, Scott is concentrating entirely on gallery paintings of the early and contemporary American West.

Cover painting for The Elks *magazine, March, 1962.*

Tracy Sugarman

TRACY SUGARMAN (1921-   ) initiated a personal assignment of reporting the student voter-registration efforts in Mississippi in the early 'sixties. Feeling strongly about the issues and wanting to make a contribution as an artist in a reportorial series of drawings, he enlisted sponsorship of the project by the Columbia Broadcasting System and the United States Information Agency.

These sensitive line and wash drawings were made from on-the-spot observation, often under dangerous conditions, but honestly and without sensationalism. Tracy made over one hundred drawings. Many of these, in addition to their original use in a documentary film for the CBS "Eternal Light" program, and exhibition by the United States Information Agency, have also been used in *The Saturday Evening Post, The New York Times Magazine* and other magazines and newspapers. He also wrote and illustrated a book based on these experiences titled *Stranger at the Gates,* published by Hill and Wang in 1966.

Sugarman was born in Syracuse, New York, and was graduated from Syracuse University in 1943. He also studied at the Brooklyn Museum Art School with Reuben Tam.

His illustrations have appeared in *Fortune, Collier's, Esquire, Woman's Home Companion, American, Parents* magazine, *Boy's Life* and *Gentlemen's Quarterly;* and he has illustrated books for Simon and Schuster, Doubleday, Random House and Scott Foresman Company.

In addition to membership in the Society of Illustrators, he has been president of the Westport Artists, the Westport-Weston Association for the United Nations, and is active in other community activities.

Demonstration, "No singing — keep it silent. Don't answer, don't answer." Reproduced without captions in The New York Times Magazine, *February 21, 1965.*

273

Illustration for Wilderness Empire, *published by Bantam Books, 1971.*

Ken Riley

The illustrations of KEN RILEY (1919-) are remarkable on many counts: strength of draftsmanship, effective composition, the color and quality of the painting and the portrayal of mood. Riley's pictures reveal that he is clearly a master of all these, particularly in his use of color. He is at home with almost every subject and period — some of his finest pictures were painted for the historical Captain Hornblower stories by C.S. Forester in *The Saturday Evening Post*. His work has appeared in most of the national publications from *Reader's Digest* to *Life* magazine and in a variety of media from line to full color.

Born in Missouri, Riley studied under Thomas Hart Benton at the Kansas City Art Institute. Then he went to New York, where he studied under Frank Vincent DuMond at the Art Students League, and under Harvey Dunn at the Grand Central School. In his approach, Riley has successfully amalgamated the viewpoints of teachers whose methods differed radically and has added to this his own personal direction.

Currently he lives and works in Arizona, exhibiting in several Western galleries. He is a charter member of the National Academy of Western Art and member of the Cowboy Artists of America.

Morton Roberts

MORTON ROBERTS (1927-1964) crowded a full career into his very short life but gave promise of much greater things to come. His command of technique was lush and full, and he applied it with equal facility to paintings for exhibition and publication in magazines. He was also a teacher of life drawing at Pratt Institute in Brooklyn.

Among his best-known pictures were those made for _Life_ magazine on Rasputin in a history of Russia, memorable scenes from the opera "Rigoletto," and an outstanding series on the "Story of Jazz." He also illustrated for many other publications, including _Collier's, True, Reader's Digest, Redbook_ and Bantam Books.

Roberts was born in Worcester, Massachusetts, and was graduated from the Yale School of Fine Arts. Among his many prizes were the Edwin Austin Abbey Fellowship from the National Academy of Design, the American Watercolor Society's Pratt Purchase Prize, and the First Altman Prize, also from the National Academy of Design.

"Jazz Hits Chicago," one of a series of paintings for Life _magazine, recording the origins of jazz. Morton Roberts for_ Life _magazine._ © 1958 Time, Inc.

Illustration for "Great Moments in American History" (1976 calendar) Benjamin Franklin, Printer.

Alex Ross.

ALEX ROSS (1909-   ), who was born in Dunfermline, Scotland, came to the United States at the age of three. With early ambitions to be an industrial designer, he studied nights for two years under Robert Lepper at the Carnegie Institute of Technology, Pittsburgh, Pennsylvania.

Otherwise self-taught, Ross got a job in the Rayart Studios in Pittsburgh. From there he progressed to Pitt Studios, and then to the Charles E. Cooper Studio in New York. Two years later he sold his first cover design to *Good Housekeeping* magazine. This was followed by a total of 130 cover paintings over the next twelve years. In the meantime, he was doing editorial illustrations for most of the other national magazines, including *Collier's, The Saturday Evening Post, The Ladies' Home Journal* and *Cosmopolitan*. He has also illustrated several books, among them *Saints, Adventures in Courage* for Doubleday and Company.

Ross, who paints many experimental pictures in watercolor and in mixed media, exhibits regularly and is a member of the American Watercolor Society and the Fairfield Watercolor Group.

His awards include the Ranger Fund purchase prize, Saxe Foundation award and Connecticut Watercolor Society award. His work is represented in the U.S. Air Force Art Collection, New Britain Museum of American Art, the Mattatuck Museum, the National Academy of Design and many private collections.

In 1953 he was awarded a Master of Arts honorary degree by Boston College.

Illustration for "One Last Date," McCall's Magazine, November 1962. Reprinted by permission of The McCall Publishing Company.

WILLIAM ARTHUR SMITH, N.A. (1918-   ) has made pictures for a broad spectrum of uses and in a great variety of media. To each picture, whether for exhibition or publication, he brings a distinctive and highly creative viewpoint.

Born in Toledo, Ohio, Smith studied at the University of Toledo, Grand Central Art School and Art Students League in New York, l'Ecole des Beaux-Arts and l'Academie de la Grand Chaumiere in Paris, and with Theodore J. Keane in Toledo.

Smith's work is represented in many collections, including the Metropolitan Museum of Art and the Los Angeles Museum; he has exhibited in nearly every important museum in the United States. He has also had one-man exhibitions in more than twenty principal cities of Europe and Asia.

Among his many prizes are the Grand Prize and Gold Medal of Honor, American Watercolor Society (twice); National Academy of Design Award (twice); Society of American Graphic Artists' Award for Lithography; Winslow Homer Memorial Prize and the Society of Illustrators Gold Medal Award for Advertising Illustration.

He has taught at the Grand Central Art School, Pratt Institute in Brooklyn, lectured at many colleges in the United States and abroad, is past-president of the American Watercolor Society, and past-president of the International Association of Art, the UNESCO-affiliated organization of painters, sculptors and graphic artists of seventy nations.

Early illustration for The Ladies' Home Journal. © *1946, 1974 by The Curtis Publishing Company.*

"Poinsettias would be Best" by Eileen Herbert Jordon; illustration (cropped) for McCall's *magazine. Reprinted by permission of The McCall Publishing Company.*

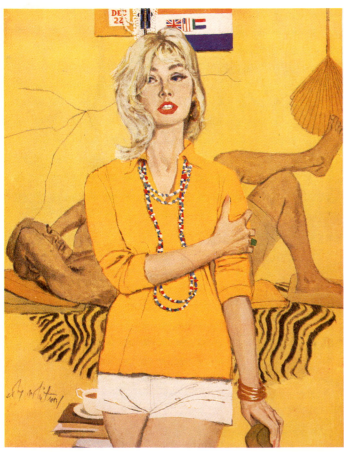

Illustration for The Saturday Evening Post. © *1959 by The Curtis Publishing Company.*

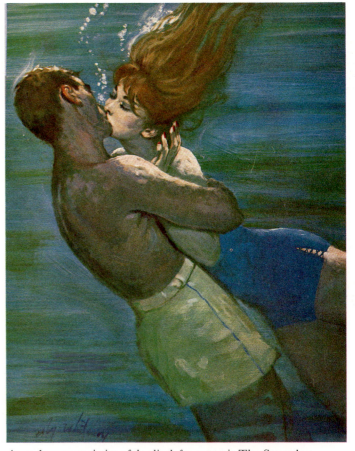

An underwater variation of the clinch for a story in The Saturday Evening Post. © *1959 by The Curtis Publishing Company.*

Illustration for "Sincerely, Willis Wayde" by John P. Marquand, The Ladies' Home Journal. © 1955, 1983 by The Curtis Publishing Company.

Coby Whitmore

M. COBURN WHITMORE (1913-   ) has described his three primary interests as "racing cars, illustrating, and smart clothes on good-looking women." The racing cars are a hobby, but he is thoroughly professional in his illustrations of beautiful women. Probably no other illustrator has been so inventive over so long a time in doing variations on the theme of "boy meets girl."

Coby was born in Dayton, Ohio, and attended the Dayton Art Institute there. Next, he went to Chicago as an apprentice in the studio of Haddon Sundblom and Edwin Henry, and attended the Chicago Art Institute nights. Following his apprenticeship, he worked for the Chicago *Herald Examiner* and the Charles Jensen studio in

Cincinnati. Then he moved to New York, for a long association with the Charles E. Cooper Studio, and also began to get illustration assignments from the major magazines, including *McCall's, The Ladies' Home Journal, Redbook, Good Housekeeping, Cosmopolitan* and *Woman's Day.* Many foreign publications purchased the second rights to publish his pictures abroad.

Whitmore has exhibited at Art Directors' shows in New York, Philadelphia, Chicago and Westchester, winning many awards and citations. He currently lives and paints from a beautiful studio overlooking the harbor on Hilton Head Island in South Carolina. He is a member of the Society of Illustrators and was elected to the Hall of Fame in 1978.

279

"Benjamin Rush: Physician, Pedant, Patriot," one of the History of Medicine *series.*

ROBERT THOM

ROBERT A. THOM (1915-1980) in 1948 took on an assignment for a series of historical paintings for Parke, Davis & Company to illustrate the story of pharmacy. To make the forty paintings constituted a monumental, ten-year effort in research and consultation in order to insure the necessary accuracy of concept and detail.

This series was followed by another equally demanding one of forty-five paintings to illustrate the history of medi-

cine. These paintings were reproduced in magazine advertisements and later enlarged and distributed widely among druggists. The original paintings have been exhibited in every state of the Union, and most of Canada, and represent institutional, and advertising art at its best. The two series won numerous awards.

Thom was born in Grand Rapids, Michigan, and had brief art training at the Institute of Fine Arts in Columbus, Ohio, and under Robert Brackman at Noank, Connecticut. He opened his own studio in Detroit, Michigan, and did commercial illustration for General Motors, Dodge Division of Chrysler Corporation, Bohm Aluminum and others prior to his Parke, Davis commissions. His career was tragically ended in an automobile accident.

Thornton Utz

THORNTON UTZ (1914-   ) likes to work out the poses of his figures with drawings — rapid, free sketches that clearly express the mood or mental attitude of his characters. Once this has been established, he then poses and photographs his models, as nearly as possible, in the predetermined positions. The photos furnish the factual details of folds and lighting which lend added authenticity to his original poses.

Utz has used this approach effectively for his humorous *Saturday Evening Post* covers as well as for the more serious fiction illustrations for *Cosmopolitan, McCall's, The Ladies' Home Journal, Redbook* and *Good Housekeeping.*

Thornton has participated in the joint Society of Illustrators-Air Force Art Program and received a citation from General Curtis LeMay for documenting the airlift of Hungarian refugees. Utz also received the Governor Bryant of Florida Award for his Freedom Posters.

He was born in Memphis, Tennessee, and studied under Burton Callicott in Memphis. He also attended the American Academy of Art in Chicago; later taught at the Chicago Art Institute. Utz, who now lives in Sarasota, Florida, presently concentrates on paintings and commissioned portraiture which has included the Carter family and Princess Grace of Monaco. He is a member of the Chicago Artists Guild and the American Artists Professional League.

Cover design for The Saturday Evening Post. © *1953, 1981 by The Curtis Publishing Company.*

1960
1970

THE DECADE: 1960-1970
Bernard Fuchs

When I got out of art school there was a great aura of glamour surrounding the top illustrators. No more. There are very few illustrators today that all the kids know about. Nobody new has come up with a style and made it stick for ten years, as once he might have.

The present-day illustrator is not like the one in those days — rich, glamorous, with a plush studio. No "characters" any more; the image has changed. We're like the new, studious baseball pro who breaks into the big league. He's a businessman now and goes about the occupation of playing baseball as a business — very serious about it. And the average ballplayer today is far better than his predecessor.

Present-day illustration, too, has changed, moved forward, since the so-called golden era of illustration. Illustration will always have a long way to go, and while now there is less of it around to do, at least it's doing a better job, in my opinion.

Today editorial people look for the guy they know will do something he hasn't done before. You may not stand or fall on each job you do — a lot of people are nice and don't condemn you for a bad one. But if a job you do reverts to what you were doing two years ago then, I think, you're in real trouble.

The greatest thing that this whole business did in the sixties was to introduce variety, not only in the freedom of the illustrators and in the fresh ways that illustration could be done, but also in opening up new sources of assignments. Added to story and advertising illustration were the new reportorial projects like those initiated by *Fortune* and *Sports Illustrated*. Several magazines experimented with art in other ways. Even articles on food have been handsomely illustrated by still life paintings in *Redbook* and *McCall's*.

It's hard for the illustrator to compete with the photographer in the news magazines, although coverage of trials, or stories like the Bay of Pigs invasion, where no photographers were present, showed what the illustrator *can* do.

Actually, it doesn't really matter whether an assignment is done by the artist or the camera. The point is, is the story illustrated right? Is there an idea in the illustration? There is no limit to the amount of freedom offered to the artist today. The only problem is the freedom within himself and how capable he is of doing this thing the way he feels it should be done. I think if you're honest about it, if you take an honest, detached approach to the solution of your problem, that will come nearer to solving it than the greatest technique. I don't care how facile you are, if you can't apply this fluency to the problem you're working on, or if you apply it falsely, you haven't done the job.

If you are "with" your own times and can translate your ideas into valid, original pictures, then you can make your own contribution. The field has never been so fast-changing and unpredictable as it was in the 'sixties — or so demanding of the illustrator's mind as well as his brush.

ROBERT K. ABBETT
THOMAS B. ALLEN
DAVID BLOSSOM
JAMES NEIL BOYLE
PAUL CALLE
MIA CARPENTER
JOSEPH S. CLEARY
TED C. CoCONIS
GUY DEEL
JACK DUMAS
NAIAD EINSEL
WALTER EINSEL
LORRAINE FOX
MARVIN FRIEDMAN
BERNARD FUCHS
MILTON GLASER
JOHN GUNDELFINGER
PHILIP HARRISON HAYS
ROBERT HEINDEL
MITCHELL HOOKS
VICTOR KALIN
SANFORD KOSSIN
MORT KÜNSTLER

ARTHUR LIDOV
FRANK C. McCARTHY
JOHN McCLELLAND
JERRY W. McDANIEL
ROBERT E. McGINNIS
FRANK MULLINS
FRED OTNES
ROBERT PEAK
JACK POTTER
RICHARD M. POWERS
ANTHONY SARIS
HARVEY SCHMIDT
DANIEL SCHWARTZ
ROBERT SHORE
SHANNON STIRNWEIS
HERBERT TAUSS
HOWARD A. TERPNING
EDWARD T. VEBELL
GILBERT M. WALKER
ROBERT WEAVER
WILLIAM H. WHITTINGHAM
BEN WOHLBERG

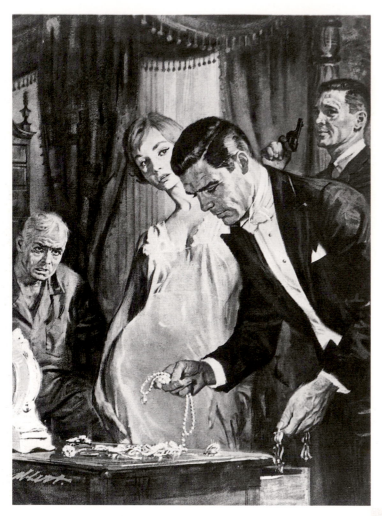

Bob Abbett

ROBERT K. ABBETT (1926-   ) was born in Hammond, Indiana. He holds a B.S. from Purdue University and a B.A. from the University of Missouri. In addition, he studied nights at the Chicago Academy of Fine Art.

He started his professional career as a writer for a public relations agency in Chicago but wanting to be an artist, became apprenticed to the Stevens-Gross Studio. He next transferred to the Bielefeld Studios, and from Chicago went to New York with the Alexander Chaite Studios.

Abbett made his first magazine illustrations for *Extension* magazine in Chicago and began to take on more assignments in New York, eventually free-lancing for such magazines as *True, Argosy, Redbook, This Week, Reader's Digest, Sports Afield* and paperback publishers, including Bantam Books, Dell, Signet, Fawcett, Ballantine and Pyramid Books.

Leaving illustration in the early 'seventies, Abbett devoted himself fully to painting outdoor scenes. Best known for his definitive work with sporting dogs, Bob has also made paintings for the stamp/print programs of several conservation groups: The Wild Turkey Federation, Ruffed Grouse Society and Trout Unlimited. Portraiture includes actor James Stewart (Cowboy Hall of Fame) and Luther Burbank (Burbank Center for the Arts), and currently he is painting a series for the National Quarter Horse Association.

Abbett taught the techniques of editorial illustration at the Silvermine Guild in Norwalk, Connecticut, from 1959-62. He is past-president of the Westport Artists and a member of the Society of Illustrators in New York.

Illustration for True *magazine, "The Gentleman was a Thief" by Neil Hickey, August, 1961.*

Tom Allen

THOMAS B. ALLEN (1928-   ) invests in his work a serious yet poetic feeling that is a stimulating combination of old and new points of view. The pen-and-ink cross-hatching method Allen uses had its vogue before the turn of the century, yet in his hands it becomes a new method for exploring form and creating an atmospheric effect. A dampened paper surface is often used to blend the lines into a tonal rather than linear rendering. In his paintings, too, Allen combines a feeling of old and new in his almost primitive style of dealing with contemporary subjects. As a result, his pictures are set apart from the usual printed material and gain increased attention for his reportorial subject matter for such publishers as *Esquire, Sports Illustrated, McCall's, Life, Redbook, Playboy,* CBS, Signet Classics and Harper & Row.

Allen was born in Nashville, Tennessee, spent two years at Vanderbilt University and obtained a B.F.A. after another four years at the Art Institute of Chicago. He exhibits regularly, is represented in New York by the D'Arcy Gallery and has won numerous awards, including the New York Art Directors Club Gold Medal and Society of Illustrators Gold Medal. He also taught at the School of Visual Arts in New York from 1958-64.

In this illustration for "A Snook Hunt along the Shores of the Spanish Main," Allen combines a Howard Pyle composition with a modern painting technique and use of color; published by Sports Illustrated, *January 3, 1966. © 1966, Time, Inc.*

Blossom

DAVID BLOSSOM (1927-   ) is the son of illustrator Earl Blossom. (David also has a son, Christopher, who is carrying on the family talent as a very promising young marine painter.) Blossom learned about illustration by growing up and living with it in his father's studio. In addition, he studied for a year at the Yale School of Fine Arts and for two years of night school at the Art Students League under Reginald Marsh.

For the next fourteen years he worked as an art director for the J. Walter Thompson advertising agency in New York.

With this thorough groundwork, David decided in 1961 to become a free-lance illustrator. He started at the top by selling his first illustration to *The Saturday Evening Post,* followed by work for most of the other major magazines, including *McCall's, Good Housekeeping* and *Reader's Digest.* He also illustrated for many national advertisers, such as Pan American Airlines and Pontiac Motor Division of General Motors.

Blossom has exhibited regularly in the Society of Illustrators Annual Exhibitions, winning Awards of Excellence, and in 1972 he was given the Society's prestigious Hamilton King Award for the best illustration of the year by a member.

He also has designed a series of postal cards commemorating famous events of the American Revolution for the United States Postal Service.

"The Consultation," cover painting for Medical Times, *August, 1972, for which Blossom won the Hamilton King Award. © 1972 Romaine-Pierson Publishers, Inc.*

Boyle

JAMES NEIL BOYLE (1931-   ) is a native of Canada, born in Granum, Alberta. He first studied at the Banff School of Fine Arts in Alberta, then for three years at the Art Center School, and for two years at the Chouinard Art Institute in Los Angeles.

His professional career has been centered on the West Coast, beginning after graduation from Chouinard, with Tri-Arts Studio and then with the association of free-lance artists called Group West. He is past-president of the Society of Illustrators of Los Angeles.

Boyle has illustrated for the *Reader's Digest, The Saturday Evening Post, Cosmopolitan, Westways, This Week, The Ladies' Home Journal* and *Argosy* magazines. He has also designed many record album covers for Capitol, RCA, Imperial, and Dot records.

Currently he is also making sculpture and painting historically-related Western subjects. His work is represented in several galleries including the Esther Wells Collection in Calabasas, California, and other galleries, in Texas, Toronto, Canada, and London, England. He recently completed a commission for Mount Sinai Cemetery in Glendale, California, a painting depicting the history of the Jewish people in America. His work is represented in many collections, including the Pentagon and Smithsonian Institution in Washington, D.C.

"Old Air Show in Southern California," illustration for Westways, *published by the Automobile Club of Southern California.*

MIA CARPENTER (1933-) has an excellent sense of composition and design which she combines with the subtle sensitivity that distinguishes her work.

Mia is a Californian, from Los Angeles, and obtained her B.A. from the Art Center School there.

Her first work was for *Seventeen* magazine in 1957, and she has since illustrated for *Redbook, The Ladies' Home Journal, Good Housekeeping, McCall's, Parents* magazines, and the *New York Times.* In addition, she has illustrated a book for Harper & Row.

Mia Carpenter's work has been exhibited at the annual shows of the New York Society of Illustrators where, in 1962, she won the Gold Medal for advertising art.

Illustration for Tanner of North Carolina, 1964.

PAUL CALLE (1928-) is probably best known for his skill with a pencil, his favorite medium; he is the author of *The Pencil,* published by North Light Publications, which recently went into its sixth printing.

Born in New York City, Calle attended Pratt Institute and sold his first work to *Liberty* magazine at the age of nineteen. He went on to illustrate for *McCall's, The Saturday Evening Post, National Geographic, Fortune* and many other magazines as well as national advertising accounts.

He was selected as an official artist of the National Aeronautics and Space Administration Fine Art Program, and he became involved with many of the NASA projects. As a related project, he designed the "First Man on the Moon" stamp for the U.S. Postal Service, one of thirteen stamps he has designed to date.

Another involvement was with the Department of Interior Artist in the Parks program which gave Calle the opportunity to travel throughout the West. This led to an interest in the history of the area and in drawing and painting the life of the early settlers.

He now is involved full time with historical pictures, which have been exhibited widely and won him a following of collectors. His works are in the permanent collections of the Phoenix Museum of Fine Arts, Pacific Northwest Indian Center, Thomas Gilcrease Institute of American History and Art, National Cowboy Hall of Fame, The National Aeronautics and Space Administration Collection, National Park Service, U.S. Department of Interior and other institutions.

"The Winter Hunter," a recent painting; the artist has also done a pencil version of this subject, reproduced in limited edition. Property of Mill Pond Press, Inc.

cleary

JOSEPH S. CLEARY (1926-   ) is a West Coast painter who finds distance no impediment to working for magazines in the East. These have included *The Saturday Evening Post, Parents, The Ladies' Home Journal* and *Argosy*.

His exhibition activities are centered in the West, however, at the San Francisco Museum of Art, the M.H. De Young Memorial Museum of San Francisco, the Jack London Show and California State Fair. He has won many awards, including several firsts.

Cleary was born in Long Beach, California, and studied at San Francisco State College, Mills College and the California College of Arts and Crafts in Oakland. He is a member of the East Bay Art Association, the Bohemian Club of San Francisco, and taught at the California College of Arts and Crafts in 1955-57.

Illustration for the story by Ray Bongartz, "The Beautiful Travelers." © *1963 by The Curtis Publishing Company.*

T. CoConis

TED C. CoCONIS (1927-   ) has done illustrations for almost every major magazine over the years, and also designed covers for record albums, book jackets, travel campaigns and motion picture posters.

Recently he has returned from several years' stay in Paris and in the Greek Islands, painting under the "incomparable Mediterranean light." He is continuing to pursue his fine art endeavors, but also does a limited number of story illustrations and movie poster commissions.

Some recent movie illustrations have been done for "Fiddler on the Roof," "Man of La Mancha," "Dorian Gray," "Breezy," "The Prime of Miss Jean Brody," "Hair," "The Other Side of Midnight" and "Waterloo."

CoConis was born in Chicago, Illinois, and studied at the American Academy of Art there. Prior to appearing in the magazines, he worked as a studio artist in New York. He has also taught at the San Francisco Academy of Art.

Poster painting for the movie version of "Fiddler on the Roof," United Artists Corporation, 1972.

287

GUY DEEL (1933-   ) has come full circle in his interest in the American West to his own family background. His grandparents began ranching in Texas in the 1880s; his father was a Texas cowboy, and his mother cooked for the ranch hands.

Deel was born in the west Texas town of Tuxedo. He was awarded a scholarship at the Art Center College of Design and after graduation, had further training with Pruett Carter. He also studied sculpture at the Otis Art Institute.

His professional career, beginning with work as an animator and background artist for a film production studio, has also included free-lance assignments from *Redbook, True, The Saturday Evening Post, Good Housekeeping, This Week, Westways, Reader's Digest* and *Esquire* magazines. In addition, he has done paperback cover illustrations for leading Western authors, such as Luke Short, Will Henry, Elmer Kelton, Clay Fisher, Lewis Patton, Gary McCarthy and Louis L'Amour. A recent project included four years' work at the EPCOT center at Disney World in Florida painting historical subjects of the Revolutionary War for the American Adventure Pavilion. Currently he is concentrating on gallery paintings based on themes of the Old West and his family history.

Cover design for After the Bugles *by Elmer Kelton for Bantam Books, 1981.*

"Man Tracks," a recent Dumas painting.

JACK DUMAS (1916-   ) was born in Seattle, Washington, where he attended the Cornish School of Allied Arts and the Seattle Academy of Art, studying under Ernest Norling.

After his first work for the *Los Angeles Examiner* editorial art department, Dumas joined a commercial art service with Ren Wicks. This was followed by a five-year Army stint, beginning in 1941, with a topographical engineering battalion. After the war, he moved to San Francisco and the helpful influence of Maurice Logan, Willard Cox, Stan Galli and Fred Ludekens.

His first editorial art published was a cover for *Argosy* magazine in 1956. This was soon followed by assignments for *Sports Afield, The Saturday Evening Post, Argosy* and Bantam Books. He has also illustrated for West Coast advertisers, notably the Weyerhaeuser Company of Tacoma, Washington.

An enthusiast of the outdoors and wildlife, he now lives in the redwood forest of northern California. The wildlife subjects which were his illustrating specialty naturally led to his doing gallery paintings of the same subject matter. His art has helped to raise thousands of dollars for conservation projects and his paintings were recently included in the North American Wild Animal Art Exhibition at the Cowboy Hall of Fame.

Dumas was a member of the Society of Illustrators for many years and is now a member of the Society of Animal Artists.

NAIAD EINSEL (1927-   ) was born in Philadelphia, Pennsylvania. She studied at the High School of Music and Art in New York City and graduated from Pratt Institute. She was an art director in the promotion department at CBS when she met her husband, Walter, then her counterpart at NBC. Their similar artistic tastes became even more alike as they worked alongside each other and soon they could collaborate at any stage of their assignments, if necessary, from concept to final rendering. The final work receives the signature of the one who originally got the assignment.

Naiad's first illustrations were done for *Seventeen* magazine in 1947. Further commissions have come from *Redbook, The Ladies' Home Journal, Collier's, Look, Parents, Woman's Day, Family Circle, Good Housekeeping* and *Cosmopolitan* magazines. Other work has included children's books, book jackets, record album covers, TV titles, package designs and movie posters. Together they designed a four-panel block of commemorative stamps, "Progress in Electronics," in 1973 for the U.S. Postal Service.

She and Walter have both exhibited their work at the Society of Illustrators, The American Institute of Graphic Arts and the Art Directors Club of New York, receiving many certificates of merit. They also currently teach at the Parsons School of Design.

"Westport 1776-1976," published in Americana Magazine, *July, 1976. This full-sized Bicentennial quilt was designed by Naiad and executed by dozens of volunteer Westport needlewomen over the period of a year. © Naiad Einsel 1974, owned by the Westport Historical Society.*

EINSEL

WALTER EINSEL (1926-   ) is a native of New York City. He attended classes at the Art Students League with John Groth and graduated from Parsons School of Design, studying under Moses Soyer.

The New York Times Magazine gave him his initial illustration assignment. This was followed by commissions from *Epicure, American Heritage, Life, Look, Time, The Saturday Evening Post, Boy's Life, Gentleman's Quarterly* and many other publications.

His first three-dimensional art object was a valentine for Naiad; other such mementos became more complex; movement was added by means of gears, ratchets, motors and springs. These became a part of his artistic repertoire and animated sculpture now dominates his work. Clients include Macy's Department Store, which built a fourteen-foot replica of his "Captain Macy," Allied Van Lines, and A.T.&T., which recently commissioned Einsel to design an exhibition for its corporate participation in the EPCOT Center, a permanent world's fair of technology in Orlando, Florida. His exhibit involves fifty-five figures, most of which move in various ways, and includes a twelve-foot ferris wheel and a fourteen-foot "Einsel Tower Phone Mobile."

"Save America" — When a coin is deposited, the knob is pulled and a plunger pushed, Uncle Sam raises his hat and opens his mouth. Printed on his tongue is "Thank you." Polychromed wood, 28 inches high.

Fuchs, who plays a trumpet himself, is a jazz afficionado and has done many excellent paintings of contemporary and historical jazz musicians. Advertising illustration for Benge Company.

"Amelia Earhart," illustration for John Hancock Mutual Life Insurance Co., 1964.

"Old Western Saloon." Courtesy, Jack O'Grady Galleries, Chicago.

B Fuchs,

BERNARD FUCHS (1932-   ) was named "Artist of the Year" in 1962 by the Artists Guild of New York, signalizing his position at the top of the illustrator's profession at the youthful age of thirty. He was also the youngest illustrator ever elected to the Society of Illustrators Hall of Fame, in 1975. His pictures for *McCall's, Redbook, Sports Illustrated, Cosmopolitan, TV Guide* and other magazines are probably more admired — and imitated — than those of any other current illustrator.

Fuchs is equally at home as a gallery painter and has done official portraits of both Presidents Kennedy and Johnson. He met Kennedy just before the Cuban crisis and subsequently painted several pictures of the late President, two of which are in the Kennedy Library Collection.

Bernard was born in O'Fallon, Illinois, and attended the Washington University Art School in St. Louis. For five years after graduation, he worked for Detroit advertising art studios. He then moved East to Westport, Connecticut, and began to do editorial magazine illustration.

He has had one-man shows in various parts of the country and participated in many group shows, including the United States Information Agency Graphics Exhibition in the Soviet Union.

Preliminary study for figure in a painting of New Orleans musicians.

291

lorraine fox

LORRAINE FOX (1925-1976), who was Mrs. Bernard D'Andrea, was an equally accomplished illustrator. Born in Brooklyn, she studied at Pratt Institute and the Brooklyn Museum Art School under Reuben Tam.

Her early professional experience was acquired in the layout departments of various New York advertising agencies. In 1947 she did her first illustration for *Better Homes and Gardens*, followed by assignments for *Woman's Day, Seventeen, Good Housekeeping, Cosmopolitan, The Ladies' Home Journal, Redbook* and *McCall's*.

She exhibited her work at the Society of Illustrators' annual shows, New York and Philadelphia Art Directors Club exhibits, the Brooklyn Museum, New York City Center Gallery and at the Silvermine Guild New England Show, winning several Gold Medals and other awards.

Lorraine taught at the Parsons School of Design in New York and was a member of the faculty of the Famous Artists School in Westport, Connecticut. In 1979 she was posthumously elected into the Society of Illustrators Hall of Fame.

Cover illustration for Anna and Her Daughters, *published by Avon Books, 1965.*

FRIEDMAN

MARVIN FRIEDMAN (1930-   ) exhibits a thorough knowledge of drawing in rendering the most complex subject matter with a direct reportorial manner. His color is vibrant and exciting; his control of values impressive.

Friedman was born in Chester, Pennsylvania, and his sound training was acquired at the Philadelphia Museum School of Art where he studied under Henry C. Pitz and Ben Eisenstat.

His first published work was for small religious publications, followed by illustrating for *Good Housekeeping, Cosmopolitan, The Ladies' Home Journal, Playboy, Changing Times, This Week, Cavalier, Redbook,* the *Ford Times, Boy's Life, Better Homes & Gardens* and *Family Weekly.*

He also has had a number of advertising accounts for clients such as the Ford Motor Company and Sharp and Dohme Pharmaceuticals. In addition, Friedman has illustrated some thirty-five children's books.

Since 1980 he has been devoting increasing time to painting. He recently won a major grant from the State of New Jersey to paint four large murals for the Burlington County Memorial Hospital. He regularly exhibits at the American Watercolor Society and other institutions, such as the Moore Institute of Philadelphia, the Society of Illustrators and the Philadelphia College of Art.

"Stripper," illustration for Cosmopolitan *magazine, 1963.*

A Midsummer Night's Dream

Milton Glaser

MILTON GLASER (1929-   ) is a native of New York where he attended the High School of Music and Art, and Cooper Union Art School. Following graduation, he received a Fulbright scholarship which allowed him to study etching in Italy under Giorgio Morandi. Later, Glaser spent another period in Italy for a concentrated eight months' study of lithography.

In 1954 Glaser was a founder, and president, of the Push Pin Studios formed with several of his Cooper Union classmates. Glaser's work is characterized by directness, simplicity and originality. He uses any medium or style suggested by the problem — from primitive to avant garde — in his designs for book jackets, record album covers, advertisements and direct mail pieces, as well as for magazine illustrations. His work has won numerous awards from Art Directors Clubs, American Institute of Graphic Arts, Society of Illustrators, and Type Directors Club.

Glaser has taught at both the School of Visual Arts and at Cooper Union in New York City.

Cover illustration for Shakespeare's A Midsummer Night's Dream, *published by Signet, New American Library, 1964.*

J. Gundelfinger

JOHN GUNDELFINGER (1937-   ) was born in Saint-Die, France, and studied at the School of Visual Arts in New York under Jack Potter and Tom Allen. He began free-lancing immediately after finishing school and sold his first illustration to *Redbook* in 1959. Since then he has added to his list of clients: *The Saturday Evening Post, The Ladies' Home Journal, Good Housekeeping, Reader's Digest, Seventeen* and *McCall's,* and has won several awards for his pictures, including a Gold Medal in the Society of Illustrators 1962 Annual Exhibition.

His non-illustrative work has been shown in numerous exhibitions in the United States and abroad. Since 1971 he has concentrated on his painting career and has placed pictures in many corporate and museum collections. He is represented by the Fischback Gallery in New York.

Gundelfinger is a solid draftsman, and his line is a strong underpinning for his tonal work as well. For several years Gundelfinger has also been teaching drawing and painting techniques at the School of Visual Arts in New York City.

"Nina Simone at the Village Gate," one of a series of six full-page, on-the-spot illustrations for Nugget *magazine.*

R. Heindel

ROBERT HEINDEL (1938-   ) "just makes pictures," without regard to their purpose, as "art" or "illustration." This is the enviable position of many contemporary illustrators who are given far greater editorial freedom than their predecessors had. However, it also imposes a higher artistic standard on those who accept the creative responsibility.

Heindel has responded to this challenge by making each painting the best possible artistic solution to the picture problem, whether it is imposed by a magazine editor, advertiser, or is self-assigned.

Born in Toledo, Ohio, his only art education was through correspondence with the Famous Artists Schools. However, Heindel's clients have included top accounts, with magazines such as *The Saturday Evening Post, Fortune, Time, Sports Illustrated, Good Housekeeping, Redbook, Woman's Day* and *The Ladies' Home Journal,* as well as advertisers including Wamsutta sheets and Waverly Fabrics. He has also illustrated *The Grapes of Wrath* in limited edition for The Franklin Library.

Heindel is a member of The Illustrators Workshop, teaching in summer sessions which have been held in New York, California and Paris. He also paints for exhibition, with a recent one-man show at Gallery One in San Francisco. Aside from many awards in the Society of Illustrators Annual Exhibitions, he won their Hamilton King Award in 1982.

"Dawn" is one of a series of studies of ballet dancers, which have been a painting preoccupation for several years. This subject was also used as the twenty-fifth exhibition announcement for the Society of Illustrators in 1983.

philip hays

In his work, PHILIP HARRISON HAYS (1932-   ) makes a deliberate break with the traditional evolution of illustration. Yet in this, he also borrows heavily from earlier eras, combining extracts from the old look with a contemporary point of view. The result is both novel and provocative and has won for him many awards from the Society of Illustrators, National Society of Art Directors, Art Directors Club of New York and the American Institute of Graphic Arts, including Silver and Gold Medals.

His work is represented in the Graphics collection of The Metropolitan Museum of Art and was included in the United States State Department Exhibition of "Graphic Arts in America" on tour in Europe including the U.S.S.R.

Hays was born in Sherman, Texas, and grew up in Shreveport, Louisiana. He attended the Kansas City Art Institute, the Ringling School of Art in Sarasota, Florida and the Art Center School in Los Angeles. He has taught illustration at the School of Visual Arts in New York City and for the last seven years has been Chairman of the Illustration Department of the Art Center College of Design in Pasadena, California.

Illustration for Cosmopolitan *magazine story by Margaret Cousins, "Paris Opening," October, 1958.*

Mitchell Hooks

The career of MITCHELL HOOKS (1923-   ), like that of many other artists of the post-World War II era, has been involved to a great extent with paintings for paperback book covers. His interpretations have a strong poster quality, in keeping with the need to hold their own on display with other competing titles on the bookstands, but also have a subtlety and sensitivity that attracts a closer and longer look.

In addition to his book designs for Avon, Bantam, Dell, Popular Library and Fawcett publications, Hooks has illustrated for *Cosmopolitan, The Saturday Evening Post, The Ladies' Home Journal, Redbook, McCall's, Woman's Day* and other magazines.

Mitchell was born in Detroit, Michigan, and obtained his art education at the Cass Technical High School there. Later he studied further with James Billmeyer in New York. After the war, and Occupation duty as a Second Lieutenant in Germany, he returned to New York to begin his free-lance illustration career.

In recent years, Hooks has become more diversified, dividing his work between magazines, hardcover books, paperback covers and advertising. Hardcover books include illustrations for The Franklin Library, Reader's Digest Books and Coronado Publishers.

This striking painting was considerably cropped, into an oval shape, when it appeared as a cover design for The Novice *by Giovanni Arpino, published by Bantam Books.*

Victor Kalin

VICTOR KALIN's (1919-   ) versatility is such that it is difficult to identify his style. Unlike many artists who develop a strong, easily identifiable technique, he is so interested in experimentation that his work looks constantly new.

In the field of illustrating for paperback books, this is an ideal qualification, for the industry is so competitive that the drive is always to look as contemporary as possible.

Kalin was born in Belleville, Kansas, and was graduated with a B.F.A. from the University of Kansas. He also taught classes there in painting and drawing in 1941-42. During World War II he did artwork for the training manuals, three-dimensional assembly drawings, and also served as a field correspondent for *Yank* magazine.

His first illustrations were done for the *American Weekly,* but for many years the majority of his pictures were painted for paperback covers. He now divides his time with additional assignments for advertising, record album covers and illustrations for hard-cover publishers, such as Reader's Digest Books, and Holt, Rinehart and Winston.

Recently Kalin appeared in a General Electric TV commercial in the role of a portrait painter, both acting and producing the art.

"Porgy and Bess" design for a record album cover for RCA Victor.

295

ARTHUR LIDOV (1917-   ) holds an A.B. in Sociology from the University of Chicago but is self-taught in art. He also believes that illustration is the only kind of painting worth doing.

This conviction is also his own challenge which he has capably met, in commissions for a wide variety of magazines, including *Fortune, Collier's, The Saturday Evening Post, Redbook, Good Housekeeping, American, Cosmopolitan, American Mercury, The Sign, Life, Sports Illustrated, Field and Stream, Parents* and *True.* Added to these clients have been commissions from most of the major drug companies and several of the medical magazines.

Lidov's paintings have been exhibited at The Museum of Modern Art, the Art Institute of Chicago, the National Gallery in Washington, D.C., and others, as well as in Art Directors Club exhibits in New York, Chicago, Detroit, Milwaukee and the American Institute of Graphic Arts, winning numerous awards.

Lidov's creative approach is exemplified here by one of his series of twenty-five paintings relating to industrial drug research, "Research at CIBA," published in Medical World News. © *1966 by Arthur Lidov.*

SANFORD KOSSIN (1926-   ) strikingly demonstrated in his powerful series of pictures for *Life* magazine's re-creation of the Bay of Pigs invasion, the role the illustrator can play in summarizing the total effect of war action in a way that the camera cannot. Each of his pictures highlights a major phase of the tragedy from the initial landing to final overwhelming defeat.

Kossin, who was born in Los Angeles, studied there for four years at the Jepson Art Institute under Rico Lebrun and Herbert Jepson.

His first work after coming East in 1953 was for science fiction magazines. He also illustrated children's magazines before graduating to *Life, Good Housekeeping, Parents, Redbook* and other national publications. As many of the magazines began to disappear or cut back on fiction in the 'sixties, Kossin became more involved with paperback art, including covers for Bantam Books, Ballantine, Pocket Books and Berkley Books.

He has also returned to more humor — his first love — in *Boy's Life, Reader's Digest* and other publications, including over a dozen children's books. For the last ten years (part time), Kossin has taught drawing at the Parsons School of Design in New York City.

Kossin is a member of the Society of Illustrators; his work has been represented in annual exhibitions there and at New York Art Directors Club shows.

"The Last Try Fails," illustration for Life *magazine article, "We Who Tried," May 10, 1963; Tusche on gesso ground. Sanford Kossin for* Life *magazine* © *1963 Time, Inc.*

J. McClelland

JOHN McCLELLAND (1919-   ) was born in Stone Mountain, Georgia, and attended the Alabama Polytechnic Institute, the Grand Central School of Art and the Art Career School of New York City. He also studied with Jerry Farnsworth.

John is especially successful in painting children and was commissioned to paint a portrait of Mrs. John F. Kennedy with her children for *Good Housekeeping* magazine. He is affiliated with Portraits, Incorporated, and paints as much for exhibition as for publication. His work has won several first prizes and other awards at shows in New York, Boston, New Haven, Hartford, Atlanta and at regional exhibits.

McClelland first illustrated for *Collier's* magazine in 1947 and has now worked for most of the national publishers, including *Woman's Day, Good Housekeeping, McCall's, Redbook, American, This Week, American Weekly* and *The Ladies' Home Journal.*

He taught at the Silvermine Guild of Artists in Norwalk, Connecticut, and for the past few years, he has created paintings for a series of Limited Edition Collector's Plates and a group of porcelain figurines. He has won awards for the collector plates including the top awards in 1980 and '81 from NALED (National Association of Limited Edition Dealers).

Illustration for story by I.A.R. Wylie in Good Housekeeping *magazine.*

Jerry McDaniel

In his work JERRY W. McDANIEL (1935-   ) relies mostly on line which he uses with a sophisticated, light touch. Combined with the line is an equally good sense of pattern employed for emphasis and visual excitement. This style has won him over two hundred citations and awards from shows at the New York Art Directors Club, Graphis Annual, A I G A, One Show and the Society of Illustrators. He has also exhibited in many one-man and group shows in New York (Soho) and in Europe.

McDaniel was born in Vinton County, Ohio, and studied at the Columbus College of Art and Design, in Ohio (B.F.A.), The New School for Social Research, the Fashion Institute of Technology and the School of Visual Arts.

He was only twenty-one when his first illustrations appeared in *Redbook* magazine in 1957, and he has since added *Good Housekeeping, Reader's Digest, Parents, The Ladies' Home Journal, Seventeen, Business Week* and other publications as clients. Since 1970, McDaniel has been Illustrator/Designer on "Marlboro" sports promotions for Philip Morris International.

He has been an active member of the Society of Illustrators, serving as Chairman of the 1965 Annual Exhibition and the Scholarship Show in 1977 and 1978. He is currently an elected officer of the Graphic Artists Guild, New York Board of Directors.

McDaniel is also a Professor of Advertising Design at The Fashion Institute of Technology.

Advertising illustration for Harlow's Restaurant, 1968.

"Tomahawk Throwing Contest," painted in 1981. Collection of Mr. and Mrs. Robert Torray.

MORT KÜNSTLER (1931-   ) has never been swayed by the vagaries of style or technique. His approach is straightforward and painstaking. For him the challenge is in the picture concept and in solving all of the problems of research.

Work with the *National Graphic Magazine* early in his career taught him the importance of accuracy, and he goes to extreme lengths to verify the authenticity of his reference material. This has been a vital necessity for his many historical recreations and for corporate clients, such as the Rockwell International Corporation, which commissioned him to do a recent series of paintings on the space shuttle Columbia.

Künstler was born in New York City and attended Brooklyn College and U.C.L.A. before switching to Pratt Institute for the illustration course. His early work was for the men's magazines, and he has also been published in *The Saturday Evening Post, Reader's Digest* and *Newsweek.* Most of his illustration has been involved with advertising, however, and his clients have included such major corporations as General Electric, Exxon, U.S. Steel, American Cyanamid and Texaco.

More recently, Künstler has been painting for exhibition; Hammer Galleries have had several of his one-man shows, and his pictures are included in many collections, among them the U.S. Air Force Museum, Favell Museum, the Diamond M Museum, the U.S. Naval Academy and the San Mateo County Historical Museum.

"Under Hostile Fire," reproduced in Frank C. McCarthy, the Old West.
© *1981 by Greenwich Workshop.*

FRANK C. McCARTHY (1924-   ) is a master technician and strong colorist whose pictures are always exciting to look at. He is a New Yorker who studied at Pratt Institute and at the Art Students League under George Bridgman and Reginald Marsh. He developed his talent early and was in his mid-twenties when he began to obtain illustrating commissions from *American* magazine and *Collier's.* These were soon followed by *Redbook, Argosy, True, Outdoor Life* and others, as well as a great many paperback covers for Bantam Books, Signet, Dell, Avon and Popular Library. In addition, he has done illustration for Ballantine, Goodyear, Warner Brothers, Columbia Pictures, United Artists, Twentieth-Century Fox and other advertisers.

In 1972, after twenty-seven years as an illustrator in the East, his transition to painting historical Westerns for galleries was completed and in 1974 McCarthy moved to Arizona. He was invited to join the Cowboy Artists of America in 1975, showing his work with such great illustrators as John Clymer, Bob Lougheed and Tom Lovell. He had two retrospective shows in 1977, at the Norton Museum in Shreveport, Louisiana, and the Museum of the Southwest in Midland, Texas. He has won many Certificates of Award by the Printing Industries of America for his limited edition prints published by Greenwich Workshop. Two books have been published on his paintings: *Western Paintings of Frank C. McCarthy* by Ballantine Books in 1974 and a limited edition book, *Frank C. McCarthy, the Old West,* in 1981 (the latter was sold out pre-publication) by the Greenwich Press.

ROBERT E. McGINNIS (1926-   ) was born in Cincinnati, Ohio, and studied both at Ohio State University and the Central Academy of Commercial Art in Cincinnati. He is a fine draftsman and painter, particularly of women — good or bad — for paperback covers. The predatory female, shown here, appeared in print only four-and-a-half inches high, painted with the dash and style of a lifesize portrait. This approach has kept McGinnis one of the busiest and most prolific painters for cover designs, totalling over 1,000, and he has worked for virtually all the paperback publishers. In addition, he has illustrated for *The Ladies' Home Journal, The Saturday Evening Post, True, Woman's Home Companion, Good Housekeeping, Guideposts, Argosy* and other magazines. He also did the titles for the Hollywood movie, "Hallelujah Trail" and has done posters for four James Bond movies, a Jane Fonda film (Barbarella), Burt Reynolds' ('Gator) and others. His painting of John Wayne for "The Searchers" was made a limited edition reproduction by the Greenwich Workshop and was awarded a Silver Medal by the Society of Illustrators. The original has been willed by the purchaser to the John Wayne Cancer Center at U.C.L.A. in California. For the past five years, McGinnis has also been selling Western paintings through the Husberg Gallery in Sedona, Arizona.

Cover illustration for one of a series of thirty Carter Brown mystery novels, featuring the "McGinnis Girl," published by Signet, New American Library in the 1960s.

FRANK MULLINS (1924-1978) used an impressionist's brush and color with very carefully controlled values to paint muted but highly effective illustrations. In this Central Park skating scene, he used yellow-greens, red-violets and blues in high key against the grayed-white surface of the ice to create a charming and festive atmosphere.

He varied his color to suit the mood, from boxing or golfing assignments for *Sports Illustrated* to fiction settings for *The Saturday Evening Post* or *Redbook*. His range of subjects was also diverse — he had illustrated for *American Heritage, The Book of Knowledge,* J.P. Lippincott Co., and a series of several paintings and drawings reporting on oceanography as experienced aboard the "Chain" out of the Woods Hole Oceanographic Institute for *Chemical and Engineering News*.

Frank was also an active member of the Society of Illustrators in New York and exhibited in their annual shows.

Cover painting for The Saturday Evening Post. © *1963 by The Curtis Publishing Company.*

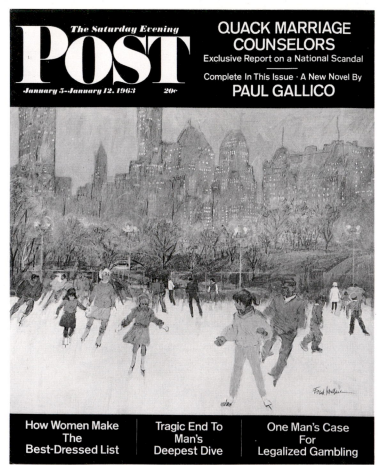

Fred Otnes [signature]

FRED OTNES (1925-   ) is a native of Junction City, Kansas; was educated at the American Academy and the Art Institute of Chicago.

His early illustrations, distinguished by expert draftsmanship, appeared in a wide variety of magazines, including *Town and Country, True, The Saturday Evening Post, Fortune, Redbook* and the *Reader's Digest.* More recently, Otnes has evolved a new approach to picture-making, incorporating collage, assemblage and printing techniques with his images. Gradually these have taken over — he now works as much with stat camera, engraver's vacuum frame and photo enlarger as with brush or paint.

The results are striking and provocative, many extremely complex, requiring the viewer to spend more time to "read" the picture message. This has made Otnes a particular favorite for advertisers and among his clients have been General Motors, Exxon, Chevrolet, Ford, Chrysler, Dobbs Hats, Italian Lines and Tennessee Gas Transmission Company.

His work has been exhibited extensively and has won over 150 awards in Chicago, New York, Detroit, Cleveland and Minneapolis Art Directors' shows. He is a member of the Society of Illustrators and received their prestigious Hamilton King Award in 1974.

"Tribute to Howard Pyle, Father of American Illustration." Assemblage created for a poster by Otnes for the 75th anniversary of the Society of Illustrators in 1976. Collection of the Society of Illustrators Museum of American Illustration.

Potter [signature]

JACK POTTER (1927-   ) prefers black-and-white to color, and his favorite line is black wax crayon or charcoal. He also insists that his drawing be only from life — that drawing from photographs is criminal! Although this point of view no longer has many protagonists, there is no question that Potter is an excellent draftsman who does not need to work from photographs and that his drawings are all the better for it. Certainly he has had a strong influence on current illustration, both as a practitioner and as a teacher. He taught for three years at the Art Center School in Los Angeles, and more recently at the School of Visual Arts in New York.

Potter is a Californian. He studied in Los Angeles at both the Art Center School and the Jepson School under Rico Lebrun. He also feels a kinship with Vuillard, Toulouse-Lautrec and the post-impressionists.

His work has appeared in national magazines, such as *Cosmopolitan, McCall's, The Ladies' Home Journal, Woman's Home Companion,* and for many national advertisers, including Coca-Cola, Northeast Airlines and L. S. Ayres & Company.

One of a series of very effective illustrations for Fuller Fabrics in 1958.

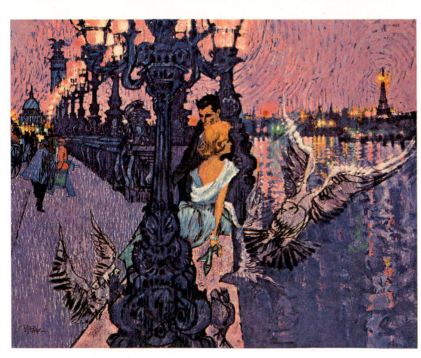

"Ritual Spectacle of a Heavyweight Championship" for "Sports' Greatest Event" by Budd Schulberg, Esquire *magazine, January, 1962.*

Bob Peak

A really skilled performer makes his artistry appear easy, and for this reason the paintings and drawings of ROBERT PEAK (1928-   ) look deceptively simple. To those who have followed his work, it is apparent that the process of simplification has gradually evolved over a period of years as a result of his deliberate effort to subordinate details to ideas. This emphasis on idea requires a lot of preliminary thought and experimentation but, once determined, the actual rendering may require only a few hours. Peak keeps his outlook fresh by rejecting conventional solutions, always looks for a new aspect of a subject or pose and prefers to work from life whenever possible.

Peak was born in Colorado and brought up in Kansas. Although he liked to draw, he first studied geology at the

University of Wichita. With time out for Army service and his interest in art revived, he followed this up with two-and-a-half years at the Art Center School in Los Angeles.

Moving East to become an illustrator, he found the first few years very difficult and groped to develop his own point of view. It was after he stopped looking at the work of other illustrators and concentrated his efforts on strengthening his own direction that he began to attract the attention of the major publishers and advertisers.

His work has since regularly appeared in magazines such as *The Ladies' Home Journal, McCall's, Good Housekeeping, Parents, TV Guide, Esquire;* and he has done more than forty *Time* covers. Advertising accounts have included French Lines, Columbia Records, Samsonite Luggage, Puritan Sportswear, Seven-Up, and he has done paintings for more than 100 motion pictures, including "Camelot," "Apocalypse Now," "My Fair Lady," "Superman" and "Star Trek." Recently Peak completed designs for the U.S. Postal Service for a series of thirty postage stamps on sports themes for the Olympic Games.

Peak's work has appeared regularly in Art Directors Clubs shows and Society of Illustrators exhibitions where he has won many awards, including eight Gold Medals. He was named "Artist of the Year" by the Artists Guild of New York in 1961 and was elected into the Society of Illustrators Hall of Fame in 1977.

One of a series of paintings made for an article on professional football. Robert Peak for Sports Illustrated © *1963, Time, Inc.*

Poster for United Artists; awarded a Gold Medal in the Society of Illustrators 23rd Annual Exhibition.

Illustration for "International Auto Racing" by Jackie Stewart for Sports Illustrated © *1973, Time, Inc.*

Advertising Design for TWA, 1964.

"Mountain Man", Courtesy of Mohawk Paper Mills, Inc.

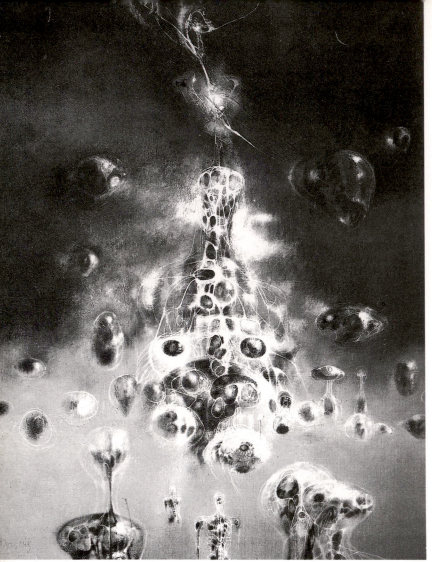

powers

There is nothing orthodox about the work of RICHARD M. POWERS (1921-   ), whether for publication or for exhibition. He cuts through directly to the picture-idea using the means as sparingly as possible; he varies his approach to fit his subject.

As an illustrator, Powers has done a number of children's books, cover designs for many of the classics of poetry and literature for Dell Publications, and a series on "Major Cultures of the World" for World Publishing Company. He has also illustrated for _Esquire, The Saturday Evening Post, Redbook, Life_ and _Natural History_ magazines.

In addition to 'straight' illustration, Powers has executed some 400 science fiction/fantasy paintings over the past three decades. In 1983 he was given the Frank R. Paul Award. Simultaneously, Doubleday has produced a portfolio of sixteen of his surrealist paintings titled "Space Time Warp."

He is associated with the Rehn Gallery in New York and has had twenty-four one-man shows. He was included in a New Talent Exhibition at The Museum of Modern Art in 1952 and has also exhibited at The Metropolitan Museum of Art, the Corcoran Gallery in Washington, D.C., the National Academy of Design and the Whitney Museum.

Powers was born in Chicago and studied at Loyola University, the Chicago Art Institute and the University of Illinois. Later he worked with Julian Levi at the New School for Social Research in New York, and studied with Jay Connaway in Maine and Vermont.

"Gof-fFlar, Quasarquark of fFlar." From Space Time Warp _portfolio;_ © _1983 by Richard M. Powers._

Saris

ANTHONY SARIS (1924-   ) researches his pictorial subjects thoroughly before planning any layouts or compositions, preferring to keep completely receptive to any new ideas suggested in the course of his inquiry. Similarly he does not make preliminary drawings but, having worked out the problems in his mind, makes his finished renderings while there is still a creative challenge to be met, rather than redo an approved sketch. This method produces some occasional failures which must be redone, but Saris works rapidly — usually in pen and ink with tone or color added — so that the time factor is not unduly important. He spends much more time in research and planning than in the rendering itself.

Saris was born in Joliet, Illinois, but moved to New York City while a boy, attended Pratt Institute, the Brooklyn Museum Art School, and the New School for Social Research. He himself has taught at Pratt Institute since 1956.

He has illustrated for most of the major publications and many national advertisers including pharmaceuticals, and his work has won numerous awards in exhibitions for New York and Washington Art Directors Club shows, the Society of Illustrators, the Outdoor Advertising Show, and the American Institute of Graphic Arts.

"Ma Rainey," illustration for "History of Jazz/Part III," published by Show Business _magazine, 1961._

Harvey Schmidt

HARVEY SCHMIDT (1929-   ), fresh from the University of Texas, with a personal and unusual portfolio, landed his first art job in New York for the graphics design department of N.B.C. Television. There he had the opportunity to design and execute the title illustrations for national network shows, learning to eliminate superfluous details that would interfere with communicating his ideas. This directness characterizes all his work for freelance magazine and advertising assignments.

Schmidt was born in Dallas and spent his boyhood between drawing and teaching himself to play the piano by ear. At the University of Texas he continued to follow both art and music, and wrote a musical in collaboration with lyricist Tom Jones while still in school. The two again successfully collaborated in "The Fantasticks," the long-running hit revue.

His first Broadway musical score was for the David Merrick hit, "110 in the Shade"; he has also worked on other Broadway scores. Schmidt recently completed a short art film with Tom Jones, called "A Texas Romance 1909," for which he composed the music in addition to doing a section of paintings along with Robert Weaver, Elaine Morfogen and Robert Benton.

Although this division of talents tends to limit his output in art, he has continued to do picture reportorial assignments for clients such as *Fortune* magazine, Abbott Laboratories' *What's New, The Lamp* — a Standard Oil of New Jersey publication, *Sports Illustrated,* and others, winning numerous top awards and medals from the Society of Illustrators and Art Directors Clubs' annual exhibitions.

Illustration for "An Assassin in Algeria," published in The Saturday Evening Post. © *1962 by The Curtis Publishing Company.*

Robert Shore

ROBERT SHORE (1924-   ) has a painter's interest in texture, color and abstract design. His subjects are presented strongly with a minimum of detail and have great impact on the printed page.

Born in New York City, Shore studied at the Cranbrook Academy of Art in Detroit, Michigan, and at the Art Students League of New York. He was awarded a Fulbright Fellowship in painting in 1952. His work has been exhibited at the Detroit Institute of Fine Arts, the Smithsonian Institution and the National Gallery in Washington, D.C., the National Academy and at Cornell University.

Shore has illustrated for a long list of magazines, including *Seventeen, Redbook, Pageant, The Reporter, Park East, Esquire, Show Business, Woman's Day;* for book publishers, such as Macmillan Company, Rinehart & Company; for advertisers, E.R. Squibb & Sons, and National Broadcasting Company.

Shore was awarded a Gold Medal at the Society of Illustrators in 1967. He has also been an instructor at the Henry Street Settlement, Cooper Union, and at present teaches at the School of Visual Arts in New York City.

Illustration for Moby Dick *by Herman Melville, published by The Macmillan Company.*

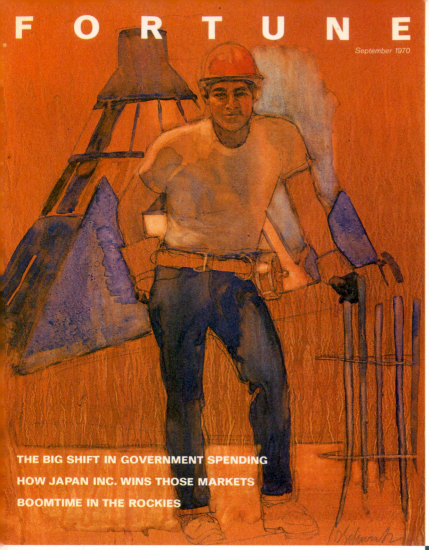

DANIEL SCHWARTZ (1929-   ) started out to be a painter and had several one-man shows at the Davis Gallery in New York City before doing his first illustrations for *Sports Illustrated* in 1958.

Schwartz is a native New Yorker and was graduated from the High School of Music and Art. His B.F.A. was earned at the Rhode Island School of Design, and he also studied with Yasuo Kuniyoshi at the Art Students League in New York. Schwartz was awarded the Louis Comfort Tiffany Fellowship in Painting in 1956 and has been an eight-time winner of the Gold Medal for Editorial Art at the Society of Illustrators exhibition since 1961, and also won the Hamilton King Award in 1978.

Continuing to combine his painting for the gallery and for publication, he has had additional one-man shows in Cincinnati, San Francisco and New York. His illustrations have appeared in many of the major magazines, including *Esquire, Life, Redbook, Playboy, McCall's, Sports Illustrated, Time* and *Fortune.*

He also has a long list of corporate clients, including CBS and NBC Television, Merrill Lynch, Mead Paper and Equitable Life.

Cover painting for Fortune *magazine, September, 1970.*

The career of SHANNON STIRNWEIS (1931-   ) has encompassed the whole range of the field from his beginnings as an advertising agency sketch artist to serving as President of the Society of Illustrators and as a Founding Trustee of the Graphic Artists Guild.

He was born in Portland, Oregon, and attended the University of Oregon for a year before studying at the Art Center School in Los Angeles under Reynold Brown, John LaGatta, Joseph Henninger and Pruett Carter. After graduation in 1954, he served as an illustrator with the U.S. Army in Europe. Upon his return, he settled in New York to become a free-lance illustrator following a four-year stint as an agency sketchman.

His first illustrations were done for *Sportsman's Magazine* in 1959, followed by work for *Field and Stream, Reader's Digest, Mechanics Illustrated, Money, Outdoor Life, Boy's Life* and *Popular Mechanics,* as well as a long list of advertising clients, movie posters and paperback covers for virtually all the publishers in New York.

Stirnweis has also participated in several special assignments for various U.S. Government agencies, involving trips to the Berlin Wall, the Everglades, Alaska and Arizona. More recently, he has been painting historical pictures of the Old West and exhibits in several galleries. His work is represented in many private and public collections, including the U.S. Air Force, the U.S. Army Historical Museum, the Department of the Interior and California Federal Savings Collections.

"Jenning, All-American Flanker-Back," commissioned by the U.S. Air Force Academy, 1971.

(signature)

HERBERT TAUSS (1929-) paints his subjects with the greatest economy of means — no extraneous detail intrudes on his picture concept. This approach requires complete technical competence to carry it off, as he does here, in this complex subject of an airport waiting room for a story in *Good Housekeeping* magazine.

Tauss is a New Yorker who received his only art training at the High School of Industrial Arts in New York.

His first illustrations were made in 1949 for *Pageant* magazine. He has grown steadily in his work for other publications which have included *American Weekly, Argosy, The Saturday Evening Post, Magazine Management, Redbook, Parents* and *McCall's* magazines.

Tauss has also painted many covers for paperback novels, including the *Kent Chronicles* which have sold over 40 million copies, and several limited edition books for The Franklin Library.

He has received numerous citations, awards of excellence, silver and bronze medals for his work from the Art Directors' Club of New York, the Society of Illustrators, and *Communication Arts* magazine.

Illustration for "Take my Hand," published by Good Housekeeping *magazine, November, 1965.*

(signature: Terpning)

HOWARD A. TERPNING (1927-) was born in Oak Park, Illinois, and studied in Chicago at the American Academy of Art and the Chicago Academy of Fine Arts. After service in the Marines in World War II, he went to New York to do advertising, editorial and motion picture illustration. Among others, he did posters for the films "Cleopatra" and "The Sound of Music."

His magazine clients have included *McCall's, Good Housekeeping, Reader's Digest, The Ladies' Home Journal, Field and Stream, Redbook, True* and *Cosmopolitan;* advertising clients: Gold Label Cigars, BOAC, TWA, Hat Corporation of America and Pendleton Woolen Mills.

More recently, Terpning has moved West and became a member of the Cowboy Artists of America in 1979. He has won top awards in their annual exhibitions since, as well as the Prix de West Award from the National Academy of Western Art. His work has also been exhibited in Peking, China, and the Grand Palais in Paris.

Typical, sensitively painted illustration by Terpning for a story in The Ladies' Home Journal. © *1966 by The Curtis Publishing Company.*

Ed. Vebell

EDWARD T. VEBELL (1921-   ) brings the same intensity to his art work as to his other major interest — fencing. He has represented the United States on two Olympic fencing teams and on one World Championship team, is ranked as one of the top epee men in the country.

Vebell is one of the top illustrators, too, a pro who can take on a difficult assignment, on virtually any subject, and do it quickly and competently. An expert photographer, he directs and takes his own reference pictures, has a large collection of costumes and props, such as guns, swords and helmets. Because of his background, he does many illustrations of war and military subjects, as well as sports.

He grew up in Chicago and attended art schools there. After a short time in his first art studio job, he was inducted into the Army. Vebell spent the war years on the staff of *Stars and Stripes* in Europe, served as illustrator-reporter in France and Italy, including the taking of Monte Cassino. Following the war, he spent an additional two years in Paris as a free-lance illustrator for French publications.

In 1947 Vebell returned to the United States and to free-lance for American publications which by now include many of the major magazines, such as *Life, Reader's Digest, Field and Stream* and *Sports Illustrated.*

In recent years he has become increasingly immersed in historical art and is a founding member of the Society of Historical Artists.

Vebell has designed fifteen stamps for the U.S. Postal Service and has also been active in the related field of First Day covers.

Illustration for "The Lost Bomber" for This Week *magazine.*

Gil Walker

GILBERT M. WALKER (1927-   ) has occasionally used other media, but he is essentially a pen-and-ink artist. And, although he attended the Art Students League for brief study with Reginald Marsh and with Robert Beverly Hale, he is otherwise self-taught. He has been a prolific sketcher since childhood and was doing professional advertising agency art work while still in high school.

The Army helped shape Walker's career, assigning him to various art projects on the West Coast. With the advent of the Korean War, he was recalled to service at the Pentagon, as an army artist, in the offices of the Chief of Staff and Chief of Information. After discharge he stayed on in Washington to do illustrations for many publications, such as *Nation's Business, U.S. News and World Report, Changing Times, Combat Forces Journal;* later moved to New York where he has continued to free-lance for other publishers, including *American Heritage, Harper's* magazine and Doubleday. This work is largely reportorial, and he has done several additional *Sketch Books* on World War II; the Korean War; U.S. Air Force; the Castro Movement; Johns Hopkins Mental Hospital; and histories of the United States Army, the American Red Cross and the U.S. Marine Corps.

Walker's work has won him Gold Medals and Distinctive Merit awards in Washington, D.C., and in New York, as well as several book awards. He also taught art at the College of the City of New York from 1957-61.

"The American Fighting Man: from Minute Man to G.I." Pen drawings for "Wide World 60," N B C Television booklet, 1960.

Here, for an Esquire *article, Weaver painted a portrait of the Presidential candidate, Jack Kennedy, symbolizing his emergence from the background of local politics to the rotunda of national statesmanship. "Kennedy's Last Chance to be President," by Richard H. Rovere, April, 1959.*

R(VEaVER

ROBERT WEAVER (1924-   ) has a strong conviction that the role of the illustrator should be a decidedly active one. He believes that the artist should make his contribution at the thinking stage as well as in painting the picture itself, whether it's for an advertising client or an editorial assignment. He has helped to create a climate for this point of view by the many creative pictures he has painted under this obligation to himself for *Fortune, Life, Look, Sports Illustrated, Cosmopolitan, McCall's, True, Seventeen, Town and Country* and *Esquire.*

Born in Pittsburgh, he studied at Carnegie Institute of Technology, the Art Students League in New York and the Accademia Delle Belle Arti in Venice.

Weaver has exhibited at the D'Arcy Galleries, American Institute of Graphic Arts, Society of Illustrators, and Art Directors Clubs in New York, Washington and other cities. The Society of Illustrators awarded him a Gold Medal in 1964, and he has had many honors since, including a Retrospective Show in 1977 at the School of Visual Arts Museum.

Weaver has also been teaching at the School of Visual Arts in New York for more than fifteen years and is a visiting faculty member at Syracuse University.

Illustration for "The Reluctant Warriors" by John Toland published by Look *magazine in 1959.*

Whittingham

WILLIAM H. WHITTINGHAM (1932-   ) is typical of today's illustrator who approaches his picture-making from a painter's viewpoint and who exploits the latest pictorial trends in either field.

He was born in Detroit and studied at the University of Michigan as well as with Reuben Tam at the Brooklyn Museum. His work won a first prize at the New York City Center and has also been exhibited at the Society of Illustrators.

Whittingham has had his illustrations reproduced in many women's magazines in England as well as in *The Saturday Evening Post, Ski* magazine, *TV Guide, Parents* magazine and Bantam Books in this country.

Ben F. Wohlberg

BEN WOHLBERG (1927-   ) had an early interest in architecture, which he studied for a year at Kansas State College. Classes in drawing stimulated him to shift his interest to art, and he transferred to the Chicago Academy of Fine Art and on to the Art Center School in Los Angeles.

Wohlberg's paintings are done in large scale, marked by bold color and strong composition yet with subtle value changes and sensitivity of form. The majority of his work has been for *Redbook,* for which he did his first illustrations in 1960, but he has also painted for *Good Housekeeping, The Ladies' Home Journal, Woman's Day, McCall's* and *Guideposts.* He has also done paperback covers for Dell, Ballantine, Pinnacle, Fawcett, Popular, Tower and New American Library, as well as hard cover book illustrations for *Reader's Digest* and The Franklin Library.

Ben exhibits with the American Watercolor Society and the annual shows of the Society of Illustrators from which he won the Award of Excellence in 1962.

This illustration was done for "The Hungry Ones" by Paul Gallico for The Saturday Evening Post. © *1962 by The Curtis Publishing Company.*

Illustration for Redbook *magazine story, "The Long Day," December, 1961.*

1970
1980

THE DECADE: 1970-1980
Murray Tinkelman

Wouldn't it be ironic if 100 years from now, the 1970's were looked back upon as a golden age of illustration? This decade is seeing the proliferation of an almost endless stream of special interest publications that are filling the void in the illustration market left by the demise of many national magazines. Because some of these smaller publications do not have large budgets, they are forced to use younger, less established artists and consequently, serve as showcases for new talent.

The paperback book field is a renaissance in itself. Westerns, adventure, gothics, fantasy and science fiction titles are published and reissued with furious regularity. Prices are often high and deadlines civilized. Styles and subjects that were thought to be obsolete have found new and appreciative audiences.

The Brooklyn Museum, the Delaware Art Museum, the Whitney Museum, the New-York Historical Society, the New Britain Museum of American Art and the Brandywine Museum, have all mounted major exhibitions in the 1970's dealing with illustration in a serious and scholarly way. Art galleries are also eagerly seeking out and exhibiting original illustrations and most newspaper and magazine reviewers are now omitting the "mere" as a prefix when discussing illustration.

The professional art schools are revitalizing their illustration departments, and are again treating the profession of illustration as a valid and viable art form.

Beautiful books on the subject have been published. Howard Pyle, N.C. Wyeth, Harvey Dunn, James Montgomery Flagg, Norman Rockwell, J.C. Leyendecker and John Held Jr. are just some of the illustrators whose work and careers have recently been documented. Happily, many contemporary illustrators have not had to wait so long for recognition, and many have already been the subject of handsome art paperbacks.

Social and sexual taboos have largely disappeared. Highly personal approaches and esoteric subject matter once considered too far out or just plain obscene are now every day images. (So much for the pious pornography of the 1950's.)

Worthy of note in this decade is the disappearance of obituaries for the field of illustration. I have not seen or read an (illustration is dead, or dying) article in years. A 1969 quote in one of the prominent trade magazines stated, "The illustrator has become a casualty to technology;" obviously the patient not only survived, it has flourished.

Illustration of the 1970's is marked by a healthy, creative, playful and highly intelligent eclecticism. Art Nouveau, Deco, Hard Edge or Funk, Magic Realism, Surrealism, Expressionism through Impressionism; all ism's are fair game and all have become part of the iconography of the 1970's. There is no dominant style, look or artist that has emerged and certainly no illustrator of this period is a

drawing by Murray Tinkelman

household name. The most significant characteristic of this decade is variety. The entire history of art has become a mammoth smorgasbord for the illustrator to feast on. The pace is frenetic, the choices and decisions infinite, but the opportunities for self expression have never been greater. More than ever the illustrator is sought after for his head as well as his hands.

The ability to act as a mirror and reflect our society's manners and mores has traditionally been the forte of the illustrator. As Mary Black, the former curator of paintings, prints and sculpture at the New-York Historical Society wrote in the catalog of the Society of Illustrators' 200 years of American Illustration Bicentennial show; "Even more than easel paintings, these illustrations offer documentary evidence and an exhilarating vision of two hundred years of American life."

I have no doubt that when we look back on the decade of the 1970's we will not only appreciate the esthetic excellence of diversity of many of the illustrators, but we will also have a vital and expressive record of the period in which they lived and worked. Maybe the good old days are now!

RAYMOND AMEIJIDE
JOHN BERKEY
SEYMOUR CHWAST
ALAN E. COBER
JOHN COLLIER
CLIFF CONDAK
JEFFREY W. CORNELL
ROBERT CROFUT
ROBERT M. CUNNINGHAM
KEN DALLISON
JACK DAVIS
PAUL DAVIS
DIANE DILLON
LEO DILLON
MARK ENGLISH
RANDALL ENOS
BART FORBES
FRANK FRAZETTA
GERRY GERSTEN
PAUL GIOVANOPOULOS
ALEX GNIDZIEJKO
DAVID GROVE
H. TOM HALL
ROGER HANE
RICHARD HESS
BRAD HOLLAND
STANLEY R. HUNTER
DOUG JOHNSON
DAVID McCALL JOHNSTON

DAVID LEVINE
MALCOLM LIEPKE
ALLAN MARDON
MARA McAFEE
GERALD McCONNELL
WILSON McLEAN
JAMES McMULLAN
ROBERT ANDREW PARKER
DAVID PASSALACQUA
JERRY PINKNEY
DON IVAN PUNCHATZ
CHARLES SANTORE
ISADORE SELTZER
MAURICE SENDAK
THOMAS SGOUROS
JIM SHARPE
BURT SILVERMAN
EDWARD SOREL
JAMES J. SPANFELLER
RICHARD SPARKS
WALT SPITZMILLER
BENJAMIN F. STAHL
GILBERT L. STONE
ROSS BARRON STOREY
MURRAY TINKELMAN
JACK NEAL UNRUH
HENRY P. VIRGONA
DON WELLER
ROBERT M. ZIERING

Ray Ameijide

RAYMOND AMEIJIDE (1924-   ) has been appropriately described as a "rainbow snipper." Certainly he uses all the colors of the rainbow in the felt cloth he uses for his medium and all the shapes must be carefully designed, cut out and assembled to make his bas relief constructions. His use of felt grew out of the need for color in earlier paper sculpture projects. Basically, the felt is glued to a stiff paper to give it the required rigidity and ability to be shaped — bent or curved — to suggest the various forms in the assemblage. Ameijide's designs are carefully planned to convey the idea like a telegram, in a happy marriage of medium and message.

He was born in Newark, New Jersey; the family name comes from northern Spain in Galicia — and he graduated with a B.F.A. from Pratt Institute. His first employment was in the Ross Art Studio in 1949. He has since, as a freelancer, illustrated for clients such as *Fortune, Vista, Discover, Money, National Geographic,* Harcourt Brace, Ginn and Company, Exxon, IBM, RCA, and Pfizer.

Ameijide has won many awards for his work as exhibited at the New York Art Directors Club and the Society of Illustrators. He also won the Hamilton King Award from the Society in 1970.

"Shepherd Boy and Wolf," felt sculpture for Mother Goose campaign by Pfizer in 1976.

BERKEY

The art of JOHN BERKEY (1932-   ), which is produced in his studio in a small town in Minnesota, looks more as though it might come off the drawing board of a team of NASA space engineers in Cape Canaveral a hundred years or more hence. And, it is likely that some of the space craft in the future will look the way he depicts them. No matter how much mechanical detail Berkey introduces in his futuristic vehicles, however, he is less interested in the nuts and bolts than in the concepts. On closer examination, the detail looks right but is not real; rather, he conjures up a vision of what might be and makes it believable.

Berkey was born in Edgley, North Dakota, and got his artistic start by producing calendar art for Brown and Bigelow in St. Paul, Minnesota. The many kinds of subject matter required, and the need to work quickly, gave him an excellent training. He has since attracted a wide variety of editorial and advertising clients, including *The National Geographic, Time, Life, Omni, Discovery, Sports Afield, TV Guide,* The Franklin Library, U.S. Steel, IBM, Texaco, Otis Sperry, Paramount and 20th Century Fox.

"Zenith Probe" for Portal Publications, 1977.

S. CHWAST

The name of SEYMOUR CHWAST (1931-   ) immediately conjures up an association with the Push Pin Studios, of which he was a founding partner in 1957, along with Milton Glaser. Their Push Pin style has had a tremendous influence on graphic art — and illustration — in all the years since.

With an eclectic approach that borrows freely and irreverently from any source, Chwast adapts his drawing style to the individual client's requirements. His clients have been among the most prominent corporations, and he has worked for virtually all the magazines, including *Time, Newsweek, New York Magazine, Esquire* and *Psychology Today.* In addition, he has designed record covers, children's books, package designs and served as editor, publisher and art director of the bi-monthly *Push Pin Graphic.*

Chwast was born in New York City and studied at Cooper Union with Sidney Delevante. His first illustrations were for *Seventeen* magazine, which was a forerunner in providing wider artistic freedom and encouraging young illustrators.

In 1970, Chwast and Push Pin Studios were honored with a retrospective exhibition at the Louvre's Musée des Arts Decoratifs, followed by showings in other major cities in Europe, Brazil and Japan. Several of his posters are in the collection of the Museum of Modern Art in New York. He is a visiting professor at the Cooper Union art school and serves on the Board of Directors of the American Institute of Graphic Arts.

"Psalliotrophobia," advertising illustration for the Strathmore Paper Company.

ALAN E. COBER (1935-   ) was named "Artist of the Year" in 1965 by the Artists Guild in recognition of his original sense of design and expressive use of line. Although Cober's work is largely linear, his is not in the traditional approach for line reproduction since, to suit his ends, he freely and effectively uses it with halftone or color.

Cober was born in New York City. He had begun the study of law at the University of Vermont before deciding to become an artist. After attending the School of Visual Arts in New York and the Pratt Institute Graphic Center, and another two years attached to the art unit in the Special Warfare School at Fort Bragg, he was able to begin freelancing. By now he has worked for all the major magazines, many Fortune 500 advertising accounts, and illustrated twenty-five children's books.

Recognition for his work has been legion; he has received numerous Gold and Silver Medals from the Art Directors Club of New York, the Society of Publication Designers and the Society of Illustrators, which also honored him with the Hamilton King Award in 1969.

Alan is president of the Illustrators' Workshop. Held each summer, it is probably the best and most intensive training an illustrator can currently obtain.

Recent projects include: painting a 31-foot mural of George Washington for the Smithsonian Institute and making life-size portraits of all the circus members (animals included!) for the Ringling Museum.
Illustration for Politics Today *magazine, 1977.*

John Collier

JOHN COLLIER (1948-) has been a consistent award winner whenever his work is exhibited. His credits include many Certificates of Excellence, five Gold and seven Silver Medals from annual exhibitions at the Society of Illustrators, and the Champion Paper International Corporation Award. This recognition is well-deserved approbation for an artist whose works are as appropriate for the gallery walls as for his many editorial and advertising clients.

Collier was born in Dallas, Texas, and received his art training from his father, Carroll Collier. He attended college in Kansas and Texas and began his art career as an assistant art director in an ad agency in Dallas. A job as staff artist in Minneapolis followed. Since then he has freelanced from Houston to New York to Lawrence, Kansas, where he presently lives. Among his clients have been *Newsweek, Time, TV Guide, The New York Times, Sports Illustrated, Redbook, Playboy,* and *Good Housekeeping* magazines; advertisers such as Mobil, Exxon, Shell, TWA, Swiss Air, CBS, and H.J. Heinz.

Collier has also found time for teaching at Pratt Institute and the Fashion Institute of Technology in New York, the Hallmark Corporation in Kansas City, and is currently teaching part time at the University of Kansas.

"Clown," cover illustration for Push Pin Graphic *magazine, June, 1978.*

Cliff Condak

CLIFF CONDAK (1930-) began attending art classes at Pratt Institute and the Museum of Modern Art School courses while still in high school. Born in Haverhill, Massachusetts, Condak won two art scholarships, is a graduate of the Institute of Applied Arts and Sciences, State University of New York, having majored in advertising art.

During two years' service with the U.S. Army in Austria, he studied painting at the Salzburg Museum; upon returning to the U.S., he attended classes at the Art Students League with Howard Trafton and later at the New School in New York with Alexy Brodovitch.

Meanwhile, he was working in various advertising agencies as an illustrator-designer. In 1958, after a year's leave for further study in Florence, Italy, he began his free-lance career. His first illustrations were done for *Gentleman's Quarterly* and *Nugget* magazine, followed by work for *Escapade, Esquire, Seventeen, Playboy, Sports Illustrated,* New American Library, Ballantine Books and various advertisers.

For several years Condak has exhibited his paintings and has had numerous one-man shows. He has also taught at the School of Visual Arts, Pratt Institute and Parsons School of Design.

"Sigmund Freud," cover design for Avon Books.

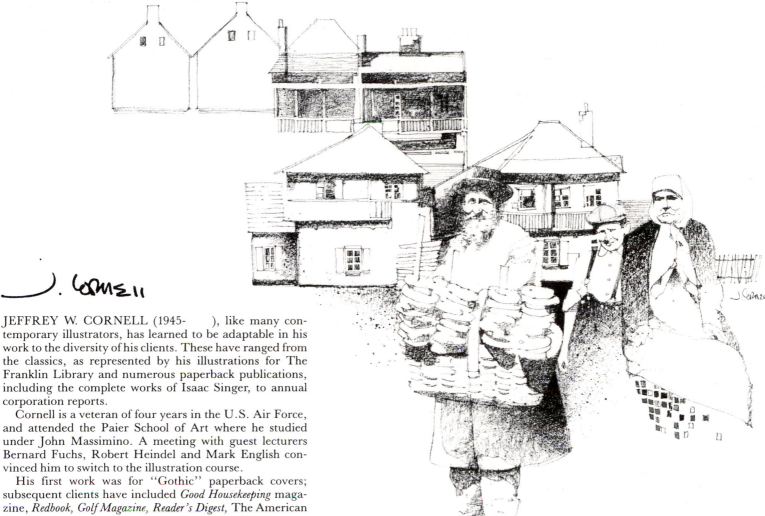

J. Cornell

JEFFREY W. CORNELL (1945-   ), like many contemporary illustrators, has learned to be adaptable in his work to the diversity of his clients. These have ranged from the classics, as represented by his illustrations for The Franklin Library and numerous paperback publications, including the complete works of Isaac Singer, to annual corporation reports.

Cornell is a veteran of four years in the U.S. Air Force, and attended the Paier School of Art where he studied under John Massimino. A meeting with guest lecturers Bernard Fuchs, Robert Heindel and Mark English convinced him to switch to the illustration course.

His first work was for "Gothic" paperback covers; subsequent clients have included *Good Housekeeping* magazine, *Redbook, Golf Magazine, Reader's Digest,* The American Stock Exchange, Bell Telephone, NBC-TV, RCA Records and Video Disks, Texaco, General Electric and the Carnegie Corporation of New York. He also designed a commemorative stamp for the U.S. Postal Service to honor the Special Olympic Games in 1979.

Cover illustration for Satan in Goray *by Isaac Bashevis Singer. Published by Fawcett books.*

Crofut

Although ROBERT CROFUT (1951-   ) received a good liberal arts education from Tufts University and the Boston Museum School of Fine Arts, he credits illustrator Harry Anderson with the guidance to get successfully started as an artist.

His first commission was a paperback cover from Tower books, and he has since done paintings for many other publishers including Signet, Berkley, the Easton Press, The Franklin Library and American Heritage, as well as magazines, such as *Outdoor Life, Field and Stream, Seventeen, Reader's Digest,* and *Science '83.* Advertising clients include M-G-M, NBC, and Exxon.

Crofut has exhibited in the Society of Illustrators Annual Exhibitions, and is represented in the Sanford Low Collection of American Illustration at the New Britain Museum of American Art. A collector of American illustration, he owns prized examples of the works of Mead Schaeffer, Harry Anderson and others.

Illustration for "Last Chance," published by Guideposts *magazine, June, 1980.*

This subject won the Gold Medal Award in the Society of Illustrators 20th Annual Exhibition.

Illustration for Pastimes: Eastern Airlines magazine, November/December 1973.

ROBERT M. CUNNINGHAM (1924-   ) has been an active professional for nearly twenty years; his first illustrations were published by *Sports Illustrated* in 1965. Yet, as his work continues to evolve, it looks fresher and more contemporary than that of artists half his age. His images are designed with great care, then simplified to the utmost, with great reliance placed on color. He likes to work with acrylic paint on paper because of its strong, bright colors and flexibility in making alterations or corrections because it dries quickly.

Cunningham was born in Herington, Kansas; he studied at the University of Kansas and the Kansas City Art Institute before moving East to attend the classes of Kuniyoshi, Corbino and Bosa at the Art Students League. His editorial work has been published in *McCall's, Redbook, TV Guide, The Lamp, Lithopinion* and other magazines, as well as many advertising clients and a series of stamps for the U.S. Postal Service.

He has been the recipient of numerous awards and medals at the annual exhibitions of the Society of Illustrators, as well as the Hamilton King Award for the best illustration of the year in 1983.

Cover illustration for Ashanti to Zulu — African Traditions *by Margaret Musgrove, published by Dial Books in 1976.* © *Leo and Diane Dillon.*

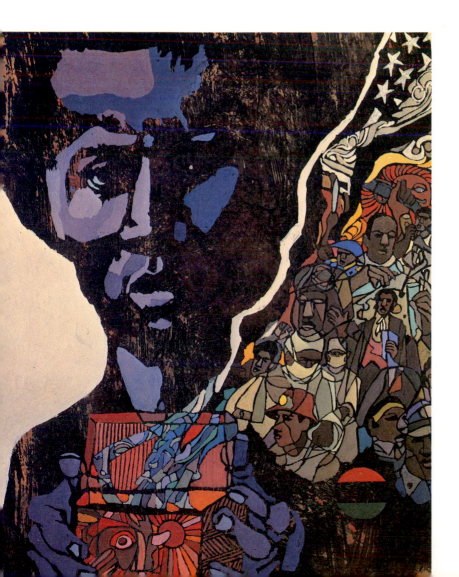

L+D DILLON

LEO and DIANE DILLON (1933-   ) were both born in March of the same year but hail from opposite coasts and different races. They began their collaboration while studying together at Parsons School of Design and the School of Visual Arts, and were married in 1957. To preclude professional jealousy, they have fused their two artistic personalities into a single and singular career, pushing each other's standards and trusting each other's input to forge a "combined artist," where each contributor critiques and takes over the other's work.

In addition to drawing and painting, the rigor of print-making techniques is evident in their work for *The Saturday Evening Post,* Caedmon records, Ballantine, Fawcett and Time-Life Books.

The Dillons are likely to employ woodcut, pochoir, stencils, airbrush, typography or Bourgess overlays in bringing the paperback cover to a high art form. This search for perfection has earned them the Hamilton King Award from the Society of Illustrators in 1976, The Caldecott Medal for Children's Book Illustration in both 1976 and 1977, and the Hugo Award for Science Fiction and Fantasy in 1971. Together they have taught at the School of Visual Arts in New York and exhibited variously in the metropolitan area at the Metropolitan Museum, the Art Directors Club, Brooklyn Public Library and the U.S. Parks Department.

Illustration for Gift of the Black Folk *by W.E.B. Dubois. Published by Pocket Books. Collection of Society of Illustrators Museum of American Illustration.*

Ken Dallison

KEN DALLISON (1933-   ) was born in Middlesex, England, where he attended the Twickenham School of Art. Moving to Canada, he obtained his first illustration assignments from *Liberty* magazine (Canada) and CBC-TV Studios in 1955. He subsequently moved to Long Island, New York, and has illustrated for many American publications including *Sports Illustrated, Esquire, Redbook, Car and Driver* and *Flying*.

Although Dallison has painted general subject matter for many advertisers and publishers, his special forte is the depiction of automobiles, and he does them all from antique racing cars to the newest experimental models.

His work has been included in shows at the Society of Illustrators and Art Directors Club shows in New York, Detroit, Pittsburgh, Toronto, Montreal and London, England.

A member of the Society of Illustrators and the Graphic Artists Guild, Dallison currently lives in Ontario, Canada, and teaches at the Ontario College of Art.

Illustration for "The Uncultured Collector," published in Car and Driver *magazine, December, 1971. Collection of the Society of Illustrators Museum of American Illustration.*

JACK DAVIS (1926-   ) is a phenomenal draftsman in the tradition of T. S. Sullivant, who can "do it straight", but finds more challenge and satisfaction in humor and exaggeration.

Davis was born in Atlanta and studied art at the University of Georgia under the G.I. Bill following three years in the Navy.

After moving to New York in 1951 and studying at the Art Students League at night, he made his first entry into the art field as an inker for a comic strip. He was soon heavily involved in comic art of every description and became one of its top practitioners for *Mad* magazine, *Trump, Playboy* and many other publications.

Davis has since graduated to the more lucrative advertising art market where his humor, combined with an ability to draw anything and to meet almost impossible deadlines has made him very successful. He has also been frequently called upon to pinch-hit overnight covers for *Time* magazine, totaling thirty-six to date. Other work includes animation and artwork for television, movie posters and newspaper advertisements, covers for RCA Records, Topps Baseball cards and a children's book for Random House.

"G.O.P. Elephant during Watergate," unpublished for Time *magazine, 1974, showing the artist's preliminary sketch and the finished illustration.*

Paul Davis

PAUL DAVIS (1938-   ) who is a native of Centahoma, Oklahoma, came East and attended the School of Visual Arts on a scholarship. There he studied under a distinguished roster of teachers — Philip Hays, Robert Weaver, Tom Allen, Robert Shore, Howard Simon, George Tscherny and Burt Hasen.

His first illustrations were published in *Esquire* in 1959, and he has since appeared in *Life, Time, Look, Sports Illustrated, Evergreen Review, Harper's, Horizon, McCall's, Show* and other magazines. He has also done record covers, book jackets and advertising illustration. Recent clients have been G.E. Theatre and Mobil for the Masterpiece Theatre programs about Disraeli, King Lear and Lord Nelson.

Davis exhibits at the Society of Illustrators, the American Institute of Graphic Arts and the New York Art Directors Club shows, winning two Gold Medals and several Honorable Mentions. He has also exhibited in the Warsaw Poster Biennial, in Lahti, Finland, had one-man shows in the Museum of Modern Art in 1975-76 in Kamakura and Kyoto, Japan, and in 1977 in the Pompidou Museum in Paris. His work is also represented in galleries in Tokyo and Rome.

"Opera Singer," poster illustration for the School of Visual Arts, 1978.

E N O S

RANDALL ENOS (1936-   ) is a satirist in the guise of a primitive, and he uses the linoleum block medium with the sleight of hand of a magician to conceal the sophistication of his renditions. He has brought this ancient technique up to date by various untraditional means. Enos may use a block like a rubber stamp, for instance, creating a whole crowd out of a single figure; he prints with many different inks on varieties of colored papers and does a lot of cutting and pasting.

Enos was born in New Bedford, Massachusetts, and attended the Boston Museum School of Fine Arts where he studied painting and graphics. After an eight-year stint as an instructor in the cartoon course at the Famous Artists School, he began to do free-lance illustration, first for *Cavalcade* magazine, then *Harper's, Playboy, Esquire, Holiday, Fortune, National Lampoon, The New York Times* and many other publications. He has also worked in animated film, designing for clients such as IBM, Olivetti, Xerox, Burlington (the famous crisscross animated signature is his design) and also some film titles, such as "The Russians are Coming."

He has taught at the Parsons School of Design for several years. His work has been exhibited in annual shows at the Society of Illustrators, Society of Publication Designers, and Art Directors Club shows, winning many awards and a Cannes TV Festival Award (1964) for animation.

"Diary of a Movie Extra," illustration for the Boston Globe, *June, 1983.*

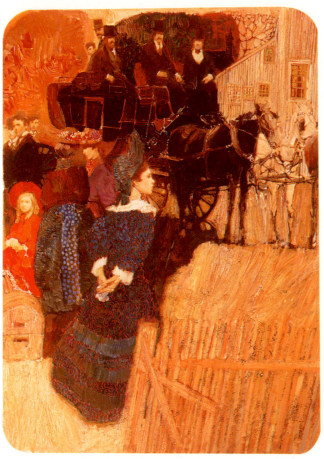

1732-1982

USA 20c

Mark English

MARK ENGLISH (1933-   ) has evolved in his work through several stages and painting styles, but each has been distinguished by his use of subtle changes in color and value while emphasizing the overall pattern of shapes.

English was born in Hubbard, Texas. He attended the University of Texas as well as the Art Center School in Los Angeles where he studied with John LaGatta and Joe Henninger.

After considerable studio and advertising experience with the automobile industry, he got his first fiction illustration assignment from *The Saturday Evening Post.* Since then he has also contributed to many other publications, including *Redbook, Parents, The Ladies' Home Journal, Good Housekeeping* and *Sports Illustrated.*

English has been making another transition to painting for exhibition. To that end he became artist-in-residence at Hallmark Cards in Kansas City, conducting teaching sessions for the staff artists. He also has been a member of The Illustrators Workshop, a distinguished teaching group of professional illustrators.

His work has been exhibited widely and has won awards from the Society of Illustrators and the Art Directors Clubs of Pittsburgh and Detroit. His paintings are also shown at the Jack O'Grady Gallery in Chicago. English was elected into the Society of Illustrators Hall of Fame in 1983.

"Taking care of Elena," by Jessie Schell, illustration for McCall's *magazine. Reprinted by permission of The McCall Publishing Company.*

Recent painting exhibited at the Vineyard Gallery.

BART FORBES (1939-   ) lives and works from his home base in Dallas, Texas. Born in Altus, Oklahoma, he was the son of Air Force parents and did a lot of moving while growing up. He graduated from the University of North Carolina with a B.A. in 1961. After serving in the Army, he did graduate study at the Art Center School in Los Angeles; one of his instructors there was John LaGatta.

After about six years as an advertising illustrator in Dallas, he received his first editorial assignment from *The American Way.* He has since worked for most of the magazines, including *McCall's, Time, Saturday Review, TV Guide, Money, Seventeen,* and *Redbook,* as well as Doubleday Books and various paperback publishers. Advertising clients have included RCA, Exxon, Eastern Airlines, American Express and Sony.

A member of the Society of Illustrators and the American Institute of Graphic Arts, he has won many awards in their exhibits. He has also had one-man shows at Washington State University, Texas Christian University, 2719 Gallery in Dallas and other galleries. Former President Jimmy Carter had seven Forbes paintings in his White House collection.

"The Death Dealer."
© 1973 by Frank Frazetta.

![Frazetta signature]

FRANK FRAZETTA (1928-) is an artistic phenomenon who has created a cult following for his fantasy paintings. His ingredients include a mixture of sex, violence, melodramatic action, exaggerated anatomy and exotic, impossible settings — and he makes it all work. Paperback publishers vie for his services; his illustrated calendars and posters sell in the tens of thousands to avid fans. Frazetta originals are too valuable for him to sell; instead, poster reproductions must serve for those who would collect his work.

Frazetta was born in Brooklyn and has had dual talents in drawing and athletics from childhood. He won the Most Valuable Player award and batted .487 in his Parade Grounds League and received several offers to play professional baseball. At the same time he had been selling comic book drawings beginning in his second year of high school, and as a promising young artist had received an invitation from Walt Disney to come to Hollywood. Frazetta decided to stay in Brooklyn to be near the Dodgers, but he reasoned

that an artist's career could be a longer one than a ball player's.

The comic book field was an excellent training ground, particularly in forcing the use of imagination, and Frazetta flourished in it. For a while he had his own strip, "Johnny Comet"; worked as an assistant to Al Capp on the "Li'l Abner" strip for several years; did some drawings for *Mad* magazine and *Playboy,* also some movie posters.

It was the chance to do a series of paperback covers for a new edition of "Tarzan" stories that started him on his present course. They were enormously successful and led to many commissions for "sword and sorcery" titles. Frazetta's covers had much to do with the success of this genre, and a whole school of fantasy artists has followed his lead. Meanwhile, Frazetta has been able to create his own market through publishing ventures which distribute his signed reproductions, posters and annual calendars, freeing him to choose his own subjects and to paint them at his own pace.

Gersten

GERRY GERSTEN (1927-   ) is a product of the Cooper Union Art School, although during his career he has contradicted much of what he learned there. (The then prevailing attitude was to damn Norman Rockwell and to praise Piet Mondrian.) Having been born in New York City and attended the High School of Music and Art, he has had a thorough grounding in the fundamentals of drawing, and they are his greatest strength. Much of his work is drawn in pencil on tracing paper, then dry-mounted on illustration board; washes or color may be added when appropriate.

Gersten is a particularly effective caricaturist. As he describes his approach, "When I get an assignment to do a character, I try to make him as universally 'readable' as I can. I try to create a symbol, so that the viewer can feel that he knows this person, perhaps he has met him somewhere . . ."

Gersten's humor and irreverence have kept him busy for clients such as *Boy's Life, The Ladies' Home Journal, Playboy, McCall's, Harper's, Time, Life, Sports Illustrated, Scholastic* and many other publications, as well as various advertising accounts.

He is a member of the Society of Illustrators and the Graphic Artists Guild and was a guest lecturer at Parsons School of Design in 1975.

Portrait of Joe Namath, "A lot of people over 10 still believe in Superman," full-page newspaper advertisement for Sport *magazine.*

Gnidziejko

ALEX GNIDZIEJKO (1943-   ) is a thoughtful, careful artist who plans and paints his pictures without artifice or ostentation, conveying a sense of dignity and strength in his work. In 1975 he received a Gold Medal from the Society of Illustrators and was awarded a Creativity Certificate of Distinction from *Art Direction* magazine in 1979. In 1980 he received advertising's Andy Award as well as an Award of Excellence from *Communication Arts* magazine.

A student at Pratt Institute and the School of Visual Arts, he first illustrated for *Playboy* magazine in 1966. He has since worked for many magazines and advertisers, including NBC, Time, Inc., *Sports Illustrated, New York* magazine, *McCall's,* Mobil Oil Corporation, *Penthouse, Good Housekeeping, Esquire, National Geographic,* Holiday Inns and Lenox China.

Gnidziejko also paints and exhibits at the New Jersey Watercolor Society, the Rizzoli Gallery in New York and the Landsman Gallery in New Jersey.

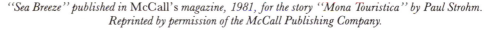

"Sea Breeze" published in McCall's *magazine, 1981, for the story "Mona Touristica" by Paul Strohm. Reprinted by permission of the McCall Publishing Company.*

"Magritte." Collection of the artist.

Giovanopoulos

PAUL GIOVANOPOULOS (1939-   ) has a Greek heritage, as his name would indicate. Born in Kastoria, Macedonia, he came to the United States as a teenager, knowing no English. The adjustment was very difficult, but his artistic aptitude won him a two-year scholarship to New York University. He next attended the School of Visual Arts for three-and-a-half years, studying under Robert Weaver.

He began his illustrating career with a commission from *Seventeen* magazine in 1961, but other work came slowly. In 1964 and '65, he won the John Armstrong Chaloner Foundation Fellowship to work and study abroad. Upon his return to New York, he found a much more favorable response to his work and obtained commissions from *Playboy, New York* magazine, *The Ladies' Home Journal, Redbook, Fortune,* and other magazines as well as advertisers.

Giovanopoulos also illustrated *The Real Tin Flower* in 1968 and *Free as a Frog* in 1969; both volumes were judged by *The New York Times* as among the ten best illustrated children's books of their respective years. His work has won many other awards, including a Gold Medal from the Society of Illustrators. He has exhibited at the Lacarda Gallery in New York, Joslyn Art Museum, Butler Institute, Norfolk Museum, National Academy of Design, Corcoran Gallery, Baltimore Museum and various other institutions. He also teaches, formerly at the School of Visual Arts, now at the Parsons School of Design.

Poster illustration for "Never Cry Wolf," a Carroll Ballard Film produced by Walt Disney Productions, 1982.

DAVID GROVE (1940-   ) has developed an interesting variation of the Coles Phillips' "fadeaway" technique by melding background and foreground colors and values. And, as demonstrated here, he has further heightened the effect by means of shared shapes. Obviously, this demands much preliminary planning for the final result to look so spontaneous.

Grove was born in Washington, D.C. and attended the Syracuse University School of Art. However, for most of his career he has worked from his West Coast studio where he does work for a wide range of clients, such as *Car and Driver, Saturday Review,* Bantam Books, Ballantine Books, Dell Publishing Company, Standard Oil, U.S. Navy, Atlantic Richfield, Western Airlines, NFL Properties, Inc., Pendleton Woolen Mills, CBS, Bank of America and Walt Disney Productions.

The artist has exhibited in New York, Los Angeles, San Francisco and Paris, winning Awards of Excellence in the Illustration West 16 and 20 shows. Grove has also taught at the Academy of Arts College in San Francisco and is a member of the San Francisco and New York Society of Illustrators and the Graphic Artists Guild.

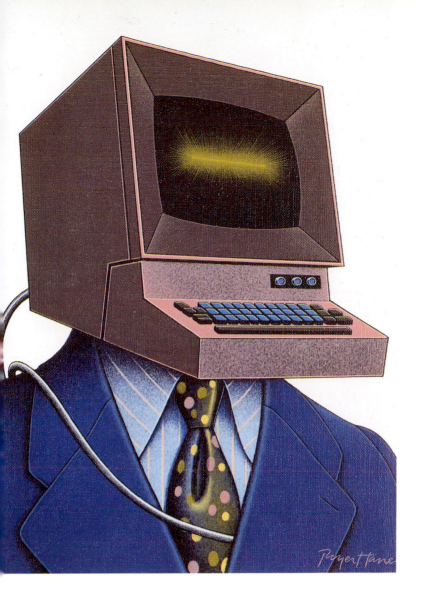

Roger Hane

ROGER HANE (1938-1974) crowded a distinguished illustrating career into a short life span. Tragically he was robbed and beaten to death in Central Park at the age of thirty-six. Just three weeks earlier he had been voted ''Artist of the Year'' by the New York Artists Guild.

He was born in Bradford, Pennsylvania, and was graduated from the Philadelphia Museum School of Art in 1961. Moving to New York, he quickly established himself as a strong new talent; his surrealist/fantasy concepts which were rendered with meticulous care found him many clients, including *Fortune, New York* magazine, *Redbook, The Lamp, Look, Vista* and *Playboy.* Simon and Schuster published his covers for the Carlos Castenada books, *Journey to Ixtlan, The Teachings of Don Juan* and *A Separate Reality,* which were perhaps his best-known pictures, and he worked for other paperback publishers, such as Avon Books, E.P. Dutton Company and Collier Books. Advertising clients included Formica, Sylvania Bulbs, De Beers Diamonds, Merck Sharp & Dohme, Inc., and he designed a number of record album covers for RCA, Columbia Records and Philadelphia International Records.

''Information Please,'' illustrated for The Lamp, *summer issue, 1972. Courtesy of the Exxon Corporation.*

R. Hess

RICHARD HESS (1934-   ) came to illustration by a circuitous route beginning with one of his first jobs as a designer of paint-by-number sets for the Palmer Paint Company in Detroit. Born in Royal Oak, Michigan, he early showed art talent but lacked formal training. However, after a short stay at Michigan State and evening classes at the local Society of Arts & Crafts, he was able to land an advertising agency job. This was his art training ground. Through a succession of agency posts in Detroit, Philadelphia and New York, he learned to handle typography, design in allotted space and to handle various mediums.

A natural primitive, Hess has not tampered with his style, and it is the strength of his ideas that has made him a successful creative art director, designer and illustrator with a host of clients, such as *Vista* magazine, which he also art directed, Random House, *Playboy, Esquire, Newsweek, New York* magazine, American Airlines, Western Union, CBS, *The New York Times,* U. S. Plywood, Champion Papers, Xerox, Westvaco and many others. His work has received Gold and Silver medals and merit awards from Art Directors Clubs in New York, Detroit, Philadelphia, Chicago, Houston, Los Angeles and San Francisco; additional awards from the American Institute of Graphic Arts, the Society of Illustrators and other organizations.

Advertising illustration for Public Broadcasting System program, sponsored by Exxon Corporation, 1981.

"Scorpions," published by Thomas Y. Crowell Company, 1977.

HOLLAND

BRAD HOLLAND (1943-   ) appears to be endlessly inventive in powerfully portraying the foibles of humanity. Using stark, unorthodox symbology, he shocks and surprises while forcing the viewer into unavoidable recognition of the underlying truth in his pictorial commentary. His talents have been ideally suited to the Op-Ed pages of *The New York Times,* which has commissioned and published some of his best work since 1971.

Holland was born in Fremont, Ohio; he grew up there and in Fort Smith, Arkansas. He was submitting cartoons to magazines while still in high school; moved to Chicago after graduation and found his first employment in a tattoo parlor and later some small illustration jobs. Moving to Kansas City in 1964, he worked briefly for Hallmark cards and formed the Asylum Press "to print eccentric projects with friends."

In 1967 he moved to New York City and began to contribute drawings regularly to *Playboy* magazine. He also worked for the underground press, *New York Free Press, East Village Other, Review, Redbook* and other publications.

His work has won many awards including Gold Medals from the Society of Illustrators and the New York Art Directors Club; he has also exhibited in the Musée des Beaux Arts in Bordeaux and in The Louvre in Paris. A book with drawings and text by Holland titled *Human Scandals* was published by Thomas Y. Crowell Company in 1977.

"Human Scandals," published by Thomas Y. Crowell Company, 1977.

"Lettuce," published by Thomas Y. Crowell Company, 1977.

Wraparound cover illustration for The Great Steamboat Race *by John Brunner. Published by Ballantine Books, February, 1983.*

Hall

H. TOM HALL (1932-   ) grew up in Prospect Park, Pennsylvania, and studied at the Tyler School of Fine Art and the Philadelphia College of Art. His teachers were Henry Pitz, Joe Krush, Ben Eisenstat and Al Gold, and he was inspired by the work of Ben Stahl and Robert Fawcett.

While stationed in Japan with the U.S. Army, he wrote a children's book to practice illustration. After returning home, this became his first illustration assignment when published by Knopf. About the same time he started working for other book publishers and *Jack & Jill* magazine. He continued to work in the children's field for about twelve years; then in 1970, armed with a new portfolio, he shifted to adult book and magazine illustrations.

Hall's credits include dozens of children's book publishers, *Reader's Digest* books and magazine, *National Geographic* books, *The Saturday Evening Post, Guideposts* magazine, Bantam Books, Avon, N.A.L., Fawcett, Warner, Ballantine and other paperback publishers.

Hunter

STANLEY R. HUNTER (1939-   ), like many other illustrators, got his professional start in Detroit as an automobile illustrator. For about ten years he did the backgrounds and figures, as well as some automobiles, for various agencies and studios.

He was born in Lansing, Michigan, and after high school attended the Society of Arts and Crafts in Detroit where he studied with Nick Beauholis and where his training landed him his first studio job.

In 1974 he moved East and has since worked for many periodicals, including *Newsweek, TV Guide, Reader's Digest, Life, Look, The Ladies' Home Journal, National Geographic,* and book publishers such as Doubleday and the Franklin Library.

Hunter's work has won many Awards of Excellence, a Gold Medal in a Detroit art show and a Silver Medal from the Society of Illustrators.

"Interior of the Café Sélect" from The Sun also Rises *by Ernest Hemingway. Published by the Franklin Library.*

DOUG JOHNSON (1940-) was born in Toronto, Canada, and studied at The Ontario College of Art. There he received a traveling scholarship enabling him to continue his painting for two years in Spain and Morocco. He then returned to Toronto and worked as a free-lance illustrator for four years. In 1968 he moved to New York City where he has been working for major magazines and ad agencies. Some of his clients have been United Airlines, Department of the Interior, *Playboy, Oui, Viva, Look, Sports Illustrated,* United Artists and Columbia Records.

In recent years he has done much work for the theatre. His advertising consulting firm, Performing Dogs, has worked on several Broadway shows, including the award-winning "Candide." He is presently Creative Director of The Chelsea Theatre Center for which he has won several awards.

Johnson has exhibited in and won awards from approximately one hundred shows and in the spring of 1977 had a one-man exhibit at the Society of Illustrators.

He has taught for several years at the School of Visual Arts and was a visiting professor at Syracuse University in the spring of 1977.

DAVID McCALL JOHNSTON (1940-) is a mid-Westerner, born in South Bend, Indiana. After completing his studies at the Art Center College of Design in California where he studied with Joseph Henninger and John LaGatta, he returned to the mid-West for his first art job as a studio artist at Art Staff in Detroit, Michigan, in 1964. Eventually, he became a partner in his own Detroit firm, Designers and Partners.

Now a free-lance illustrator, he has done work for a wide variety of clients, including Signet, Bantam, Harper and Row, Franklin Mint and The Franklin Library. Johnston has also created designs for Steuben Glass, with some pieces in museums.

He regularly exhibits his work, which has been included in annual shows of the Art Directors Club of Detroit, winning both Gold and Silver Medals, and the Society of Illustrators.

"The World of Ike and Tina Turner," record cover for United Artists Records, 1973.

Advertising illustration for Coty, 1973.

Illustration for How to be a Celebrity *by Elsa Maxwell, published by Doubleday & Company, Inc.,* © *1962 by Elsa Maxwell.*

"Lyndon Johnson at Sea," Look *magazine, March 4, 1969.*

Self-caricature by David Levine, which demonstrates that he can take it as well as dish it out; 1968.

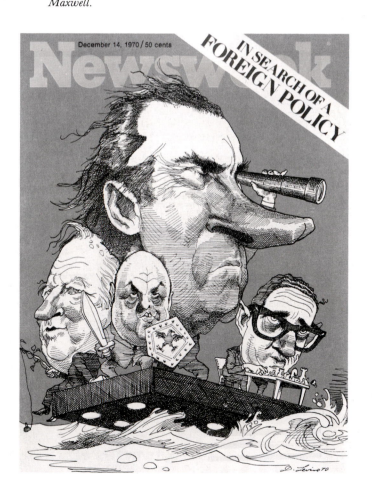

D. Levine 70

DAVID LEVINE (1926-   ). If anyone deserves the mantle of political cartoonist Thomas Nast, it is surely David Levine, who wields perhaps the sharpest satiric pen today.

Levine studied at the Tyler School of Art in Philadelphia, and for a year with Hans Hofmann in New York, although his influences run from Will Eisner and Harold Foster to Edouard Vuillard and Thomas Eakins.

He began by free-lancing for *Esquire* in 1958 and since the early 'sixties has become a mainstay at the *New York Review of Books,* where he has caricatured a virtual encyclopedia of great literary, artistic and political figures. One of the most notorious of these depicted Lyndon Johnson displaying his appendectomy scar in the shape of Vietnam. He escalated from there to lambaste Richard Nixon on the covers of *Time* and *Newsweek.*

Several books of his drawings have been issued, most recently *The Arts of David Levine* published by Alfred A. Knopf in 1978. The Forum Gallery in New York exhibits his pen-and-inks as well as his non-illustrative work: very sensitive portraits, beach scenes and cityscapes in watercolor.

Newsweek cover, December 14, 1970.

Liepke 1983

MALCOLM LIEPKE (1954-   ). One of the most traditionally painterly of current illustrators, Malcolm "Skip" Liepke has had no formal schooling in art. "In constantly striving to become a better artist," he says, "my teachers have been Velasquez, Whistler, Sargent, Chase and many others in the great museums around the country." Liepke was born in Minneapolis, Minnesota, and did not complete college.

Since 1976, however, when he made drawings that appeared in titles for the ABC-TV show "Rich Man, Poor Man," he has gone to the top of the profession with covers for *Time, Forbes, Newsweek* and *Fortune* magazines. In addition, his illustration clients include The Franklin Library, *Reader's Digest, McCall's, Good Housekeeping* and *The Ladies' Home Journal.*

He has accumulated impressive awards for an artist under the age of thirty: a Gold Medal from the Allied Artists, a Purchase Award from the National Academy of Design; and from the Society of Illustrators, a Gold Medal, Norman Rockwell Award and Past Chairmen's Special Award.

He has also exhibited prominently at the National Academy, American Watercolor Society, Allied Artists, National Arts Club, Salmagundi Club, and has taught at the School of Visual Arts in New York.

Portrait of composer Janáček, album cover painting for Nonesuch Records, 1982.

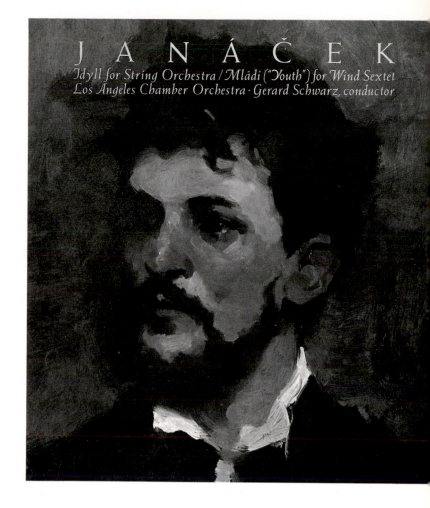

J A N Á Č E K
*Idyll for String Orchestra / Mládí ("Youth") for Wind Sextet
Los Angeles Chamber Orchestra · Gerard Schwarz, conductor*

ALLAN MARDON (1931-   ) grew up in the town of Sarnia, Ontario and went to the Ontario College of Art, the Edinburgh School in Scotland and the Slade School in London. After returning to Canada, he set up a studio in Toronto and began to free-lance. Putting together a portfolio of his work, he called on *Sports Illustrated* and landed his first assignment in the States. After a lot of flights between Toronto and New York, he moved to Connecticut and has developed a large clientele since. Among them are *McCall's* magazine, *The Ladies' Home Journal, Redbook, Time* and *National Geographic.* Other clients include many of the large corporations, such as Gulf and Western, Exxon, American Express, Mohawk Paper, Lightolier and numerous pharmaceutical accounts.

Mardon's crisply rendered work is usually in mixed media, reinforced by pen line which reveals the sure draftsmanship of his Slade School training; he has won several awards from Art Directors Clubs in New York and Boston and an award of merit from the Society of Illustrators.

Cover design for program, First Day of Issue Ceremony, Franklin D. Roosevelt stamp. Client, United States Postal Service.

333

McAfee

The art of MARA McAFEE (1934-1984) is almost an anachronistic throwback to the era of Norman Rockwell. Furthermore, she was a very capable painter who could paint as realistically as he did. However, there the resemblance ended. Like the *National Lampoon,* with which her work is most closely associated, her outlook was irreverent, and instead of glorifying the past, she ridiculed the present.

McAfee was born in Los Angeles and went to school at the Chouinard Art School there, before moving East to study at the Art Students League under Frank Mason. Her first illustrations were done for *Playboy* and along with *Ms. Magazine, New York, Esquire, Redbook, Oui, Viva* and other magazines, she also painted paperback covers for publishers such as Pocket Books, Bantam and Fawcett.

She was an accomplished portraitist as well, represented by Portraits, Inc., and exhibited her paintings in a number of galleries in addition to the annual shows at the Society of Illustrators. Her work won many awards, from the New York Art Directors Club, the American Institute of Graphic Arts, the Society of Publication Designers and others.

A book, *The Art of Mara McAfee,* was published in 1981 by Simon and Schuster.

Cover design for the National Lampoon, *February, 1979.*

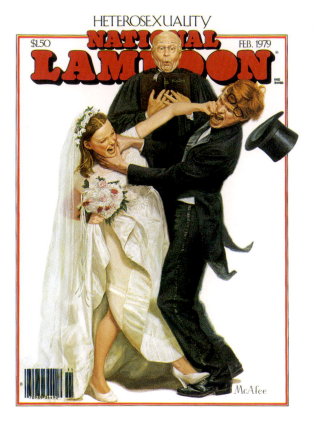

Gerald McConnell

Born in East Orange, New Jersey, GERALD McCONNELL (1931-   ) studied at the Art Students League with Frank Reilly and simultaneously apprenticed under Dean Cornwell. It is not easy to pinpoint an influence on his work, however, since it covers such a range of stylistic approaches and applications.

Starting with Pocket Books in 1953, McConnell concentrated on Western covers for most of the major paperback publishers. When he began making assemblages in 1967, an entirely different (and better paying) group of clients became patrons. And when he won the Society of Illustrators' Hamilton King Award in 1981, it was for his ultra-rendered pencil drawing of Grand Central Terminal. A Gold Clio award was won in collaboration with photographer Cosimo Scianna on a complex construction of a mummy. Other awards include "Best in Show" of the Real Show in 1979 and numerous certificates from Art Directors Clubs. He has also exhibited his work in galleries and museums, including the U.S. Air Force Museum in Dayton, Ohio, NASA Museum and the National Parks Department in Washington.

McConnell has long been a backbone of the Society of Illustrators, serving on the Executive Committee for over ten years, as House Chairman, and as Editor of the Annual Books. He is also National Vice-President of the Graphic Artists Guild, and has taught at Pratt Institute.

Of late, McConnell is concentrating on his publishing ventures, Madison Square Press, and Annuals Publishing Company.

"America Sings." An assemblage created for RCA Records in 1979.

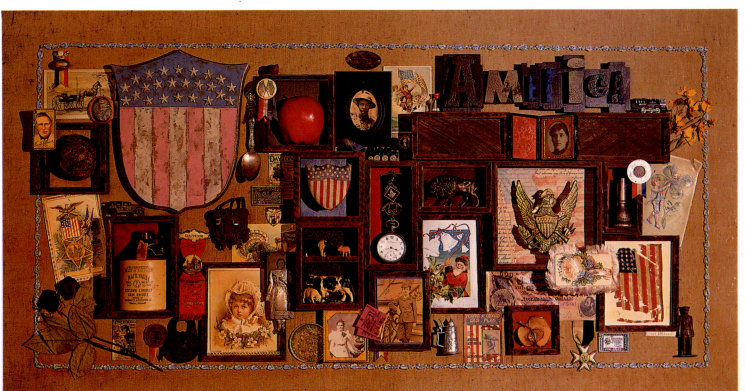

WILSON McLEAN:

WILSON McLEAN (1937-   ) was born in Glasgow, Scotland, moved to London at ten. With no art training, he landed his first job making magazine layouts. This led him to try free-lancing in Copenhagen, but he found London better, and returned to free-lance there until making the big decision to move to America in 1966.

The decision was well-timed. His carefully designed, meticulously rendered compositions found immediate acceptance and have had a strong influence in the field. He has illustrated for virtually all the magazines, including *Esquire, Sports Illustrated, Time, McCall's, Redbook, New York, Intellectual Digest, Saturday Review, Playboy, Oui, Penthouse,* as well as a number of advertising clients.

McLean has taught at the School of Visual Arts and Syracuse University. He also has been a regular participant in the annual exhibitions of the Society of Illustrators where he has received several awards. In 1980 he was also the recipient of the Society's Hamilton King Award.

The subject for St. Joe Minerals Corporation won the Award for Excellence in the Society of Illustrators 19th Annual Exhibition.

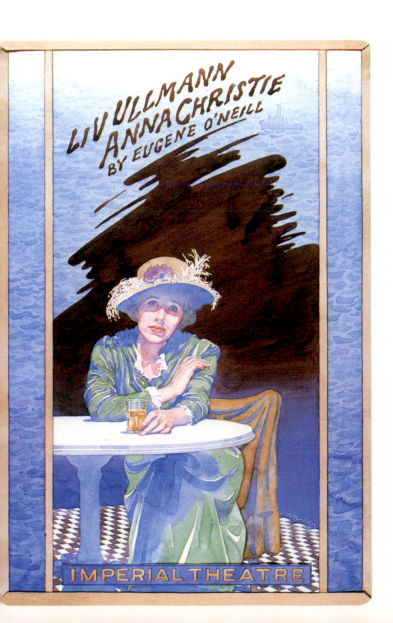

James McMullan

JAMES McMULLAN (1934-   ) comes from a missionary family and was born in Tsingtao, China. His boyhood was divided between China, India and Canada, followed by service in the United States Army. He graduated from Pratt Institute in Brooklyn and began an art career that has been marked by great diversity of clientele and use, but consistent in the intensity of his artistic outlook.

Among his activities has been work for T V animation, record jackets, posters, book covers, magazines and advertisements. McMullan was associated with the Push Pin Studios from 1965 to 1968 and has since formed his own organization, Visible Studio, Inc. He has designed a number of theatrical posters for Alexander H. Cohen and in conjunction with Robert Blechman created an animated Christmas film for Public Television in 1977.

McMullan has also been active as a director of the American Institute of Graphic Arts and was one of the founders of the Illustrators Guild. A member of the Society of Illustrators, he received their Gold and Silver medals in 1981. His book, *Revealing Illustrations,* was published in 1981 by Watson-Guptill.

"Anna Christie," illustration for the play produced by Alexander H. Cohen, January, 1977.

JOSEF VON STERNBERG'S THE BLUE ANGEL.

Robert Andrew Parker (signature)

ROBERT ANDREW PARKER (1927-   ) has had multiple careers in the gallery world and on the printed page (as well as in film) without particularly intending it. Some of his watercolors of battle scenes done for his son were published by *Esquire* magazine and led to commissions from other magazines, including *Fortune* which sent him on several major reportorial assignments around the world, *The Lamp* magazine, *Playboy*, *Sports Illustrated* and *New York* magazine.

The movie projects included doing all of the artwork for "Lust for Life," comprising those in the studio and others "in progress" as though being painted by Kirk Douglas as Vincent Van Gogh. His own watercolors accompanied two films on the poetry of Wilfred Owen and Keith Douglas.

Parker, who was born in Norfolk, Virginia, and studied at the Art Institute of Chicago was really preparing for a fine arts career. Following a stint in the Army Air Force as a flight engineer on a B-25 bomber, he won a scholarship to the Skowhegan School of Painting and Sculpture in Maine, studying under Jack Levine and Henry Varnum Poor.

He participated in his first show at Atelier 17 in New York in 1952 — then with Young American Printers, in 1953. The following year he had a successful one-man show at the Roko Gallery, including a purchase by the Museum of Modern Art. Since then he has appeared in many exhibitions, received numerous awards, and his works have been acquired by private and public collections.

In addition, Parker has found time to teach at both the Rhode Island School of Design and at Parsons School of Design in New York.

"The Blue Angel," illustration for The Lamp, *Fall, 1976.* © *1976,* The Lamp, Exxon Corporation.

Passalacqua (signature)

Much of the work of DAVID PASSALACQUA (1936-   ) conveys a feeling of intensity and energy, like the artist himself. His work is also very diverse, ranging from sensual line drawings to pastels, markers, watercolor, collage and assemblage. His clients too, are diverse, including most of the national magazines, such as *The Ladies' Home Journal, The Saturday Evening Post* and *Sports Illustrated;* many paperback book publishers, among them Bantam Books, and a long list of advertising accounts — Celanese Corporation, Standard Oil, Dayton-Hudson, Universal Studios and Warner Communications.

His drawings are represented in the Boston Museum of Fine Arts, the Singer Collection, the Don Padilla Collection, the Celanese Corporation and in numerous private collections.

Passalacqua was born in San Francisco and studied at the Chouinard Art Institute in Los Angeles as a Disney Scholarship student. He also attended the Otis Art School and the County Art Institute.

In addition to his active illustration career, he currently teaches drawing and illustration at the Parsons School of Design, Pratt Institute and Syracuse University. He has also lectured at universities and art schools across the country and abroad.

Portrait of Fidel Castro for the cover of The Saturday Evening Post, *June 8, 1963.* © *1963 by The Curtis Publishing Company.*

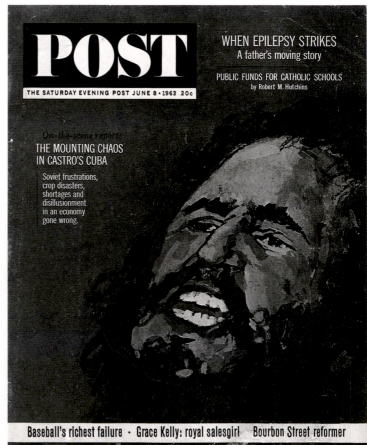

POST
THE SATURDAY EVENING POST JUNE 8 • 1963 20c

WHEN EPILEPSY STRIKES
A father's moving story

PUBLIC FUNDS FOR CATHOLIC SCHOOLS
by Robert M. Hutchins

On-the-scene report:
THE MOUNTING CHAOS IN CASTRO'S CUBA
Soviet frustrations, crop disasters, shortages and disillusionment in an economy gone wrong.

Baseball's richest failure • Grace Kelly: royal salesgirl • Bourbon Street reformer

JERRY PINKNEY (1939-   ), who was born in Philadelphia, studied at the Philadelphia Museum College of Art. In 1960 he moved to Boston and obtained his first work in a design studio as a designer-illustrator. Later he became one of the founders of Kaleidoscope Studio, leaving after two years to free-lance. During this time he was actively involved in design work for the Boston National Center for Afro-American Artists and served as the visiting critic of the Rhode Island School of Design.

Since 1971 he has been located in Croton-on-Hudson, New York, and handles a wide range of assignments for clients which have included *Seventeen, American Home* magazine, *Woman's Day, Essence, Boy's Life, Scouting,* Dial publications, Harper and Row, Dell publications, Coward, McCann and Goghegan, Seagram Distillers, S.D. Warren Paper Company and others.

His work has received Gold, Silver and Bronze Medals from Art Directors Club shows in various cities, other awards from the Society of Illustrators, the Council on Interracial Books, and *The New York Times'* Outstanding Book of the Year in 1975. Pinkney's work has also been exhibited in the Boston Museum of Fine Arts; Black Artist exhibition, New York and Boston, 1971; Studio Museum, Harlem, New York; and North Florida State University.

Illustration for Seagram's Black Historical Calendar, 1975.

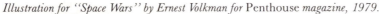

DON IVAN PUNCHATZ (1936-   ) is a transplanted Texan. He was born and went to school in Hillside, New Jersey. A member of the National Honor Society, he won a full scholarship to the School of Visual Arts in New York City. Among his teachers were Burne Hogarth, Bob Gill and Francis Criss. While still in school, he found an advertising agency job, continued evening classes at SVA and later at Cooper Union.

An interruption for Army service, in which he was assigned to do medical illustration and training films, gave him further experience. Following discharge, he worked as an art director in Pittsburgh for nearly five years. During the latter part of this period he began to do free-lance illustrations. In 1966 he broke away to full-time free-lancing and in 1970 formed his studio, the Sketch Pad, in Arlington, Texas.

Among his clients have been *Playboy, Penthouse, Esquire, Omni, Time, Look, Horizon, Redbook, McCall's, New York* magazine, *National Lampoon, Oui,* Dell publishing, The New American Library, Avon Books, Alcoa, IBM, RCA, U.S. Steel, Martin-Marietta, General Electric and many others.

Punchatz has received numerous professional awards from Art Directors Clubs in various cities, the Society of Illustrators, the Society of Publication Designers and others. He also paints for exhibition and is represented in the permanent collections of the Dallas Museum, the George Eastman House in Rochester, New York, and many private collections. In addition, he is currently teaching at both Texas Christian University (since 1970) and East Texas State University.

Illustration for "Space Wars" by Ernest Volkman for Penthouse *magazine, 1979.*

Charles Santore

CHARLES SANTORE (1935-   ) has that ideal combination for an illustrator: a good solid base of the traditional fundamentals of picture making, along with a very contemporary outlook. A good designer, his pictures are dramatic and arresting.

He is from Philadelphia and attended the Philadelphia College of Art, studying under Henry Pitz and Albert Gold. His first assignment was for the Armstrong Cork company in 1958, and he has gradually added a long list of clients which include many of the top advertising agencies in New York and Philadelphia as well as *Redbook, The Ladies' Home Journal, The Saturday Evening Post, Reader's Digest, Time, Life, Newsweek, Penthouse, Playboy, TV Guide, Esquire,* and other magazines.

Santore has received three Gold Medals at the Philadelphia Art Directors Club show, Awards of Excellence from the Society of Publication Designers and the Society of Illustrators. In 1972 he received the Society of Illustrators Hamilton King Award. He had a one-man show at the Tyler School of Art/Temple University, and his work can be found in the College of Free Library of Philadelphia, the New York Museum of Modern Art, as well as in many private collections.

"Alice in Wonderland," an advertising illustration in 1974 for Pfizer Pharmaceuticals to depict vertigo, symbolized by Alice's fall into a dark hole.

Isadore Seltzer

ISADORE SELTZER (1930-   ) credits the Push Pin Studio as his professional training ground. Certainly his work has the "Push Pin look" but with his own unpredictable variations of it.

He was born in St. Louis and attended school at Chouinard in Los Angeles for two years, interrupted by Army service, and was graduated after another two years at the Art Center School. Following school he found a few free-lance jobs doing shoe ads and record album covers, but it wasn't until he moved to New York and joined the Push Pin staff in 1960 that he began to hit his stride. After four-and-a-half years, he was invited to join the stable of artists represented by Harvey Kahn, beginning an association of over twenty years. During that time his work has appeared in *The Saturday Evening Post, Time, Newsweek, Esquire, The Ladies' Home Journal, Redbook, McCall's,* and *Playboy,* and for many advertising accounts. He has also done several movie posters, for "The Hotel New Hampshire," a Woody Allen film and a four months' project doing all of the tattoos for the movie, "Tattoo."

Seltzer does not exhibit but does paintings, watercolors and woodcuts for himself. He also teaches, both at the Parsons School of Design and Syracuse University.

Illustration for Mickey Rooney TV Special, sponsored by the ITT Corporation.

Illustration for Where the Wild Things are, *story and pictures by Maurice Sendak. Copyright © 1963 by Maurice Sendak. By permission of Harper & Row, Publishers, Inc.*

MAURICE SENDAK (1928-   ) shook up the whole tradition of children's book illustration when his volume, *Where the Wild Things are,* appeared in 1962. Many critics, librarians, and parents complained about the text and his depictions of horrifying beasts, which ran counter to accepted norms of proper subject matter for impressionable children. Fortunately, the kids loved the books and their psyches have apparently not suffered. By now, the public acceptance of Sendak's work is virtually unanimous, and Sendak has received a Doctor of Humanities award from Boston University, the Hans Christian Anderson award

and the Caldecott award, among many others.

Sendak was born in Brooklyn and attended the Art Students League where he studied under John Groth. His book illustrating career began with a title for McGraw Hill as early as 1948 and included more than a decade of non-controversial picture-making prior to his sudden notoriety. Additional pace-setting books have included *In the Night Kitchen,* and *The Juniper Tree — Tales from Grimm,* in two volumes.

Other facets of his career have included theatrical ventures, such as "Really Rosie," an animated TV musical, which he and song writer Carole King wrote and later adapted for the stage, and set designing for several opera and ballet productions. Sendak has also found time to teach at Parsons School of Design.

Illustration for In the Night Kitchen *by Maurice Sendak. Copyright © 1970 by Maurice Sendak. By permission of Harper & Row, Publishers, Inc.*

THOMAS SGOUROS (1927-   ) describes himself as "teacher/illustrator/artist," and he works at it full time. Currently he is chief critic in the European Honors Program for the Rhode Island School of Design in Rome, Italy. He has been associated with the Illustration Department of RISD in various capacities since 1962, graduating from there with a B.F.A. in 1950. Following school, he free-lanced for several years in Boston, New York and Providence, his work published by *Time, Life, Reader's Digest, Yankee, Ford Times,* Ginn & Company, Random House, Brown University Press and for many advertising accounts, including TWA, Ford Motor Company, U.S. Steel and Coca-Cola. His work, exhibited at the Society of Illustrators and Art Directors Club shows in New York, Boston, Providence and Denver, has won six Gold Medals, eight Silver Medals and fifteen Merit Awards.

Simultaneously, he has been painting for exhibition regularly; has had several one-man shows; is a member of the Boston Society of Watercolor Painters and the American Watercolor Society. His work is represented in the Cleveland Museum of Fine Arts, the Jacksonville Museum of Fine Arts· and the Rhode Island School of Design Museum of Fine Arts, and in many private collections.

Illustration for Yankee *magazine; July, 1976.*

BURT SILVERMAN, N.A. (1928-   ), like many current illustrators, paints both for the printed page and gallery exhibition. He has had fourteen one-man shows in galleries in New York, Philadelphia, Houston, Washington and Boston, and won more than fifteen awards and prizes from annual exhibitions of the National Academy of Design and the American Watercolor Society, and various other regional and national exhibitions.

Born in Brooklyn, he attended the High School of Music and Art and the Art Students League where he studied with Louis Bouché and Reginald Marsh. He also earned a B.A. at Columbia University in 1949. His first work was published by *Sports Illustrated* in 1959, and he has added a long roster of other periodicals since, including *Time, Life, Fortune, Esquire, The New Yorker, New York, Redbook, McCall's, Newsweek, Discover, People* and *Psychology Today.*

In 1964 and '65 Silverman taught at the School of Visual Arts; he has been teaching privately since 1967.

"British Prime Minister Margaret Thatcher." Cover painting for Time, *June 20, 1983.* © *1983 Time, Inc. All rights reserved.*

340

Edward Sorel

EDWARD SOREL (1929-   ) is a satirist with a waspish sting. No institution is safe from his attack; politicians are particularly vulnerable. His training ground was in the underground press, but the militant unrest during the Vietnam period gave him a more mainstream audience. *Esquire* magazine published his work regularly for a feature, "The Spokesman," and he did "Unfamiliar Quotations" for the *Atlantic*. When *New York* magazine was started, he became a contributing editor. His work has also appeared in *Harper's, Time,* the *Village Voice* and *Ramparts.*

Sorel was born in New York City, attended the High School of Music and Art and Cooper Union. He was a founding member of the Push Pin Studios in 1953, prior to free-lancing. Currently he and his wife, Nancy, are collaborating on a series called "First Encounters" appearing every other month in the *Atlantic* which she writes and he illustrates. He is also the author and illustrator of several books: *How to be President, Moon Missing, Making the World Safe for Hypocrisy* and *Superpen.*

Editorial illustration for The New York Times, *1974.*

The art of JAMES J. SPANFELLER (1930-   ) appears to have more kinship with the British illustrators Harry Clarke and Aubrey Beardsley than any American influence. He has their same fascination with the macabre and intricacy of distorted detail. The result both disquiets and intrigues the viewer.

Spanfeller has had a thoroughly American background, however. He was born in Philadelphia and attended both the Philadelphia College of Art and the Pennsylvania Academy of the Fine Arts. His first illustrated book, *Where Did You Go? Out. What Did You Do? Nothing.* by Robert Paul Smith was on the Best-Seller List for more than a year. He has since worked for many other book publishers, including Ballantine Books, Harper & Row, Time-Life and Random House. Magazine appearances include *Seventeen, Playboy, The Ladies' Home Journal, McCall's, Redbook, House Beautiful, Charm, Columbia, Avant-Garde* and others.

He was named the Artists Guild's "Artist of the Year" in 1964; received the *Herald-Tribune* Children's Book Award in 1965; Gold and Silver Medals from the Society of Publication Designers. He teaches at Parsons School of Design and is an active member of the Society of Illustrators.

"Halley's Comet," published in Mineral Digest *magazine as a full color, four-page centerfold in 1973 to illustrate "Star Dragon," an essay by Loren Eiseley.*

JIM SHARPE (1930-) is a native of Vernon, Texas, and attended Texas Tech in Lubbock as an advertising design major. He then entered the Navy and served as a jet fighter pilot for four years. Returning to school, he enrolled in the Art Center School in Los Angeles and was graduated with honors in 1964.

His first positions were in art direction and studio illustration in Detroit. In 1968 he moved to the New York area to begin his free-lance career. Early work included many paperback covers for Bantam, Dell, Fawcett, Warner, Signet, Ballantine and others. Advertising agencies have also commissioned his work for the 3M Company, U.S. Steel, Armstrong Tires, General Electric and many other corporations. He did over twenty covers for *Time* magazine between 1970 and 1979; has painted more than a dozen covers for *TV Guide;* two for *Newsweek;* and other covers for *Golf Digest, True,* and *Field and Stream,* as well as editorial illustration for *Woman's Day, Scouting, Reader's Digest, Popular Mechanics, Cosmopolitan, Boy's Life* and many others. The Franklin Library commissioned him to do three limited edition titles; he has also made paintings for the National Parks Association. He recently worked with the producers and directors of the ABC Television News program "20/20" making illustrations for the major theme of a story which could not be recorded in film. One such was on Howard Hughes, another on "The Death of Elvis Presley." He himself has also appeared on the "New York Today" NBC television program. Another commission has been from the U.S. Postal Service for six commemorative postage stamps for the Performing Arts Series, and a design featuring the late Dr. Ralph Bunche.

Premier Chou En-lai, portrait for Time *magazine cover, February 3, 1975.* © 1975 Time, Inc. All rights reserved.

R. SPARKS

RICHARD SPARKS (1944-) started out aiming to be an architect and received his degree in architecture from Texas A. & M. University. Realizing that he really wanted to be an artist, he enrolled in the Art Center School of Design in Los Angeles where he studied under Harry Carmean, Donald Puttman, and Joseph Henninger. There he met and married his wife Barbara, also an illustrator. They free-lanced in Amsterdam, Holland, for three years before returning to the States and the New York art market.

Sparks found acceptance quickly, and his work has been published by *Time* magazine (several covers), *Fortune, Sports Illustrated, Esquire, Forbes, Redbook, The Ladies' Home Journal, Psychology Today, McCall's, New York, Reader's Digest, Cosmopolitan, Boy's Life, Family Circle, Woman's Day,* and other periodicals. Recently he completed a postage stamp design portraying George Mason, author of the Bill of Rights, for the U. S. Postal Service. His portrait painting for a *Time* cover of Mstislav Rostropovich was placed in the National Portrait Gallery in Washington, D.C. Other paintings are in the Franklin D. Roosevelt Library and the Academy of Art College in San Francisco. Sparks has received a Gold Medal and an Award of Excellence for his work exhibited at the Society of Illustrators. Other honors and national recognition have come from the American Institute of Graphic Arts, *Graphis, Print* magazine, *Art Direction* magazine and *Communication Arts* annual.

"Budapest Quartet," painted for album cover, CBS Records in 1979.

WALT SPITZMILLER (1944-   ) is from St. Louis, Missouri, and was graduated from Washington University there with a B.F.A. in 1969. His first free-lance artwork was for advertising agencies, and he supplemented his income with part-time teaching at St. Louis Junior College and Washington University.

McCall's magazine gave him his first editorial job and Spitzmiller, who now lives in Connecticut, has since gravitated to sports subjects. He has done over twenty assignments for *Sports Illustrated* and works regularly for publications such as *Golf, Golf Digest, Sports Afield, Outdoor Life,* Playboy books, The Franklin library and *Signature* magazine. He has collaborated with Carlo Fassi on *The World of Figure Skating* published by Charles Scribner & Sons and is currently working on a project for the United States Football League and the 1984 Olympics.

He has had several one-man shows and won awards from Art Directors Clubs across the country; has exhibited many times at the Society of Illustrators. One of his paintings is included in the Rodeo Museum in Colorado Springs, Colorado.

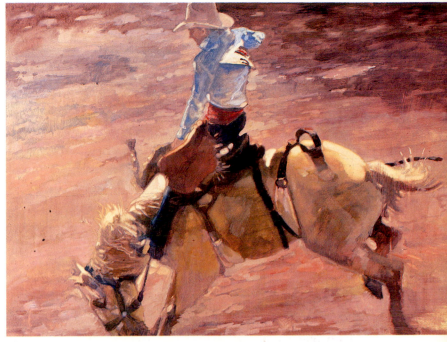

"Sunlit Palomino." One of a series of paintings for *"Ride 'Em! The Real Rodeo Lives,"* published by Sports Illustrated *in 1981.* © *W. Spitzmiller. Collection of the Society of Illustrators Museum of American Illustration.*

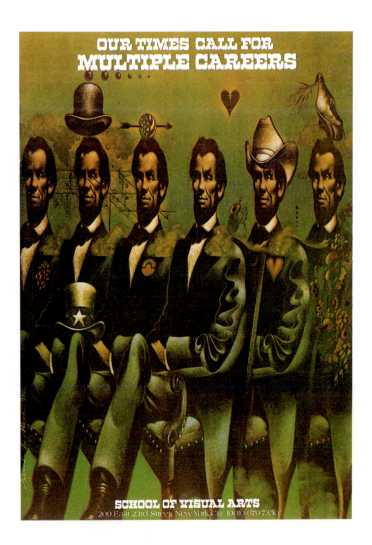

GILBERT L. STONE (1940-1984) made an illustration career out of presenting a unique, sidewise compressed vision of the world. The optical illusion conferred itself to the picture content as well, adding an element of mystery and forcing the viewer to interpret its meaning. The effect was intriguing and very successful in attracting the attention of the reader.

Stone was born in Brooklyn and went to the High School of Art and Design. He attended Parsons School of Design on a scholarship, then furthered his education at New York University, graduating with honors. In the years following, he was active as a media artist, exhibited regularly and taught at the School of Visual Arts for many years. His published work appeared in *Playboy, McCall's, Redbook, The Ladies' Home Journal, Esquire, Oui, Sports Illustrated* and *New York* magazine, winning many awards when exhibited in Art Directors Club shows, and three Gold Medals of the Society of Illustrators Annual Exhibitions.

Simultaneously, he had three one-man shows and participated in six group shows in New York. Most recently he was represented by the Frank Rehn Gallery. His pictures are in many collections, including the Brooklyn Museum, the Joseph Hirshorn Collection and the Smithsonian Institution, as well as several corporate and private collections.

Cover design for catalog, School of Visual Arts, 1972.

Cover design for The Illustrations of Murray Tinkelman.

Cover illustration for The Sheep Look Up, *published by Ballantine Books, Inc.*

MURRAY TINKELMAN (1933-   ) has had a major impact on contemporary illustration both by the example of his work and through the enthusiasm of his teaching and lectures.

Born in Brooklyn, Tinkelman was graduated from the New York High School of Industrial Art (now named the High School of Art and Design) and served in the Army. He returned to study at the Cooper Union art school for two years, then switched to the Brooklyn Museum art school on the Max Beckman scholarship to study under Reuben Tam. Although originally intending to pursue a career in painting, he became disillusioned by the commercialism in the galleries and decided to become "honestly commercial" as an illustrator. Taken on by the Charles Cooper Studio, then the most prestigious association of illustrators in New York, Tinkelman quickly made a name for himself. The studio staff learned as much from him as he from them, for he led a whole group of name illustrators back to school to study under his mentor, Reuben Tam.

When the studio dissolved in 1964, he became a freelancer and has since worked for a wide range of clients, including *The Saturday Evening Post, Playboy, Boy's Life, The Ladies' Home Journal, Good Housekeeping, American Heritage, Family Circle* and *Field and Stream.* He has done twenty-five children's books for publishers such as Harper & Row; Coward, McCann, and Geoghegan; Macmillan, and Knopf, as well as a large number of fantasy book covers for Ballantine Books (H.P. Lovecraft) and an even larger number of Zane Grey Western covers for Pocket Books. He has often appeared on the Op-Ed page of the *New York Times,* made a series of drawings for the National Park Service and is currently following the rodeo circuit working on one or more book projects.

All this is in addition to an almost full-time career as a teacher. He served on the illustration faculty of Parsons School of Design for many years; at present he is a professor of art, College of Visual and Performing Arts at Syracuse University. He has also written several articles for *American Artist* magazine and lectured on the history of illustration to various art groups around the country and on public television.

He was selected as "Artist of the Year" in 1970 by the Artists Guild in New York and has been awarded numerous Gold and Silver Medals by the Society of Illustrators, Art Directors Club of New York and Society of Publication Designers. His book, *The Illustrations of Murray Tinkelman,* was published in 1980, and his latest book, *Rodeo Drawings of Murray Tinkelman,* in 1983, both by Art Direction Book Company.

"Rodeo Rider," published in North Light *magazine, 1982.*

BF STAHL

BENJAMIN F. STAHL (1932-   ) has always scrupulously avoided trading on his famous illustrator father's name, rarely signing his work and for years using a pseudonym. In developing his own style and identity, Stahl's work is marked by its combination of strength and sensitivity. He depicts young people particularly well and has won American Institute of Graphic Arts awards for Children's Book Illustration in 1977 and '79 and was included in Outstanding Science Books for Children (National Science Teachers Association, 1976).

His art has been commissioned by most of the major publishers, including Houghton, Mifflin; Little, Brown; Putnam; Coward, McCann and Geoghegan; Random House; Scribner's; The Franklin Library; Limited Editions Book Club; Bantam Books; Reader's Digest; Warner Publishing Company and Holt, Rinehart and Winston.

Stahl was born in Chicago and grew up with illustration, never having a formal art training. He, however, is an excellent teacher; for various periods between 1955 and '70 he taught at the Famous Artists Schools, Bridgeport University and at the Ringling School of Art in Sarasota, Florida.

B. Storey

ROSS BARRON STOREY (1940-   ) has been an active illustrator since the age of twenty.

Born in Dallas, Texas, he studied the Famous Artists Course and attended the Art Center School in Los Angeles. Storey's first illustrations for publication were for the Sunday magazine of the New York *Journal American,* followed by *This Week* magazine, *Woman's Day, Children's Digest, Time, National Geographic, Saturday Review* and various paperback publishers, including Avon, Fawcett and Pocket Books.

He has also done numerous advertising illustration assignments and received awards for his work from Art Directors Clubs in New York, Los Angeles, Denver and Dallas, as well as a Gold Medal from the Society of Illustrators in 1976.

Storey has taught at Pratt Institute and the School of Visual Arts in New York. His studio is now located in San Francisco.

Illustration for The People Therein, *Signet paperback cover.*

"Race between Horsepower and Steam." Illustration for Boy's Life *magazine, 1980.*

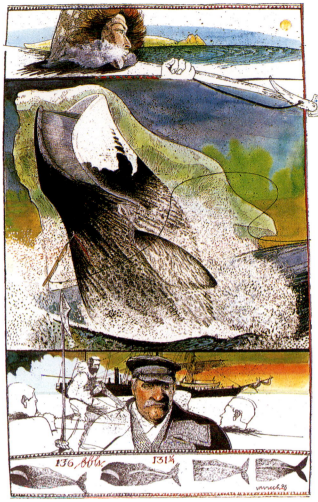

The art of JACK NEAL UNRUH (1935-   ) has
evolved considerably during his career, becoming increasingly linear and disciplined in drawing with more emphasis on pattern.

The son of an Air Force father, Unruh was born in Pretty Prairie, Kansas, and moved a lot during his childhood. He was graduated with a B.F.A. from Washington University in St. Louis, Missouri, having studied under Bob Cassel. He then started a studio with a partner, in Dallas, Texas, but was called to active military service during the Berlin Crisis in 1961-'62. Upon his return, he started to free-lance as an illustrator with a Dallas group called Portfolio. Since 1981 he has been on his own.

During these years, his work was appearing in many magazines, including *Redbook, Seventeen, Sports Illustrated, Quest, Boy's Life, Oui, Outdoor Life* and *National Geographic.* He has also illustrated the annual reports for LTV, Dresser Industries, Borg Warner, Triton Oil and others, as well as advertising illustrations for American Airlines, Braniff, NBC, Hyatt Hotels, ITT, Kimberly Clark, Exxon and Twentieth Century Fox.

A member of the Society of Illustrators, Dallas Illustrators and the Dallas Society of Visual Communications, Unruh has also taught drawing and illustration at East Texas State University from 1969-'78.

Illustration for "Arctic Odyssey," published by the National Geographic, *July, 1983.* © *National Geographic Society.*

HENRY P. VIRGONA (1929-   ), better known as "Hank," stopped doing illustration to devote his time to "Fine" art, about ten years ago. However, he has found that his current endeavors also have a place in the commercial world and have been published in *The New York Times Magazine,* Op-Ed and Book Review Sections, *Harper's* magazine and other publications, including a recent cover for a book by Yevgeny Yevtushenko for Marek Publishers.

Over the years his work has appeared in *Fortune, American Heritage,* Bantam Books, NBC-TV, *Seventeen, Pageant,* Ballantine Books and many pharmaceutical companies. In the process, he has won a Gold Medal and several other awards from the Society of Illustrators, as well as Awards of Excellence from the New York and New Jersey Art Directors Clubs and the American Institute of Graphic Arts.

Actually, he has had a parallel career right from the beginning. Born in Brooklyn, he went to evening classes at Pratt Institute, studying under Francis Criss. He has participated in many group exhibitions over the past years and had one-man shows at the Roko, FAR, Summa and Washington Irving Galleries in New York, four shows at the Rittenhouse Gallery in Philadelphia, and others in California, Michigan, Florida and Connecticut. His work is in the Metropolitan Museum of Art and New York Public Library Print Collections, The Smithsonian, the Butler Institute of American Art, Slater Memorial Museum and in many private collections.

His book, a collection of satirical etchings, titled *The System Works,* was published by Da Capo Press in 1977.

Aquatint reproduced by The New York Times, *April 17, 1983, for an article by McGeorge Bundy, "MX Paper: Appealing, but mostly Appalling."*

Weller

The illustrations of DON WELLER (1937-) are like the performances of a juggler — he successfully keeps all of the elements of his pictures: form, color, shapes, and a bit of spatter, all in the air. He also uses distortion with good effect; there are a lot of accidentals and surprises in his pictures that make them effective.

Weller is a West Coast illustrator; he was born in Colfax, Washington, and earned his B.A. at Washington State University. His first published work was a cartoon for *Western Horseman* magazine. He has gradually added a long list of publications as clients, such as *Time, T.V. Guide, Sports Illustrated, Boy's Life, Westways, Seventeen, Emergency Medicine, Road and Track, Communication Arts, Bon Appetit* and *Idea* magazine. His work has been exhibited in many shows on both coasts, and he has won Gold and Silver Medals from the Art Directors Clubs of New York and Los Angeles, various Merit awards and the Society of Illustrators of Los Angeles' Lifetime Achievement Award in 1982.

Cover painting for Communication Arts *magazine, 1978.*

ROBERT M. ZIERING (1933-) is a specialist in line — an expressive one that effectively conveys the feeling of shape and motion, along with the multiple imagery he often uses to indicate the animation of his subjects.

Ziering was born in Brooklyn, New York. He attended the High School of Music and Art before going on to the New York University School of Education and the School of Visual Arts in New York City.

His first professional illustration was done for *Coronet* magazine and has been followed by commissions from *Time, Life, Esquire, Runner, Redbook, Print* magazine, *The* *Chicago Tribune, McCall's, Saturday Review* and other publications, as well as advertisers, such as T.V. Guide, Barton's Chocolates, Arista Records, NBC, Mobil Oil and IBM.

Ziering's works appear regularly in the exhibitions at the Society of Illustrators, the Art Directors Club of New York, the A.I.G.A., and have also been exhibited at the Butler Institute of American Art, the Carroll Reece Museum, East Tennessee State University, the Museum of Modern Art, the Alonzo Gallery in New York and Heritage Arts in New Jersey. In addition, he has taught high school art and at the School of Visual Arts in 1982.

"Fred Astaire," for the Film Society of Lincoln Center, 1973.

BIBLIOGRAPHY

Abbott, Charles D., *Howard Pyle, A Chronicle,* New York & London: Harper & Brothers, 1925.

Advertising Arts & Crafts, Volumes I & II, New York & Chicago, Lee and Kirby Inc., 1924

Allen, Douglas, *Frederic Remington and the Spanish-American War,* New York: Crown Publishers, Inc., 1971.

Allen, Douglas and Allen, Douglas Jr. *N. C. Wyeth; The Collected Paintings, Illustrations, and Murals,* New York: Crown Publishers, Inc., 1972.

American Art Annual, Washington, D.C.: American Federation of Arts, 1898 to 1936.

American Art by American Artists, New York: P. F. Collier & Son, 1914.

The American Historical Scene as depicted by Stanley Arthurs, Philadelphia: University of Pennsylvania Press, 1935.

Amstutz, Walter, editor, *Who's Who in Graphic Art,* Zurich, Switzerland: Amstutz & Herdeg Graphis Press 1962.

Annual of Advertising and Editorial Art and Design, New York: The New York Art Directors Club Yearbook, 1921 and annually thereafter.

Annuals of American Illustration published for the Society of Illustrators, New York: Hastings House and Madison Square Press, 1959 through 1983.

Arts Yearbook I, *The Turn of the Century,* New York: The Art Digest, Inc., 1957.

Bama, James, and Ballantine, Ian, *The Western Art of James Bama,* New York: Charles Scribner's Sons and Peacock Press/Bantam Books, 1975.

Baragwanath, John, *A Good Time was Had,* New York: Appleton-Century-Crofts, Inc., 1962.

Beam, Philip C., *Winslow Homer's Magazine Engravings,* New York: Harper & Row, Publishers, 1979.

Biographical Sketches of American Artists, 5th Edition, Lansing, Michigan: Michigan State Library, 1924.

Bloch, Maurice E., and others, *The American Personality; The Artist-Illustrator of Life in the United States 1860-1930,* Los Angeles, California: The Grunwald Center for the Graphic Arts, University of California, 1976.

Bolton, Theodore, *American Book Illustrators,* New York: R. R. Bowker Company, 1938.

Broder, Patricia Janis, *Dean Cornwell; Dean of Illustrators,* New York: Balance House, Ltd., 1978.

Buechner, Thomas S., *Norman Rockwell, Artist and Illustrator,* New York: Harry N. Abrams, Inc., 1970.

Calkins, Earnest Elmo, *Franklin Booth,* New York: Robert Frank, publisher, 1925.

Clark, Eliot, *History of the National Academy of Design 1825-1953,* New York: Columbia University Press, 1954.

Cornwell, Dean, *The City of the Great King,* New York: Cosmopolitan Book Corporation, 1926.

——, *The Man of Galilee,* New York: Cosmopolitan Book Corporation, 1928.

Craven, Thomas, editor, *Cartoon Cavalcade,* New York: Simon and Schuster, Inc., 1943.

——, *A Treasury of American Prints,* New York: Simon and Schuster, Inc., 1939.

Creative Artists, 1940, New York: Sackett & Wilhelms Lithographing Corporation.

Darton, F. J. Harvey, *Modern Book Illustration in Great Britain and America,* London: The Studio Limited, New York: William Edwin Rudge, 1931.

DeShazo, Edith, *Everett Shinn 1876-1953,* New York: Clarkson N. Potter, Inc., 1974.

Downey, Fairfax, *Portrait of an Era as Drawn by C. D. Gibson,* New York and London: Charles Scribner's Sons, 1936.

Drawings by Thulstrup and Others, New York: E. R. Herrick & Co., 1898.

Dunn, Harvey, *An Evening in the Classroom,* Privately printed at the instigation of Mario Cooper, 1934.

Dykes, Jeff C. *Fifty Great Western Illustrators; A Bibliographic Checklist,* Arizona: Northland Press, 1975.

Eggenhofer, Nick, *Horses, Horses, Always Horses, The Life and Art of Nick Eggenhofer,* Cody, Wyoming: Sage Publishing Co., Inc., 1981.

Ellis, Richard Williamson, *Book Illustration; a Survey of its History and Development,* Kingsport, Tennessee: The Kingsport Press, 1952.

Elzea, Rowland, and Hawkes, Elizabeth H., editors, *A Small School of Art: The Students of Howard Pyle,* Wilmington, Delaware: Delaware Art Museum, 1980.

Fawcett, Robert, *On the Art of Drawing,* New York: Watson-Guptill Publications, Inc., 1958.

Ferber, Linda, and Brown, Robin, *A Century of American Illustration,* New York: The Brooklyn Museum, 1972.

Fielding, Mantle, *Dictionary of American Painters, Sculptors & Engravers,* (from Colonial times through 1926), Flushing N.Y.: Paul A. Stroock, publisher, 1960.

Fischer, Katrina Sigsbee, *Anton Otto Fischer; Marine Artist,* Brighton, Sussex, England: Teredo Books, Ltd., 1977.

Flagg, James Montgomery, *Roses and Buckshot,* New York: G. P. Putnam's Sons, 1946.

Frost, A. B. *A Book of Drawings,* New York: P. F. Collier & Son, 1904.

Gallatin, Albert Eugene, *Art and the Great War,* New York: E. P. Dutton & Co., 1919.

The Gibson Book, A collection of the published works of Charles Dana Gibson in two volumes, New York: Charles Scribner's Sons, R. H. Russell, 1907.

Gill, Bob, and Lewis, John, *Illustration: Aspects and Directions,* New York: Reinhold Publishing Corporation, and London: Studio Vista, Ltd., 1964.

Glackens, Ira, *William Glackens and the Ashcan Group,* New York: Crown Publishers, Inc., 1957.

Goldsmith, Oliver, *The Deserted Village,* Illustrated by Edwin Austin Abbey, New York and London: Harper & Brothers, 1902.

Goodrich, Lloyd, *The Graphic Art of Winslow Homer,* Smithsonian Institution Press, 1968.

Gottschall, Edward M. and Hawkins, Arthur, editors, *Advertising Directions,* New York: Art Directions Book Co., 1959.

Graphic Artists Guild Directory 1981-1982, New York: Annuals Publishing Company.

Guitar, Mary Ann, *22 Famous Painters and Illustrators Tell How They Work,* New York: David McKay Company, Inc., 1964.

Guptill, Arthur L., *Drawing with Pen and Ink,* New York: The Pencil Points Press, Inc., 1928.

____, *Norman Rockwell — Illustrator,* New York: Watson-Guptill Publications, Inc., 1946.

Hall, W. S., *Eyes on America,* New York: The Studio Publications, and London: The Studio, Ltd.

Halsey, Ashley Jr., *Illustrating for The Saturday Evening Post,* Boston: Arlington House, 1951.

Harmsen, Dorothy, *Harmsen's Western Americana,* Flagstaff, Arizona: Northland Press, 1971.

Harrison Fisher's American Beauties, Indianapolis: The Bobbs-Merrill Company, 1909.

Hassrick, Peter H., *Frederic Remington,* New York: Harry N. Abrams, Inc., 1973.

Helck, Peter, *The Checkered Flag,* New York: Charles Scribner's Sons, 1961.

____, *Great Auto Races,* New York: Harry N. Abrams, Inc., 1975.

Held, John Jr., Weinhardt, Carl, Connelly, Marc, and Hayes, Bartlett H. Jr. *The Most of John Held, Jr.,* Brattleboro, Vermont: The Stephen Greene Press, 1972.

Held, John Jr., *The Works of John Held, Jr.,* New York: Ives Washburn, publisher, 1931.

Holme, Bryan, *Advertising: Reflections of a Century,* New York: The Viking Press, 1982.

Holme, Charles, editor, *Modern Pen Drawings: European and American,* Special Winter Number of ''The Studio'' 1900-1901, London, Paris, New York, 1901.

Horn, Maurice, editor, *The World Encyclopedia of Cartoons,* New York and London: Chelsea House Publishers, 1980.

____, editor, *The World Encyclopedia of Comics,* New York: Chelsea House Publishers, 1976.

Hornung, Clarence P., editor, *Will Bradley; His Graphic Art,* New York: Dover Publications, Inc., 1974

Hutchinson, William Henry, *The World, The Work and The West of W.H.D. Koerner,* University of Oklahoma Press, 1978.

Hydeman, Sid, *How to Illustrate for Money,* New York and London: Harper & Brothers, 1936.

Hyland, Douglas K.S., and Brokaw, Howard P., *Howard Pyle and the Wyeths: Four Generations of American Imagination,* Tennessee: Memphis Brooks Museum of Art, 1983.

Johnson, Fridolf, editor, *Treasury of American Pen & Ink Illustration 1881-1938,* New York: Dover Publications, Inc., 1982.

Johnson, Merle, compiler, *Howard Pyle's Book of The American Spirit,* New York and London: Harper & Brothers, 1923.

____, Compiler, *Howard Pyle's Book of Pirates,* New York and London: Harper & Brothers, 1921.

Kent, Norman, editor, *The Book of Edward A. Wilson,* New York: The Heritage Press, 1948.

Kery, Patricia Frantz, *Great Magazine Covers of the World,* New York: Abbeville Press, 1982.

Landgren, Marchal E., *Years of Art,* The Story of the Art Students League of New York, New York: Robert M. McBride & Company, 1940.

Lucas, E. V., *Life and Work of Edwin Austin Abbey, R.A.* in two volumes, New York: Charles Scribner's Sons, London: Methuen and Company, Ltd., 1921.

Ludwig, Coy, *Maxfield Parrish,* New York: Watson-Guptill Publications, 1973.

Lyon, Peter, *Success Story: The Life and Times of S. S. McClure,* New York: Charles Scribner's Sons, 1963.

McConnell, Gerald, editor, *Twenty Years of Award Winners,* published for the Society of Illustrators, New York: Hastings House, 1981.

McCracken, Harold, *The Charles M. Russell Book,* Garden City, New York: Doubleday and Company, 1957.

____, *The Frederic Remington Book,* Garden City, New York: Doubleday and Company, 1966.

Mahoney, Bertha E., Latimer, Louise P. and Folmsbee, Beulah, editors and compilers, *Illustrators of Children's Books 1744-1945,* Boston: The Horn Book, 1947.

Mahoney-Miller, Bertha, Viguers, Ruth Hill, Dalphin, Marcia, editors and compilers, *Illustrators of Children's Books 1946-1956,* Boston: The Horn Book, 1958.

Mallett, Daniel Trowbridge, *Mallett's Index of Artists,* New York: R. R. Bowker Company, 1935. Supplement published in 1940.

Marshall, Francis, *Magazine Illustration,* New York: The Viking Press, Inc., London: The Studio Ltd., 1959.

Mather, Frank Jewett, Jr., Morey, Charles Rufus, and Henderson, William James, *The American Spirit in Art,* from the "Pageant of America," Vol. XII, New Haven: Yale University Press, 1927.

Meglin, Nick, *The Art of Humorous Illustration,* New York: Watson-Guptill Publications, 1973.

Meyer, Susan E., *America's Great Illustrators,* New York: Harry N. Abrams, Inc., 1978.

____, *James Montgomery Flagg,* New York: Watson-Guptill Publications, 1974.

____, *Norman Rockwell's People,* New York: Harry N. Abrams, Inc., 1981.

____, *Treasury of Children's Book Illustrators,* New York: Harry N. Abrams, Inc., 1983.

Moline, Mary, *Norman Rockwell Encyclopedia,* Indianapolis: The Curtis Publishing Co., 1979.

Morse, Willard S. and Brinckle, Gertrude, compilers, *Howard Pyle — A Record of his Illustrations and Writings,* Wilmington, Delaware: The Wilmington Society of the Fine Arts, 1921.

Munce, Howard, *The Animal Art of Bob Kuhn,* Westport, Connecticut: North Light Publishers, 1973.

Munce, Howard, and Fawcett, Robert, *Drawing the Nude,* New York: Watson-Guptill Publications, 1980.

Murrell, William, *A History of American Graphic Humor,* New York: The Macmillan Company, 1938.

Official Directory, American Illustrators and Advertising Artists, Washington, D.C.: American Federation of Arts, publisher, 1949.

O'Rourke, P.J., and Charles, Milton, *The Art of Mara McAfee,* New York: Pocket Books, 1981.

Packer, William, *The Art of Vogue Covers,* New York: Harmony Books, 1980.

Pennell, Joseph, *The Adventures of an Illustrator,* Boston: Little, Brown and Company, 1925.

____, *Modern Illustration,* London and New York: George Bell & Sons, 1895.

____, *Pen Drawing and Pen Draughtsmen,* New York: The Macmillan Company, 1889.

Perlman, Bennard, B., *F. R. Gruger and His Circle; The Golden Age of Illustration,* Westport, Connecticut: North Light Publishers, 1978.

____, *The Immortal Eight,* Westport, Connecticut: North Light Publishers, 1979.

Phillips, Coles, *A Young Man's Fancy,* Indianapolis: The Bobbs-Merrill Company, 1912.

Pitz, Henry C., *The Brandywine Tradition,* New York: Weathervane Books, 1968.

____, *Howard Pyle,* New York: Bramhall House, 1965.

____, *Illustrating Children's Books,* New York: Watson-Guptill Publications, Inc., 1963.

____, *Ink Drawing Techniques,* New York: Watson-Guptill Publications, Inc., 1957.

____, *The Practice of Illustration,* New York: Watson-Guptill Publications, Inc., 1947.

____, *A Treasury of American Book Illustration,* New York and London: American Studio Books and Watson-Guptill Publications, Inc., 1947.

____, *200 Years of American Illustration,* New York: Random House, Inc., 1977.

Reed, Henry M., *The A. B. Frost Book,* Rutland, Vermont: Charles E. Tuttle Co., 1967.

Reed, Walt, *Great American Illustrators,* New York: Abbeville Press, 1979.

____, *Harold Von Schmidt Draws and Paints the Old West,* Flagstaff, Arizona: Northland Press, 1972.

____, *John Clymer; An Artist's Rendezvous with the Frontier West,* Flagstaff, Arizona: Northland Press, 1976.

____, compiler, *The Magic Pen of Joseph Clement Coll,* Westport, Connecticut: North Light Publishers, 1978.

Renner, Frederic G., *Charles M. Russell,* New York: Harry N. Abrams, Inc., 1966.

Rockwell, Norman, as told to Thomas Rockwell, *Norman Rockwell — My Adventures as an Illustrator,* New York: Doubleday & Co., Inc., 1960.

Rubinstein, Charlotte Streifer, *American Women Artists,* Boston: G.K. Hall & Co., New York: Avon Books, 1982.

Samuels, Peggy and Harold, *The Collected Writings of Frederic Remington,* New York: Doubleday & Co., Inc. 1979.

____, *Contemporary Western Artists,* Houston, Texas: Southwest Arts Publishing, 1982.

____, *The Illustrated Biographical Encyclopedia of Artists of the American West,* Garden City, New York: Doubleday & Co., Inc., 1976.

____, *Frederic Remington, A Biography,* New York: Doubleday, 1982.

Schau, Michael, *"All-American Girl," The Art of Coles Phillips,* New York: Watson-Guptill Publications, 1975.

____, *J. C. Leyendecker,* New York: Watson-Guptill Publications, 1974.

Schnessel, S. Michael, *Jessie Willcox Smith,* New York: Thomas Y. Crowell, Toronto: Fitzheary & Whiteside Ltd., 1977.

Schoonover, Cortlandt, *Frank Schoonover, Illustrator of the North American Frontier,* New York: Watson-Guptill Publications, 1976.

Schreuders, Piet, *Paperbacks: USA,* San Diego, California: Blue Dolphin Enterprises, Inc., 1981.

Scott, David, *John Sloan,* New York: Watson-Guptill Publications, 1975.

Sears, Stephen W., *The American Heritage Century Collection of Civil War Art,* New York: American Heritage Publishing Co., Inc., 1974.

Simon, Howard, *500 Years of Art in Illustration,* New York: World Publishing Co., 1942.

Stebbins, Jr., Theodore E., *American Master Drawings and Watercolors,* New York: Harper & Row Publishers, Inc., 1976.

Suares, Jean-Claude, editor, *Art of The Times,* New York: Universe Books, 1973.

Taft, Robert, *Artists and Illustrators of the Old West 1850-1900,* New York: Charles Scribner's Sons, 1953.

Thirty Favorite Paintings by Leading American Artists, New York: P. F. Collier & Son, 1908.

Tinkelman, Murray, and Kagan, Daniel, editor, *The Illustrations of Murray Tinkleman,* New York: Art Direction Book Company.

Traxel, David, *An American Saga; The Life and Times of Rockwell Kent,* New York: Harper & Row, Publishers, Inc., 1980.

Watson, Ernest W., *Forty Illustrators and How They Work,* New York: Watson-Guptill Publications, Inc., 1946.

Wenzell, A. B., *The Passing Show,* New York: P. F. Collier & Son, 1903.

Whiting, John D., *Practical Illustration, A Guide for Artists,* New York and London: Harper & Brothers, 1920.

Who's Who in American Art, Washington, D.C.: American Federation of Arts, publisher, New York & London: R. R. Bowker Co., 1936 to present.

Who's Who in Graphic Art, Zurich, Switzerland: Amstritz & Herdeg, Graphis Press, 1962.

Wortman, Denys, *Mopey Dick and The Duke,* New York: Fairchild Publications, 1952.

Wyeth, N.C., and Wyeth, Betsy James, editor, *The Wyeths,* Boston: Gambit, 1971.

The Year's Art/The Quarterly Illustrator, New York: Harry C. Jones, publisher, 1893, 1894, 1895.

INDEX   *The first number following the artist's name refers to the biography. Other references are indicated in italics.*